PORTRAIT OF
A GREEK
IMAGINATION
◼

PORTRAIT OF A GREEK IMAGINATION

◘

AN ETHNOGRAPHIC BIOGRAPHY OF ANDREAS NENEDAKIS

For Tingjun, extraordinary teacher, extraordinary student, have you keliou de xueshengj, laopi de laoshi

MICHAEL HERZFELD

THE UNIVERSITY OF CHICAGO PRESS
CHICAGO & LONDON

MICHAEL HERZFELD is professor of anthropology at Harvard University. The editor of *American Ethnologist,* Herzfeld is the author of six books, including *The Social Production of Indifference.*

The University of Chicago Press, Chicago 60637
The University of Chicago Press, Ltd., London
© 1997 by The University of Chicago
All rights reserved. Published 1997
Printed in the United States of America
06 05 04 03 02 01 00 99 98 97   1 2 3 4 5

ISBN 0-226-32909-7 (cloth)
     0-226-32910-0 (paper)

Library of Congress Cataloging-in-Publication Data

Herzfeld, Michael, 1947–
    Portrait of a Greek imagination: an ethnographic biography of
Andreas Nenedakis / Michael Herzfeld.
        p.   cm.
    Includes bibliographical references and index.
    ISBN 0-226-32909-7 (alk. paper).—ISBN 0-226-32910-0 (pbk.:
alk. paper)
    1. Nenedakēs, A. N.—Biography.   2. Authors, Greek (Modern)—20th
century—Biography.   I. Title.
PA5625.E54Z64   1997
889'.334—dc21   97-24232
                                                        CIP

■

CONTENTS

■

PREFACE

This book emerged from a particular friendship and, I hope, expresses important dimensions of that friendship. At the same time, I owe a considerable debt of gratitude to numerous other friends who helped guide it to completion. I am especially grateful to those who read the manuscript in earlier versions and whose critical insights have been crucial in giving it whatever coherence I have been able to achieve: Margaret Alexiou, Begoña Aretxaga, Ruth Behar, Melissa Caldwell, Vangelis Calotychos, Maria Couroucli, Henk Driessen, Kenneth George, Stratis Haviaras, Tracey Heatherington, Gail Holst-Warhaft, Jane Huber, Michael Jackson, Arthur Kleinman, Aristidis Tsandiropoulos, and Kay Warren. It was in long conversations with Aristidis Tsandiropoulos in Rethemnos that this project really took its initial shape. Eva Kodrou was a marvelously helpful guide in Stockholm and her insights proved invaluable. In Paris, Rethemnos, and Stockholm, too, I would like to thank those who graciously allowed me to interview them in person or over the telephone; some are mentioned by name in the book (and in Andreas's books). At Harvard, my assistants Panos Tsokas and Pantelis Hatzis, enthusiastic transcribers of my interview tapes, also provided useful reflections and insights.

At the University of Chicago Press, David Brent has always been a special source of encouragement and warmth. I am deeply grateful to Kathryn Kraynik for her editorial skill, patience, and perceptiveness. Matthew Howard was always ready with practical assistance and advice. And other Press staff, too, have demonstrated an intensity of commitment that I have found both refreshing and reassuring.

Not only was Cornelia Mayer Herzfeld a critical and, at crucial times, encouraging reader of this book in draft form, she was also an inspiring presence in the entire project as it developed and is actively engaged in the friendship with Andreas Nenedakis and Elli-Maria Komninou that has made it all possible. To her, my gratitude is not to be measured with words, but whatever they can weakly convey here will have to suffice on the printed page. Nor can words even begin to express the warmth, humor, and delighted sparring and teasing that have marked our friendship with Andreas and Elli, one of the most profound human encounters it has been my privilege to enjoy. I hope that they will both find in these pages some reflection of that extraordinary friendship, which for me, at least, has dissolved differences of age, culture, and experience in a truly astonishing effervescence of *anthropiá*—of everything it means to be human.

1 ▣

ANTICIPATIONS

This is a book about a novelist. It is, strictly speaking, neither a literary biography nor an ethnography, but fuses elements of both. Unlike most ethnographies, it is focused on the life, writings, and ideas of a single person: the Cretan-born Greek novelist Andreas Nenedakis; unlike most biographies, it is less concerned with the personality of the central character than with the significance of his life and times for a tangle of intersecting social worlds.

I have called this study an "ethnographic biography," not simply in order to signal the deliberate transgression of genre boundaries but also because I try to engage Andreas's writings in a contrapuntal conversation with the concerns of ethnographers, including myself, who have tried to make sense of more or less the same places, movements, institutions, and events. The story of the novelist's life, while important in its own right, appears here as the vehicle of other concerns—and this is as he too wishes it to be, for his own way of striking a heroic pose is to disdain the trappings of fame that have eluded him for most of his nearly eight decades.

The tactic of ethnographic biography allows us to move along the trajectory of a life that has bisected many histories and of a person who has dwelt in many communities rather than staying (as most conventional ethnography does) within a single place. It is true that Andreas Nenedakis and I first met in his birthplace, which also happened to be my field research site at the time, and that our absorption in that place—the Cretan coastal town of Rethemnos—gave this project its initial impetus and grounding. But we soon discovered many other common interests, and these—issues of gender, political injustice, aesthetics, the role of the state in national consciousness, the meaning of the past, to name but a few—deepened our friendship and sense of mutual engagement.

While partially anchored in the detail of ethnographic observation, the approach I have attempted here offers a perspective more in harmony with the restless experiences of our times than do some conventional ethnographic strategies. Furthermore, instead of focusing on a single place, such as a village, it allows us to see how a particular social actor—the novelist—makes sense of a variety of social entities and settings. Of course, a single person's observations cannot substitute for the full description of a local community—in any case the writing of fiction has quite different goals—but the juxtaposition of the two genres may generate mutual insight: existing ethnographic resources provide a lively commentary on ideas and facts the novelist takes for granted, while the highly personal insights of the novelist begin to overcome the distance between social analysis and lived experience.[1]

I had the good fortune to meet Andreas Nenedakis in the courtyard of the drafty, high-ceilinged, but remarkably well-stocked public library in Rethemnos. I knew of him mainly as the author of a local history. He showed me the newspaper materials he had collected, from around the time of his birth when a significant Muslim community still existed in the town, and told me he was thinking of incorporating them into a novel. Ever the literal-minded academic, I told him I thought it a pity not to put such rich material to more scholarly use. Little did I know that he was working on what was to be his most successful—but also his most controversial—book to date.

He wrote his novel. (As we shall see, there are those who dispute whether it really *is* a novel.) I carried on with my fieldwork. And in time we met again. We talked about the town itself and about artisanal apprenticeship, a subject on which Andreas's childhood recollections proved interesting and helpful for the research I was doing. Andreas blithely ignored—forgave?—my earlier solecism, although he still remembered it with amusement two years later; but when I finally talked with him about it, I had passed through an entire education at his hands. I cringed now at the memory, but found absolution in his gentle amusement at my expense.

His forbearance was remarkable: I was a British subject now working at American universities; he was a Greek communist who had been condemned to death by his pro-British Greek wartime military commanders on the Middle East front. He impishly told me that he did not think of me as a scholar and hoped I would not mind—he actually meant it as praise. He is some three decades my senior. He had certainly had time to realize how circumstances could change one's perspectives—had even described his own "conversion" in his fiction. He also taught me—and

---

1. For some of my own observations on the relationship between differences of viewpoint and affect, in an essay written partially in contemplating my project in this book, see Herzfeld 1997b.

this was the theme of his personal conversion—that pride in one's national identity does not automatically mean chauvinism: a valuable insight and modulation at a time when both media and scholarly critics increasingly treat nationalism as something one is either for or against.

We have enjoyed many quietly animated conversations since that first meeting. We have talked over food at a seaside restaurant in Rethemnos, and, one summer, we sipped the fiery Cretan grappa in front of the back-alley cottage that he had rented there. In his Athens apartment, surrounded by paintings and drawings (including two of himself) by his many friends in the Greek art world, he is content to talk about his life, answering my often naive questions with occasional impatience at my obtuseness (hardly helped by our both having hearing problems), then with proprietorial satisfaction serving up an austere but tasty meal of beans and fish washed down with a light wine. On some occasions when I visit his apartment, he detours to the kitchen to stir a simmering pot of bean soup before we remove ourselves to the spectacular balcony view of Athens—a heritage from his father-in-law, a distinguished physician—poised in the smog-laden but still shimmering afternoon summer light between the Acropolis and the monastery church atop Mount Lycabettus. The view is breathtaking. But the inward focus of our shared enthusiasm is Crete, especially Rethemnos. Andreas certainly understands my love for his hometown and island, and that passion—which we share across the divide of entirely different experiences and motivations—undoubtedly directed our conversations as well as the development of this book.

We have disagreed, too, for Andreas shares the official Greek view that Greece has no ethnic minorities, while I have been attacked in some sectors of the Greek and Greek-American press for my critical response to this position and its consequences. On the other hand, while Andreas sometimes chides me with a sorrowful (or testy) allusion to such disagreements, which he chooses to interpret as signifying obdurate ignorance on my part, he also finds little political disagreement with me on most other matters. Moreover, he respects consistency of opinion virtually above all else. In any event, disagreement has never threatened the warmth of our engagements. When I had to make a decision about whether to fight against a British university press's decision not to publish a book about Macedonia for fear of hypothetical risks,[2] I remembered thinking that while Andreas might disagree with much of the book's argument he would have made the decision to fight, just as he had decided to leave the Communist Party over the 1966 Moscow show trials of dissident intellectuals Yuli Daniel and Andrei Sinyavski. When I told him that this

---

2. For a partial discussion of the case, including indications of some reasons for the complexity of the relevant Greek attitudes, see Gudeman and Herzfeld 1996.

had been in my thoughts at the time of my own moment of decision, his face crinkled with pleasure and unreservedly warm approbation.

Elli-Maria Komninou, a painter to whom he has been married for nearly three decades, has been an observant participant in these encounters. Elli (as she is more informally called) occasionally walks into the room and offers affectionately sardonic comments on the gap between his views and his practices (especially concerning the right of women to hold opinions) or, in a much louder voice intended to overcome his long-standing deafness, bluntly disagrees with some detail of his recollections. She often disagrees with his pugnacious responses to his enemies, thinking that he should not bring himself down to their level of abuse. But she knows that here he operates within a masculine code that leaves him little room for compromise and that his self-respect will not allow him to heed his wife's objections—and that she does not possess the weapons of Cretan village women for intervening in fights and then bearing the "blame" for their husbands' failure to fight.[3]

Moreover, her interest in the talk was, above all, that of an artist. One day she decided to sketch us as we spoke and captured all the vivacious enthusiasm of those precious moments. Andreas's hands move vigorously; the cassette recorder lies on the sofa between us, almost forgotten, as Andreas's exposition reaches a momentary climax. Elli looks quizzically at us, adjusts a detail in her sketch, and continues. I am aware of what she is doing, but it has become as fully naturalized an aspect of the interaction as the little cassette recorder: each holds out a promise to inscribe the fleeting but intense pleasure of the encounter in something more durable than human memory.

I have tape-recorded many of our conversations. This was especially valuable because it allowed me to compare Andreas's oral recollections with passages in his novels—an important issue when addressing the relationship between chronicle and novel, and all the more so in the context of post–World War II Greek literature with its deliberate reproduction of oral narrative styles (Tziovas 1989). Andreas, too, seemed perfectly at ease with this arrangement, perhaps even pleased: it created an archive of his recollections. At other times, I would simply jot down points of particular interest. It would have been disingenuous to pretend that I was not going to record anything that might have relevance for this project.

I think Andreas enjoys our encounters in part because he finds my interests intriguingly different from those of most scholars he has known. I have nothing at stake in the debates about style, quality, and promise. But I also suspect that he is often amused by my preoccupations. Twice

---

3. Women are often involved in peacemaking in Cretan pastoral communities because their "interference" gives the men an ethical alibi for what would otherwise (and may anyway) be construed as cowardice (see Herzfeld 1985: 61).

The novelist and the ethnographer: passionate memories (pencil drawing by Elli-Maria Komninou).

he has wordlessly handed me a newspaper in which a scholar who happened to be a friend of mine—once an anthropologist, the other time a literary scholar—had come under fire for allegedly holding views on Greek culture that Andreas found disturbing or wrongheaded.[4] But he does not belligerently demand to know how these people dare to hold such views. On the contrary, a whimsical shake of his head suggests that, while he now has good reason to wonder about the intellectual company I keep, he prefers our friendship to remain untroubled by matters of which he has no direct knowledge. Such moments leave in my memory a lingering half-smile at the ponderous preoccupations of academics. Indeed, he reacted in much the same way, by letter, to some of the more theoretical passages in an earlier draft of this book: he wants to make sure I get the story right, but what I actually do with it can safely be left to my peculiar set of priorities. He only says that he likes the idea of what I am doing; and that is cause enough for content.

This book does remain a scholarly work, although I hope—especially

4. See Faubion (1993) and the critique by Pesmazoglou (1994); Jusdanis (1991) and the equally bitter critique in question in Kayalis (1994). These disputes appear to arise in large measure from a deeply distrusted—they intimate—introverted foreign academic establishment. The foreign side stands for a theoretical sophistication that its Greek critics charge with insensitivity to, or ignorance of, Greek realities.

The ethnographer and the novelist: entangled expositions (pencil drawing by Elli-Maria Komninou).

given Andreas's sense of priorities—that it can be read for other reasons as well. It is about issues that have recently been central in anthropology: the self and personhood, the social and cultural construction of history, literature and society, the crossing of disciplinary boundaries, critical reflections on anthropology itself. The encounter between my anthropological interests and Andreas's writing has helped me to understand how he has negotiated the engagement of his cultural background, his sense of tradition and of value, with the encompassing enormities of his times. It has also helped me to think through some of the constraints of anthropological writing.

This is a straightforward goal, and it may lead to some more general insights into the connections between personal idiosyncrasy and culture. Even so, one may wonder why an English-speaking reader should even care about one necessarily selective portrait of a novelist, however talented, who has never even been published in English. And what business does an anthropologist have trying to ask for such a reading?

My answer lies particularly in two areas. One is the long-standing anthropological concern with the cultural problem of motivation, while the other concerns the implications of a novelist's claims to realism for the work of an ethnographer describing the same or similar places.

First, then, motivation—a familiar zone of confusion and doubt for anthropologists, who are trained to describe only what they see and hear and are consequently reluctant to engage in intuitive judgments.[5] I still largely share that hesitation; but Andreas does depict motive and desire in his novels as well as in his conversation, and presumably expects people, if not to believe these portraits, at least to consider them *socially* plausible. This is the same distinction that we confront in asking about the excuses that people make for their errors and mishaps: since belief is indeed ultimately and irreducibly private, I can never tell whether you really do believe my protestations, but I can certainly try to present them in a form that will make it socially awkward for you to question them.[6] (Greeks conventionally question the possibility of knowing others' intentions—"How can you know someone else?" they rhetorically demand—even as they try to divine these very intentions from such telltale signs as past history or present habits and friendships.) It is in this social sense that Andreas's particular attributions of motive, in the imaginary world of his fiction and in the reported news of his milieu alike, are genuinely illuminating of what Greeks regard as plausible representations of psychology.

The second challenge, that of realism and its implications, lay in Andreas's own complicated view of what he was doing when he wrote about institutions, places, even particular people or families I had already met in the course of my own research. Was my writing more "real" when I described the lives (often in their own words) of animal-stealing shepherds engaged in feuds like those that had animated Andreas's father's life, or when I tried to portray the political and social maneuvering of people among whom Andreas had grown to maturity and whose affectations he satirically deflates in his most recent novel?

In fact, the description of motive and desire is itself an important aspect of any claim to realism in the Greek context. Like most Greeks, Andreas both doubts the possibility of knowing another's thoughts and recognizes the existence of conventions for doing so. This is a conundrum

---

5. See especially Leavitt 1996; Needham 1972; Rosen 1995. In many ways the richest ethnographic argument is delivered by Crapanzano (1980; see especially pp. 8–10 on biography, the case history, and the shaping of selfhood in the narrative encounter—a clear demonstration, if one were needed, that something of the quality of intersubjective encounters can be conveyed through committed description). Warren (1993; 1997), by examining the connections between genre and idioms of self-fashioning in their political context, also shows how motive can be communicated and shared.

6. This is the logic of the approach to self-justification that I present in *The Social Production of Indifference* (1992).

one meets in many cultures—Kaqchikel Maya, for example, say that "each mind is a world" (Warren 1995)—but ways of exploring its practical consequences vary from setting to setting. As with Maya public intellectuals, moreover, so too with Greek writers: their responses to the conundrum are grounded in particular social and historical circumstances (such as the need for collective secrecy under conditions of persecution) and take culturally specific forms, which require informed interpretation. In Greece, where fiction draws heavily on the conventions of oral narrative, a novelist describing the most sophisticated milieu must observe at least some of the verbal and stylistic conventions of everyday gossip, and this reveals a great deal about collective expectations of personal motive.

As is clear in the following passage from *The Daisies of the Saint,* a collection of short stories about the experiences of political prisoners under the military dictatorship of 1967 to 1974, Andreas knows that these conventions for talking about others are part of the rhetoric used to exonerate the self. A military truck has been parked outside some political prisoners' cell window in Athens. The author's voice is heard asserting that this was to prevent passersby from peering into the jail. Not everyone was of the same opinion:

> "Others said this was done to bully the prisoners. The sick imaginings of political prisoners! They think that everything is done on purpose. To kill them off. Systematically.
>
> "An elderly teacher, who was lying in a corner between two men younger than himself, says, 'It is not systematic, nor are these things done on purpose. If you take these people one by one you'll see that they're not very different from you and me. These things happen because civilization teaches them this behavior.'" (*Daisies,* p. 56)

In this exchange, Andreas is consistent both with the conventional Greek ambivalence about guessing others' motives and with his own reflective reluctance to prejudge even the most brutalized camp guard as inherently evil. Above all, he avoids totalizing characterizations. He knows all about the profusion of conspiracy theorists who infest every political discussion in Greece; but he finds their rhetoric unpersuasive precisely because it relies so heavily on attributions of character and motive. Or is he being ironic himself? "The sick imaginings of political prisoners": whose voice do we hear? Perhaps it is that of the military authorities, not of the detached observer? In the end, the opacity of his own intentions reminds us that *no* attribution of motive is transparent. We do not really know what (if anything) the authorities intended by their actions, or what the prisoners intended by their guesswork—or what the author intends by his description; and it is this uncertainty, uniting the narrative moment with the narrated events, that makes the scene descriptively plausible (see especially Bauman 1986).

Such descriptive agnosticism is thus ethnographically realistic and goes far beyond generalizing accounts of what "Greeks do": it is about how Greeks—many Greeks, at least—argue about what Greeks do. Andreas refuses the lure of abstract, introspective speculation, preferring instead to clothe individual portraits in the garb of ordinary social discourse. His portraits work, in part, because we recognize common social devices and everyday rhetoric in the characters about whom he writes, not because he has captured the exact word or phrase that would be so vital to the ethnographer's description or the historian's chronicle, and certainly not because he claims to know what moves people to act as they do—he is caught up in their perplexities, and so, in consequence, are we.

I find the implications of Andreas's realism absorbing, not only because the relationship between ethnography and fiction has long bemused anthropologists, but also, and especially, because—in a directly comparable debate—Andreas has for years been engaged in sometimes vehement public arguments about whether he is truly a novelist or a historian. For him, this question is vital; and his preoccupation holds a revealing mirror up to anthropology. What are the social and cultural circumstances under which such issues come to mean so much, and what can they tell us about the preoccupations of our own writerly craft?

This is a key aspect of the current interest in literature among anthropologists. Some anthropologists are uncomfortable with the idea of a close relationship between ethnography and fiction, but few would dispute the notion that the relationship requires elucidation. Anthropologists' professional training generally—and, in my view, reasonably—inclines them to descriptive realism. Some use literary sources entirely within that realist mode, to reconstitute social processes now long past. Even this mode of investigation is fraught with a peculiar difficulty because of the all too common absence of contemporaneous counterweights to artistic license in the form of detailed historical archives, but it does open up important topical possibilities that compensate precisely those lacunae (for example, Couroucli 1993; Danforth 1976; Papataxiarchis n.d.; Sant Cassia and Bada 1992). Perhaps mindful of what has happened to the uses of myth as a source of historical and anthropological insight, these writers have taken care to check their readings of novels—which are aptly called *mithistorímata*, "myth-narratives," in Greek—against archival data and personal experience.

Others, with equal caution, have variously explored literary themes in order to open up ethnographically underexplored facets of modernity (see, for example, Faubion 1993; Panourgiá 1995). A linguist, Deborah Tannen (1983), has written a sympathetic literary and feminist biography of Lilika Nakou, the author of a controversial semi-autobiographical novel set in Andreas Nenedakis's hometown of Rethemnos and dealing with its confrontations with cosmopolitan morality (see Herzfeld 1991a: 24–26 and passim). All these approaches, exemplified here by works specifically dealing with the rich context of Greece, indicate that novels challenge the anthropological imagination to go beyond a concern with social institutions and structures and especially to let individual and collective agency subvert the conflation implied by the ever-present definite article: "*the* values of *the* Greeks." Panourgiá's study also takes the vexed issue of the "native" anthropologist beyond the usual platitudes about insiders and outsiders, using the confrontation of what she calls "fables of identity" with the brute fact of mortality to elucidate the intimate complexities lurking behind the usual stereotypes and generalizations.[7]

These illustrations of the relationship between literature and ethnography are drawn from Greek materials, but it is an increasingly popular topic at a much broader level. It has been at issue at least since novelist Joseph Conrad and anthropologist Bronislaw Malinowski, two expatriate Poles and mutual friends, each produced some of the most impressive English-language writing about cultural difference in his particular genre.[8] Rather than surveying what has become a minor cottage industry, I would like simply to note some aspects that have proved especially illuminating to me in contemplating my friendship and intellectual relationship with Andreas.

Three works should particularly be mentioned at the outset. Judith Okely's (1986) critical biography of Simone de Beauvoir provided some rich insights against which to assess Andreas's occasional and partial echoes of a Sartrean sensibility, as well as his struggle to make sense of women's predicaments in the emergent heyday of the Greek bourgeoisie. Okely's exploration of the impact of de Beauvoir's writings on her own emergence as a feminist and an anthropologist suggested helpful analogies: Andreas, like de Beauvoir, is not a professional anthropologist, but, perhaps for that very reason, illuminates questions that are of central concern to anthropologists.[9] Richard Handler and Daniel Segal (1990) have mined the novels of Jane Austen for evidence of the play of agency in a superficially rigid system of manners, showing that a cultural account of literature, far from being reductionist, can analytically disengage

---

7. On the issue of the cultural positioning of the ethnographer in the Greek context, see especially Bakalaki 1993; Gefou-Madianou 1993.

8. See the debate between Hsu (1979) and Leach (1980); cf. also Meunier 1987.

9. "De Beauvoir has in part done an anthropological village study of specific women, but without the anthropological theory and focus" (Okely 1986: 71)—these being aspects of Okely's own work for which de Beauvoir was nevertheless a partial inspiration (Okely 1986: 157).

agency from a surface appearance of studied formality. And Nigel Rapport's (1994) subtle comparison of E. M. Forster's novels with his own ethnographic explorations of an English village reveals some common goals of novelist and ethnographer in ways that partially anticipate my strategy here.[10]

Such approaches, as Handler and Segal (1990: 135) have pointed out, furnish a usefully complicating counterpoint to the work of anthropologists, "who have generally assumed a more unitary and authoritative voice in texts self-consciously constructed to be nonfiction." In a very different way, Andreas, while sometimes inclined to posit a "traditional" culture every bit as homogeneous as the normative fictions of the ethnographer's craft, nonetheless shows in his portrayals of inner conflict—an art student rebelling against her bourgeois family's respectability, a young Cretan lad discovering that the conventional bromides of his patriotic provincialism had equipped him poorly for accepting the kindness of a Turk or facing his own cowardice, Andreas's own proud father humbly begging his enemy's pardon—that tradition always entailed the possibility of multiple *responses* to norms perceived as fixed and culturally inalienable. Andreas's personal experiences were his usual guide to such complexities, making biography an appropriate medium for their exploration here. And his inconsistency on the degree to which tradition could be read as unitary was itself the best evidence that, for him as for me, in the final analysis it could not. Had matters been otherwise, motive, too, would have been tediously transparent, the outcome only of an entirely predictable collective will.

Repeatedly the prisoner of brutal right-wing thugs, despised as a folkloristic provincial by parts of the self-appointed cultural elite in the capital, and constantly impelled to express his identity and ideology in impetuous acts of self-marginalization, Andreas expresses in his writings all the pain and pleasure of being Greek (and Cretan) that his personal predicament exemplifies. His marginality reproduces that of his own society in the larger world: Greece, spiritual ancestor of the powerful lands to the west, is also their poor and sometimes embarrassing cousin. But marginal people and places, as I have already argued for Greece, are the best source of critical insight because they pose provocative questions about what brought that marginality into being.[11] What does the Greek condition tell us about "Europe"? What does the life of Andreas Nenedakis tell us about the bourgeois society, at once fawning and prickly toward its self-

10. See also Behar and Gordon 1995; Couroucli 1996; Gokalp 1996; Hauschild 1995; Nikolopoulos 1995; Postel-Koster 1977; Poyatos 1988; Verdier 1995.

11. This project is explored in some detail in my *Anthropology through the Looking-Glass* (1987a).

appointed mentors and protectors, in which he moves? Marginalities lead us to an understanding of the powers that define them as such; narratives written against the grain of those powers complicate—and thereby enrich—social analysis, crisscrossing its assumptions of cultural homogeneity and predictability with alternative visions of human experience (see also Rosaldo 1989: 147–67). Andreas's principled but impish self-exclusion is no exception, and his contradictoriness offers more insight than any normative description of Greek society.

I have thus availed myself of his willing presence in order to explore through metaphor and allegory some of the puzzlements of a society that itself challenges the complacency of such categories as "Europe," "bourgeoisie," and "modernity." Andreas is an unruly and challenging actor in all these mutually entangled social universes. My interest in them is not exactly the same as his, but it is complementary to his. It is as an anthropologist meeting a writer that I first made Andreas's acquaintance; it is in these identities, too, that we meet in the pages of this book.

The paths of Andreas Nenedakis have been varied, full of joy as well as pain, mapping a complicated tangle of friendships. I owe that first meeting in the Rethemnos public library to one of my closest friends in the town, George Leledakis, a former bootmaker who now presides over the local Cultural Society. He is related to Andreas, and both are adventurous products of families originally hailing from legendarily wild hill villages to the west of the town. Another time, I met Andreas with his maternal cousin, Paul Stavroulakes, when they came to eat at the "Pantheon" restaurant, a seaside summer eatery run by another good friend and one of my most frequent haunts. It is a place popular with local scholars, perhaps in part because the owner's wife, Aspasia Papadaki, is an accomplished scholar of Venetian Crete (see Papadaki 1995). Among the learned customers is the tall, stooped, and ascetic figure of the distinguished prehistoric archaeologist and historian of Cretan Renaissance literature, Stylianos Alexiou, who has edited some of the major works from that period. Alexiou is a generous and unpretentious sage who published my own first feeble attempt at an academic article in 1969 when I had just graduated from my undergraduate university. His response to Andreas has been similarly open-minded. When Andreas published a critical edition of the seventeenth-century Cretan poet Tzane Marinos Bounialis's *The Cretan War* and claimed the right to intrude on the academic domain on the grounds that he had a more intimate knowledge of the Cretan dialect than any learned professor, Alexiou—apparently alone among established scholars—unequivocally recognized that some of Andreas's emendations represented a genuine contribution.

The company at the Pantheon is a real celebration of the recovery of Crete's Renaissance past. Not all those involved are directly engaged in academic research on the subject. Andreas's cousin, Paul Stavroulakes, a doctor who lives in the United States, is known to many as an active promoter of undergraduate study in Greece.[12] He was also instrumental in securing for the city of Rethemnos a major seventeenth-century painting of the town in all the glory of its Venetian masonry. Andreas—experienced in the ways of the art trade—had tracked this painting down to an auction house in London; thanks to the two of them, it now hangs in the Rethemnos town hall, the pride of a municipality increasingly glad to acknowledge its Renaissance past.

Not all Rethemniots have been equally delighted with their town's elevation to the status of a Venetian historical monument, which has brought upon them the controlling hand of the national historic conservation bureaucracy. Many householders, especially the poorer among them, resisted what they saw as the insensitive expropriation of their domestic spaces by the agents of this official apparatus. I had come to Rethemnos in 1986–87 for the specific purpose of observing this contest over the ownership of the past and the refraction of nationalist historiography and cultural representation—a topic that I had also explored—through the ever-shifting divisions and alliances of local politics.[13] But the intelligentsia, including many faculty members from the University of Crete and a large Rethemniot diaspora in Athens and abroad, was unanimous in celebrating the importance of the Venetian heritage. Andreas, long a resident of Athens, was no exception. Indeed, he had—in the face of skepticism and even hostility from members of the scholarly community—justified his own critical edition of Bounialis's *The Cretan War* on the grounds of the special knowledge of the poem's distinctively Cretan dialect, which he attributed to his family's rural background. The talk at the Pantheon delicately skirted the edges of these past disagreements: after all, Andreas and his cousin had given the town an image that impressively affirmed its living Venetian past.

Most of the interviewing I did for this book took place in Greece. Some was embedded in other projects, especially a study I was conducting on apprenticeship in Rethemnos.[14] In Paris and Stockholm, however,

12. He promoted the Aegean Institute, a study program for North American undergraduates, for some years after the death of his first wife, Niki Stavroulakes, who had founded and directed it.

13. See Herzfeld 1991a. The relationship between the official production of cultural discourse can be studied both in its locus of production (such as state agencies) and at its site of consumption—where, however, it is also *reproduced* and also transmuted through the agency of local social actors—a point that commonly escapes "macro" analyses of nationalism and similar phenomena.

14. The research on apprenticeship was supported by a research grant from the National Science Foundation (award no. SBR-9307411). I am most grateful for the support and take full responsibility for the research findings.

where Andreas still maintained contacts from his time of exile early in the military dictatorship of 1967 through 1974, I was also able to make use of openings afforded by professional invitations to both cities.[15] In Paris one such contact, Yannis Angelopoulos, turned out to be a close friend of my own colleagues there, while in Stockholm Yannis Tsipras turned out to be an anthropologist himself. Andreas had other, more indirect connections with the program in modern Greek at the University of Birmingham in England, where I had received graduate training in the early 1970s under Margaret Alexiou, now my colleague at Harvard. Another Harvard friend, Stratis Haviaras, as a very youthful writer made the acquaintance of Andreas in an Athens literary circle—"I always remembered a lad [that is, Haviaras] who used to stand on his own at the Loumidis [café] and suddenly you handed me a critique of my book *Tsingos* that you'd done in [the newspaper] *Mákhi*," Andreas recently reminded him in a letter (1 September 1993). Both Alexiou and Haviaras have read and commented on this book as I was working on it.

Recounting such unexpected links is not just a matter of setting the scene or of emphasizing that a work of this kind cannot be a traditionally site-bound ethnographic study. Its significance is, above all, that all the actors are enmeshed in a tangle of tracks connecting areas of our social lives that we ordinarily think of as discrete, and it suggests that the tactic of ethnographic biography may offer one route—a trajectory through multiple social worlds—to an ethnography of transnational intellectual communities.

It is true that the idea of the totally isolated community seems to be vanishing from anthropological discourse—where, in retrospect, it was never much more than a convenience and a convention, and possibly a barrier to understanding at that. But these crisscrossing trajectories signal something more than the abandonment of an outmoded way of thinking. They provide a context for an objective I was trying to reach with Andreas: an ethnographic attempt to reverse the usual ethnographic emphasis of pattern over experience, the collective and the cultural over the range of idiosyncrasy that the members of a society are prepared to tolerate.

Yet cultural specificity is also central to understanding Andreas's views, especially his attributions of motive and desire. These clearly elicit recognition from his Greek readers. So, too, do attacks on his own motives by his critics. By using these clashes to explore his—and their—culturally specific assumptions about human nature, I intend to show

15. The Department of Social Anthropology of the University of Stockholm (together with other units of that institution) and the École des Hautes Études en Sciences Sociales were my gracious hosts on these occasions.

how his portrayals of character evoke such a strong sense of collective familiarity among his readers, both friendly and hostile. The arguments about motive and morality play out, in a literary and even a scholarly idiom, feuds that in earlier generations began with bitter insults and often spiraled into cycles of bloodshed.

These transformations of physical into intellectual violence are not, of course, necessarily typical of modern cultural debates in Greece. But they do remind us of a more general point. In any country, intellectual life and values may be much more culture-specific, and more deeply rooted in local social practices, than the universalizing rhetoric of art and scholarship ever implies.

This does not mean "explaining" Andreas in the terms of "his own culture"—a condescending and theoretically naive undertaking under any circumstances.[16] I have tried instead to describe the common sense on which Andreas relies in his readers, and on which he plays in multiple, creative ways that reflect the tumultuous vagaries of his life. His descriptions of emotion and motive, and of values and ideology, are personal refractions of collective representations, and they elicit personal responses that also invoke collective models. Much the same can be said of anthropologists: they make idiosyncratic use of the conventions of their discipline—a point that this book should exemplify. In writing an ethnographic biography, then, I hope to balance the advantages of the usual anthropological focus on collective phenomena against the complicating presence of an individual who is himself engaged in exploring issues, conjunctures, and places that have interested anthropologists, as well as many phenomena that have hitherto seemed beyond their locally focused perspective. In a purist's sense, the result is neither ethnography nor literary biography; but I hope that it will at least suggest the potential advantages of such cross-pollination.

This study is thus something of an experiment, although it is by no means a unique effort in that regard. In that it is not a conventional biography, I am not especially concerned to tell a sequential story of Andreas's life, although in some sections I will pursue that trajectory in order to sketch the inspirations and reactions that have influenced his perspective. The dominant narrative mode, however, is episodic, in accordance with his own preferred idiom as well as my aims here. If male autobiographies are often self-congratulatorily "progressive, linear, unidimensional works" in contrast to the "disjunctive narratives" and "episodic" styles of women (Jelinek 1980: 15; 1986: 104), we should beware, as Marianne Gullestad (1996: 280) wisely cautions, of turning such generally useful observations into essentialized caricatures. Indeed, Andreas—although

16. See Fabian (1983) for a more general critique of such stances.

often aggressively masculine in manner and ideology—cannot be so easily reduced to a neat formula. He has written some of his most biting yet empathic allegories of inequality as first-person female narratives.

Furthermore, he openly exhibits his hesitations and self-questioning in virtually every conversation and every piece of writing in which he engages. What he calls the "punishment" of authorship is the realization, every time he returns to the lived world from the ecstatic solitude of writing, that "no book of mine pleases me." The escapist pleasure of authorship is punctuated by bouts of self-disgust, irritation, ennui. Life itself is hardly more stable. Thus, a more episodic and less teleological style seems more apposite here, as I sketch the vicissitudes, full of reversals and distractions, of an idiosyncratic self traversing eight unpredictable decades.

It also seems a better idiom for a study intended to complicate cultural description through a highly active and imaginative personality, especially one as alive as Andreas is to the fertile uncertainties of human existence. Anthropologists have long considered as one of their primary tasks the decoding—or, more precisely, "defamiliarization"[17]—of what seems self-evident to the members of a given society. Yet people often encounter situations that disclose to them the conditionality of the received wisdom or common sense of their everyday lives, so that the obvious no longer seems obvious at all. Paradoxically, perhaps, they may cling to the familiar categories just at the moment when, and precisely because, they suddenly perceive this fragility, or—much like anthropologists seeking formal elegance in the messiness of field experience—they may try to reduce this disturbing turmoil to a new sense of order and coherence. Others more readily embrace the dislocation of the everyday. Most people exhibit both proclivities in unstable proportions, shifting their emphasis in response to mood, force, logic, even sheer caprice. Such is the contradictory condition of the thinking human being—of the serendipitous explorer of life's multiple possibilities.

Andreas exhibits this contradictoriness in rich measure. This is "the Cretan who, within the peaceful man, noisily quaffs the grappa-glass of life, baring a big set of big strong teeth at death and all its miseries" (Raftopoulos 1963: 46). In a series of episodes, recounted in both his writings and our conversations, he condemns chauvinism but exalts Greekness; expresses empathy for the plight of women in his androcentric world but condemns his political enemies in the masculinist rhetoric of his youth on Crete; and oscillates between emphatic assertiveness and modest self-deprecation, sometimes in the same breath. One of his first-person characters, a female art student, adopts the medieval image of jousting—one that I have heard used by Cretan male highlanders to talk

---

17. On this concept, see particularly Stacy (1977).

about card games, and with strongly sexual overtones[18]—to express the deeply internalized sense of conflict that gives meaning to life—or so Andreas and his characters argue, using an image of social relations as ideally grounded in tension that is widely expressed in Greece. This character is bound to her lover ("S") by precisely these stormy emotions of resentment and dependence, and they infuriate and delight her at one and the same time (*Manuscript*, p. 126). In Andreas's hands, her life becomes an allegory of the play of personal autonomy and dependence in a society in which the banality of bourgeois cliches routinizes unyielding, humorless structures of power.

His own language is rich with these tensions. His habits of speech tease at the edges of propriety and time. His speaking voice is hesitant and peremptory at the same time, ringing with pride in his achievements, but doubting them too, and rushing forward even as he worries about whether he has explained the background first. Like his Cretan shepherd forebears, and perhaps in half-deliberate imitation of them (and especially of his father), he may sometimes dramatize his self-confidence by a powerful display of restraint. Such performances by the mountain shepherds may put unworthy opponents to shame, through a sudden and dangerous stillness, far more effectively than would unrelieved braggadocio. In a similar mode, Andreas displays personal self-confidence through dismissive modesty about his achievements and gentle mockery at his own expense. While clearly pleased at my undertaking this book, he kept remarking that it was really unimportant to him.

(And what of my own diffidence, as surprising to me as it might well be to others—what does that mean? Hardly a retiring person, I nevertheless experienced acute discomfort at the thought of juxtaposing large segments of my published ethnographic writings with the passages from Andreas's works and from the interviews, as I had originally intended. Was I simply afraid of appearing too self-serving? Did I find the device uninteresting, repetitive, or merely impracticable inasmuch as it might have lengthened the text beyond any publisher's tolerance? Is there some other cause that I am still unwilling to acknowledge? My motives were hardly less ambiguous and opaque to me than were his. To call either his diffidence or mine disingenuous would beg the question of how far social actors themselves experience their intentions as clear and explicit imperatives, let alone expose them to others' perceptive understanding. Since I am still quite unsure about the reasons for my own hesitation, I find the ways in which Andreas's critics and friends construct his motives far more interesting than my own guesswork on that score.)

Andreas's diffidence is, in any case, as unpredictable as his narrative

18. See Herzfeld 1985: 149–62.

style is episodic. He can be precipitate, even abrupt, all hesitation temporarily banished by a particular provocation to dearly cherished ideas. He recalls going to a public reading by a Rethemniot poetess:

● But I didn't like the way she read it and I tell her, "Give it to me and I'll read it to you." It was the first time I'd taken them [in my hands]. So I read it to her and she says to me, "But you've read them before?" "No." Well, look here, she'll have said to herself, "Eh, it's because he's an author that he knows how to read." It's not that at all! I know authors who can't. . . . I had been taught by people how to r[ead].

The reading of Greek is one of very few areas in which Andreas expresses confidence about the superiority of his knowledge, which he traces to an austere old Rethemniot teacher who claimed to know how to reproduce the cadences of ancient Greek in the modern language.

But even here he is more open-minded than his manner of speaking might imply. Yannis Tsipras, who shared Andreas's brief exile in Stockholm at the beginning of the Papadopoulos dictatorship,[19] and who still lives in that city, is a specialist in historical and anthropological linguistics. Tsipras was interested in the pronunciation of ancient Greek and asked Andreas to seek out all the bibliographical references he could find in Greek about the so-called Erasmian pronunciation, the (West) European standard for the ancient language originally formulated by Erasmus and significantly different from the pronunciation of modern Greek. Tsipras eventually wrote his analysis using the sources that Andreas had provided to launch a blistering attack on the Erasmian system, whereupon Andreas criticized him for his excessive zeal—attributable, said he, to the linguist's youth. When I saw Tsipras in Stockholm in 1994, I had, only the day before been treated in Athens to a Nenedakis tirade against Erasmus. "That," said Tsipras, with some satisfaction, "is a subsequent position of Andreas's." And he continued: "That is the significant thing. He has the virtue of *hearing* his fellow-humans. . . . In the first phase, however, he may not hear them . . . but then he has something to think about . . . he goes off, and afterwards he is ready, open, like a decent person (*ánthropos*[20]) to apologize—for the intensity he's exhibited the night before." These comments convey a sense of the thinking process— the negotiation of ideas through time—that sometimes makes Andreas seem as inconsistent as he is emphatic. Especially in matters concerning

19. George Papadopoulos led the triumvirate who assumed dictatorial powers through the coup of 21 April 1967. See chapter 7 for more discussion.

20. This term expresses less the Enlightenment vision of the perfected human being than notions of social solidarity and decency—a fellowship of the flawed. Greeks stereotypically uphold this model as appropriate to their way of life, placing more emphasis on good fellowship than on formal morality.

the Greek language, he indeed exudes deep passion. But this does not mean that he has never been swayed by the views of others. An ironic self-awareness tempers all his debates with others—sometimes only after the fact, at other moments in a moment of hesitant shyness that invites reflection like a lake suddenly calm after a tempest—the tempest (*trikimía*) that Tsipras described as Andreas's first reaction to many things.

Andreas often speaks forthrightly, bluntly, because the time for talking is too precious to be wasted on hypocritical courtesies. He can be obstinate in claiming special knowledge, especially in matters concerning the purity of food and the discipline of the body—symbolic domains for the exploration of the purity of his Cretan descent and the honest toughness of his Cretan stock. One of his old friends from the time of his exile in Stockholm during the military dictatorship remembers his "wonderful feel" for such matters as the purity of Cretan olive oil, and recalls:

● There may be a cook, for example, who really knows all about cooking, but Andreas won't agree with him—not with the very best professional. A typical case: I said to Andreas, "Some lady taught me that the use of onion is basic in cooking. And Andreas said, 'That's what *I* said! She must have heard it from me!'"

In these memories, affectionate friends recapture Andreas's headstrong caprices. But was that what these outbursts really were? Was there no tinge of the ironic self-deprecation we see in so many other stretches of his conversation? His obstinacy can be vivid and perhaps too strongly colors the interpretation of remembered eccentricities.

Another Stockholm friend, the poet Kostis Papakongos, remembers meeting Andreas for the first time in a café in that city:

● Then, after I'd been talking a long while, and Andreas had said very little, Andreas—I didn't realize anything—he, in that way of his, said, at the end of the conversation, "Do you know," says he, "I didn't understand any of what you said!" [*At this point I interjected (sympathetically, in part because of my own poor hearing), "In other words he was deaf and you were deaf too!"*] "Why's that, Andreas?," I ask him. "I don't hear well," he tells me. [*Laughs*] "I've got the same problem," I tell him. [*Laughs again*]

They had been talking at each other, neither hearing the other, for two hours. And so Papakongos invited Andreas back to his apartment, where they could enjoy the quiet they both needed in order to communicate. They soon became close friends.

Andreas was at first embarrassed to admit to his deafness. (He has only very recently begun to wear a hearing aid, now that it can be incorporated into his glasses—but even the glasses are a matter of embar-

rassment to one so concerned with bodily health.) Such masculine pride
in wholeness can also yield to trusting self-deprecation, or Andreas would
never have told Papakongos of his disability. When he was younger, I
was told, he would say that, when he had to wear such aids to sight and
hearing, "I'll be altogether in a state of collapse!"

But he does allow friends to perceive these marks of an entirely human weakness. Behind the aggressive masculinism, too, his contemporaries have noted a persistent streak of painful diffidence, and they have a
ready explanation for it. For them it is as much a social and historical
phenomenon as it is a personal trait. According to them, he has learned—
as a Communist forced into exile on remote island prison camps for long
periods following the 1949 rightist triumph in the Greek Civil War—the
harm that precipitate haste can do. During World War II, having fought
in the front line at El Alamein, he was sentenced to death for his participation in a mutiny and was saved from execution only by the twists and
turns of Greek politics. One old friend from Stockholm attributes his
sudden hesitations—and specifically the combination of precipitate obstinacy with equally sudden bashfulness in his speaking style—to the fear
drummed into all victims of the right-wing regimes that ruled Greece from
the end of World War II almost continuously up to the collapse of the
military junta in 1974.

One dimension is clear: his hatred of arbitrary power permeates everything he says and writes. It even colors his occasional forays into legal
language with equally rare but unmistakably flashes of Cretan accent in
his otherwise Athenian speech—an ironic way of poking fun at authority
that especially struck Panos Tsokas, one of the Greek undergraduates
who helped me with the transcribing of the interview tapes. His predicament and his heritage perhaps explain how such an aggressively male
person is able to write comfortably in a woman's voice (although there
were certainly many precedents for doing so, both in Greece and elsewhere); how, although an active Communist, he is proud to have broken
decisively and irrevocably with the communist parties in Greece and castigated the Soviet Union in the 1960s for its repression of free speech; and
why, although he is an impassioned patriot, he deplores the excesses of
unthinking nationalism as a yielding of the moral high ground and reacts
with profound contempt to the recent critic who recast his portrayal of
these events as a betrayal of Andreas's own father's patriotism.

These complexities admit of a variety of explanations. Some are offered by Andreas's close friends; others are laid bare, confronted, in his
writings. But such explanations may be after-the-fact justifications and,
as such, best understood primarily as the reflections of social circumstances. Yet even this may be too dismissive. Cultural explanations that
offer little more than a convenient closure, allowing analysts to ignore
the anecdotal and the marginal, always risk reproducing the convenient

fictions of those who wield power (see K. Stewart 1996). Much recent anthropological work on literature has, significantly, emphasized writing as a site of critical reflection on the normative power structures of, for example, gender (Behar and Gordon 1995) and ethnicity (Rosaldo 1989). Besides, what would be the point of complicating well-rounded cultural accounts through an individual critical voice, if in the end we simply standardized that voice again by overwhelming it with a generic cultural description? Conversely, what is the point of writing an anthropological account of a writer's life, unless it is to show how cultural analysis can temper simplistic attributions of motive and individualistic character? Clearly a more dialectical approach can offset the temptations of closure.

In this sense, the project can work to identify, isolate, and subject to critical scrutiny the conventional assumptions that a knowledgeable (and in this case especially a Greek) reader would bring to Andreas's writings—and, by extension, to any utterances made by Greeks about many of the topics on which Andreas touches. In particular, deeply entrenched presuppositions of national as well as individual character die hard, especially when they are sustained by political attitudes. Andreas, a highly recognizable representative of the disillusioned Greek left-wing tradition, attracts predictable commentary, the very conventionality of which—often repeated in his own writing—makes it especially amenable to the cultural, collective focus of an ethnographic approach. The ethnographic biography offers one way of exploring the cultural world of post–World War II political and intellectual life, showing how some of its characteristics are grounded in values that, because they are deeply submerged in a locally generic common sense, are not always readily apparent to the participants.

By the same token, however, the exercise is also highly salutary for anthropologists. It encourages us to question easy assumptions about cultures, conceptualized as homogeneous and clearly bounded entities in a way that disturbingly reproduces such reified notions as national culture and national character (see Handler 1985; Rosaldo 1989). While anthropologists are often sensitive to the dangers of overgeneralization, the voices of local intellectuals and their critics, especially when these can be grounded in local as well as national contexts, can provide varieties of insight not normally accessible in ethnographic studies.[21]

This, in broader theoretical terms, is a call to explore the mutual entailment of agency and structure (see Giddens 1984; Karp 1986). At this level, my goal is to capture some of the resulting dialectic. I have therefore striven here for an openly uneasy interplay between cultural explanation and the quirky unpredictability of Andreas's responses to his world. That, and an episodic rather than a smoothly sequential flow,

21. See my argument in *Cultural Intimacy* (1997).

seemed to supply the idiom most faithful to his own restless representations of his life and times. The episodic mode also challenges the sense of predestination—of an overdetermined telos—that so often seems to direct the biographies of better-known public personalities. In an uncertain world described by the ambivalent voice of critical marginality, this seems the most appealing and consistent strategy of representation.

If this book belongs to a hybrid and uncertain genre, for that very reason it participates in what it describes. For Andreas's own writings have becomes the object of sometimes heated arguments within Greece about their generic identity: some critics explicitly deny that Andreas writes novels all. To his chagrin, they dismiss him as a chronicler—something less prestigious than an academic historian in a society that arguably views the creation of a literary canon as a prerequisite for entering "Europe" (see Jusdanis 1991; Tziovas 1986). (His own derision for the slavish pursuit of "Europe" in modern Greek cultural politics makes him personally quite impervious to such criteria.) Having dismissed him as a mere recorder of facts, moreover, these critics can then castigate him for misrepresenting those same facts. (There have also been benign compromises, as when his personal friend, the left-wing literary critic Dimitris Raftopoulos [1959b: 150], praised a book by Andreas as a "novelistic chronicle.") The arguments about Andreas's work are interesting, not because they are right or wrong, but because they clearly mattered enormously to their protagonists, whose debates highlight an extensive politics of knowledge and aesthetics, and because they matter to Andreas. What we call our writings radically affects how they are read: the attribution of genre is in this sense always a political act.

An ethnographic concern with aesthetics thus addresses not only the stylistic criteria but, more particularly, the politics of taste. This subject is also vital to much current literary criticism. When Raftopoulos praises Andreas's stylistic "austerity" while taking another Rethemniot (Yannis Dalentzas) to task for "the burden of comparisons and personifications, the verification, and the many idiomatic (that is, local dialect) expressions, which are a naturalistic tendency of form of a populist folkloristic genre (*mias ithoghrafías laïkistikís*)" (Raftopoulos 1959a: 150; cf. 1959b), he is engaging in precisely this kind of critique. The same applies to other themes that are central to this account: the alleged recognition of variation in artistic ability, ideological distinctions between art and craft, and arguments that pit historical and cultural precision against inventiveness. But while the ethnographic perspective means that I will be less concerned than the literary analyst with specifically stylistic issues, I will be more interested in placing such issues in the context of the forms of local social practice.

From the ethnographer's perspective, perhaps the greatest advantage of juxtaposing ethnography and fiction lies in the solution it offers to the problem of representing subjectivity—an area where anthropological theory and local practice both converge and clash in revealing ways. Against conventional wisdom about the impossibility of representing "psychological inner states" ethnographically (Needham 1972; Rosen 1995), a view that corresponds strikingly to proverbial wisdom in Greece, John Leavitt (1996) has argued persuasively that, while we may think we cannot portray motives and desires but in fact do so often and well: in practice ethnographers are at their most successfully descriptive when they relinquish the doctrinaire rigor that requires them only to describe what is objectively observable. Pragmatically, as Amelie Rorty has suggested, the evidence shows that "we understand the psychology of others surprisingly well. We would [otherwise] have died of thirst and isolation long ago" (1995: 220). Responding to a similar insight and concerned to become "better able to imagine myself into individual minds" (1994: 275), Nigel Rapport read several of E. M. Forster's novels and his own ethnographic data from an English village into a comparative framework. The description of feeling necessarily remains a matter of evocation rather than of analysis.

Anthony Cohen (1994: 180–91) suggests analogous reasons for paying serious anthropological attention to works of fiction. Novelists, he argues, already step in where anthropologists fear to tread. To pursue Cohen's insight it is not necessary, although it may be useful and instructive, to write ethnographic novels (for example, Jackson 1986). On the contrary, our task, I suggest, is to treat novels and novelists ethnographically—to ask searching questions about their audiences, cultural resonance, and social trajectories.

But this goal itself implies that we must recognize the differences as well as the similarities between ethnography and fiction as genres, and between their respective sets of preoccupations. It is precisely because in this book I can claim *not* to be writing fiction that I can present Andreas's works in their social and cultural contexts and am able to ponder them in terms of the relationship between individual creativity and collective representation—or, in more current terms once again, the relationship between agency and structure.

Thus, maintaining the distinction between fiction and ethnography is less a matter of definition (usually a poor reason for doing anything) than of tactics: it recognizes both Andreas's and my own stated intentions, and clarifies them for the reader. On the division of emotional labor between expository and fictional writing, Wolfgang Iser offers a clear discrimination:

> Strangely enough, we feel that any confirmative effect—such as we implicitly demand of expository texts, as we refer to the objects they are meant

to present—is a defect in a literary text. For the more a text individualizes or confirms an expectation it has initially aroused, the more aware we become of its didactic purpose, so that at best we can only accept or reject the thesis forced upon us. (1980: 53)

This is nowhere more apposite than in the exploration of intimate thoughts, where fiction is perhaps the richest source of representations to supply the deliberate deficiencies of ethnographic writing.

The point becomes especially cogent in the Greek context. In a novel, the contradiction between the generic affirmation that one cannot read others' minds and the specific desire to do so—at once a paradox and a cliche for most Greeks—does not usually create a problem because the author continually draws attention away from the contradiction, allowing it to live in the text as it does in everyday subjective experience. But reading novels against the grain of ethnographic description brings the sense of paradox back into focus, providing a suddenly intense vision of the absurdity of treating culture as a consistent and ordered set of norms. If we now note that Greeks commonly typecast themselves as unruly and insubordinate, the relief this approach provides from rigid models of social structure becomes both welcome and logically appropriate.

As Michael Jackson—himself an ethnographer, poet, and novelist—has pointed out, moreover, the key difference between novels and ethnographies is not a technical one but concerns authorial intentions[22]—which means that we, too, are engaged in guessing motives. The novelist may freely invent, in effect constrained only by the audience's taste, credulity, and so on. The anthropologist makes an ethical commitment to engage in an act of representation that concerns other, living human beings. The difference does sometimes become blurred, as do the divisions among history, chronicle, and fiction—a matter of great concern to Andreas, since it radically affects the critical interpretation of his writings and, in an ironic illustration of what I have just written, the assessment of his underlying motives. For Andreas is always aware of writing in a small social world, and his motives never escape the scrutiny of small-town gossip. As a result, the cultural setting constantly and productively trans-

---

22. Michael Jackson, personal communication (marginal notes on an early draft of this book). He makes the crucial point—often overlooked in some of the literary criticism of ethnographic writing—that there is an important difference between using "novelistic *techniques* (tricks of the trade) such as narrative, reported dialogue, scene setting, sensible aspects of context" and "*making things up* (fiction)." See also Jackson 1995: 160–70. These points are extremely consequential for any discussion of ethnographic realism, especially when juxtaposed with the *ideological* realism of, for example, the Greek poets of Andreas's generation, who were reacting against the self-indulgence of a metaphorical discourse that appeared to reinforce the status quo (see Calotychos 1993: 257–76).

gresses the abstractions of theory—notably genre—and, far from subverting the specificities of the genres in question, invests them with social and cultural immediacy. This is fitting, given both Andreas's dislike of pure academicism and my own view that honest cultural scholarship must always include itself in its analytical scrutiny. If for Sartre good novelists cannot be among those drudges who "never bet on uncertain issues" (1949: 30), for Andreas that excitement—what Iser (1980) treats as a "transgression" of reality—often lies in a cheeky invasion of the immediate social world: by parodying the pompous he provokes their literal-minded anger, trapping them (intentionally or otherwise) in an ironic replay of what he appears to describe. It is precisely because he is a novelist, and insists on that identity, that he can and does refuse his readers and critics the right to tell him what to do (or not to do).

Thus, when Andreas's writings have seemed to me to illuminate familiar ethnographic questions—dowry and other gender issues, nationalism, ideologies of blood and kinship—from unfamiliar angles, it is because I read him as a novelist, not as an *ersatz* anthropologist. Our mutual engagement grew out of the complementarity, not the sameness, of what each of us was doing, although for me much of the fun of our encounters came from daring to imagine the difference as sameness. This is because Andreas's company, in person and in text, compensated me for some of my more obvious deficiencies and liabilities. A novelist's accounts of personal feelings, for example, may console the anthropologist who has encountered and perhaps gained intuitive empathy with individual subjectivities without the confidence to describe them. Ethnographic description, in turn, should illuminate the social constraints on individual action, particularly the largely invisible operation of culturally specific ideas about what is self-evident or universally true—the sort of detail that Sartre also saw as constantly threatening a novel's appeal once the common experiences of authors and their audiences had faded from memory:

> people of a same period and collectivity, who have lived through the same events, who have raised *or avoided* the same questions, *have the same taste in their mouth;* they have the same complicity, and there are the same corpses among them. That is why it is not necessary to write so much; there are key words. (1949: 68; author's emphases)

Ethnographers cannot rely on sharing so much knowledge with their readers; they must analytically describe that "taste in the mouth," much as literary scholars and historians must infuse unfamiliar contexts with reconstituted reality. But these scholarly activities explore some of the same social and cultural domains of human experience as does the creativity of the novelist. Rather than living in asocial authorial spaces constituted only by our respective imaginations, Andreas and I both participate in complicatedly overlapping and mutually illuminating *social worlds*.

Instead of trying to merge or assimilate the two genres—ethnography and novel—to each other, I prefer to exploit the acknowledged differences between them: by treating the novelist's voice as that of a member of the larger society, however idiosyncratic or disaffected, I recognize that whatever images of subjectivity may result from the encounter are still necessarily refractions of collective representations. When Andreas draws on his own experiences to describe pain, loss, loneliness, frustration, and intense desire to illustrate his characters' inner lives, he uses a socially salient vocabulary and images, much as we all must when we attempt to convey the common grounds of intensely private experience (see Abu-Lughod and Lutz 1990: 11–13).

Thus, even when he writes of his personal feelings and reactions, what Andreas says is always tailored to an imagined audience—not so much Eco's (1979) "Model Reader" as a Greek who will recognize both the common cultural grounding and the individual specificity that makes it interesting. The novelist thus makes the personal and the social palpable through each other. It is particularly in the social arena that Andreas leaves much unsaid, presumably because he can reasonably assume that his audience shares a common framework for interpreting his use of nuance and context. Many of what to me are revelations about a social universe are simply self-evident truisms for Andreas—for example, the internalization of a social world that admits of far more "jousting," to use the art student's image of perplexity, than many readers of this book will know from their own social universes. Part of my present task is to spell out some of these implications for readers who do not share this background knowledge—to provide what Sartre described as the taste in the mouths of those who live in the same cultural world as Andreas—without allowing them to become the crude determinants of a complex and idiosyncratic life.

◙

In the following chapters, I quote extensively from Andreas's writings and from interviews with him and others. All translations of Andreas's writings are my own. The sources of short quotations are clarified in the text. For greater convenience, however, block quotations are marked as follows: excerpts from published works by Andreas Nenedakis (listed below) have a justified right margin and are introduced with a rectangle ▮, while all block quotations from interviews have a ragged right margin and bear an oval ◗. The interviews were conducted in Athens, Crete, Paris, and Stockholm, during the 1993–94 academic year and in the summers of 1995 and 1996. The tapes and a full set of transcriptions are currently in my personal field archive, together with detailed notes and other documentation, including photocopies of letters from Andreas Nenedakis's personal records and a set of critical reviews, artwork, and photographs.

MAJOR WRITINGS BY ANDREAS NENEDAKIS

Bir Hakeim (1954)
White Fences (1959)
Oranges Are Bitter in October (1960)
The Daisies of the Saint (1962)
Anthology of Narratives 1900–1963 (1963)
Prohibited (The Diary of Youra) (1964)
The Painter Tsingos in War and in Prison (1965)
Svart April (published by Raben & Sjögren, Stockholm) (1969)
Black April (Greek version of *Svart April*) (1974)
The Cretan War (published by Tetradia tou Riga, Lund and Nicosia) (1969)
Ten Women (1973)
The Brave (1974)
The Manuscript of the School of Fine Arts (1976)
Rethimno (published in English and German) (1978)
The Cretan War *of Marinos Tzane Bounialis* (1979)
Old Photographs (a photographic collection) (1979)
Fortezza di Retimo (1980)
The Policemen of Stockholm (1981)
Efedhropateras: The English Strangled the Resistance on Crete (1982)
Rethemnos (A Town for Thirty Centuries) (1983)
Aristidis Stavroulakis (1984)
The Seine, My Home (1984)
Voukéfali (published by Kedros, Athens) (1991)
In Parallel with R. (published by Kedros, Athens) (1991)
George Nenedakis (1996)

2 ◘

PROVINCIAL BEGINNINGS

Andreas Nenedakis was born in a sleepy, impoverished, but architecturally stately provincial port town on the north coast of the island of Crete. Many years later, when Andreas's friend, the poet Kostis Papakongos, asked him for permission to publish one of his short stories in Sweden and tried to get him to supply some basic biographical details, Andreas wrote gruffly back:

> "Dear Kostis: Why are you asking me if you'll get my book? or whether you'll get my story? Well, take it, and do your thing if it suits your purposes. Just don't ask where I was born, write 'in Crete,'" says Andreas.—"Health and joy,[1] Andreas." So now I take up a letter to write to Andreas, and I tell him, "Look here, Andreas," I tell him, "I know you were born in Crete and I thank you for letting me publish it [that is, the story], but you haven't written to me when you were born and in what place." So now Andreas answers me: "Dear Kostis: Do you think the Swedes have nothing better on their minds than to wonder when and where Andreas Nenedakis was born? But since you insist, write that I was born in 1918 in Rethemnos."[2]

Yet Andreas is certainly proud of his birthplace: his impish self-deprecation does not hide that pride. Rethemnos, "the town of letters," *A Town for Thirty Centuries* in the title of Andreas's attempt at a local history, had been a great cultural center during the years of Venetian rule in the high Renaissance. In those days, it was the home of poets and playwrights who wrote in the local Greek vernacular (but using the Italian alphabetic system), their imagery and subject matter a product of the twin

---

1. This is a standard salutation in both speech and informal writing among Greeks.
2. Kostas and Kostis are both affectionate forms of Konstandinos (Constantine). Papakongos uses Kostis as the first part of his pen name.

The Venetian harbor of Rethemnos: traces of a lost tranquility (watercolor by Elli-Maria Komninou).

influences of village traditions of improvisatory verse and the imported literary models of the Italian Renaissance.[3] The rich conjunctures of urbane and local styles encountered in Andreas's life and work have a long history in Rethemnos, where vernacular poets and chroniclers continued to record the life of the town until at least the middle of the present century.

The Venetian occupation brought Cretan art and letters into the wider orbit of the European Renaissance but brutally exploited Crete's natural and human resources for its ambitious mercantile and military ends. The powerful influence of the Venetians on local art and, especially, architecture, and the literary florescence in vernacular Greek that accompanied it must be viewed in a context of religious intolerance, forced labor, and the brutal military repression that provoked one revolt after another while conspicuously failing to protect the local rural population from the increasingly bold depredations of pirates as well as the Turkish fleet.

In 1645, the Turks made a serious onslaught on Crete, and Rethemnos fell within a few months; the rest of the island was already

3. See M. Alexiou 1991. On military and mercantile aspects of Venetian rule, see Maltezou 1991; on literature, M. Alexiou 1991; Holton 1991b; Vincent 1980; and the several editions by S. Alexiou; on social life, see, most recently, Papadaki 1995.

largely under Turkish control, although Candia (now Iraklio) held out from 1648 until 1669. A Greek observer at the time, Marinos Tzane Bounialis, wrote the dramatic poem *The Cretan War*, of which Andreas Nenedakis published a critical edition to which I shall briefly turn later.

Of the larger towns, Rethemnos was the most profoundly affected demographically by the Turkish conquest. Together with Islamicized Greeks, the Turks eventually came to constitute the majority of its population. Rethemnos, lacking road connections to the other towns, its cultural glories no longer of interest to its occupiers, began a slow economic decline that was somewhat cushioned by the still cosmopolitan character of its remaining trade.

The decline was, nevertheless, inexorable. In his novel *Voukéfali*, Andreas paints a vivid picture of the process in its final stages; in the 1950s the Rethemnos-born novelist and essayist Pandelis Prevelakis described the continuing decline in an affectionate portrait, *The Tale of a Town* (1961). World War II brought new hardship and devastation. But the final blow to the town's established economy came in the early 1960s. Until that time, the local soap industry had always had a secure source of raw materials in the olive-oil producers of the hinterland and a steady outlet in the European trade. But factory-produced detergents suddenly flooded the Balkans and wrecked the town's sole firm economic base. Only with the rise of tourism in the mid-1970s did an alternative begin to reverse the sense of terminal decay; but the larger lesson had not been learned, and today the same tendency to rely on a single economic resource again places a fragile local economy at risk. The sudden mushrooming of a "New Town" largely supported by the tourist industry—and latterly by the newly established (1979) University of Crete—cannot disguise the nervousness of those who live off tourism. Their brave assertions about the spiritual blessings that a reduction in the level of tourism might bring emphasize a deep concern, sometimes almost verging on desperation, more than they conceal it. But at least a few of the poorer residents of the "Old Town" have been able to extract resources from the state's historic conservation authorities in time to skim a small profit from the romanticism of the tourist trade.[4]

The gradual economic decline of Rethemnos during the eighteenth and nineteenth centuries followed the progressive erosion of Turkish political authority through internal revolts and external shifts in the balance of global power. Turkish control of Crete came to a limping, ignominious end. First, a major revolt in 1866 ended in the Turkish massacre of the monks of the Arkadi monastery, along with the unarmed villagers who had fled there for refuge. This event stirred the indignation of pro-Greek

4. This process is discussed in detail in my *A Place in History* (1991a).

activists in several European countries, including the novelist Victor Hugo, the folklorist and traveler Dora d'Istria, and the Italian revolutionary leader Garibaldi, and the pressure for real change began to build in earnest. Two decades before Andreas's birth, yielding to international pressure and still plagued with local insurrections and lawlessness, Turkey recognized Cretan autonomy, with the Greek king's second son, George—later succeeded by a professional politician—as High Commissioner. A scant five years before Andreas's birth, in 1913, Crete became part of the Greek territorial state, which had declared its independence from Turkey in 1821.

The family of Andreas's father hailed from Asi-Gonia, a highland pastoral village in the Khania province close to the border of the province of which Rethemnos is the capital. The village was well known as a proudly independent community, active in resistance to foreign invaders and linked to neighboring communities by reciprocal animal-theft and by the ties of spiritual kinship through which such mutual hostility was converted into an often tense form of alliance. It has been so described by a philhellenic scholar-traveler (and, at the time of writing, British ambassador in Athens—see Llewellyn Smith 1965) and an anthropologist (Machin 1983). Known to the English-speaking world as the home of the author of *The Cretan Runner,* a heroic tale of local and Allied resistance to the Nazi occupier of Crete (Psychoundakis 1955), it still commands international journalistic attention for its ongoing feuds (Smith 1996). The village men were constantly at war with villages in the neighboring district of Sfakia. On one famous occasion around 1878, in the midst of a major uprising against the Turks, twenty Sfakians and three Asi-Goniots—one of whom was Andreas's father—swept down on horseback on the eastern end of the island, no mean feat in the days of poor or nonexistent roads, and carried off a series of devastating raids in the fertile Messara Plain. They then promptly returned to their mountain home, fighting off Turks as they went—although Andreas, always skeptically attentive to the details of any grand story, recalls that the pigs would not be budged from their sties and that few of the stolen animals of other kinds actually survived the trek back to Asi-Gonia.[5] Whatever one may think of such heroic legends, with which Sfakia is especially well endowed (see Damer 1988), these were times of enormous unrest, with the Turkish rulers increasingly on the defensive and virtually no official policing of violence in the rural communities.

Indeed, Andreas's father, Nikolaos, as a member of the proud Nenes

---

5. Pigs are notoriously hard to coax away in silence, although I have heard that a sponge soaked in butter and attached to a tether will do the trick.

clan,[6] was caught in the revenge cycles of this strongly patrilineal society that had driven so many before him into enforced exile in order to avoid annihilation. He had killed a man to avenge his own twenty-year-old brother, himself the victim of a fatal encounter with Sfakian sheep-thieves. To save his skin, but also to avoid further provocation with the attendant threat of wholesale massacre, Nikolaos moved to the comparatively sedate ambience of Rethemnos, and then to the mainland Greek port city of Piraeus (where there were many Cretans at the time).

But he did not manage to lead a peaceful life even then. He became actively interested in Greek national politics. Crete had by this time become a nominally autonomous political entity, free of Ottoman control, but most Cretans regarded this as a provisional situation and expected unification with Greece at any time.[7] He sided with the progressive faction of the national political spectrum, a group headed by the politician Charilaos Trikoupis, and, in the course of a political brawl, he struck the police chief—or so a self-designated witness alleged when Nikolaos Nenedakis was unlucky enough to testify at least a year later, at an unrelated trial at which the witness claimed to recognize him. In jail, serving a life sentence, his toughness earned him the coveted job of coffeeshop manager (the role also of a highland villager of my acquaintance who had killed his brother's assassin—under circumstances so remarkably similar that one is tempted to speculate on the extent to which familiar narrative structures may actually shape events in a setting culturally predisposed to recognize such "social dramas" [see Herzfeld 1985: 79–82, and Turner 1974: 31–42]); the prison authorities wanted someone who could control the other inmates, of whom many were Maniats from the southern Peloponnese—men whose reputation for ferocious violence was matched only by that of the Cretans.

As coffeeshop manager, Nikolaos Nenes suddenly had access to the prison's regular supply of newspapers, brought in for the staff and for prisoners awarded leisure time for their good behavior; his response was to teach himself, at long last, how to read with some degree of fluency. He had no expectation of early release, but suddenly the fighting against Turkey in Macedonia created an urgent need for fighting men, and Nenes

6. Cretan clan names tend to become family surnames with the distinctive -akis ending, suggesting either a diminution of the owner's persona or an affectionate form of reference. Locally, it is said that the Ottomans insisted on these names in order to humiliate Christians. But it seems more probable that this form originated from the idea that those who are members of a given patriclan (or patrigroup, as I preferred to dub it [in Herzfeld 1985]) are in a sense "sons" of the group: hence Nenedakis, the "son" of (or "little") Nenes.

7. The first high commissioner was a son of the Greek king, and he was succeeded by a Greek politician. During this period, Crete issued stamps and currency and ran its own police authority and legal institutions.

Manhood triumphant: Andreas's father and the captured flag (photograph in Andreas Nenedakis's personal archive).

had hopes of heading for the front. Many of the young village men who did manage to gain their freedom at this time had learned the hardy arts of survival in hill country from Nenes himself. Several of them were his kinsmen; some were former apprentices (*tsirákia*) and ten years his junior. But they now jealously protected their own chances of command and heroism in the new emergency, thinks Andreas, and did not call for Nikolaos Nenes to join them. It was only when his patron Venizelos returned to power through the military coup known as the Goudi Revolt in 1909[8] that Nikolaos Nenes, now recategorized as a political prisoner rather than as a common criminal, walked out of prison to his freedom. The doughty old warrior finally got his chance to fight in the wars of national expansion. So he closed his shop and, now in his mid-forties, went off to join the struggle in Epirus.

8. The 1909 Goudi revolt, in which discontented army units stationed near Athens threatened to march on that city, triggered a series of political events that eventually led to the election of Venizelos as prime minister for the first time in December 1910 (see Vournas 1957).

From Epirus he brought back a Turkish flag as a trophy. It was kept in the house, recalls Andreas,

● and I didn't know what it was. And it got destroyed and my mother didn't take care of it, so to speak; afterwards [that is, at this later date], it was destroyed during the German Occupation. Our things were broken up, you know, the Germans stole them and so forth.

A nephew remembers the eventual fate of the flag differently. According to this source, the flag remained in the house until the colonels' coup d'état in 1967. But then, fearful of being accused of harboring pro-Turkish sympathies and being discredited altogether, this uniformly communist family destroyed the flag: for the military dictators conflated all alleged national enemies—Turks, Slavs, communists—in a single conspiratorial threat that they invoked to justify their harsh repression. Whatever the actual circumstances of its destruction, the flag itself does seem to have existed; the recent charge that it did not, which was bracketed with the accusation that Andreas had portrayed his father in a pro-Turkish light (Tsouderos 1995: 8) shows that the game of nationalist name-calling dies hard.[9]

In any event, Nikolaos Nenes was never far from any fray that fed his political loyalties. In 1920, when Venizelos was ousted by the royalist elements whose poor leadership was then credited with the collapse of the Greek irredentist adventure in Asia Minor two years later, some Cretan Venizelists broke into the prisons and stole a huge number of weapons from the warders' stores. The house of Nenes became a major cache. As a result, Nenes and many other known Venizelists were arrested and sentenced to "exile" (eksoría)—banishment under close surveillance—in the then overwhelmingly royalist district of Tripoli, in the Peloponnese. Thus the father bore punishments that, in form if not in degree, anticipated the sufferings of his son in the years ahead.

Andreas's mother came from a village in the reputedly gentler Amari valley—a village that nevertheless was also then known even in the wilder mountain communities, as indeed it still is, as the haunt of notably skilled, audacious animal-thieves. It was in fact through animal-theft that Andreas's parents came to marry. His mother's family was riven by internecine feud originating in the bad relations between the respective sets of children of a man's two successive wives. The sons of a daughter of the first wife talked Andreas's father, who was already feared for his prowess in raiding and admired for his reserved hauteur and unflinching convictions, into joining in their plot to destroy the sons of their mother's half-

---

9. See chapter 8 for a fuller account of the charge and Andreas's response to it.

sister—their first cousins. Such open hostility among close kin is relatively unusual, but, when it does occur, it seems to be correspondingly intense: more is at stake, both morally (in terms of a sense of betrayal) and materially (in terms of shared prospects of inheriting property from common antecedents). Nor is the use of an unrelated ally entirely unexpected: when the point is to destroy a local rival, especially a kinsman, it is advisable to have an accomplice from relatively far away, an agent and scapegoat who can carry away the booty as well as a goodly share of the blame for what otherwise carries the stigma of internecine aggression.

In the event, the raid was successful: all the sheep and cattle belonging to one of the hated cousins were spirited away. Despite the ploy of using an unrelated ally, however, the victims managed to identify the culprits. Andreas does not say how they managed to do so, but it is usual in such cases for the victim's kinsmen to make inquiries, using their own connections (usually spiritual kin) as agents to locate the missing livestock; while ostensibly they are not told the names of the culprits, nothing prevents them from drawing their own inferences from such data as the location of the missing animals or reports of their having been sighted. Such inferences can coalesce, over time, into moral certainties (see Herzfeld 1985: 197).

A quarter of a century later, Andreas's father—after his return from Epirus with the captured Turkish flag—returned to Rethemnos, where he ran a *tavérna* (restaurant). One day a kinsman of his erstwhile victim came to find him at the tavérna and suggested that Nikolaos should now, in the more generous atmosphere created by the uneventful passage of years, marry his victim's daughter and so put an end to the feud once and for all.

❶ And of course he did accept the alliance, and they were married. Still, it is very strange. . . .

Alliance was (and still is) a conventional resolution to feuds in the Cretan hill communities, but Andreas grew up in a world of increasingly different social values—first amid the provincial gentility of Rethemnos, where the signs of wilder origins are demurely suppressed, and then in the cosmopolitan whirl of Athens; and after that, although with deep misgivings, abroad. To him, such an arrangement would indeed seem both perfectly natural and "very strange." At the same time, he subscribes to the conventional view that animal-theft was a legacy of resistance to the Turkish occupier:

❶ In former times the thieves didn't rob poor people. They used to steal from the Turks or from the very rich, let's say, those who collaborated in some way with the Turks, do you understand? Theft had a heroic character back then; later, of course, those who were hungry used to steal, and now they've made a business out of it.

Andreas thus attributes the origins of animal-theft to the period of Turkish rule, when, he says, "there wasn't even a cigarette to be had in the villages." His account conforms in every respect to that offered to this day by the inhabitants of those villages where the practice remains endemic.[10] It is also fully consistent with larger patterns in Greek culture, above all the refusal to see as autochthonous anything that might offend a "European" standard of decency. The attribution of blame to others—here, "hunger" caused by the Turks—fits a political cosmology, a way of explaining misfortune,[11] in which Andreas also follows a series of distinguished critics of foreign intervention in Cretan (for example, see Papamanousakis 1979) and Greek affairs.

But it also reproduces village rhetoric in another important respect. That the villagers had nothing to eat figures substantially in the rhetoric of self-exoneration for the collective taint of animal-theft. Andreas suggests that this privation generated a "leftish tendency" among the poorer Cretans of the time: "Imagine that for the whole district, the whole town of Rethimni [a formal version of the name], which then had a population of about ten thousand, three or four handcarts went in" with all the agricultural supplies that were available. Andreas also links this austerity, learned early in his life and still reflected in his personal habits and his prose style alike, with his own political disposition. Local memory suggests, however, that in the hill villages meat was already a major source of food. It was, and is, the quintessential shepherds' produce and the ultimate symbol of their masculinity. For many years now it has been a minor component of Andreas's diet, but one to which he still accords sentimental importance.

Andreas's father conformed in many respects to the idealized image of the tough mountain shepherd, meat-eating and all. He had been a fearsome animal-thief, as one had to be to survive in the competitive social world of these highland Cretan shepherds. Once arrived in Rethemnos, on the surface a place of genteel provincial urbanity, he retained his fearsome reputation and even enhanced it. In the face of any contrary argument he was wont to declare, "I'm the Prosecutor here!"—an ironic gesture of legal authority from this former animal-thief and blood-feud hero but, for that very reason, a fair index of how thin a conceptual barrier separated constitutional authority from socially based ideals of leadership

10. See the account in Herzfeld 1985: 21–22.

11. This is what I have elsewhere (1992: 5–8) called "secular theodicy"—in the sense that evil requires explanation, especially from state structures that have seemed to guarantee some measure of redemption.

in Crete. At the same time, true to the patrilineal principles on which the blood-feud is based, he held that blood itself was the physical carrier of male virtue—an idea that villagers often celebrate by maintaining that the red wine drunk to resolve a feud or to celebrate a marriage is the blood of the patriline and thus the means of ensuring the birth of many sons. Once, when Andreas (then six years old at most) cut his knee, his father told the boy, "Quiet there! You have gold in your blood. Do you hear? You'll be well right away!" On this argument of blood, all Greeks, Andreas maintains, claimed their superiority over their foes, the Turks, invoking a truly ancient ancestry.[12]

Thus it was that the Cretan highlanders could so easily reconcile localism, patriotism, and extremes of insubordination toward the state. Drawing on the same logic that allowed the Greeks to claim spiritual ancestorhood over all of Europe even while contemplating their present political and economic dependence on the continent's more powerful countries, the Cretans—recently absorbed administratively into a nation-state that often seemed to treat them as savages—looked to the still deeper antiquity of their island culture: "What I'm telling you, that is, what my father told me about our golden blood and all that, all the Greeks were that way—and the Cretans more so!"

When Nikolaos Nenes moved from his native village to the town of Rethemnos, he did not adapt easily to the urbanity around him. Andreas was later to recall his embarrassment at what, as a schoolboy, he felt to be his father's uncouth language—an attitude he radically reversed in later years. Nikolaos opened a grocery store and, later, a tavérna. The latter was a simple affair: Rethemniots did not habitually eat out in those days, even on special occasions, and establishments like the one owned by Nikolaos Nenes catered primarily to the rural folk who came to town to buy supplies; indeed, such cookshops still exist. Running an establishment of this kind was logical work for the former shepherd as he gradually accumulated the signs of urbanity and social expertise, but it also maintained his visible identity in the urban setting as someone who dealt with food and, especially, with meat.

Andreas remembers that his father never gave up these meat-eating habits:

● I'm in Sweden, now, during the [Papadopoulos] dictatorship with my wife and so on. So I came into conflict with various other Greeks, discussions, political matters, etcetera. So once some Macedonian[13] told me, "You've come here," says he, "and you've filled yourselves up with

12. See Roger Just's (1992) extremely lucid discussion of these matters.
13. Here, presumably, a native speaker of Greek from the Greek province of Macedonia.

meat, in Sweden." I didn't say anything back to him, but I was on the verge of weeping, because I am remembering that in our house, all my life long, he [Andreas's father] used to hang up a lamb in the house every day. Because my father was a carnivore, he didn't eat anything else. That's what he was accustomed to. So I went to Sweden to fill myself up with meat? Since my whole life long. . . . If I'd told that man—who was a good fellow, but that's just the way he expressed himself, let's say—he wouldn't have believed it. Do you see? Or other kinds [of food], let's say, cheese, things like that. There was, [as] I told you, in those houses like ours a plentiful supply.

Andreas brings to the narrative of his former years a strong sense of connection among food, body, and person. Typically, too, for the older mountain shepherds of Crete, he sees no contradiction between a memory of plentiful meat and the image of a time of hunger. The shepherds used to complain of hunger even though they had a plentiful supply of meat, because their rough transhumant lifestyle meant that they could only rarely enjoy the luxury of a home-cooked meal.[14]

It is clear from his account that his father retained the dietary habits that went with the studied insouciance and aggressive masculinity of the mountain shepherd. But these stances ill matched the specialized acumen of the merchant role to which Andreas's father aspired. Completely unable to withstand—or understand—the 1929 global stock market collapse, locally exacerbated by three successive years (1928–30) of agriculturally disastrous weather, the elderly shepherd-turned-merchant turned increasingly to drink for solace. Andreas has a particularly humiliating recollection of seeing shepherds making off with some of the sheep that his father owned and then watching the thieves heedlessly digging up the bean plants and greens to cook in the evening because they had become sick of a diet composed only of cheese and milk. There was nothing he could do against a group of armed and desperate shepherds.

But the worst blow was treachery close to home. The elder Nenes was cheated by his own partner, a kinsman, and was consequently unable to meet his mounting debts at a time when other, more prescient merchants who had acted early to buy imported rice in bulk were able to survive the crash. This experience gave an unusually ugly twist to the local adage that one "should eat and drink with kin but should have no business dealings with them."[15] The ordinary sense of this saying is that

14. See especially Herzfeld (1985: 134). As one of the primary symbols of masculinity, unalloyed meat-eating could imply the endurance of hardship rather than the pleasures of domestic luxury.

15. This saying must be interpreted in the context of Greek social rhetoric, which often exaggerates in pointed ways ("You speak Greek better than we do!"). But there is also a

kin tend to expect favored treatment to an extent incompatible with making profits. In fact, business partnerships often did involve even close kin, but these rarely survived a single generation as the complexities of local norms of property transmission—which require that each asset be separately and equally divided among all coheirs—placed too much financial strain on the relatively fragile obligations of kinship. For this reason, too, friendships were often easier with more distant kin—even with those, as Andreas recalls, who did not bear the same surname.

This observation is important for another reason. Those who shared a surname were patrikin, a more serious basis of association in feud-ridden Crete than in many other parts of Greece. Nikolaos Nenes's partner belonged neither to his own nor to his wife's patriline—a detail the importance of which will become especially apparent much later in this book when we look at the social organization and cultural emphases of a specifically *literary* feud. Here I am more particularly concerned to note that Cretans of Nikolaos Nenes's background were always interested in showing off their extensive networks of kin, and especially the strength of their respective patrilines. As shepherds, they could both afford to increase their flocks in proportion to the number of their sons and enjoy greater security from raids in proportion to the number of their agnates with useful connections in the other villages of the region. The habit of boasting about one's enormous patriline was predictably widespread among the fierce shepherds of Sfakia, the rocky district of the island's southwestern corner:

❯ Listen to me: I don't know if you're aware of what *Sfakianosingénia* [literally, "Sfakian kinship"] means? That is, in former years, and nowadays too, this [attitude] is still kept up somewhat. . . . In former years people wanted to present themselves as having . . . belonging . . . or to look like [coming] from a big patriline [*yeniá*], so to speak. This thing, in the Ionian Islands, means that it's a noble house [*spíti arkhondikó*] and is inscribed in the *Libro d'Oro*.[16]

I have noted the contempt Andreas feels for those who, in his view falsely, claim noble status in Rethemnos. Here he pokes gentle fun at the pretensions of his own shepherd stock but notes that their concern with high status is not very different from "noble families in Europe, but we'll take an example [from] the Ionian Islands, they have few members." In Rethemnos, even today, patrilineal kinship ties are an especially potent

---

practical dimension: kin have expectations on which they sometimes insist to excess, and they are morally hard to gainsay. People often fear the economic consequences of sharing space (except socially) and avoid entanglements.

16. This is the Venetian register of ennobled families.

bond, to be invoked especially for the purpose of recruiting support in political campaigns. As for *Sfakianosingénia,* it conferred the great advantage that one could hail a large number of men by a suitably vague kinship term such as *thíe* ("uncle") without knowing—or particularly caring—what exactly the relationship was.

This ethos of imprecision—which extends to matters of time, money, and even the most sacred ties of godparenthood—stands in direct opposition to the pedantry and calculation that such men discern in formal institutions such as the bureaucracy and the educational system (Herzfeld 1991a: 168–74). In this society, a true man, a "captain" (*kapetánios*), must constantly show that he cares not a whit for material gain or political advancement: he masters events, not they him. Above all, he despises the petty exactitude of the law. The ideal world, nostalgically imagined, is one in which the spoken promise—the "word of honor"—renders the contemptibly distrustful institutions of the contract irrelevant and ridiculous. But this does not mean that such a man does not calculate at all. On the contrary, to the precise extent that his actions belie the merest hint of calculation they tangibly increase the social value of the *kapetánios* himself. The disavowal of material interests confers material advantages. Old Nenes was neither unaware nor very pleased that, at a time when there was virtually no new construction, one of the more successful merchants had succeeded in building a brand-new hotel—a well-financed piece of social climbing that Andreas was to satirize more than six decades later, thereby throwing new fuel on the fires of interclan feuding.

In fact, his father's vicissitudes fed more than agnatic loyalties in the young Andreas. The cataclysmic effects of the great financial crash can hardly have failed to impress a hot-headed youth already avidly reading supposedly subversive writers like Friedrich Engels and introducing his classmates to them. Also, his father's adherence to the local contempt for pedantic precision may have prepared the way for Andreas's later disgust with the academicism of much Greek art—a disgust that he expresses very much in terms of admiration for the wild mountain fighters against the foreign ("Bavarian") pen-pushers who tried to capture their bodies in prison and their untamed spirit in the fussy, pastel-shaded art of officially sanctioned schools.

For all his swashbuckling ways, the elder Nenedakis was certainly no uncouth braggart, nor did he lack an appreciation of knowledge to which he could not himself aspire. Notably, he made his sons, including Andreas, go to school and insisted that they try to learn French. (Andreas's surviving sister did not receive this schooling—not, Andreas avers, because their father objected in principle to having his daughter educated, but because by that time the family fortunes had sunk to a low financial ebb.) Neither this attempt at formal schooling nor Andreas's brief period of study under Lilika Nakou, the French-educated high-school teacher and future novelist who was to chronicle Rethemniot school life and small-town morality (and who many years later became an enthusiastic reader of Andreas's own writings), did much for his French. In 1968, while in political exile in Paris, he could barely articulate a few words of the language. As a schoolboy, he was simply not interested; as an adult, he was already seriously deaf—the result of constant exposure to heavy gunfire during the battle of El Alamein—when it occurred to him that he might have found it useful to learn more of a foreign language.

Today Andreas looks back on his adolescent years with regret for opportunities missed. He is puzzled that he and his brothers were all un-ruly pupils and did not measure up to their father's determination to offer them every chance of breaking free from the limiting world of villagers and laborers. He contrasts his wildness then with the seriousness of his own son. The latter is named Nikolaos for Andreas's father in accordance with a customary practice that supposedly identifies name, character, and blood with each other,[17] but Andreas is no rigid genetic determinist de-spite his occasional habit of linking common descent with shared physical traits. Certainly he perceives change from one generation to the next:

> Nowadays, that is, I think about or [rather] compare my son's behavior toward me, for example, I say, "But these . . . these are saintly lads"— [not just he] but the lads all around, so to speak. All those things they say about youth these days, they're absurd.

And he went on to describe his participation in a dynamite bombing at-tack against a local politician, in order to show how he spent the time his father wanted him to devote to self-improvement.

Surely it is Andreas himself we hear in the reactions of an older man who finds himself among a group of youths quietly entertaining them-selves and talking with sad foreboding in a *boîte,* or informal musical club, in Athens on the night of the coup of 21 April, 1967:

> A young man had seated himself at the piano and silence again fell in the hall (*sála*). He played an unknown piece of popular music. He was a young composer. Someone clapped as soon as he began and he responded with a backward gesture of his hand. He played a long time. No one talked. They were all plunged into their innermost selves. In their thoughts. You might have been in a village council of elders (*dhimoyerondía*). And then they talk about the hooliganism that currently afflicts today's youth.
>
> "When I was younger I was livelier," said the author. "Not just livelier; I was a great troublemaker. We set our neighborhood by the ears. We broke windows, played practical jokes, didn't leave a soul in peace. I remember

17. See Herzfeld 1982b; Kenna 1976; Sutton 1997; Vernier 1991.

one evening, after a long tour of the streets singing in a way that made everyone really upset, we passed the house of a French teacher. What's odd is that French teachers were peculiar people. That's the way it seemed to us, but the truth was they'd been taught a whole different culture and behaved accordingly, like, so to speak, beings from outer space. So do you know what we did? He was married and had children, and would have been asleep at that hour. We jammed up his bell with a bit of candlewax. The house was in uproar. The whole neighborhood woke up, they called for an electrician—but where were they going to find one at such an hour? They turned on all the lights and were in the streets until dawn since they couldn't figure out what was wrong. Well, every time has its personality. But these days, who plays such jokes?" (*Black April*, pp. 28–29)

Andreas's father organized his children's entry into polite society down to the last detail:

● Every autumn, do take note of this! he bought us umbrellas. So that we would not get wet. Caps, clothing, suits, that is—everything. And I remember that we used to go for walks, on outings. And I remember that it impressed me, gave me pleasure, that others would look at me, because I was better dressed than the others. And this was due to my father, who was. . . . What can I tell you, it was not just that he was dispos[ed] . . . wanted to dress his children well, but I have the impression that he was . . . he had a . . . what's it called? something inside himself, he wanted, so to speak, he *liked* it. He himself was always very well dressed, a smartly turned-out person.

In the same way, the young Andreas, having begun to read poetry on his own initiative, gloried in his new-found erudition and sought to turn it to social advantage—a mark of distinction that transcended the immediate horizons of Rethemnos. Speaking of one of the anthologies circulating at the time, he recalls with more than a hint of self-mockery:

● I remember down by the waterfront where we young people used to take our evening strolls, so to speak, I would say in a loud voice, "I've read Polemis's poetry collection," so to speak, in order to impress people that I was . . . that I was reading.

Thus, in the early upbringing of the future communist activist, we see a formative alchemy that turned village notions of self-regard (*eghoïsmós*) into unmistakably bourgeois preoccupations with good form.

Such marks of distinction, moreover, were more striking in the narrow frame of the provincial prewar Greek economy than they would be amid today's riotous consumerism. Books were a rare commodity, umbrellas obviously a luxury. More comprehensively, Andreas points out that prices were much higher in relation to wages than they are now; an oke (about 2¾ pounds) of oil, for example, often exceeded a laborer's daily wage (twenty to twenty-five drachmas). As a youth, each New Year's Day he received five drachmas as a ritual gift (the *kalí khéra*, or "good hand") from his father, whose hand he formally kissed. But there were no opportunities for an eager young man to earn some cash independently. Manual labor was done by a few specialists—painters and plasterers, for example—of low status:

> ● They were [certain specific] families. And they would sometimes take someone on—especially Asia Minor refugees, so to say. But I don't know of a single family at that time whose children worked . . . as they work in America. . . . Where, you know, I read that Truman used to sell newspapers, let's say, or, you know, something like that. If that had happened with a family, if the son of any family at all had sold newspapers, people wouldn't have talked to the . . . They had a class-based view of things, so to speak, about all that. Work, jobs of that kind for example, were considered very humiliating, very demeaning.

But, notes Andreas, this was not purely a matter of social ideology: aside from the shoemakers, who constituted a true proletariat, "the labor market was very narrow." The humblest of all were the smiths, new urban residents whose customers were almost all rural folk with animals to shoe and harness; while these artisans took on apprentices from their home villages, they studiously avoided hiring close kin, seeing their lowly status as a temporary humiliation through which succeeding generations of ambitious rustics would pass.[18]

Such fragile distinctions are not a far cry from the village context, in which small advantages created large prestige differentials and where the claims of some clans to be of high status (*kalósiri*) were always subject to contest. In early twentieth-century Rethemnos, while a more lasting system of class discrimination had begun to emerge, the few "hearths" (*tzákia*, semi-aristocratic clans) were mostly of recent village or merchant origin and had achieved their new status through wealth rather than ancestry. The means by which they could hope to perpetuate their status were limited and fragile. Under these conditions, it is not surprising that Andreas's proud and ambitious father would seek to enter his children in the competition for social rank or that, years later, one of them—Andreas himself—would provoke the ire of these grand families by poking fun at their insecure pretensions.

---

18. See also note 15. Distrust of kin is often grounded in a material context and is always especially bitter. The avoidance of hiring close (especially agnatic) kin as apprentices reduces the risk of clashes over accusations of exploitation and maltreatment.

Andreas's mother had already been somewhat exposed to such preoccupations at the time of her marriage. She came from a relatively well-to-do family; her father was a local party organizer for the Cretan Liberal politician Eleftherios Venizelos, who later became prime minister of Greece. She brought with her a substantial dowry in gold coins and further enhanced her husband's social standing by bearing him six children. While he maintained an aloof dignity and rarely showed his family the depth of his affection for them, she sang to the children and tried to temper their father's austere pride with a warmer presence. But there were six children to make demands on her time and emotion, so that sometimes they felt that they were not getting enough individual attention from her—for, as Andreas rhetorically demanded, "which one was she supposed to embrace first?"

Her family at least provided her with a vicarious outlet for hidden ambitions. She thirsted for more knowledge than the restrictive ambience of provincial Crete could offer. Thus her brother, although an educated man and himself a schoolteacher, could not countenance the prospect of a sister able to rival his own sophistication. Whereas their father had been more than willing to let the young woman go on to secondary school and to a possible career as a teacher, her brother forcibly dragged her away from school, concealing his own motives in the categories of a traditionalist ethic: "back then girls, women, didn't go to school; it wasn't allowed."

His mother's experience never ceased to disturb Andreas, who attributes so much of his own literariness to her influence on his childhood. In his novel *Ten Women*, a character describes the traditional inculcation of a sense of inferiority:

▌ I often thought, why did people say we women were bad? And I believed when I was little that I couldn't be a woman because I wasn't bad. I respected my father and never looked at him straight in the eye; I never argued with him in all my life, even when I was a little girl. But nor did he ever yell at me because he wasn't one of those people who speak nastily. But I often wondered, when I used to see other parents caressing their children, why my father had never once petted me. He wasn't tender either with me or with my mother. He took care of us; we lacked for nothing at home; he bought me dresses, shoes, whatever I needed; but the only time I could talk to him was at table at midday or the evening or, occasionally, on Sundays, when we all went together for our afternoon walk. Later, when I grew up, he took me out of school, "because too many letters aren't good for women," as he used to say. And because I was upset I didn't see or speak to him all that time. He, however, said—and knew—that I would get over it. (p. 183)

But that was a self-fulfilling prophecy: the father, arguing from a position of strength, presumably would know that his daughter could not, and would not, sulk for long. Here, in fact, Andreas satirizes the notion that a father not only knows what is best for his daughter but can establish to his own satisfaction that she has internalized and accepted that outcome. This portrayal of her innermost thoughts is patently false—and is intended to be read as such. For Andreas was to experience successive right-wing regimes' attempts to control the leftists' hearts and minds by forcing them to sign so-called declarations of loyalty to the state (or of repentance for their supposedly past ideals); he knows that such literal-minded readings of outer appearances as the exact expressions of innermost thoughts represent the kind of self-deception in which only those with unchallenged power can afford to indulge.

So much, then, for the dutiful daughter. Her father seems to be a composite of Andreas's mother's brother and his own notably undemonstrative father; the attitudes are those we meet in a more dramatic strained form in the heroic figure of Captain Michalis in Nikos Kazantzakis's novel *Freedom or Death* (1956).

Andreas learned from his mother's experience that resignation was not really the same as acceptance. For, despite this early discouragement, Andreas's mother kept her appetite for reading, and Andreas—who thinks she had a "natural genius"—remembers that she subscribed to a locally produced journal, of which Pandelis Prevelakis, author of *Tale of a Town*, was the editor during the first couple of years of Andreas's life.

She also decorated their home with prints of famous paintings; Andreas especially remembers a heroic Delacroix depicting the Greek national struggle. Andreas's father, however, had artistic skills of his own—skills in which we can perhaps discern the source of Andreas's involvement with "representational [that is, visual] [artists]" (*ikastikí*) as well as of the deep respect that he has always evinced for the technical skills of artisanship:

> However . . . let me tell you something now that will surprise you, perhaps. That old father of mine, when he was in jail—here perhaps all the prisoners did and still do just jobs—made *komblén* [embroidery named for the famous Parisian tapestry factory of Gobelins]. *Komblén. Komblén* is a cloth on which one embroiders, and, now, it's a branch, so to speak, of the visual arts (*kládhos . . . ikastikós*), so to speak, do you understand? There exist two [such] works of his, which we have at home.

In this modest way, Andreas became intimately familiar with the arts of visual representation. The designs included religious illustrations. And old Nikolaos Nenes even taught his younger sister how to sew. His sewing skills took a practical turn: he knew how to mend shirts and stitch the heavy shepherds' boots that are still *de rigueur* among young mountain shepherds. Andreas recalls that it was then usual for shepherds to stitch (or at least patch up) their own boots. "But to sew shirts is a very difficult thing." Andreas's recollections of his father warn against easy assumptions about "traditional" gender roles. Given his artisanal view of the writer's craft, moreover, these recollections perhaps indicate one source of his ability and eagerness, in later years, to write in the female first-person voice—although, to be sure, there were several important antecedents as well as contemporary Greek writers who made the same move, all of them familiar figures of his universe.[19]

But the main source of this empathy with the plight of women in Greek society was certainly his mother. Andreas seems to have brooded all his life on the injustices of her position and on her seemingly infinite capacity for self-sacrifice. Unlike many men of his generation, he did not take her sufferings for granted, as part of the divinely ordained condition of women, but identified with her role as a woman whose intellectual goals were thwarted by a brother's jealous ambition.

He also marvels yet at the extent of her self-effacing ability to nurture. She even sacrificed the trappings of her body for her children:

> She was from a well-to-do family, and so forth. Do you know—a baker told me this—that it came to the point that this woman didn't have bread to eat? Why's that? Because it was—I was in exile [in prison camps], my brothers in jail, and she had nothing, just the house she lived in—nothing! Just think of the woman's misery. I'll tell you something very . . . let's say . . . moving. I remember that she had a row of gold teeth—she had no real teeth, so to speak, and so on. When I returned from exile, I asked her—I saw she didn't have any [gold teeth] left: "What have you done with your teeth?" Well, I found out—she didn't tell me herself—that she had sold them and made [food] parcels out of them for me (*mou ta ékane dhémata*) to send to me in exile. That means I ate her teeth. Can you understand the meaning of such a thing?

In an arresting metaphor of reversal, Andreas drew nourishment from the body of his mother—whom, in a dramatic conversational reversal of normative gender ideology, he also represents as the quintessential male figure who withstands the worst hardships with fortitude: "She was blind for eight years. Not a sigh was heard from her. She was a *pallikári*"— the ideal type of the young male fighter, whose enemy this time, however, is neither Turk nor German but sheer privation.

"I ate her teeth": a few astonished words enfold a tale of dignity

---

19. Earlier writers include Stratis Myrivilis, Alexander Papadiamantis, and George Vizyenos; modern writers include Kostas Taktsis and Stratis Tsirkas.

salvaged—scavenged, even—from the depths of a family's humiliation at the hands of a vindictive police state. They look forward to many of the moral commitments that Andreas was later to take up in his writing, and they describe the self-reliance on which Andreas would need to call as a political exile in various prison camps and abroad. In particular, the specter of the intellectually gifted village woman thwarted in her dreams of education and committed to an arranged marriage, dowry and all, haunts the heroine of the book he wrote from the perspective of a young woman desperately resisting a similar background in order to create a career in art, *The Manuscript of the School of Fine Arts;* the story of the teeth also appears in a more specific and indeed thinly disguised form in one of the tales of imprisonment that constitute *The Daisies of the Saint* (pp. 106–10), while in *Ten Women* (p. 187) we get an even clearer appreciation of the magnitude of such a sacrifice when we learn that a set of ordinary false teeth, bought on credit, could take five years to pay off. Both his mother's self-sacrifice and the art student's tribulations—similarly drawn from actual events about which Andreas came to hear—make a woman's inner, embodied life the site of a dignity that no amount of petty bureaucracy or harsh political persecution can even touch.

Andreas's mother was a woman whose thwarted intellect and cosmopolitanism as well as her devotion to family had always led her to express a special interest, says Andreas, in the activities of those family members who had emigrated to distant places. But she ended her days isolated by blindness, as though her ceaseless giving of moral resilience had exhausted her own physical resources. For Andreas to write in the female voice appears, from this perspective, as an act of reciprocal redemption. Indeed, the expression whereby he explains that his mother turned her teeth into food recalls the language in which an adroit sheep-thief converts the stolen livestock—counters in a male game of reciprocal provocation—into "real" animals (*tá 'kana próvata;* Herzfeld 1985: 220) by incorporating them into the flock that is his and his family's source of livelihood. A similar phrase denotes the conversion of goods into money. The link I am suggesting might seem far-fetched were it not for Andreas's own emphasis on his familiarity with rural idiom (*Cretan War,* pp. 10–15, 165–67). Rather than seeing a direct connection here, however, we should probably simply interpret the similarity as marking a basic social principle: the realization of highly prized possessions as consumable capital.

But Andreas came to appreciate his mother's sacrifices through an empathy that went beyond formal reciprocity or acknowledgment. He knew that frustration over her thwarted dreams of advanced schooling could not have been assuaged by the generous dowry with which her family sent her into matrimony. On the contrary, the idea that an excess of education might actually threaten a young woman's marriage prospects, reducing her *timí* ("social worth") by more or less the same degree as that by which it would have enhanced a man's, became deeply offensive to Andreas, who makes the heroine of *The Manuscript of the School of Fine Arts* the victim of precisely this kind of calculation. His mother belonged to a rural family just beginning to enter the bourgeoisie. Her brother, as a teacher, had broken free of the pastoral economy and culture but clearly felt that his new status would be jeopardized—and perhaps also that his own achievement might also be diminished—by granting his sister access to the same advantages.

We have already seen how bourgeois ideas of cutting a fine appearance subsumed rural self-regard in the young Andreas's sartorial vanity. Here, more perniciously, we see that bourgeois notions of respectability could also call on supposedly traditional *exclusions* to enforce gender inequality more violently than it had been maintained in the poorer, less worldly and ambitious past of these people's pastoral forebears. It was not, after all, the father of Andreas's mother who had kept her out of secondary school. On the contrary, he had actually sent her there. It was her more educated brother, representative of her own generation, in whom a new kind of class ambition would not tolerate such hubris in a woman. His actions provide a cautionary tale against anthropological assumptions about the "traditional" character of female submissiveness in Greek society and suggest that intrusive, class-based models of propriety may have played a much greater role than has generally been recognized in generating that pattern (see Bakalaki 1994; Clark 1983).

Although given no choice in the matter of her education and thrust into a marriage of convenience in which her primary duty was to bear a large brood of children, Andreas's mother never lost her love of letters, and, until overtaken by blindness, always found time to read—she followed political events to a degree that was probably unusual for a woman of her time and background—and she encouraged her unruly offspring to do the same.

But their father was no insensitive yokel either. On the contrary, he held writers in great respect; among his comrades in the fighting in Epirus were the poets Lorentsos Mavilis and Dionisios Romas, and he often mentioned them thereafter; he also declined the chance of commanding his own brigade on the grounds that the Rethemniot historian Khristos Makris would bring it far greater distinction. Andreas was later to encounter major figures of the Greek literary and artistic scene in various prison camps. Military life for the socially ambitious father and political exile for the socially and politically skeptical son: through these respective experiences of shared struggle, they forged bonds of personal affection that expanded their horizons ever outward.

In the comportment of Nikolaos Nenes, the reserved dignity of the indomitable mountain shepherd always remained untouched by the years of economic hardship. These years nonetheless took their toll. Many of his contemporaries became rich enough to claim the quasi-aristocratic status of *tzákia*, a pretension for which I have already noted Andreas's contempt, while his father became deeply disillusioned and increasingly marginalized. The old man nevertheless never lost his sense of personal dignity or his hopes for his wild offspring.

And wild they certainly were. Andreas remembers stealing two-drachma pieces from his father—"I think all the children did it in those days"—and paying no attention to his schoolwork. "What injustice children do to their parents," muses Andreas as he reflects on his and his siblings' insubordination and contrasts his father's unrelenting moral toughness with the fact that the old man never once struck any of his children—an act that would have betrayed weakness rather than strength (see Campbell 1964: 190): "Our father never struck us . . . I think he . . . well, poor Kostas [one of Andreas's brothers] on one occasion . . . but just once. While we were very unruly, I can tell you he worshipped us." And that one occasion was itself revealing of his restraint: old Nenes, informed that Kostas had stolen from a local man, hit the boy in the man's presence; when Kostas protested that being struck by his father as well by the other man seemed a doubly unfair punishment, his father—incensed by the idea that another had usurped his authority over his own son—himself struck the man. When the latter had him brought to court, Nenes went straight to his victim and kissed his hand in unconditional apology. To Andreas this seemed the epitome of self-discipline: in a society where weakness is fatal, it took a special kind of strength to humiliate oneself voluntarily twice—first to one's own son, then to the aggrieved party—and all the more so where socially, if not legally, old Nenes would have been considered in the right and his enemy an intemperate bully.

The virtue of a restraint that indicated true strength informs all Andreas's recollections of his own contemptuous reactions to the guards who mistreated him at the several prison camps to which he was sent. That restraint probably, he thinks, saved him from even worse forms of torture. He gave it dramatic expression in *Ten Women*, where a businesswoman testifying in court describes the virtues of a man accused of abetting abortion. She had taken him on to manage her beekeeping farm:

▌ "The strange thing is that his underlings, for he immediately took over the management and general supervision, now worked harder and more productively, even though he made no effort to make them do so. It was enough for him to give the order for a particular job and it would be carried out without any waste of time or delay. Nor did he supervise them the way it's ordinarily done, with shouting, threats, and dismissals. Everyone who was under his authority worked the way I told you before, for the sole reason that he didn't rush them, he didn't threaten them, he didn't talk to them at all, nor did he calculate or measure the product of their labor. And yet the result was incomparably superior to every other time." (p. 125)

In this passage there appears an understanding of human relations of which traces do appear in ethnographic writings but that seems remarkably absent from the more stereotypical accounts of Greek social norms—even from descriptions generated by most Greek observers.

This restraint—judicious severity rather than random violence—is truly crucial to a society in which vengeance plays an important role. To be effective, vengeance must always conform to the strict requirements that then also legitimate its considered, occasional use. Restraint is the background against which the message of vengeance achieves its impact. The kind of restraint that it requires appears dramatically in Andreas's very personal introduction to the critical edition he prepared—in conscious defiance of the professorial monopoly of the philologists—of the late Renaissance poem, *The Cretan War*, by Marinos Tzane Bounialis. Both here and in his prize-winning *Voukéfali* he recounts his father's refusal, during the 1922 collapse of the Greek armies in Asia Minor, to allow his fellow-Asi-Goniots to massacre all of the "Turks"—most or all of them Greek-speaking Muslims, in all probability—who had taken refuge in the town. Against "two hundred guns" old Nenes declared that they, his kin, would have to kill him first if they wanted to get at the Muslims: "If you want to fight a war, go to Asia Minor!" This act expressed an important distinction between the obligations of friendship and those of patriotism. It also protested the indiscriminate extension of the feud. By facing his own coreligionists and telling them that they would have to kill him first, Nikolaos Nenes demonstrated—as if they had not already known it—that he was no coward. By forcing an unwelcome restraint upon them, he also captured the highest moral ground.

For Andreas—whose *Voukéfali*, not coincidentally, in 1994 won the prestigious İpekçi Prize, awarded by a joint Greek-Turkish committee of pacifist intellectuals—his father's action was one of unimpeachable morality. Veteran of vicious fighting in the Balkan Wars, Andreas's father was certainly prepared to take up arms against the Turks when the occasion so demanded. But he also had a strong sense of social obligation. Local Muslims ("Turks") worked in his tobacco fields, and he shared grazing areas with Turkish shepherds.

There were thus other, more intimate ties to consider—neighborliness and friendship especially—beyond those of a generic patriotism.

Given the extent to which nationalism draws on such intimacies for all of its imagery, these local ties had a more fundamental force than the more abstract virtues enjoined by the state ideology: without them, the latter would itself have no power to appeal. Knowledge of this is deeply ingrained in everyday social experience. Little Andreas, six years old when the last Turks departed in 1924, played with some of their children, although his memory of these playmates is now very vague. He does remember the house of their wealthy Muslim neighbor and family friend, the merchant Ali Vafi, one of those his father saved from the Christians' revenge in 1922:

● In those days the transportation of imported goods, so to speak, dried pulses, rice of various kinds, sugar, all those things, was not motorized, it was done with those four-wheeled handcarts. Well, they were loaded and unloaded by the people we used to call *khamálidhes* ("porters"), that is, barefoot men who around the beginning of the 1920s [literally, "of 20"] were Turks.

Andreas also recalls his own childhood impressions of the constant activity around Ali Vafis's house, which was also the Turk's warehouse:

● There weren't hundreds of them, there were twenty or thirty people, barefoot, with their turbans, with big mustaches [*moustákes*], and what not. . . . I was a little child. I can tell you that I was even afraid to pass by there, but I can't forget the noise there was around that house.

It was this house that Nikolaos Nenes refused to accept as a gift from his old friend, as Andreas recounts in *Voukéfali*, because he did not wish to be accused by his fellow-Christians of profiting from his defense of the Muslims. Recent reactions to *Voukéfali*—notably the charge that Andreas has impugned his father's memory by representing him as a Turk[20]—suggest that this was a wise precaution.

In business dealings with Muslim merchants, Nikolaos Nenes—always at heart the village *kapetánios* who disdained the pedantic precision of the law—no more demanded a formal contract than he would have of a fellow-Christian: regardless of religion, a man's word of honor sufficed to seal any bargain and a request for more formal ratification would have conveyed an insulting lack of trust. Guided by local concern with the obligations of hospitality and asylum, moreover, and aware that these particular "Turks" were neighbors, friends, and fellow-merchants whose murder would merely provide further incitement to revenge on the part of their coreligionists, he saw the greater strength in restraint, not in indiscriminate violence—an important element in Andreas's own modernist

20. See Tsouderos 1995, Andreas's response (in *George Nenedakis*), and chapter 8.

conception of personal strength. His willingness to stand up for specific people in the face of a generic enmity in which he himself participated, as is evident in his eagerness to join the fight for the liberation of Epirus from Turkish rule, is another instance of the common Greek tendency—often explicitly noted by local and foreign observers alike—to distinguish between hatred for a generalized category and fondness for those of its individual members one actually knows. It also set an example of tolerance that the young Andreas could scarcely fail to find harmonious with his own emergent internationalism.

To hear Andreas tell of his schooldays, the restraint that he later developed to such a marked degree was not yet much in evidence. J. K. Campbell (1964: 280–82) has noted that the Sarakatsani (Northern Greek transhumant shepherds) he studied demanded *palikariá*—a mixture of tough masculinity, courage, and bravado—of young men before marriage; after that watershed, it came to seem increasingly incompatible with steadily increasing family responsibility. I found much the same pattern among Cretan shepherds, among whom animal-theft is thought to be more appropriate before than after marriage. I do not wish to overemphasize the parallel, but it does nonetheless suggest yet again that Andreas's understanding of his world and of his own role in it are grounded in the very values and perceptions that the tag of "modernity" would deny—and yet the awareness of such things as traditional is itself a definitive mark of modernity. Once again the links between past values and present attitudes underscore the historical contingency of the modern.

Rethemnos, known in Venetian times for its flourishing literary culture, now offered scant inspiration for a young man's literary yearnings. In Andreas, the first stirrings of literary interest came from his mother's attempt to make sure there would always be some reading material in the house. Young Andreas consumed these periodicals avidly; visiting his mother's family in Amari, the regular arrival each Saturday of Athens periodicals he had ordered—mail delivery was a very public affair—evoked real scorn and hostility from adults who claimed to be enthusiastic about the spread of literacy but thought the young should not be reading "periodicals": "And the [very] word bothered them."

In town, things were little better. Secretly, insatiably, he pored over almost any printed matter he could find:

● But in our house, I was still going to high school, we didn't have electricity in the house. We had a petrol lamp, we had some oil lamps with two or three of those [wicks]. I remember I had a room whose windows let in the wind and the lamplight used to flicker. But I would read all night—novels, various things, whatever I could find, I had periodicals.

He could not imagine a private house filled with books:

● But there were no books or libraries in people's houses (spíthia[21]). There were [personal] libraries, let's say, in the offices of lawyers, the [volumes containing the] laws. I don't recall ever having gone into a [private] house and seeing a library. In the City of Letters [Rethemos], so to speak. A strange business. . . . Perhaps there were some in houses I didn't go into. I don't know.

He also managed to gain access to the personal archive of the great Rethemniot folklorist Pavlos Vlastos, scion of one of the great Constantinopolitan families with which the Byzantine emperor Nikiforas Fokas (Nicephorus Phocas) had repopulated Crete in 961 after the emperor had driven out its Andalusian Arab ("Saracen") occupiers and author of major treatises on the customs of Crete. It was here, soon after he left school, that he first read an edition of *The Cretan War*, the seventeenth-century account of the Turkish occupation of Crete that he was one day, in 1979, to republish in a controversial edition of his own.

Teachers certainly played some part in Andreas's early learning despite his disobedience at school. A local doctor owned an encyclopedia and let the precocious but rebellious schoolboy read it in his office. Andreas's parents, like most provincial parents of the time, did not involve themselves in his schoolwork beyond asking whether he had done his assigned homework and noting his grades. There was, in any case, little they could do to discipline him. Although whenever they asked him whether he had studied they used the conventional phrase *dhiávases?* ("have you read?"), only his mother had more than a utilitarian appreciation of what reading meant.

It is important to get some sense of what it meant more generally in the cultural milieu in which Andreas grew up. In particular, the standards of originality and realism to which he would later be held accountable were not necessarily those of a Western European intellectual universe and must therefore be carefully traced to their cultural sources and described. The poetic idiom of the Cretan highlands included a vigorous tradition of improvised verse duelling and satirical commentary, in which a person could claim authorship of a verse less on the basis of *textual invention* than because of a strikingly original *use of a verse in context.*[22]

---

21. Here Andreas uses a characteristically Cretan pronunciation of the—in Athens—more usual *spítia*. This suggests that he associates the older memories with a more distinctively local Cretan speech style. He also occasionally slips into Cretan phonology when using highly formal legal language, as Panos Tsokas noticed while transcribing one of the interview tapes; in that context it suggests irony or mockery.

22. See Herzfeld (1985: 141–49) for a more detailed discussion of these verse duels.

This view of artistic invention encountered a sere academicism among the educated, who attributed authorship strictly on the basis of a very literal understanding of novelty: words were combined in a new text—however conventional, banal, or simply dull the end product may have been—and that was enough. Such was the respectable bourgeois "verbalism" (*verbalismós*) against which left-wing critics, Andreas among them, still rage today.

The schoolboy Andreas himself mastered the techniques of this arid verbalism with disdainful ease. He composed a poem of remarkable pomposity—

> Around me, laurel crowns
> of green, o ye dead!
> sobbing cries, incense, bended knee
> at the tombs . . .

—which he entered for a competition and for which he received second prize. One of the judges was his own headmaster, who flatly refused to believe that Andreas had written it. The boy was deeply affronted at the suggestion that he had stolen the words: "What should I copy, now? And where should I copy it *from?*" But the skeptical headmaster only knew him as an unruly schoolboy. Moreover, as Andreas today concedes:

● It is *verbalistikó,* that is, in reality, words of that kind—bombastic—and so forth, that I found here and there, that I'd heard. It's not poetry, actually, it's verse, versification, but in any case in those days such things were popular, so to speak, and were considered poetry, so to speak. Well, then there were none of today's . . . modern poets, and even the translations of foreign [works] had not yet been done—how would they know, let's say, how Eliot was writing?

Thus Andreas justifies this early potboiler—which indeed was at least no less original by the standards of modern literary criticism than were either the serviceable but well-tried verse ripostes of the villagers or the pedantic poetic models with which he was fed at school.

But it is amusing to note that Andreas in turn was later to doubt his friend Thanasis Tsingos in much the same way. The scene is a British detention camp in Sudan where they were both incarcerated for mutiny in 1944. Andreas used to scold Tsingos for the quality of his Greek; Tsingos retaliated by challenging his fellow-prisoners to a poetry contest:

▮ [Tsingos] read some of his poems. I told him they were not his, because I liked them and, although I'd seen him writing occasionally, I didn't think he wrote poems. Then he said we should write eight-line poems to a prearranged rhyme scheme, because his poems were in free verse. He really silenced us when, a little while later, we saw his eight-liners. Perhaps the only thing wrong with them [that is, our own verses] was our rhyme scheme. (*The Painter Tsingos in War and in Prison*, p. 156)

In these incidents, separated from each other by nearly a decade, we see how Andreas's original bruising by such skepticism reappeared in his own doubting stance. Expectations of deceit and fakery are instilled at an early age in Greece (Friedl 1962: 78; Hirschon 1992); such lessons may reproduce themselves well into adulthood. Children are taught to expect sly practical jokes and to develop a sense of reciprocal cunning, through sometimes merciless teasing: a favorite uncle is said to have died suddenly when in fact he is safe and sound, a promised treat is withheld at the last instant, an apprentice is constantly thwarted in his attempts to learn his master's craft.

These experiences create the sense that certain forms of deceit are usual, perhaps even a sign of affection and intimacy, and may prove useful in the defense of the very setting—often the family—in which they are learned. In this agonistic social idiom, personal autonomy requires a belittling of others but may reflect positively on one's own kin or at least serve to protect their interests: learning to deceive from an early age is thus a moral education. In refusing to credit the young Andreas with authorship of those conventional verses, his headmaster was being fully consistent with the expectations of their social milieu: a schoolboy was expected to cheat and, if he had not done so, the experience of being accused of it would still prepare him for the skepticism he would encounter throughout his life. Such was the conventional representation of motive: what a person thought was less important—since it could not be known—than how easily it could be matched to a model of predictable human duplicity. Even as a boy, Andreas, who had composed the verses himself and who sought pleasure in writing, was hurt at being reduced to the cipher of a banal social expectation. It may well be that this personal experience of rebuff was what made Andreas willing to concede victory to his friend Tsingos—a good example of his growing capacity for rethinking his assumptions about others when the evidence suggested that he might have misread them.

Equally characteristic is the way Andreas scoffed at his friend's command of Greek. At an early age he had absorbed a deep respect for the Greeks' Classical heritage. This may seem surprising, given his later contempt for the insipid neo-Classical art of the foreign-dominated Athens establishment, not to speak of the Left's usual disinclination to play along with the conservative adulation of ancient Hellas. In fact, however, there is no contradiction here. The respect that Andreas expresses for the Classical past is not that of the educational establishment: unfettered by academic precision, it springs as much from his father's admonition to take pride in the "gold" of his ancestral blood as it does from any of what he learned at school—hence his early fascination with the relationship of Classical Greek to the correct pronunciation of the modern tongue. The exact sound of the ancient language remains a matter of heated—and sometimes fiercely ideological—debate. Certainly there has been enough change to make modern spelling a pedagogical nightmare: children can easily learn to read sounds off printed letters, but knowing how to write from oral dictation is quite another matter. Andreas's teacher was undaunted by the incompleteness of the available information. He told his impressionable pupils to lay a heavy emphasis on *all* the ancient diphthongs even when the modern vowel was short, so that a stressed sound would serve as the phonetic shadow of a once-broad vowel sound. If this sounds tortuous to readers brought up on English, one can only respond by saying that it offers a fair measure of the neo-Classicists' deep penetration of thought, speech, and action even among the liberal and left-wing sectors of the population. Indeed, this kind of imaginative reconstruction was consistent with the left-wing philology of the pre–World War II period, in which a romantic nativism turned to folklore in order to recover the ancient past from a foreign-inspired scholarship that focused only on morphology rather than on deeper connections and values.

But for all his adolescent enthusiasm for this exercise, Andreas ruefully concedes, "it couldn't be managed. It must happen from a young age, let's say, and be taught by the parents and so on; this is something that cannot be taught in a [classroom] lesson." For even a well-intentioned teacher was still a teacher—and Andreas's love of the ancient past remained obdurately free of the slightest trace of academicism. Despite his skepticism about the feasibility of fully recapturing the ancient style of pronunciation, moreover, he retained a conviction that he knew better than most other Greeks how the language should maintain a sense of its ancient rhythms. Even a partial grasp of the ancient past, however fanciful and however free of strictly philological precision, confers a moral authority that few in Greece, outside the academic establishment, would want to challenge; it is an affirmation of their collective claims to a place in "Europe." Indeed, that authority rests in part on contempt for the pedantry of the academic approach. The possession of "golden blood" is itself a guarantee of knowledge, much as, at a humbler level, the ability of any foreigner to speak even halting Greek is more or less automatically attributed to the flow of Greek blood: "Don't you have a Greek mother or a Greek father?"

Andreas's reading was eclectic. Even his mother would perhaps have been puzzled by his early enthusiasm for Engels's treatise on the origins of the family, lent to him by a member of one of the town's then very few openly communist families. But Andreas attributes his revolutionary ardor less to his reading of Marx and Engels than to the general feeling of insurrection that was prevalent in Crete at the time. Indeed, Andreas doubts whether even the few declared communists of Rethemnos in the pre–World War II years were prepared to challenge the social order with which they had grown up, being thoroughly imbued (*zimoméni*, literally, "kneaded [like dough]") with the values of small-town hierarchy. They would rebel against particular leaders, but, Andreas demands, "How could an unknown barber become a parliamentary deputy, now?" This was simmering rebellion, but it lacked both focus and direction.

More conventional fare than Marxist treatises, but still appealing to his insubordinate spirit and very much of a piece with the local mood he associates with those turbulent years, were the tales he read about brigand captains: for the most part of mainland Greek authorship, they recounted the deeds of men who carried on the glorious revolutionary traditions of the fight against Ottoman tyranny into a modern era in which the enemy were now the office hacks of the new bureaucratic state. Here too, however, Andreas used these stories as raw material on which to practice his own writerly craft, and his use of the nonlocal term for brigand captains (*lístarkhi*) suggests an early disposition to project his Cretan interests onto a larger national stage. Like an artisan faced with shoddy work— his admiration for basic artisanal skill was often to outshine his respect for artistic originality—he took these popular tales, much as he was later to do with a private diary that became the core of his novel *The Manuscript of the School of Fine Arts,* and rewrote them until they were more to his liking. His headmaster again had not the faintest idea that his wayward pupil was reading such subversive literature (and would have been sure to forbid it had he known, Andreas thinks), or that he was reformulating it stylistically.

Andreas was indeed a disobedient schoolboy; but he was probably no wilder than his contemporaries. Lilika Nakou's autobiographical account of a schoolteacher's life in prewar Rethemnos, *Madame Do-Re-Mi,* gives us what Andreas—whose own writing evidently greatly pleased the redoubtable old lady in her later years—himself ruefully acknowledges as an accurate picture of the wild atmosphere of the classroom, although he also insists that some details, notably the prevalence of Cretan costume among the boys of village origin and their bearing of firearms in class, betray a measure of poetic license.

Andreas, son of a man in search of urban respectability, was quite wild enough even without these accouterments of rural ferocity. At the age of seventeen, fired by his reading of Engels and perhaps also by his literary experiments with the brigand tales, he played an active role in getting his schoolmates involved in the local uprising against the newly established fascist dictatorship of Metaxas. As he recalls it, all the young people of Crete were afire: they were "revolutionized" and "politicized" by the recent memories of the Cretan struggle for freedom. Many of them were already armed as a matter of habit; they occupied the school build- ing as well as a nearby hill and sent off a formal announcement: "The Rethimni High School places itself on the side of the Revolution." Back came the chilly response—"a cold shower," says Andreas—from the lo- cal insurrectionary leader, an army general: "The Rethimni High School is to return to its desks." This ignominious dismissal did nothing to de- flate the ardor of the young Andreas, but it did squash the boys' immedi- ate attempt to recreate their glorious revolutionary heritage.

Occasionally, what Andreas read was politically more innocent than ignorant local officials thought. When during the virulently anticommu- nist Metaxas dictatorship the liberal politician Sofoklis Venizelos paid a visit to Rethemnos, Andreas climbed onto the wall of the Municipal Gar- den and yelled, "Long live the son of Lefteris"—an allusion to the politi- cian's famous father Eleftherios, patron both of Andreas's father and of his maternal grandfather, and perhaps also to "freedom" (for which the Greek is an etymological cognate, *lefteriá*). For this escapade, he was haled into the police station. At that moment he happened to be carrying a book by Tolstoy. No matter that for Andreas Tolstoy was, if anything, a foe of communism. He was, after all, a Russian; Russians were Slavs; and, in the right-wing imagination, Slavs were automatically Commu- nists—and therefore anti-Greek—by instinct and blood.[23] Although not much happened at that moment, the incident made him an immediate suspect in later troubles. As Andreas says, "That was the level of educa- tion among the police, so to speak, and of . . . of *all* those who are against the left, that's the education they had, that was their level of cultivation." And, one might add, a very convenient ignorance it was for the purposes of political harassment.

The young Andreas often acted in defiance of his father's desires, especially on the political front. Although Nikolaos Nenes was a "pro- gressive" who supported Venizelos, he did in at least one case allow per- sonal friendship to override his political convictions. That exception in- volved a member of parliament for the rightist and anti-Venizelist Popular Party by the name of Sfinias. Andreas remembers that the old- style politicians, many of them tough mountain shepherd-fighters by ori-

---

23. Such practices and attitudes proved remarkably durable. Many years later, in the early 1960s, a teenage girl was summoned to an Athens police station because she had agreed to feed her neighbors' dog, which was named for one of the Russian space satellites: "Is it true that you have been feeding the communist dog Lunik?" (Dimitra Dimitra, personal communication).

gin, maintained such friendships across party lines, and it may be that this memory has influenced Andreas's own ability to recognize human qualities even in those who were nominally his worst enemies—police officers in particular, men whose humble origins could also excite his political sympathy even when they rejected his views. In particular, he recognized that many of the policemen of his youth were the children of shepherds and peasants, beneficiaries of a systematic drive for their parents' votes that the elder Venizelos had developed. Moreover, the class divisions that he was later to describe for prewar Rethemnos were not of long standing, which is why he found the affectations of the elite so pretentious; by the same token, people could move up or down the social ladder with relative ease, and few of those on the way up had entirely lost contact with their origins. He could thus appreciate the human worth of some police officers even while viscerally regretting their lack of cultural sophistication or their antipathy to him personally. He, too, was of village stock.

Andreas, then, was an independent youth. He and some friends concocted a homemade bomb consisting of a large and bulbous finial taken from a decorative marriage bed and stuffed with dynamite, and set it off against Sfinias. The politician, who escaped with his life, offered a reward of 5,000 drachmas—a princely temptation in those days—for the successful identification of the culprits. He never did discover who they were: "think what would have happened if it [the culprit's identity] had been discovered—the man would have been astonished!" Nor did Andreas's father ever learn of the young man's involvement. "*No one* learned of it!" And while that silence may have saved Andreas from a painful showdown with his father, it was especially fortunate for another member of that boisterous gang who went on to an immaculate career in the judiciary!

It was in fact in a confrontation with the law that the young Andreas was able to give his father tangible proof of his filial devotion. In 1912 or the following year, Nikolaos Nenes had bought a house from one of the growing number of Turks who saw that their future on Crete was increasingly at risk and were consequently selling their properties at low prices in order to save at least some goods and some dignity from the impending debacle. True to the ethos of the word of honor, he disdained the very idea of a legally validated contract. In 1924, however, as a result of the Treaty of Lausanne that officially ended hostilities between Greece and Turkey in Asia Minor, the remaining Muslims departed for Turkey and several times as many Christians from Asia Minor came flooding into Crete. The legal status of Muslim properties and the urgent need to house the refugees led to a series of legal arrangements for the official transfer of Muslim property as "exchange items [that is, property]" (*andaláksima*) for that lost by the Christian refugees. These arrangements were largely entrusted to a national bank, which in some cases sold off the properties in order to cover their overhead expenses. Thus, in 1935, Andreas's father discovered that the house he had used as a shop for over two decades, and that he regarded as his own property, was suddenly up for auction: words of honor from a departed national enemy—a Turk—counted for little in the context of integration into the capitalist economy of a highly centralized nation-state. Andreas's mother hastily sold off at a ruinously low price some fields she still owned in Amari and so raised 60,000 drachmas. Thus it was agreed that Nikolaos Nenes could buy back his shop.

The scene that followed conveys something of the chaotic conditions of the time:

● So, they had fixed a day for arranging the contracts. Eh . . . the lawyer comes, [. . .] was his name, a fine person, one of the best lawyers, who was godfather to ["had baptized"] my brother, we had major relations with him, so to speak, and he knocks on the door, and I was having . . . I remember that I was asleep, it was morning, I was asleep in a cistern that was full of water, I was having a bath. [*Laughs.*] And he says, "If the contract isn't signed today you'll lose the shop." It was the final deadline. Think of it, now. . . . I rush off—the other children were at school—I go to the Tax Office, I find the tax inspector, I tell him, "I'm So-and-so, and what not, let's draw up the contracts." Well, anyway, they start in on drawing up the contracts, they do some calculations— and they came up with a sum, eh, 70,000 [drachmas], I don't remember how much, somewhere around there. For the *rents*, if you please! The shop had been put up for auction at [a starting price of] 250,000 drachmas; in those days—it was a dizzying price for those days. An American had come up with it [the price?], eh, a Greek-American had come from . . . So he brought it up to 250,000 drachmas, but my father wouldn't let it go, told him, "I'll buy it at a million, you're not going to get it, because I have children, how will my children live?" Anyway, he [the American] let it go to the old man. But there was rent to pay on the period [in which Nikolaos had not technically been the owner of the property]—[*laughs*]—the banks calculated it; all that time, he . . . he'd never paid, I tell you—one could see it was his [property]! And we were paying the rent, and one o'clock comes around, and the contracts had to be signed. And the tax inspector says, "They've closed. . . . The cashier's office has closed," says he. The business with the cashier's office is as follows: the Tax Office, in order to make up contracts, buys government tax stamps. [The number of] this tax stamp is copied onto a certain page, he [the tax inspector] signs, and the sales ledger of the cashier's office can close, so to speak. And . . . the cashier's office had closed, the cashier had gone home. Says the tax inspector, "You've lost the deal, you've lost the shop, because (*dhióti*[24]) it's not. . . ." So I—I'd paid 70,000 drachmas so we could draw up the contracts. If the cashier's office had closed, what . . . *who* was responsible? Had *I* closed the cashier's office? I fell right on . . . I was just a lad, of course, but . . . on the tax inspector, I grabbed him right here: "You cheated me," I tell him. "*Shame* on you, stealing from me, a child! What will I go [and do], can I look at my family, what am I to . . ." He realized, truly, what he . . . And he makes this [gesture], and calls to one of the staff and tells him, "Go and call the cashier." He'd gone home. So he goes there and calls the cashier, who comes from his house, he tells him, "This is what's happened. We are responsible, you must open up a *new* section, we'll draw up a . . ." They drew up, let's say, a page, they wrote on it the justification of a new page [in the ledger] for the sale of the tax stamp for the contract being drawn up. That's how it happened . . . and . . . well, it was written down, and we kept the shop! The next day when he's signing the contract I stood right there in the middle, flexing my muscles like this, proud that I'd pulled this off; and the tax inspector tells my father, who was an old man, I didn't look as though I was his son, says he, "This lad, whose is he?" And my father says, "He's mine." Laughing now, although I'd grabbed him by his necktie. . . . But, well, I was a lively lad, he liked that . . .

The literal-mindedness of Greek bureaucracy has not changed greatly since that time, and Rethemniot men still love to recount their clashes, often similarly casting themselves in the role of violent but honest crusaders for justice—against the tax office or, in recent years, the historic conservation authorities. Andreas, although a wild and disobedient young man, was not disloyal to his family: on the contrary, loyalty to kith and kin often went hand-in-hand with a disposition to defend them to the last quixotic drop of a youth's blood. Moreover, Andreas knew perfectly well that loss of the shop would have spelled total ruin for them all; they were already facing the dire effects of the economic disaster that had struck them in the crash of 1929, a mere six years earlier.

This incident not only illustrates the strength (and even violence) of Andreas's family loyalty, but also demonstrates the acuity with which he observed the world around him and his ability to put his conclusions to work for practical ends—a quality that would later save him from destitution. He gleaned a useful knowledge of many skills simply by watching his father's and other merchants' laborers at work. In this way

24. This is a neo-Classical (*katharévousa*) form, suggesting an attempt to use rhetorical authority.

he acquired, for example, a detailed understanding of tobacco processing. His father never offered him verbal instruction in these matters; that would in any case have been highly unusual—the only difference between a son and an apprentice in this regard being that a son would not *actively* be prevented from acquiring the technical mastery since, unlike the apprentice, he would probably not try one day to set up in direct competition with his father's business. At that time, as we have already seen, parents did not directly engage in their children's formal education, and sustained verbal instruction in any task was rare. Dignified silence and mental self-reliance were also the marks of pastoral masculinity. Indeed, Andreas's personal antipathy to "verbalism" has roots deep in the social ethos of Cretan manhood.

3 ◘

CRETE, ATHENS,
THE WORLD

Class considerations narrowed the career options for a young man of Andreas's background. As the son of a merchant, he was on nodding terms with the artisans he saw every day as he walked through the streets of Rethemnos, but it would never have occurred to him—nor would his father have permitted him—to apprentice himself out to any of them. Only the sons of the economically desperate Asia Minor refugees, some of whom had owned considerable properties in their former homeland, accepted that degree of social demotion; they were already prepared for such discrimination, their children having been segregated educationally in what is known to this day as the "Turkish school." For Andreas, an artisanal career in Rethemnos was not a socially acceptable option.

At the same time, clearly, Andreas's unruly school career did not augur well for his father's social ambitions for him. But he was also not prepared to accept the yoke of an office job—the Greek term for "employee," *ipálilos,* means "one [who serves] under another person," a demeaning category in the Cretan value system—or otherwise become beholden to a politician for favors. His powers of observation and invention, however, had already been keenly developed. And even though his father had not been a notably successful merchant, he still attributes his own enthusiasm for trade to an environment rather confusingly rendered here by the familiar metaphor of blood: "So it seems as though I had in my blood this commercial yen, this merchant's genius, what can I tell you? This was because I had a lot to do with my father's shop."

At the age of twenty, in 1938, Andreas left for Athens. He had not finished school in Rethemnos, so he was obliged to do so in Athens. His earliest adventures away from Crete exhibit both his tough stance toward life's slings and arrows and some of the experiences that made him as unpredictable in his communism as he has been in so much else. For he certainly discovered the creative joys of petty capitalism in his youth.

Soon after his arrival in Athens, he started working for a friend who manufactured cooking butter. Before long, however, he realized that he could easily imitate the production technique in his own apartment. He promptly set up independently and began to make a substantial profit—although from that day on he has never used butter "because I know how it's made!"

But World War II was well under way. Already raging on Greece's frontier with Albania from the end of October, 1940, that conflict was now closing in on the capital. The Greeks, who had succeeded in repelling Mussolini's attempt at invasion and had even counterattacked with some success, faced a far more ruthless foe in Hitler. By the time the German invaders had marched into Athens on 27 April 1941, Andreas had established a very satisfactory network of creditors, including the owners of numerous restaurants around Omonia Square in downtown Athens. At this point, however, all outstanding profits were lost, and all he could do was trade on his credit for a few meals before sneaking out of Athens to join the war himself.

He saw the German army arrive in Omonia Square. His recollection is distinctively about the positioning of the self and the oddity of his predicament—a man who was not what he must have seemed to be:

● And there wasn't another person in Omonia! I was the only one! I didn't support the Germans. I just had nowhere to go. I stood there and watched the . . . And they were watching me, they must have said to themselves, "That man," they'll have said, "he must love us to be standing right here!"

And his bemused discovery of another equally assertive self in the same place is an acute narrative portrait of Greek male self-regard. Many years later, Andreas read that the author Yorgos Ioannou had also been there and had also thought himself to be the only Greek watching: "So since Omonia is big, he must have been over here and [I] over there . . . Only he and I were there!"

The situation was now extremely dangerous and Andreas was not sure what to do. His first reaction was perilously inept. In a nearby hotel there were some soldiers newly returned from the front. One was an airman, a fellow-Rethemniot who, Andreas knew, still had his gun with him. (I should add that this man, who belongs to the newly wealthy faction of Rethemniots with whom Andreas is now more than ever at loggerheads, was an extremely gracious informant during my earlier researches there.) Andreas, no doubt with quixotic thoughts of armed solo resistance, tried to get the hotelier to give him the returned soldier's weapon. Not surprisingly, the hotelier turned his request down; also not surprisingly, the soldier heard about the attempted theft and, thoroughly irritated, made sure that the story made the rounds in Crete upon his return.

Thwarted in his attempt to start a one-man resistance in the big city, unable to connect with any organized resistance (the left-led EAM guerrillas had not yet organized in the mountains[1]), short of food (bread coupons were the only available form of exchange ensuring a minimal subsistence), and unable to translate his credit into more than the occasional meal, Andreas—able-bodied, hotheaded, and full of revolutionary fervor—saw no reason to remain in Athens. It was time to join the struggle abroad. He decided to head for the Middle East.

He left Athens almost penniless. He speaks ruefully but matter-of-factly about the exigencies that soured his parting with his Athens landlady:

● A good woman, but I don't know what became of her . . . and two children, one [a son] was on the Albanian front; her daughter . . . when I was leaving she said to me, "Leave me your blanket for my daughter." But I wanted to sell it, because I needed it [the money] for the journey, so to speak.

The journey became unexpectedly complicated. First, the ship Andreas boarded was supposed to sneak out to Chios, which was close enough to the Turkish mainland to give the fugitives a chance of making their way to the war then raging in the Middle East. But matters proved unexpectedly complex:

● And yet in *Bir Hakeim*, which I've published as a book, I describe the adventure, it's a fine adventure, that is . . . heroic, as happened with all the people of that time.

Here, however, let us continue with Andreas's oral narrative, returning a little later to his literary treatment of the same experiences.

● We went this way, we went that way, from Piraeus, in a ship, in a three-master; it was an old . . . sailship, in other words. Five hundred people, but it was, ah, a dirty great beast of a boat, something like . . . a big boat of that period, so to speak. With . . . it had sails, of course, but it also had an engine. *Doúkou-doúkou, doúkou-doúkou* [the sound of the engine], we got here in twenty-four hours, at Anavisos in Piraeus. After

1. EAM (National Liberation Front) was founded in September of 1941. Its military wing, ELAS (National Popular Liberation Army), was a major force in the resistance to Nazi rule. The membership of EAM-ELAS was not exclusively communist in origin, but the communists soon asserted leadership, and it was out of this movement that the left emerged to fight the Civil War. See Eudès 1972; Hart 1996; Hondros 1983; Mazower 1993; *Studies* 1987.

that we got to Tziá [Kea], and from there we got to Tinos. It took thirty
hours. A long journey, slow. . . . But there was a storm. So, in the ship,
in this boat, there were lots of people of every kind and profession, and
so forth. In any case, an experienced eye would have told one what people one was dealing with. I, of course, was not then experienced . . . in
life, and all that, but in any case I understood people, who they were
. . . So I'd figured out that some of those who were on board that ship,
that boat, were not islanders [that is, of Tinos]. As indeed it turned out:
when we arrived at Tinos they went to stay in a certain hotel. So how
I got into contact with them I don't remember, but one evening they
deserted the boat and embarked on a little one, a little boat of eight
tonnes, with an engine, so to speak, very fast. And I managed to get on
board myself. By means of various devices, don't you know!

At this point I asked Andreas how he managed to persuade the others
to take him along:

● Among them was a Cretan. And that's important [that is, for creating
solidarity]! And they took me along, anyway. But they didn't know who
I was or anything. It turned out to be a good thing they took me along;
I'll tell you why. As soon as we left—it was nighttime, midnight—we
set off to go to . . . Turkey. Not to go to Chios. Because that big boat
was going to Chios. So as soon as we left Tinos we swung by Tsiknias.
Tsiknias is a promontory of Tinos. A *terrible* storm! So, these people
were all Greek army officers . . . and they'd been issued with Turkish
tick . . . er, passports . . . so they could cross Turkey on their way to
the Middle East. I—I was the only one who didn't have one. But they,
in the storm, all got into the hold to shelter from it. Out of *fear*—I'm
telling you that right out—I didn't get in the hold, because I thought,
"[What] if it gets turned upside down?" Because there was reason to
fear that we'd be up-ended, that is, I'd be drowned, whereas if I'm on
the outside I'll [be able to] swim, eh? Ridiculous things [to think] now,
at midnight, in the night, a storm in the middle of the sea, what could—?
Still, that's what I thought. . . . So, the captain was a real *kapetánios*
[tough man and leader]. From Alikarnasos [in Asia Minor, the Turkish
Bodrum], a tough guy (*palikári*), an old man. Eh—an old man? He was
then forty-five years old, fifty, but I was a kid then. So he saw that I
was, I don't know, he thought I was . . . like him, a real tough (*palikarás*), eh? And he calls to me, "Come here! Go to the prow, there's
something there . . . it's the compass, bring it to me here." So I went
and he says to me, "When it goes this way—*nighttime, now!*—call to
me, 'A quarter to port!' and when it goes that way call to me, 'A quarter to starboard!'" So I went . . . I put it there in its place and started
calling out, as soon as I saw the needle [move], "*A quarter to port! A*

quarter to starboard!" So the captain, accordingly, well, he turned his wheel. We couldn't get to Turkey, we came back again. He managed not to get us . . . that is, we almost capsized, but he was a fine sailor. And we came back again to Tinos. Well, since I was shouting out from sheer fear, they thought I was the bravest guy [*laughs*], did those officers who were down below! And then they hugged me and took me to their hotel. "Bravo, well done," that sort of thing, we got to know each other. And of course I got all puffed up with pride and . . . didn't tell them how frightened I'd been! [*Laughs.*]

After responding briefly to a question from me, he went on:

❯ The next day we left again, of course, and arrived at Chios. Then the captain had . . . the officers, someone said, had decided to tie the captain up so that we could go to Turkey. *He* was capable of tying all of *us* up! He was a very overbearing fellow, he proved it. So anyway, he agreed to take us to Chios. And there the Germans took us in charge. So I recall . . . But I don't think I write about that [in *Bir Hakeim*]. I remember that I went out . . .

There was, further discussion revealed, another major incident that Andreas did not write about in *Bir Hakeim*, which may be the first time he showed the characteristic pride that was so often to disconcert other tormentors in the years ahead:

❯ We arrived in Chios; the Germans rounded us up. So there was a guy in civilian dress who interrogated us, a German, but he knew how to speak terrific Greek. And he asks me, "What are you?" I had a close-cropped head. . . . Say I, "I'm a Cretan," say I. Right after the Battle of Crete [in which many of the invading German paratroopers were killed by ordinary civilians as they landed]! That's significant! "I am a Cretan," I tell him, "but my mother's family is from here, and I'm going to [her folks?] because I can't go to Crete on account of what's happened there [that is, the German landing]." And he says to me, "Oh, so you're a Cretan, are you?" [I] didn't say anything. He tells me, "Stand over there!" Say I, "Now I've had it!" I don't know what the man thought, but afterwards a gendarme told me—there were some . . . Greek . . . gendarmes[2]— "You are to come and report in to the police station every day." But that was a good thing—because they arrested others immediately and sent them in chains, sent them to Thessaloniki and from there they went

2. Technically, only Athens and Patras had a police (*astinomía*) force, while the remainder of the country, including Piraeus and Thessaloniki, had a gendarmerie (*khorofilakí*). The terms are used more or less interchangeably in speech, especially since the post-junta abolition of the distinction.

to those German [concentration camps] . . . and . . . *kaput!* The German
camps. So I reported in . . . each day . . . and so forth, and one day I
was told by a Cretan who again was a gendarme, "Don't come back,"
says he, "they've stopped asking about you." And so there was I, then,
with some fellows, in that place . . . and one evening, we slipped across
to the other side . . . to Turkey, and . . . I write about all of that in *Bir
Hakeim,* so to speak, what kind of time we had, all that, what . . . Very
. . . I don't know if I told you yesterday that we were received by a . . .
They arrested us, of course, but one evening they let us sleep in a house
belonging to a mayor in one of the villages. And the man received us,
looked after us, well—there was a . . . Half the Turks were pro-
German, others were Anglophiles.

As matters turned out, he was able to go on from there and made his
way to the fighting in the Middle East, first with the idea of joining the
Foreign Legion and then finally linking up with the Greek army-in-exile
under Allied command. Thus it was that he came to fight at El Alamein.

Several points of similarity connect this narrative with *Bir Hakeim,*
for which Andreas says he drew directly on these experiences of escape
from Axis-occupied Greece. In the book, moreover, the youthful Cretan
Xopateras, who fades from the scene before the culminating slaughter
on the Bir Hakeim battlefield itself, closely approximates a self-portrait. I
shall return shortly to the progressive discovery of tolerance that Andreas
brings to life in this character. *Bir Hakeim* begins with an immediately
recognizable series of nautical commands—commands that are, clearly,
indelibly imprinted on his memory, since they appear in the same manner
in the oral recollection we have just heard, lending a characteristically
oral tone to the fictional account:

■   "One quarter to starboard!"
The compass needle went through a full quarter.
"One quarter to port!" (*Bir Hakeim,* p. 9)

The compass needle continues to swing madly.

■   "Two quarters to starboard!"
Xopateras, barefoot and stripped to the waist, bent over the compass
and watched in agony as the needle jumped this way and that like a crazy
thing and changed direction every minute.
And at brief intervals he would yell, "Two quarters to starboard!"
And from hour to hour the young navigator expected the sailing craft
to capsize and sink into the sea! (p. 9)

The fugitives do eventually make landfall in Turkey, where they are
rounded up by the local authorities. The account that follows parodies

Greek stereotypes and documents the growing awareness of the young Cretan, torn by the fortunes of war from the security of a prefabricated national history. It is hard not to see Andreas himself in the portrait of Xopateras. The story he tells is one of self-discovery—of learning about the meaning of courage and fear, about bigotry and war, about love of the land, and, above all, about the dismaying capacity of the inner person for both unrestrained excess and self-disgust. It is a parable about the onset of maturity.

It did not take Andreas long to discover how much the official ideology depended on a highly selective reading of the past. He knew that claims of fearless bravery, much invoked in the patriotic rhetoric, concealed the greater courage—the courage that deals with the reality of fear. In this, he is close to the Cretan shepherds who still embroider tales of their terror during raids on others' flocks, thereby highlighting all the more dramatically the personal qualities that allowed them to persevere: through the endless narratives of tough men, fear becomes, like fate, an inescapable chill on the landscape of the social imagination that only a fool would deny or ignore.

Andreas has faced death in the terrible crossing to Chios that he describes at the beginning of *Bir Hakeim*, in battle at El Alamein, and at the hands of the military judges who ordered his execution. He also had the example of his father's protection of their hapless Muslim neighbors; while this was a mark of strength in the face of violence, however, Andreas here shows more interest in the political foresight with which, he claims, his father prevented the creation of martyrs for the cause of Turkish expansionism. This is not inconsistent. Andreas recognizes the reality of multiple motives: his time in the death cell and on the battlefield taught him that courage is never unambiguous or unmixed with other emotions. It may lie, above all, in recognizing one's own capacity for fear, which in turn may be overcome by a concern for the consequences for others of one's own risk-fraught actions. These attitudes call into question the simplistic stereotypes of traditional values and suggest that the truly crass perspectives are those propagated by a chauvinistic leadership and dutifully absorbed by a complaisant bourgeoisie.

What dawning maturity taught him was thus not a rejection of the values he had absorbed, especially from his father, but a new and more comprehensive understanding of their meaning. He remained, and remains, a convinced patriot, utterly uncompromising in his espousal of such articles of faith as the significance of the Classical heritage for the Greeks of today. He has never forgotten that he has "golden blood." These convictions sometimes lock him into arguments that, to a non-Greek, may seem exasperatingly narrow or misconceived—over whether the name "Nenes" is genuinely (that is, according to Classical philology)

Greek or not, for example. At the same time, his new perspective allowed him to transmute these cherished and ostensibly traditional ideals into an internationalist view more in keeping with his growing commitment to communism. In this part of his story, therefore, lie many of the sources for the ideological positions that inform his subsequent writings as well as the political and personal storms into which they led him.

For example, the reflections on the ambiguities of personal courage in *Bir Hakeim,* could also, and for Andreas clearly did, lead to a critical reevaluation of official historiography. If the nation-state implicitly posits a transcendent similarity among the selves of its constituent individuals, as Benedict Anderson (1983) in effect suggests, then the critical self-examination of those individuals could shed a very disturbing light on the essentialized "national character" propagated by the state. Andreas takes the logic of nationalism at face value and, with quietly devastating irony, shows where its misdirected perversions can lead.

His irony reads more as a defense of national integrity than as an attack on the idea. In passage after passage, as well as in his conversation, he draws unequivocal attention to what he sees as the Greeks' fundamental moral strength and cultural sensibilities—corrupted by a pretentious elite, but ever ready to resurface in the hardy peasantry. In this respect, Andreas's Hellenism has often been much closer to that of his enemies than either he or they could afford to admit.

Representing his views as traitorous—as anti-Greek—was the goal of the rightist thugs who tried to brutalize him in the political island prisons of Makronisi and Aï-Stratis. Hung by his then luxuriant shock of hair, subjected to humiliating insults and deprivations, he was able to withstand this process of psychological attrition in part because he flatly refused to play his tormentors' game of categorizing people: he understood that the bureaucratic obsession with classification masked a more insidious obsession with purity—ethnic, ideological, and moral—that served to relegate all nonconformists to a limbo in which their very existence might eventually be terminated with impunity.

People merit judgment for their individual actions, not their collective attributes. While Andreas is sometimes ready to pronounce on the characteristics of Swedes or Parisians, for example, he takes what Greeks often emphasize as their common habit of differentiating between stereotypes and actual people almost to the point where the stereotypes melt in the heat of his ironic evocation of them—although he is more willing to apply them to those, the dominant nations and classes, with whom he has less sympathy. His refusal to condemn others for their ideology or their background—we shall later meet him praising a police officer who eventually joined the resistance against the junta—arises partly from a realization that people may serve the state for good and decent reasons, only later discovering how easily its power may corrupt and distort their innocence. He also recognizes that his own ideas have grown out of experience that others may not share. This generosity gives his patriotism what for many is perhaps a discomfitingly undogmatic quality. Again, the courage to recognize the dangerous stupidities of self-inflation, whether personal or national, owes much to his unwillingness to accept authority on faith.

Andreas is proud to be Greek. He carefully emphasizes the distinction between corrupt military regimes and the absolute imperative of military defense against foreign invaders. He showed me a beflagged photograph of his son in his conscript's uniform with manifest pride, at once paternal and patriotic. But this same man knows the ambiguities of physical courage at first hand. He thus also knows that, by extension, there can certainly be little point in trying to generalize about national claims to virtues such as bravery (although this does not stop him from doing so in the heat of conversation or when writing about the Greek heritage of his family and ancestral village). Not only could a Greek lose a trial of physical or political power with Turks, but the Greek might also be morally compromised in the process—although, again, Andreas is sufficiently imbued with the conventions of Hellenist ideology that he usually seeks a specific historical explanation for such lapses.

Ever alert to the shocking force of self-revaluation, in *Bir Hakeim* Andreas provides a remarkable portrait of both the absurdities of ethnic categorization and the self-understanding that can, with enough provocation, penetrate the most stridently chauvinistic education. The anthropologist Peter Loizos (1988), writing of Cyprus during the Turkish invasion of 1974, provides a trenchant account of how such an education can license psychopathic thugs to maim and kill and can raise them to the status of national heroes. Andreas gives us the other side of the picture: the doubt and skepticism that less gratuitously violent people—those whose inner strength proofs them against dependence on public adulation—bring to the grandiloquent imperatives of war. He also shows us the equally unsettling capacity of scoundrels and criminals, the rejects of polite society, for acts that in a different institutional frame would have been classified as heroic. All this adds up to the insight that true strength rarely requires either publicity or violence and that it often shuns both.

Bir Hakeim opens with fear; and it is through fear that Andreas eventually discovers the humanity that he shares with these social misfits. Fear is the dominant emotion painted in this tale of a group of men who have fled the Nazi invasion of Greece—human sinners fleeing an inhuman evil—and who are now attempting to cross the stormy seas between Athens and the island of Chios, on the first stage of their escape to Turkey in a nearly uncontrollable, elderly boat. At first, their fear is simple terror at the power of nature. But soon it begins to take new and subtler forms.

The stormy sea successfully navigated, they now face a different kind of fear, that of being refugees in a hostile land. From Chios, a rowboat ferries them across to the Turkish coast. Soon thereafter, exhausted and hungry, they are arrested and brought before the mayor of the nearest town. Before long, the fugitives must face the most intractable tyrant of all: the fear in themselves. But let us first follow the story for a moment.

The mayor, an avaricious scoundrel who uses customs and excise laws to confiscate any gold he can find on the helpless refugees who end up in his hands, has an interpreter whose dialect shows that he is a Turkish-Cretan.[3] When the other Greeks are led off to the barracks to spend the night in detention, the interpreter turns to Xopateras, the Cretan who dominates much of the tale and who had wanted to spend the night with his mates:

▌ "Hey, sindeknáki, I'll take you to my hut," he told him, and held him back. "Where do you come from, lad?" Turk or Greek, if you were born in Crete you can't be anything but Cretan. And the interpreter, all things considered, had his local patriotism! (Bir Hakeim, p. 18)

There is a rueful recognition here that Cretans are notorious for such local patriotism in Greece and Turkey alike, to a degree that transcends the larger national enmities. The interpreter hails Xopateras as sindeknáki ("little spiritual kinsman"), a form of address in which endearment (the diminutive -áki ending) is combined with a conspicuously Cretan dialect word (síndeknos), which to a literalist would make no sense on the lips of a Muslim: sindekniá, spiritual kinship established through sponsorship of the rite of baptism, is a Christian institution.

But matters are not so simple. Among the Greeks who are now in the mayor's hands are a madam and her eight "girls"; unlike many prostitutes, Madame Margot had not the slightest intention of pleasing the Nazi invaders. The standard metaphor for betrayal or collaboration with an enemy, whether a foreign invader or the bureaucratic agents of the state, is "pimping" (Herzfeld 1991a: 92–96). The language with which Andreas notes her attitude is thus thoroughly imbued with the symbolism of purity and pollution:

▌ Mamma Margot was the madam of a bordello in Karlovasi [on Samos]. As soon as the Italians invaded, she hopped on a row-boat and made it to Turkish soil. She was the only Greek among the prostitutes (pastrikés[4]) of the Occupation who had no prospects. . . .

3. Many Muslims on Crete were native speakers of the Cretan dialect of Greek. Some of the descendants of the original refugee community that arrived in Turkey after the 1924 exchange of populations continue to speak Cretan among themselves by preference.

4. This euphemistic term—"clean/tidy women"—underscores the play of ideas about purity and pollution here. It also conveys the sense that prostitutes had to be especially attentive to their appearance and spent a great deal of time on their toilette.

A "girlie" for years all over Greece, she had no truck with pimps. She made her money on her own. And when it grew, she stopped kicking the heavens with her feet and made her own "house" with ten pairs of thighs, which brought her enough gold to take over whole street blocks of property in Athens. Now she was leaving all that behind her and going away.

All the same, she knew that the merchandise she had with her would have value wherever she went. She would rebuild her four-storey apartments if she ended up losing them first. She just had to sit out the storm. (*Bir Hakeim*, p. 15)

In *Ten Women,* a book explicitly subtitled *A Novel about Social Issues,*[5] Andreas makes even clearer his sympathy for the plight of women forced into prostitution. He recognizes their financial desperation. A prostitute, appearing as a deeply compromised witness in the courtroom, lashes out at her humiliation:

▌ "Do you want me to tell you the truth? As soon as I see someone approaching me at night when I'm walking the streets, my first words to him are about the price. When you are not in a well-known brothel [literally, "house"], where they come specifically to find you and pay by the visit, when they pick you up on the street, most of them aren't keen to pay because they think they've won you over with their dashing masculinity. A girl's got to let them think that, if she knows her job properly. Because they all behave like generous gents when they think the women find them worth the trouble and good at the game. But why am I sitting here telling you all this for so long? You, gentlemen of the bench, know it all better than I do. In society people always keep their hearts empty and self-interest doesn't leave even one corner free for them to warm a helpless person with a brief word or by the way they behave." (*Ten Women*, p. 232)

Prostitutes have a hard life. There is even a rumor that the U.S. armed forces' separate jurisdiction protects violent servicemen from the prostitutes' complaints:

▌ And for a whole month discussion went on in the bordellos of Athens about whether there was such an order or condition and they would have gone all the way up to the prime minister to determine if it was true. (*Ten Women*, p. 217)

Money is the key: a prostitute can create her own dowry if she earns enough (*Ten Women*, p. 232), thereby finding her way to marriage and a late respectability. After all, as Andreas has the same prostitute point out, all work comes down to the same thing. Sympathy, she tells the bench, is wasted on rich customers (p. 233): "Just imagine if you people

5. In Greek, *Mithistórima kinonikoú provlimatismoú.*

were not paid for the work that you're doing today! Whoever worked without being paid?" In this way, Andreas, who is similarly unromantic about his own occupation as a writer, also manages to bring the judges' power and majesty down to the same level.

For Madam Margot he perhaps evinced less sympathy than for her "girls," and he does make her male assistant rail furiously against her avarice and her blunt exploitation of everyone who worked for her, but he clearly has greater respect for Madam Margot, who fled from the Nazis, than for the vast numbers of prostitutes whose profession gave new meaning to the symbolic equivalence of "pimping" with collaboration and betrayal. The term "*pastrikiá*," literally a "clean and tidy woman," is at once euphemistic—prostitutes in Greece are, as elsewhere, a notorious source of venereal disease—and ironic: the ultimate impurity is that of betrayal, the actual metaphor for which is "pimping" (*roufianiá*), and a prostitute has ceased to guard the sexual core of any family's—and, by extension, any nation's—reproductive essence. (Again, the bitter allusions to official Greek pronatalism in *Ten Women* show that Andreas is fully aware of this parallel, especially as it is the prostitute in that novel who voices them.) Madam Margot is not intended to be an admirable figure. Her avarice represents another kind of betrayal: she will do *almost* anything for money. But at least she will not betray her country to the bestiality of the Nazis, and her confident sense of principle in this one respect at least provides a powerful foil to another portrait: the naive young Cretan Xopateras, full of self-righteous patriotism, finds that hating the Nazis licenses neither his contempt for Madam Margot and her troupe nor his all-consuming, school-nourished, monotonously simplistic chauvinism.

Andreas's description of that conversion, with its slow and painful introspections and its occasional apparent reverses, exemplifies the particularly advantageous perspective on a culturally specific subjectivity that a novelist's work can offer an ethnographer. It is clear, and Andreas has confirmed this, that Xopateras is none other than the young Andreas. The name, however, is one that he borrowed from the heroic figure of a Cretan priest who died a century and a half earlier while resisting the Turks. This background adds poignancy to the conversion of Andreas's fictional Xopateras:

▌An April night. The soil of Asia Minor smelled fresh and appealing from the most recent rains. The trees swelled at the edges of their branches. The earth nourished the young shoots. Here and there, as they rippled, the crops glowed in the moonlight. Over toward Vourla a forest made a black mass. From its silence leaped the shrieks of jackals making love.

The village started to fall asleep.

The mayor of Uzunköy was a widower. His only son was a student in Izmir. Tonight, for company, he had the Turkish-Cretan and two other middle-aged men. The one was bald and short and dressed in Western style. The other was skinny, of medium height. On his dried-out chest was pasted the waistcoat of a *salvári* [accompanying pair of baggy trousers] and on his thighs tightly bound felt spats. On his head he wore a velvet cap that was turning green with age. He sat Xopateras down next to him. He had been quite taken with him from that first moment when Xopateras had unhesitatingly given him his golden ring.

Opposite, at a separate low table, the women were gathered together. Everyone is solicitous and hospitable at such times! These are eight women! Foreign women, in a foreign place. In your house. One word from you and they're loaded on a boat for Chios! Another, and they go to Alexandria! This is not a joking matter!

The mayor of Uzunköy watched with pleasure. He and his friends had downed a small bottle of ouzo apiece. The women across from them took pains to respond to every movement and every toast he made.

They too were drinking and nibbling tidbits. (*Bir Hakeim*, pp. 18–19)

And so the mischief begins. The mayor is master in his own house, and hospitality gives him even greater power than the official power of which Andreas makes it the symbol. This was a dynamic that his Greek hostages—for such, in effect, they were—were culturally well equipped to understand: in both countries the act of hospitality confers a momentary moral advantage on the host even when the guests are formally more powerful.[6] The Greek fugitives thus faced serious handicaps in the mayor's mastery of this game and in their vulnerable status as illegal aliens in the country of their traditional foe. These factors turned their personal predicament into a metonym of international relations. Moreover, the moral economy of sexuality, so important in the ethnographic analysis of Greek society, exposes these hapless Greeks to insult through their association—however involuntary—with the easy sexuality of Greek prostitutes. It would have done them no good at all to protest that they had come together with these women by the merest chance; in the logic of local politics, the sexual degradation of a family's women demeans its men as well. Here, all Greeks have become a virtual family, in the conventional spirit of nationalistic imagery. The madam's title of "Mamma" (mother) sarcastically strengthens the sense of a collective moral identity modeled on that of the nuclear family. Andreas uses this

6. On Crete, the idiom of hospitality has become a means of both emphasizing local distinctiveness (expressed as moral superiority over the supposedly stingy mainlanders and foreigners), and relegating potentially powerful guests to an at least symbolically dependent role (see Herzfeld 1987b).

explosive scene to explore the basis of national pride: he suggestively reproduces the terms in which chauvinism draws on the aggressively sexual
idiom of everyday social contest—the "agonistic" mode through which
men humiliate one another by impugning each other's ability to control
the alleged sexual appetites and adventures of daughters, wives, and even
mothers.[7]

Mamma Margot recounts how she and her girls had been seam-
stresses whose good fortune, after fleeing Samos, was to fall into the
hands of the mayor—"a man of gold!" Indeed, the mayor was truly
gilded—by his greedy confiscation of all the gold he could find on his
involuntary guests. And indeed, too, Mamma Margot's "girls" had
"worked" hard at their "sewing machines" during the early days of the
Italian occupation of Samos.

The meaning of these innuendoes gains clarity, becomes obvious, as
the drink begins to take effect. Finally, the Turks set the young women
to dancing. As they dance, at first willingly and then with growing reluctance, they begin to strip off their clothes:

▌ The mayor of Uzunköy was transfixed in his chair. With his hands on his
knees he insatiably watched the girls' bodies and his eyes had grown round.

His tongue was caressing his fat lips. His body was shaking as though
it felt a deep cold. The other two men had tensed. One of them nervously
twisted his hands together without cease. The other was fidgeting from his
waist down as though he were sitting on needles.

The interpreter twirled his moustache and one of his eyes had narrowed
while the other had widened to double its normal size. Xopateras had gone
a deep red color. He kept looking from these elderly men to Mamma Margot and back, and his cheeks were aflame with the anger and the deep
shame that he felt. Xopateras was neither shy nor prudish. But this spectacle could only wound his self-regard. Brought up in the history of his homeland, with its fables about glorious rebels and legends of guerrilla captains,
he felt that these [Turkish] people at whose expense all these things had
been developed were battering his nationalism and making a mockery of
his manhood.

And now, at this moment, he was silently selling out the women of his
homeland—whatever they were—to those same people whom he could
only view as enemies. (*Bir Hakeim*, p. 22)

With this, Andreas confirms that the sexual politics of contest inform
the passions of nationalism. At home, the proud Cretan would have seen
in these women only the lowliest rejects of society, the cast-off moral

---

7. This is especially evident in symbolic male contests such as the card came (Herzfeld
1985: 152–62) and in the forms of blasphemy used in quarrels (Herzfeld 1984).

failures not only of other families but particularly of other places, since—or at least so I was told in Rethemnos—no woman would dare to sell her body in a place where she had kin (see Herzfeld 1991a: 27). Even Mamma Margot's humble but resentful male assistant, named with appropriate familism Barba-Kostas ("*Uncle* Constantine") and debarred by some implicit respect for the rules of virtual incest from ever sleeping with her girls, tells Xopateras (p. 17), "The two over there are Cretan. Have you ever heard of a Cretan prostitute?" In this, at least, he shares the Cretan view that Cretan women do not enter such shameful occupations. But for Xopateras the presence of the two Cretans becomes irrelevant—or at most an added reason to resent the Turks' treatment of these women—in the face of such national humiliation. In the segmentary logic of cultural pride and the protection of collective intimacy, he shares Mamma Margot's view (p. 16): "Whatever we are, that's nobody else's business. Nor are we going to ask you who you are and what you want here. Here we must all back each other up so we don't make fools of ourselves in front of the Turks!"

But the fact remains that Mamma Margot's troupe *does* contain two Cretan women. The absolute facticity of long-cherished stereotypes is already at risk. Moreover, segmentary or relativistic models of social relations—in which the most intimate entities, such as the family, become the emotive metaphor that marshals support for the large abstractions of nationalism—are inherently unstable; anything that exposes the grand truths about morality and the nation as a system of levels and analogies rather than as absolute verities can undermine the most self-confident bigotry. If even Cretan women can be prostitutes, it is only a single step—albeit a painful one—to questioning the elaborate mythology of female purity and the Greek male heroism that supposedly guards it. Xopateras, already bemused by the Cretan interpreter's local patriotism and appalled to discover how reluctant he is to prevent the humiliation of the women, now faces his conversion experience in all its disruptive force.

His story is all the more poignant because a conventional tale, widely heard in the villages of highland Crete, recounts how the Turkish *aǧa*, a local official, would humiliate entire villages by forcing its young women to dance for him. (The story usually ends with a heroic local youth slaying the aǧa and freeing the women.) To make the spectacle still more humiliating, physically as well as morally, the women were made to dance on a floor strewn with roasted chickpeas. Villagers still recount this tale in the midst of seemingly contrary assertions that their villagers were bastions of freedom during the years of Turkish rule. They thus show some awareness of just how conditional their freedom was, an awareness that is never made explicit in their rhetoric. For Xopateras, the revelation of contingency is less an acquisition of new knowledge than a bringing into consciousness of what his entire environment has steadfastly denied. His—and Andreas's—conversion to a broader vision is under way.

First, he discovers that power is not just a matter of relations between nationalities; in the new Turkey that succeeded the Ottoman empire the *rayádhes* [singular *rayás*, from Turkish *reaya*], the human chattels, were not always Christians:

Xopateras, leaning on his oarlock, lets himself dream as he gazes after the furrow left behind it by the little steamboat. Around him is a jumbled mass of people. Hardworking Turks with their tools. The new *rayádhes* who have now taken on the role of the *gavur* ("infidel"). Further away, fair-haired men in civilian clothes, with brown- and black-haired girls at their side. The policy of "neutrality" does not stop these blond "travelers" from playing the role of the worldly knight-errant (*kavaláris*). In deep armchairs, enormously fat Turks smoke their big hubble-bubble pipes. Only the fezzes are missing from these ağas, who have changed their color like chameleons. (p. 29)

On the street the next day, Xopateras meets one of the girls, but, when she tries to talk to him, he turns his back on her. He runs into Mamma Margot with her whole entourage, and again he turns his back:

He didn't go out of the hotel again. He waited for the day when they would leave for Syria. The others came and went. They talked about the beauties of the city, about the Burnova district, about the old town where there still stood the burned houses and the churches left from the time of [the Turkish invasion and burning of Smyrna/İzmir in] 1922. They talked about the beautiful Turkish women, the activity and wealth in the new town; and he cared not a whit. In a dark mood, unspeaking, without a word, without any life, Xopateras had been struck in the most sensitive point of his very being.

His Nationalism was the creation of his environment. Every public event in his village, every movement in his town, revolved around that point. When he was a little child, he would hear his father talking about his exploits and his achievements. How many Turks he'd killed, how many guns he'd taken off them, and how many he'd captured alive. In the villages where he wandered in summertime, all the stories he heard, old and new alike, had the same enemy, the same heroes, the same victors! The victors were always the Greeks. At school, in all history, he only read about victories of the Greeks. Only the Greeks were *pallikária!* Often, as he read that history of 400 years of slavery,[8] he was so enthusiastic with the life of the

---

8. This conventional phrase obscures the fact that the various phases—including the Ottoman (*Tourkokratía*)—of foreign dominion over what is today the territory of Greece did not last for equal lengths of time in all areas.

slaves, and it was presented to him in such an idyllic light, that he would have wholeheartedly have preferred to live in that period.

It is rare for a catastrophic horror to be described as it was in reality. In books the story was wrapped in a golden covering that blinded him.

That's why, in Uzunköy, he felt entitled to demand that the Turks respect him and the others, since they were descendants of those same people—of those Greeks who wore blinders when they dealt with history—and still do, on everything, especially *pallikariá*, as people do all over the world.

He was furious with himself. Didn't he have many an example to show him how one man on his own could take on a thousand? How had he let them insult him and make a fool of him in this way? He began to wonder if he was really the person he had believed himself to be. Often, in his sleep and in his waking hours, there had boiled within him a white-hot desire for sacrifices and heroic deeds and he had been sure that at the first opportunity he would show himself equal to them. And now he had lost that opportunity. Or was something else happening to him—something that would restore the faith that he had in himself? There it was: that the opportunity wasn't worth the trouble, or that these particular women were not worth sacrificing one's life for. Yet this explanation did not satisfy him, and from the next day on all his credos began to fall apart.

He began to think:

"On his own he could not have done anything; nor could anyone have done anything, ever!" (pp. 30–31)

And the painful lesson continues. One morning, they were all put on a train. The places they passed were well known to him from his nationalistic reading. These were places where the ancient Greeks had established colonies that came in time to equal and even surpass the mother cities as intellectual and mercantile centers, or sites of the confrontations between Arabs and Byzantines, the latter represented by the fractious border barons (*akrítes*) whose leader, Digenes, was elevated in the years before the ill-fated Greek attempt to recapture the whole area in the war of 1920 through 1922 to the status of a national hero, with an epic of Homeric proportions to match:[9]

▌   In his mind the Ten Thousand [the Athenian troops whose retreat from Persia at the end of the fifth century B.C. was documented by Xenophon[10]] became confused with the horseback-riding Byzantines. The *akrítes* and all

9. The "epic" was recovered from a series of manuscripts. Its relation to numerous folksongs has also been the subject of extensive philological reconstruction, most of it heavily ideological in emphasis. See Herzfeld 1982a: 120–21.

10. The story is the central theme of Xenophon's *Anabasis* (1972).

the versions of Digenes with the skirted soldiers (*évzones*) of [the Greek-Turkish war of] 1922.[11] And then, as though he had fallen from the sky, he got his feet on the ground and looked reality in the face. He tried to distinguish between the [Greek] refugees he knew and the Turks he was seeing now. The same faces, the same coloring, the same human beings. And he himself more closely resembled the Turks than he did many Greeks.

Then, too, these seemed like good people. From the train window he could see them early in the morning as they ran to their fields with their animals, with their children. He often played with the thought that among them there might be someone like the interpreter or the mayor, but he dismissed it, or compared their behavior with acts of the same kind committed by his own compatriots when they happened to enter a village or town belonging to the enemy. And he would shake his head, blaming himself first of all because he had never entertained such a thought before! What a strange business! That rhythmic beating of the wheels on the railroad tracks stirred him and brought him thoughts and opinions he had never had before.

There—once again, he recalled the Turkish shepherd on the beach at Çesme. He was hungry and exhausted from walking. The Turk watched him and smiled. Xopateras took courage and remembered that the Turks called bread *ekmek!*

"*Ekmek*," he said to the man, with a longing that betrayed his hunger. And the Turk smilingly brought out of his bag a whole loaf, still warm, and gave it to him. He remembered how wonderful the bread had smelled. Never before could he have eaten plain bread with such an appetite. Nor could he remember anyone ever giving him anything with such generosity and kindness. And that with a laugh and without reserve.

Xopateras slowly cut into the bread, looking at the shepherd with gratitude, and gave him back half the loaf. He [the shepherd] thwacked a wild olive stump with a whirring slash of his staff, whistled at his sheep, and hurriedly made off—perhaps to avoid Xopateras's thanks or so as not to have take back the half-loaf! (pp. 32–33)

Xopateras understands full well the double-edged implications of hospitality. In his own village, Andreas's Greek readers would probably assume that Xopateras would have been no less generous to any Turks who chanced his way. In creating moral boundaries between insiders and outsiders, hospitality and warfare—as Edmund Leach once noted of the latter (1965)—are both effective ways of translating the abstractions of

---

11. The *évzones* wear the distinctive *foustanéla*, or pleated skirt, that was common among several Balkan populations, including those of the Greek mainland and parts of Albania, in pre-Independence times; it is closely associated in the popular imagination and in nationalist iconography with the klefts and their role in the War of Independence.

social classification into palpable practice. Hospitality, ostensibly an act of generosity, may be competitive or even hostile, and it serves to draw a line between insiders and outsiders that always carries the implicit threat of violence if all does not go well.

Now Xopateras is the recipient; and Andreas, his modernist sensibilities rebelling against the ambivalent possibilities of hospitality as much as his traditionalism embraces them, draws Xopateras into the same shocked recognition of a common humanity that transcends national classification. (In his home today, Andreas plies his guests with all of the enthusiastic generosity of his shepherding forebears; unlike them, however, and with an exquisitely modernist etiquette that places personal consideration over the pressure of social obligation, he insists that his guests only eat as much as they really want.) In the Turkish shepherd, Xopateras recognizes the epitome of moral worth as he had learned that virtue at home in his own village: the poorer the giver, the more admirable is even the humblest of gifts and the more powerful the moral message that it conveys. But if a Turk is capable of such generosity, then—and this is the force of the antimodernist revelation now vouchsafed to Xopateras—this Turk, perhaps any Turk, is not a stranger, a foreigner, an *outsider*, at all.

It is not only chauvinism that Andreas challenges here. Xopateras also meets a romantic view of courage head-on. It is a view that differs significantly from the bravery of a villager engaged in animal-theft or vengeance-killing. It characterized, among others, the philhellenes who in the years between 1821 and 1833 flocked to the cause of Greek national independence and were disgusted to encounter what was (from their perspective) contemptuously dismissed as "Turkish warfare": the mountain fighters were more interested in hit-and-run raids that yielded stocks of Turkish weapons while entailing minimal risks to their own lives than in reproducing the hopeless heroism that a romantic Europe attributed to their ancient forebears (St. Clair 1972: 35–38; Dakin 1973: 72). Fighting for a collective, abstract goal and sacrificing personal interests and even one's very life for such a goal had little meaning for these guerrillas. They were interested in booty and self-preservation. That was not the image that the state promulgated, however, and local historical narrative in Crete and elsewhere had effectively been assimilated to the official hermeneutic long before the time in which *Bir Hakeim* is set. Xopateras now found that such modernist heroics were of little use to him. Like Andreas trying to steal the airman's gun in Athens in order to fight the invading Germans, Xopateras was capable of quixotic heroism, but he also learned that there were enemies—the Nazis—far worse than the Turkish bogey. Suddenly the logic of state-directed patriotism, with its corollary of violently anti-Turkish sentiment, had become suspect.

In nationalistic logic, the death of individuals in war is redeemed by the collective immortality of the nation (Anderson 1983: 17–19). The rationality of this view, to which nationalistic and philhellenic discourse has successfully attached an ancient pedigree, is not self-evident for the characters in *Bir Hakeim*. Even in the cynical society of an ethnically heterogeneous collection of hardened ex-convicts serving in the Foreign Legion, each with his own sense of failure in the wider world, good reasons for self-sacrifice can be entertained; the irrepressibly ingenuous Greek from Thessaly, Kitsos, for example, hates the Nazis and believes in people's right to own the land that feeds them. But the reasons of the bureaucratic state, with their cold rationality masking the symbolism of aggressive masculinity, have little appeal for him.

Xopateras, initially more accepting of these ideas, comes to repudiate them in a correspondingly more extreme fashion. At one point (pp. 76–85), the legionnaires fall into a lengthy discussion of why people go to war. Their almost lackadaisical chatter provides a counterpoint to the gloomy introspection of Xopateras. Both discourses lead in one direction only: away from the mindless heroics of the modern nationalist project. For these are personal histories, working against the collective imagery espoused by bureaucratic states, charting the progressive realization of an unspoken doubt that has in fact—as Andreas subtly intimates to his readers—been present all along.

Andreas has opened up one of the most painful internal contradictions of modernist heroics. On the one hand, in the nationalist view, the death of individuals is redeemed by the life of the nation—indeed, in the case of Greece, by a veritable resurrection, since the new nation-state was constructed as the reincarnation of ancient Hellas, mediated by the Orthodox Christian imagery of the Resurrection of Christ. The promise of immortality is perhaps the warring nation-state's greatest hold on the loyalty of its citizens. On the other hand, modernism also entails the full recognition of individual subjectivities, identities, and rights. This exposes a basic contradiction: if immortality can best be earned by submerging the self in the common good through the ultimate act of self-sacrifice, what of those who exercise the right to dissent and survive? What of those who in their lifetimes have already been rejected by their respective nation-states? *Bir Hakeim* is full of such characters.

Andreas's novel of the Foreign Legion is not about idealized heroes fighting for their country but about a collection of misfits, criminals, and (in some cases) rather stupid men, several of them unable to return to their homelands, who can only gain a measure of redemption from their checkered pasts in death. Some of them have understood that Nazism represents a far greater evil than their personal crimes. But their cause is not unambiguously a collective or an ideological one, and the Foreign

Legion does not really offer them an encompassing identity to which they would willingly surrender their personal sense of self.

Nor does military glory offer much solace. Resurrection, if it comes, will be a coldly impersonal reward for them. Because of who they have been in the past, the legionnaires understand that they also have no individuated future. That makes their appeal all the greater in a skeptical age. A well-known critic, Kleon Paraskhos (1954), found that these characters "make us live their drama almost as our own, or at least as a drama that deserves all our sympathy." As they face certain annihilation in the battle of Bir Hakeim on 10 June 1942, one of their number cries to the French NCO, Dugnard:

▌ "In due course, when the Nazis leave Paris, they'll take your bones, Dugnard, and they'll bury them with the bones of Napoleon. And they'll have parades and they'll sing and dance because you were killed and they'll talk about Bir Hakeim so that their hair will stand on end. But, Dugnard, they won't want to hear or talk about how Bir Hakeim was won for them by Paul the Strangler, Pedro the smuggler, and Dugnard the murderer! They'll be too ashamed to talk about it. They won't be able to say it. Have you realized that? They didn't want us alive, Dugnard, and when we're dead they'll put us in the Monument to those fallen in the War! Spit, Dugnard! Go on—over there to the north! Spit, I tell you! The heaven on which you should spit is over that way! Spit! there, in the north! At this very moment they are putting the incompetent drivers and petty thugs [literally, tram-drivers and the knife-pullers] on trial! Ha, ha! Spit, Dugnard! Over there to the north! Tomorrow they'll come to the parade which will take place in your honor. Spit, I tell you! Can't you see the regimental flags? A whole forest of them is passing under the Arc de Triomphe! Look, monsieur Artin [an Armenian character in the story] is carrying the flag of Bir Hakeim . . .!" (pp. 168–69)

Amidst the pressures of the deracinating environment of the Foreign Legion, Andreas has placed two rather naive young Greek men who must puzzle it all out for themselves. The Cretan Xopateras, the erstwhile chauvinist, gets the larger shocks. Through Xopateras's dawning comprehension, Andreas brings the fundamental contradiction of modern nationalism into focus: it is no longer clear that one's loyalty is to the national hearth and home, and the ironic imagery of sex and death—prostitutes as the receptacle of national purity, death as the obliteration of a criminal past rather than as the apogee of a glorious one—irrevocably complicates the certainties promulgated by the bureaucratic state.

For Andreas's philosophical stance toward national identity, his separation of ethnic pride from state nationalism is replicated in his impatience with the bureaucratic embodiments of state power. His view of the class character of bureaucratic border controls is strongly expressed in *Bir Hakeim* (p. 12) when he describes the arrival of Greek refugees from the Nazi invasion on Turkish soil and their fear of forcible repatriation:

> ▌In reality borders do not exist for those who travel from country to country. They have a passport with stamps and visas. The custom house [personnel] pats them down, bows to them a few times, and looks the other way.
>
> How is this fuss any different from the entry of a theatrical troupe or a circus? Only the length of time needed for the formalities. But then, for what person of equal status do borders exist? Borders are for the hunted, for refugees, for those without hearth or home.

This is the voice of a maverick patriotism indeed. It is nonetheless fully consistent with the view from the Greek left: the present-day bureaucratic state is a foreign imposition on the instinctively democratic and egalitarian *ethnos*.

Throughout *Bir Hakeim*, in fact, Andreas repeatedly pokes fun at the nationalist preoccupation with purity. Among the gang of ruffians who make up this particular microcosm of the Foreign Legion, the pretensions of a world-conquering Hellenism start to look distinctly seedy. For the wide-eyed Thessalian, Kitsos, whose name recalls the stereotypical "kleft," or guerrilla, of the Greek War of Independence, the new war is not about national pride but is about defending the fertile fields of one's native village from the destructive hand of international fascism. Unlike the intensely introspective Xopateras, Kitsos does not worry about national and sexual purity. And this leads him into a pleasurable adventure that mocks the more extreme forms of Greek irredentism.

The legionnaires are in a village near Beirut and an amiable middle-aged Syrian, Emin, is persistently trying to befriend young Kitsos:

> ▌It's now been several days since Emin has been inviting Kitsos to his home. Kitsos knows that the Syrians are hospitable and is not perturbed. Then, too, he knows that the Syrians are Greeks. That's what all the Syrians say. In all their houses there's a framed picture of Alexander the Great, just like those of the Virgin and of Christ. Those who are *grik ortodoks* have a picture of Alexander the Great along with their icons. And the other Christians have a single icon: Alexander the Great. Even the Mohammedans have Alexander the Great. They're all descendants of Alexander the Great. That's what the Syrians say. (p. 108)

The claim that Lebanese *grik ortodoks* are descended from Alexander the Great—are, in fact, kin to the *Roúmi* (Greeks) who have appeared so suddenly among them—also appears in Andreas's memoir, *The Painter Tsingos in War and in Prison*, where we also find Egyptian Bedouin invoking the same glorious ancestry and the same kinship with the Greeks

(p. 106): "And, what is most important, they say that we have the same enemies"—which by this time meant the British military, who had imprisoned Andreas and his comrades.

In *Bir Hakeim*, Andreas turns the Lebanese Arabs' claim to be the descendants of Alexander into an ironic allegory of Greek national claims. Emin's eventual success in luring Kitsos into his house leads to a hilariously polyglot conversation: "And Emin claps him on the back and tells him in Arabic and French and English all mixed together—all the races (*óles i fáres*[12]) [of the world] have passed through Syria—that he is *goot mboy* and *camarade* and *suwayah*" (p. 110). "All the races have passed through Syria": that phrase, cast in a characteristically agnatic idiom of thinking about ethnic identity, is immediately reminiscent of the way Greeks talk about their collective ancestry, a rueful acknowledgment of everything the ideology of national purity denies but that language as well as physical appearance must always betray. Indeed, it turns out, the object of all this international cordiality is to get Kitsos into bed with Emin's young wife, Nabiha. Emin is impotent, but he desperately wants a child. And so it comes to pass: a month later Nabiha is pregnant. Andreas is not averse to sending this modern young Alexander to regenerate the Orient, but we are left in little doubt that this is in no sense a Greek privilege—indeed, the whole Foreign Legion has access to such delights— and that the Greeks, similarly an oft-invaded nation, are themselves liable to comparable treatment. "It's days now since the legionnaires have left. . . . Soldiers pass by, leaving dust, money, and children!" (*Bir Hakeim*, p. 111).

But Andreas reserves his most sardonic portraiture for the French in whose name these ragtag soldiers of ill-fortune are fighting (*Bir Hakeim*, pp. 127–28). The scene is Damascus after a smashing victory and the antihero is Artin, a cynical Armenian:

> In Damascus tonight not a single legionnaire will be left in solitude, and after a few months more children will be born than legionnaires died in the slaughter [of battle]. Tonight the very earth is steaming. Sprouting greenery covers the lawless rites and the scent of the hashish-bush gets mixed up with the stink of the army boot and mingles with aromatic herbs and jasmine.
>
> The Samliyeh are female creatures with black eyes and a complexion of sallow ocher. And the legionnaires are middle-aged, tough, and wild in their appearance and their manners.

---

12. The *fara* is a patriclan or patrigroup equivalent to the agnatic sense of *yeniá* or *sói*, for which it serves as a synonym on Crete (as it apparently did among at least some of the guerrilla bands during the period of the War of Independence and immediately before and after).

Tonight the legionnaires are drunk on hashish, on the Damascene women, on *arak* [a hard liquor] and gunpowder.

In Damascus tonight, the legionnaires are making merry. And when the legionnaires make merry, many people will weep. Damascus is taking a violent thumping from the victors. In the bars and the brothels, victory undresses, and the victors are like ravenous male beasts who have abandoned everything in order to sate themselves on female flesh.

"Vive la Légion!" is what the Damascenes hear all night, and they don't know whether to bless or to curse the victory, the Legion, and all armies.

"Vive la Légion!" cries toothless Artin, and he laughs and he cackles and beats his breast from the joy and enthusiasm he feels.

"Vive la Légion!" shrieks the Samliyeh woman who is hugging Artin in the *café chantant*[13] and who is extraordinarily tender with Artin because as soon as he came in he flashed a crisp ten-pound note at her. For a while now she's been admiring Artin. For a while now *he* has been telling *her* about the battle. About Kitsos, about Slateff. For a while now Artin has been talking about Artin, about victory. For a while now Artin has been talking about things he neither believes in nor knows anything about. And Artin is true to himself and many a time he thinks out loud and shouts, "I sh——t [abbreviation in the original] on the Legion and on all armies! *Vive toi et moi . . . !"*

And he shouts again along with the whore, "Long live you and I . . ." And he drags her outside, stumbling and spitting, and as soon as the door closes behind them he turns her upside-down in the middle of the street. . . .

And the Damascene woman drunkenly and with her feet in the air (*anáskela*) sings the Marseillaise . . . !

Artin is the archetypical opportunist, a man who lived off a good old woman's desire to believe he was her long-lost son and cursed her whenever her desperate attempts to earn a little money for him failed, and who manages to come out of every military engagement physically unscathed and with a profit as well. Andreas uses this stock character to make fun of the French, in whose name the Legion fights. If there is merit to be found in patriotism, and of this Andreas has no doubt, it is metaphorically turned on its head here: the woman with her legs in the air (*anáskela*) emblematizes sexual abandon and hence betrayal; being "feet-up" is to violate all social norms.

The prostitute who sings the French national anthem with her legs in the air completes the unveiling of the sexual and androcentric under-

13. One urban music style extremely popular in Asia Minor before 1922 and then introduced into Piraeus by Greek refugees was known as *kafé santán* (*café chantant*). Andreas uses the image here to emphasize the "levantine" cosmopolitanism of the setting.

pinnings of nationalism that begin with the self-discovery of Xopateras—
a man whose serious respect for his own country is the precise antithesis
of Artin's heedless pursuit of self-gratification. For both narrow chauvinism and cynical self-absorption are, for Andreas, ways of destroying what
is best in human society. One brings the Nazi horror within the gates
and reproduces it there. The other lets it trample the world underfoot
and makes a profit out of the resulting mayhem.

Andreas also plays ironically with the theme of national resurrection—a potent image in Greek: the national War of Independence is often
represented as both the rebirth of the Classical spirit on its native soil
and metaphorically as a replay of the Resurrection of Christ. Twice in a
few days the two actual Frenchmen in the gang think themselves resurrected. The first time they see British tanks coming to their rescue; "the
legionnaires hurled themselves out of the trenches like the damned of
hell, with their faces blackened with the growth of their beards and their
eyes wild. They leaped out and started to dance" (p. 181)—and the case-
hardened French captain, Dugnard, turns to his compatriot, exclaiming,
"This is like a Resurrection, Paul! Do you believe in miracles?" And then
their hopes are smashed on the rocks of a bitter deception—for those
tanks are a Nazi ruse.

The second moment is no less bitterly ironic. For just before the great
battle of Bir Hakeim itself, the climactic event with which the book concludes, the legionnaires hear over the radio that Allied forces, and especially the Free French, are coming to their rescue.[14] Now it is Paul's turn
to hope against hope. Dugnard reminds him that they are themselves
French. And Paul replies:

▌ "We came close to forgetting that, Dugnard. Now, however, we've been
reborn. I've forgotten everything! Now I'm a lad again. Now I'm twenty
years old, Dugnard. That's how I see you too. . . ." (p. 184)

Soon after this "rebirth," the battle starts up again with rekindled ferocity. Except for Xopateras (whom illness compelled to take an extended
leave from the Legion) and Artin (whose instinct for self-preservation
served him as well as ever), all these men, rejects of society, die heroes'
deaths—although, in a final irony, they know they are also dying anony-
mously, denied in their moment of greatness the personal "resurrection"
that the survival of a name confers. Their names die away with the narrator's voice: "Ten hand grenades fell on the trench and Paul, Pedro, and
Dugnard stayed together with Juan forever at Bir Hakeim. . . ."

Like his hero Xopateras, Andreas was already far away from his erst-

14. On the battle of Bir Hakeim, see Koenig 1971; Laffin 1974: 123; Porch 1991: 482–
83.

while comrades when the battle of Bir Hakeim took place. His book not only charts his own dawning comprehension of nationalism but pays tribute to the discovery that in every ruffian—and the language of *Bir Hakeim* alone bears witness to the pains he took to know his comrades well—events may sometimes surprise a compelling humanity. A resurrection, albeit an ironic one, is vouchsafed to such as these; it is not the prerogative of fascists and chauvinists. This is the inverse of what Loizos has discerned in the nationalistic ennobling of psychopaths; these legionnaire psychopaths—the strangler and all the rest—are not concerned with legitimating the evil within them but simply with escaping from its consequences in a manner that restores their self-esteem. They are not admirable men, and Andreas does not disguise their faults; to have done so would have subverted his purposes. They are proof that what passes for villainy in one context may appear as heroism at another historical moment. While Andreas here comes close to Loizos's observation, he also urges us not to judge individuals in excessively simplistic terms. The most animal-like of human beings is also a creator, an artisan. He does not absolve them of their past crimes but places them in the context of the far more comprehensive evil of Nazism.

That was the force against which, with no prospect of a bearable life in Greece, he eventually joined up with the Allied forces in the Middle East. Two of his brothers had already fought in the Albanian campaign of 1940 against Mussolini, a campaign that drew off enormous numbers of men from Crete and left the island open to invasion by Hitler's forces. Andreas was not called up at that point; the German invasion caught him in Athens, as we have seen. Of the two brothers who fought in the Albanian campaign, one, Yannis, suffered severe leg injuries which continued to plague him in old age. The other, George, went into hiding in the Cretan hill villages but drank polluted well water from which it was said—although this is medically implausible—that he contracted the meningitis from which he died.

This brother was fair-haired and blue-eyed. Andreas repeatedly emphasizes these features when he invokes his memory, in a move that belongs to the same rhetorical set as Xopateras's surprise at discovering that many Turks resembled his own people. Many Cretans make a point of emphasizing the fair coloring that is common on the island, especially those who—like Andreas's father's line—could claim descent from the legendary Sfakian mountain villages where no Turk, it was somewhat implausibly maintained, had ever set foot. Andreas also writes in his controversial novel, *Voukéfali,* of one noble Turk who stood out among the pitiful remnants of the Muslim community in Rethemnos, attributing his fair complexion to an admixture of Venetian (rather than ancient Dorian) blood. In a country torn between orientalizing and occidentalizing self-images, racial arguments—protestations that racism does not exist in Greece to the contrary—map out degrees of social distance, even in the most intimate family politics. Neni Panourgiá remembers that as a child her fair sister "looked as if she belonged in a Renaissance painting"— obviously a *Western* Renaissance painting. In the early inculcation of distrust and anxiety that Greek children learn, her own dark skin earned her threats of being sent back to the Gypsies, jokingly called her own *sóï* ("family" or even "patriline") if she did not behave (1985: 23–24). For Andreas to dwell so insistently on this theme in his memories of his brother George does not make him a racist, and both his handling of Xopateras's self-discovery and the warm portrayal of his Arab and African fellow-soldiers in the short stories collected in the volume titled *White Fences* show him as resolutely opposed to anything of the kind. But the vocabulary of popular genetics dies hard, and it provides the fertile ground on which others can build much more destructive ideologies of human difference.

This persistent streak of admiration for European ideals of bodily beauty is not the least significant of the paradoxes that we meet in Andreas. As recent debates have dredged up the memory of his brother in an especially unsavory way, Andreas has again become more inclined to recall the physical features that distinguished George among his fellow-Cretans. But it was in the fellowship of war that Andreas, like Xopateras, began to discover the irrelevance of such distinctions for assessing the value of one's companions. Like a colonial anthropologist genuinely struggling to do without words like "primitive," Andreas found he could not entirely divest himself of this vocabulary, especially when he was speaking about his hometown and his own proud patriline. But the revelations of human fellowship were far more powerful forces in the development of his moral imagination. Like George Orwell and Jean-Paul Sartre, two authors who also wrote with passion against tyranny and prejudice, Andreas Nenedakis came to mature awareness of his opposition to these evils in the smoke and heat of the war that their presence in the world had called into being.

4 ▣

DISILLUSIONMENTS
OF EXILE

Andreas himself never fought at Bir Hakeim. Instead, from Turkey he found his way to Lebanon. The professional officers of the Greek army in exile were noticeably unenthusiastic about the arrival of eager recruits newly escaped from their occupied country. When Andreas's friend Thanasis Tsingos arrived, he was asked why he had not stayed behind and carried on with his profession as an architect:

> ▌A strange business. Who could have hoped that as soon as he set foot in the Middle East he would be told that he did wrong to come? It was the worst disappointment a person could experience. After enduring so much just to get there. After so many torments and travails. And all this advice [to stay where he had come from] to be given him by someone who in all his life had his mind set only on making sure his mess tin was brimming over. Where had he ended up? (*Tsingos*, p. 19)

The Painter Tsingos in War and in Prison is an artful description of the origins of the growing dissension and eventual outright revolt among Greek soldiers who, having fought with distinction at El Alamein, found themselves increasingly alienated from the British-dominated Greek government-in-exile in Cairo. Andreas lived through these events; while he does paint an austerely affectionate portrait of his friend, the book can also be read as both autobiography and political analysis. Written in 1965 immediately after Tsingos's lonely death, it documents the rising tide of disenchantment among those who had idealistically fought against an external enemy only to fall prey to the creeping corruption of repression from within.

These Greeks had left home too soon to join the guerrilla forces in the mountains. As they tramped from the steamy towns of Syria to the Egyptian desert beset by the hot, gritty *khamsin* (summer sandstorm), they dreamed endlessly of returning home as liberators. News of the Resistance meanwhile began to filter through, gnawing away at the men's consciousness. Tsingos, although a military policeman now, was by temperament highly susceptible to the implications of the changes. Andreas was aware almost from the beginning that the young architect-turned-officer had refused to observe the customary separation of officers from enlisted men. Their own first meeting was symptomatic: Tsingos led the unsuspecting Andreas into a highly incriminating conversation about the officers in his unit, only to reveal his true identity as a "gendarme" (p. 14): " 'Now,' I thought, 'he may turn me in. But so what? He had said even more.' " In fact, this was to be the basis of an enduring if difficult friendship: bound to Tsingos by personal attraction and a growing awareness of shared political convictions, Andreas subjected him to merciless tirades over his increasingly heavy drinking.

Tsingos had already seen the brash young Cretan in action before they ever came face to face. Their brigade was languishing in a camp in Baalbek, Lebanon, becalmed amid the storms of war by the stultifying factionalism of their leaders. Among the officers were many whose sympathies lay with the democratic (Venizelist) tradition; some belonged to a secret but rather heavy-handed antifascist organization. On the political right, the secretly pro-Nazi Falangists were agitating for a full withdrawal from the war; the Royalists, like the king himself, did not dare alienate the Allied command by opposing the war openly but became experts at dragging their feet. Meanwhile, the troops were dangerously bored and the seeds of future conflict began to germinate. Left-wing groups organized for the internal struggle ahead; right-wing spies compiled dossiers on the leftists' every spoken word. The file on Tsingos would provide inexhaustible ammunition for his enemies a scant two years later.

When Australian and New Zealand units passed through Baalbek on their way to the fighting then at a crescendo in Egypt in 1942, the frustrated Greek soldiers began to jump on the troop carriers in order to get to the front. Discipline was collapsing fast. The commanding officer, a democrat, sympathized entirely with his troops but had to resort to fomenting open revolt among his own NCOs in order to force the right-wing officers to back him.

▌ Later Tsingos told me that he recognized me from that time. All the brigade NCOs had been gathered together, and the brigadier was hearing their reports. Everyone expected a pronouncement from the ASO [Antifascist Military Organization], but none of the NCOs dared talk about what was really bothering the brigade. Most of them asked him to deal with the NCOs' problems, whether personal or collective, and time was going by. Then, suddenly, the idea occurred to me that someone should tell him about the soldiers' mood, about the war, and how if he didn't do something about it he'd have a lot of trouble on his hands.

I stepped forward a few paces and, with a salute, I gave my report in the regular manner: "Sergeant . . . beg to report on behalf of the brigade NCOs that we wish to be led to the front."

[Brigadier] Katsotas jumped. "On behalf of the NCO's? What are you? How do you come to represent them?"

"I'm a sergeant, Brigadier, sir."

"Which is your unit?"

"First antitank squadron."

"What's your special assignment?"

"Detail leader."

"So they're the only ones you represent. What do your men say?"

"What I told you, sir."

He wanted to protect me. He knew that there was a [left-wing] organization in the brigade and imagined that I was "authorized" to demand what was being written about for us to read in the "subversive propaganda" [literally, "rodents"] put out by the ASO.

He turned to his officers and said, "Do you see that . . . ? I congratulate him. . . ." And he turned back to look at me; but I was petrified and while he was speaking to me I saluted and had huddled in among the back rows.

Many of the staff officers were smiling, while others wore an inscrutable expression. (*Tsingos*, pp. 41–42)

It seems to have been quite in character for Andreas, having diagnosed the brigadier's predicament, to plunge into the fray in this manner. His terror was also not unreasonable: the right-wing officers were marshaling their considerable power in reaction to what they saw as communist subversion. His frank acknowledgment of that fear, years later, follows the moral and narrative aesthetic of rural Cretan manhood: a Cretan sheep-thief is expected to own up if directly accused but may later enhance his claims to manhood by admitting that the mere prospect of confessing to a furious rival filled him with fear at the time.

Fear again: for facing down one's own fear confers moral as well as practical advantage. Andreas's scorn for the cowardice of the right indeed knew no bounds. With Rommel bottled up in El Alamein, the British were able to reassert control in Egypt and Andreas sneers (p. 44) at the rightist Greek officers who had fled in the conviction that the Allies were on the run and who now "returned from Sudan and South Africa—it's a mystery why in their haste and fear they didn't reach the South Pole without realizing it."

Whether or not as a result of his daring intervention, a detachment of antitank troops had meanwhile been dispatched to Cairo for battle training. Andreas was among those selected. There he and his mates drilled all summer. Meanwhile, the rest of the brigade trained in the dusty Palmyra desert. The British were keen to deploy the Greeks against the Italians, who had already failed in their initial attempt to spearhead the Axis invasion of Greece two years earlier, and the great day arrived.

In the decisive battle that October, Rommel's troops were put to flight. On the Allied side, the Greeks, Andreas and Tsingos among them, acquitted themselves with distinction and took part in the rout of the German troops across the desert to Tobruk. But again the rightist officers tried to hold back, in the leftists' eyes at least. They failed in their first attempt: their democratic colleagues and the enlisted men wanted none of this apostasy.

Andreas's literary treatment of the right wing's foot-dragging tactics gives some insight into the genealogy of events that he and his comrades wished to construct. Throughout the early pages of *Tsingos* it is the foot soldiers and the democratic elements in the officers' corps who represent the military virtues; the fascists and royalists are guilty of "indiscipline" (p. 54). The battle against the Nazis for the preservation of Greek freedom gradually reveals itself as a replay of the Greek War of Independence. For where British historiography especially charts the incompetence and factionalism of the Greek guerrillas and attributes the ultimate achievement of independence to a combination of historical accident and eventual western leadership, in Greece a strongly Marxist tradition sees the foreign "protectors" as cynical opportunists who installed quislings—including a Bavarian monarchy—over the heads of the true heroes of the revolution at the earliest opportunity.[1] This is the history of Greece before Crete became part of it. Andreas consistently transforms regional values and identities into national ones: in turning the Cretan yokel Xopateras into a thoughtful Greek, he also strips away his gullibility toward the official rendition of history—and so challenges the claims of chauvinists to represent true patriotism.

In the aftermath of El Alamein Andreas saw the story of brave klefts and conniving foreigners all over again. In this historiography, the Greeks fought for their freedom only to find themselves under a new tyranny, orchestrated by foreign powers and staffed by corrupt Greeks. The main impetus invariably comes from outside.

We shall meet this theme again. It permeates much of modern Greek historiography and informs the exegetical frame whereby many Greeks—

---

1. This is locally replicated in the historiography of Crete. See, for example, Papamanousakis (1979), as well as Andreas's own attack on the British role in German-occupied Crete in his O *Efedhropateras.*

in academic and everyday discourse alike—address the frustrating limitations on the national sense of independence. This is not the place to debate its accuracy or the relative merits of scapegoating conspiracy theories
(the so-called "foreign finger") versus accusations of Greek hysteria and
irresponsibility—although, from the first democratic elections fought by
parties respectively owing their allegiance to the British, the French, and
the Russians to the well-documented U.S. tolerance of the colonels' coup
of 1967, it is clear that at the very least there is a repetitive pattern of
foreign connivance with internal political and military forces. What interests me here is the way in which Andreas manages the imagery of the past:
a "social drama," in V. W. Turner's (1974) sense, renders a succession of
events as tales of local heroes and their humiliation—in *Efedhropateras:
The English Strangled the Resistance on Crete* (p. 33) Andreas records
the British contempt for Greeks as "natives"—by ungrateful, contemptuously powerful foreigners and their local stool-pigeons. In social dramas,
the truths of a political theodicy are confirmed: the actors repeat history,
immediately attempting in this way to wrest the agency of interpretation
away from impersonal events and from hostile players. By occasionally
spelling out his sense of historical parallelism, Andreas confirms the sa-
lience of this kind of self-modeling for the way in which historical events
are turned into personal and collective experience.

   Indeed, Andreas arguably expressed the least equivocal version of
this depressing vision when he recreated the reaction of an Asia Minor
refugee to the allegedly CIA-backed military coup in Athens in 1967. It is
a mark of his ironic skill that he manages to capture both the unattractive
whining quality that such complaints often possess and the disturbing
accumulation of layer upon layer of factual plausibility that often further
reinforces one's distaste for its inexorable logic:

▌ But it's not our fault. When did they ever let the Greek people be master
of its own house? Ever since the 1821 revolution we have had Foreigners
on our backs [*svérko:* literally, "hair on the back of the neck"], ordering
us around even as they feed us at their breasts. Foreigners set up the land-
owners (*kotzambásidhes*) and killed Capodistrias.[2] They were the ones who
brought Otho [I, first King of the Hellenes] and the Bavarians [that is, advisers from Otho's father's court in Munich], accepted by the people as the
price of being delivered from hunger, anarchy, and the Anglo-French occu-

2. Ioannis Capodistrias, first president of Greece immediately after Independence, was assassinated by two brothers, members of a powerful Maniat clan. Given the general irritation
with Capodistrias within and outside Greece, it is easy to see how one perception might
have it that the assassination served certain foreign interests—always a popular exegesis,
and one that often has some basis in fact. It was in the aftermath of the assassination that
Greece became a monarchy.

pation.[3] The king's Bavarian regents created the administration that rules us yet. It put Kolokotronis in jail[4] and taught the people lying, deceit, trickery, violence, injustice—and stole its bread. Greece had become a province of the Bavarians. "Europeans, the failings of the Greeks people belong to you; you taught it to them [that is, the failings]. Like a little child brought up by a worthless parent. From you it awaited illumination, and you twisted its character." Over the Eastern Question the Anglo-French brought back their army, even to Piraeus, because Otho . . . liked the Russians. Then, when they kicked Otho out, they brought us the Dane, Glücksburg,[5] who was a tool of British policy. In 1897 they gave us a loan and we're still paying off the interest. It's been paid off a hundred times over already, and still we can't get free of our debt. (*Black April*, pp. 81–82)

And so the sad tale continues; the basic theme remains always the same.

So, too, it was with World War II (*Black April*, p. 82): "What Europeans fought against the Nazis and fascism as did the Greeks?" The charge of British ingratitude for the contribution of the Greeks at El Alamein (and for the Cretans' role in keeping the Germans busy at home) belongs to a long genealogy of discontent going back at least to the notion that the Greeks "gave the light to Europe" and received nothing but betrayal and contempt in return. If this seems no less disingenuous than what it attacks, it at least leaves the speaker with some dignity, in a culture where the play of fate and character provides that framework for an enormous range of situations from the allocation of blame for bureaucratic mishaps to the explanation of national crises: "our" successes and "your" failures are the products of character; "your" successes and "our" failures, of the action of destiny and of forces conceptualized in fate-like terms.[6]

Among the resulting convention is the view that at the end of World War II the Great Powers acted like fate (*míra*)—or, what amounts to the agent of the same force, a parent casting lots for the division (*mirasiá*) of property among the children—in that Stalin, Roosevelt, and Churchill

3. In May of 1854, British and French troops occupied Piraeus to forestall an attack on the Ottoman Empire that they construed as harmful to their national interests, exposing the country's restricted freedom of action in international affairs (as well as the adventurism of the Greek king, Otho, who thought that his troops could take on the Ottomans successfully).

4. Theodore Kolokotronis, a hero of the War of Independence, found himself increasingly alienated from the mainstream political leadership and was tried for conspiracy against the state.

5. The second king of Greece, George I, son of a prince who subsequently became king of Denmark, founded the dynasty to which all subsequent Greek monarchs belonged.

6. See my *The Social Production of Indifference* (1992: chap. 5) for an extended discussion of images of fate in the etiology of personal and political humiliation in Greece.

"divided up" the world at Yalta. Andreas has his passionate orator in *Black April* faithfully reproduce this idiom (p. 82).

In his handling of this rhetoric, Andreas is unusual only in his willingness—others have the capacity, as they often show in more intimate settings—to acknowledge the errors and moral failures of his own side as well. Later, when (like many other left-wing Greek intellectuals) he broke with the Communist Party over Soviet policies and practices, he was being entirely consistent. Communist ideology was not the only acceptable face of patriotism for him. Many of those who fought with EAM-ELAS in the early days only became known as communists because, says Andreas (*Efedhropateras*, p. 31), the British persistently so labeled anyone who would not play their game. This habit was enthusiastically adopted by the Greek rightists, who saw to it that even participation in the battle of El Alamein would count for naught against a charge of communist sedition.

It was the rightists, too, who so determinedly called many of their critics "Slavs." The names of suspected Greek communists—by now the largest single group among the officers—suddenly started sprouting Slavic-sounding "-*ov*" endings in official records. It sounded as though the country was full of Slavs even far away from the Bulgarian and Yugoslav borders.

> How it came about that in Crete, the Peloponnese, and the islands so many Bulgarians had been born and raised was a mystery. Many said that the Bulgarians would be quite right after the war to raise the issue of minorities even in Crete, since the Greeks themselves maintained that position with their documents and their rumor-mongerings. (*Tsingos*, p. 101)

This is especially interesting in that Andreas follows the official line in insisting that there are no real minorities in northern Greece. From his point of view, the entire minorities issue was largely created by the rightists' heavy-handed policies.

A distinguished officer whose name was slavicized in this way was officially called a Bulgarian on the grounds that his ancestors had come from Eastern Thrace (*Tsingos*, p. 119)—a part of present-day Bulgaria once heavily populated by Greeks and thus one of the territories coveted by Greek irredentists. Such bureaucratic categorization betrays not a hint of its central paradox: that the territory is essentially Greek even though a left-leaning Greek from the area must, for political reasons, be Bulgarian. Although Andreas does not share the current anthropological view of ethnicity, he captures a crucial aspect of what continues to be a festering problem in Greek internal and international politics.

In March of 1943 the Greek government-in-exile in Cairo reacted to the increasingly vociferous demands of rightist elements by replacing all the battalion commanders. The men rose up in revolt. For a brief while, the British refused to intervene: as Andreas notes, they could hardly attack a brigade that had so distinguished itself in battle. When certain officers of rightist sympathies demanded to be given ministerial posts in the government-in-exile, however, the British joined forces with these new leaders and began to impose their own authority on the Greek troops. Discontent swiftly became more sharply defined among the rank and file.

Tsingos, as an officer, was also forced to define his sympathies more clearly. Here Andreas gives us another vivid portrait, not unlike the one he draws of Xopateras in *Bir Hakeim,* of the agonies of self-doubt that lead to the reformulation of political sensibility. This time Tsingos is the subject, although again Andreas's ability to imagine himself into another's consciousness might plausibly be taken to indicate an autobiographical element in this account also. Tsingos, an erstwhile Nietzsche enthusiast, finds the political realities of army life deeply disturbing. Once again, the proximate cause of disaffection—at least in part—is the discovery of cowardice where it is not supposed to exist, this time in the officer corps of which Tsingos has been made a member. His ideas soon fell into disarray. As Andreas wryly remarks: "Whatever remnants were left were dispelled by the army, the desert, the trenches; and the supermen with their gold-braided caps adorned with laurel-leaves appeared as they actually were—for the most part naked, weak, clueless" (*Tsingos* p. 55). Yet many were people drawn from Tsingos's own social class. Tsingos experiences an irritation with bureaucratic literal-mindedness that we meet often in Andreas himself: "When officers refuse to give chase to the enemy because of some kilometer limit, then, if they're not mad, they're enemies themselves" (*Tsingos,* p. 56). In describing Tsingos's respect for the ordinary soldier, on the other hand—"he had greater rights than any gold-braided officer" (p. 55)—Andreas also signals his own. Soldiers could and did think, no matter what their officers chose to believe or tried to impose.

While Andreas—again through the paradigmatic figure of Tsingos— believed in the importance of discipline, bodily as well as social, he did not see it as incompatible with independent thought. On the contrary, as was to become explicit in his postwar writings, it was in the tension between the discipline of self and technique on the one hand and the intensely private and sometimes subversive ferment of ideas on the other that art, for him, successfully escaped the conventions—at once enabling and constraining—of craft. What makes this insight especially poignant in Andreas's writings is that he is able to discover and express it in the aesthetic exaggeration of a tension between formalism and spontaneity that also forms an important aspect of the dualistic Greek self-stereotype, where it is grounded in the constant struggle between extremes in the politics of culture—in language, in music, in architecture, in the historic conflict between klefts and Bavarians or, later, between communists and royalists and in the preoccupation with both idealizing self-presentation and equally idealizing demonstrations of spontaneity and intimacy.

The communists, although strongly opposed to the neo-Classical formalism of the right, had their own powerful sense of discipline: this is one area where their fondly assumed kinship with the unruly klefts, the guerrilla heroes of the Greek War of Independence, who in many regards were closer to the mutually marauding Cretan shepherds than either were to the Western European notion of a military force, begins to unravel. With this discipline, socially translated into a high level of grassroots organization, they were eventually able to incorporate many other political elements outside the royalist camp.

Many who fought against the Nazis in Greece or who began to organize the antifascist campaign within the military were not initially communists.[7] Those who rejected the moral and political authority of the royalists and falangists, however, soon found themselves so defined. As a result, they soon found even their Greekness challenged: in a process that was reiterated and reinforced in the slavicization of their names by rightist officials, communism was defined as a "foreign dogma," antithetical to the "European individualism" of true Greeks. The communists offered discipline and resistance to those who were already being pushed into their arms in this way, and their numbers swelled.

Andreas himself was already a committed Marxist at the outbreak of war. His youthful reading gave definition to what he was now seeing in the army, whereas Tsingos—scion of a merchant family already three generations deep, although, like Andreas, witness to a father's humiliation in the 1929 financial crash—still had to work his way into the skepticism about the social and political order that army experience now seemed to demand.

The soldiers dreamed of returning to Greece, where the guerrilla resistance forces, both communist and royalist, had kept up enormous pressure on the German occupiers. The British, however, were afraid to strengthen the increasingly well-organized, communist-led ELAS liberation army there and kept the Greek troops in the Middle East occupied with mindless exercises and low-level guard duties. In the spring of 1944, a naval revolt triggered a parallel revolt among the ground and air troops. Andreas and Tsingos were among the active leaders. Theirs was the most disciplined force of all:

▎ The only Greek unit which had not in the slightest degree declared its position was the First Greek Brigade. Every day now we performed landing

7. Among many useful works on the Resistance and communist organization in Greece, see Hart (1996) and *Studies* (1987).

exercises in the desert using real or model ships. The Brigade had a full [antifascist] organization now, trained and armed. It was the model unit in exercises. Seven thousand men from all over Greece divided into three infantry battalions. One artillery regiment and an equivalent antitank unit for each battalion. A separate antitank squadron, an anti-aircraft unit, engineers, with an experienced staff of officers and liaison. (*Tsingos*, p. 88)

The British apparently had no idea what was brewing.

The Greek government-in-exile had declared its intention of reaching an accord with the left-wing Resistance authorities in Greece, the so-called Government of the Mountains. This was not acceptable either to the king or to the British, however, and the Greek prime minister soon reversed himself. This provoked the progressives in the military to demand a commitment to reconciliation and to declare their intention of refusing, upon returning to Greece, to turn their weapons on their compatriots—their "brothers" in the fight against the Nazis. Soon the whole military was in turmoil. Tsingos, as Andreas notes (*Tsingos*, p. 90), was in a particularly odd position, as a "revolutionary" military police officer trying to secure the complaisance, at least, of the large number of "reactionaries" among the enlisted men. The rebels prevailed and the troops, demonstrating more than ever their exemplary military discipline, began drilling with the ELAS insignia on their caps in place of the Greek army badge:

▌That was when the strangest thing happened. The British from all around rubbed their eyes. How did it suddenly come about that all the brigade members were communists? Where had they been hiding? Their liaison officers all fell into disfavor and were castigated. So many years living with those anarchists and not to have smelled a whiff of anything? But they were all wrong.

The soldiers were all Greeks. Nothing else. Besides, what they were told in their battalions was neither communist nor anarchist: "We want to go back to Greece and not end up killing or being killed by other Greeks." That's what they were hearing. (*Tsingos*, p. 102)

In other words, it was often the reactionaries themselves who created the new communists.

Eventually the British, who had succeeded in squelching the revolt elsewhere first, trained their own heavy guns on the First Greek Battalion; their own troops—who might have balked at killing their erstwhile comrades-in-arms from El Alamein, and whose own political sympathies were not entirely certain—were told that the rebels were really rioting Italian prisoners of war. Faced with total annihilation or with, at the very least, starvation, the Greeks surrendered.

In that electric moment, one again sees both the creation of communists in the present and the emotional claim on a kleftic past that this generated. Andreas's spare, disciplined prose captures an insight into the affective symbiosis of patriotism with an internationalist ideology in an immediate way that my own more self-consciously explanatory mode cannot begin to reproduce:

▌ In the end, and after several days of standing upright, the soldiers were required to choose between two gates.

They had opened up two barbed wire fences and they marched the entire brigade up to the entrances to these. The right-hand gate was the gate of salvation and of purification. Whoever passed through the right-hand gate was received with cans of food and water and led to salvation. Whoever passed through the left-hand gate was cursed and struck and continued to be hungry and thirsty. Such was the mockery that soldiers known to be right-wingers as well as people who throughout the siege had been indifferent and uninvolved went in through the left-hand gate, preferring hunger and thirst to the paradise of canned food.

The left-hand exit filled up. However they shoved them they could not contain them all. The English and the officers from [an earlier right-wing revolt at the Egyptian encampment at] Merdj Ayum, who now suddenly found themselves at liberty, were furious [because the confusion threatened their own newly acquired liberty].

And suddenly from thousands of hungry soldiers arose a din and a roaring of song that spread around the whole desert of Bourg-el-Arab: "Olympus thunders, Giona flashes with lightning. . . ."

They threatened to mow them down with machine-gun fire, they cursed them, they threw whatever filth they could find at them. But the song continued until late into the night. (*Tsingos,* p. 111)

It is impossible to understand nationalism unless one first accepts the moral and emotional force that such a moment brings to bear—in actuality and again in the reading of an account such as this—on the most disaffected listener or participant, a professionally skeptical academic like myself who is removed in time and place or one of those present who "throughout the siege had been indifferent and uninvolved." For, as Andreas rightly notes, these men were not all (or perhaps even in a modest plurality) convinced communists, still less anarchists; but such a catalytic moment could fuse the desire to resist the international economic and military juggernaut with the well-established sentiments of nationalist grievance that, as Andreas assumes (and what Greek would disagree?), all these men must have shared.

There is ample evidence that the antiroyalist forces in the Resistance had not initially been strongly communist in orientation. Andreas confirms this:

● Nowadays of course they blame everything on the Communist Party. In those days there was a certain perception about all that situation, but unfortunately it's been forgotten. So what was it? The people then had fought against the Germans. And most of them were patriots. They went into EAM.[8] Of course, EAM's spine consisted of communists. But the rest weren't communists. They were just patriots, who used to listen to a party member, that sort of thing, telling them certain things—but they were in agreement. Because what he was telling them wasn't . . . it was patriotic, it was that kind of thing. Even EAM's seizure of power was justified. Because, up to this point, until that period, those who had power were the politicians—and we know what they were, so to speak—what we meant when we were talking earlier about favor-peddling, things like that. Greece was . . . well, going from catastrophe to catastrophe.

In this view, communists, and revolutionaries in general, emerge in response to the stupidities of oppressors. Andreas even discovered that when those who had already surrendered to the regime in power were still tortured beyond endurance, they could suddenly rediscover their pride. By the time he wrote *Tsingos*, Andreas had already lived through the prison-camp hell of Youra. There, when the prison-camp authorities continued to brutalize even those prisoners who had cravenly agreed to sign declarations of loyalty to the royalist state, these erstwhile cowards suddenly found the courage to revoke their declarations (*Prohibited*, p. 315). At such moments, there is suddenly only a single, common foe.

Thus, too, at the end of the siege of the Greek troops, the realization that theirs was a common enemy—a mighty foreign power intent on its own interests—invested resistance with an aura, at once patriotic and revolutionary, that united all the Greeks in a shared disgust—a significance that perhaps only a song in the kleftic style could adequately express. Its formulaic opening lines are in an idiom most commonly associated with the klefts who fought for Greek independence. Purified of any association with selfish interests, ethnic or social diversity, or brigandage pure and simple, these songs had already entered the official canon, from which they returned to their local sources and entered the repertoires of the rest of the country. They became perhaps the most important vehicle of state-driven cultural unification. When, as here, the country divides into opposed camps, the texts are the common vehicle for the claims that both camps make to represent that unity. The opposing interpretations point up the divergences between the two sides—a process that reproduces what had continually happened to the songs before folklorists tried to distill them into fixed texts.

8. See chapter 3, note 1.

This song fits a pattern whereby the leftists adopted—and often adapted—kleftic themes to express their own revolutionary ardor (for the text in translation, see Hart 1996: 215; see also Van Boeschoeten 1991). It is the reservoir of formulaic expressions that allows these songs to cross historical boundaries, both through their textual durability and in the sense of making the historically disparate events they celebrate with virtually identical words serve as recurrent demonstrations of larger and more generic truths. And even in the most terrible silence, as surviving communists like Andreas were to find later in the Civil War prison camps, a *sotto voce* song could provide relief from the beatings and the relentless forced labor—the fact of singing itself, any kind of singing, had a value that no brutality could entirely suppress (*Prohibited*, p. 37). And more explicit, collective singing about past and present heroes sustained their successors' defiance in the face of death.

The kleftic genealogy appears often in Andreas's work. In his art criticism, it carries the heroism of the klefts into an attack on the effete academicism of the foreign-inspired representational styles that sought, almost literally, to capture the klefts in paint. In the biography of Tsingos, that contest is acted out—to use the metaphor of the social drama again—in the conflict between democrats and fascists. Others might and do draw such distinctions in very different ways. But the principle is one shared by all of the political factions that engage in the contest to define national history.

In jail many months later, he and his comrades learned of the death of the ELAS leader Aris Velouchiotis. Juxtaposed with the evocation of the klefts, we also hear the Christological metaphor of resurrection. Indeed, as the anthropologist Renée Hirschon (1989: 139) reminds us, we should not be surprised to find such ideas among professed Marxists whose culture is nonetheless suffused with the symbolism and thought of Orthodox Christianity: she has demonstrated that the social organization of domestic and public space intimately follows the conceptual patterning of religious practice. Nor is the *political* opposition between Christianity and communism necessarily reproduced in the symbolic and ideological spheres: there is a global tradition of conceptual accommodation between them, from Liberation Theology to the more pragmatic adjustments of communist parties around the world to local religious forms, notably the Italian communists' massive absorption of Catholic symbolism (Kertzer 1996). Roger Lancaster (1992: 173) has described how the Nicaraguan Sandinistas' original attempts to coopt the local symbolism of Christianity rapidly yielded to a fusion of the Marxist with the Christian tradition in the construction of a new, hybrid identity (Lancaster 1988: 57). Begoña Aretxaga (1997), again, has shown how richly revolutionary imagery in Northern Ireland draws on the Christological tradition. In Greece, that tradition has similarly inspired an entire generation of post–Civil War writers of leftist persuasion (see Calotychos 1993: 285–96). One imagines that the earlier absorption of pagan symbolism by the then new religion of Christianity nearly two millennia ago entailed very similar processes of symbolic and cultural synthesis (see C. Stewart 1991).

Andreas expresses a more determinedly atheist and Marxist version of this accommodation. His perspective recalls the popular anticlericalism of both Greece and Spain, especially in the contrast he draws between church venality—embodied in the unctuous Father Prokopios, the companion and servant of right-wing thugs in his novels of prison-camp life—with the historically attested decency of a purely human Christ:

● In reality I'm an atheist. [. . . .] About Christ, I'll tell you this much: I consider that no better human being ever appeared on earth. Or at least, he was one of the best. But I have seen Christs, very many of them, in my life. Communist Party members. Of course. And right-wingers too. The people who were being shot by the Germans, for instance. The people who were dying before the firing squads. For the sole reason that they wouldn't sign a declaration of repentance (*mia dhílosi metánias*). Those people are of the worth of Christ. Well, what did Christ do that was greater? Of course, what he said was a major matter for that era. The theme—"love one another," because at that time . . . not a person had appeared to say such a thing.

Andreas's words could almost have been taken out of a Cretan highland villager's diatribe against the parasitic church, with one important qualification—that the villagers, for whom religious identity is social as much as it is spiritual, do not usually declare themselves to be "atheists," a term they conventionally reserve for Muslims ("Turks"): "I believe . . . in God . . . in Christ. That is, I believe as a Christian, let's say, and all that, basically I do believe. But I don't want to go to church or to set eyes on priests!" (a Cretan villager, quoted in Herzfeld 1985: 241). For the self-aware Marxist intellectual, such a fusion would be a betrayal of principle. Despite this clear difference, there is a strong element of continuity between the rural anticlericalists and the urban intellectual atheist. That continuity lies in the use of Christ as a symbol of suffering decency— as the understanding culture hero who legitimates the practice of animal-theft for the shepherds (Herzfeld 1985: 40–42), as the political martyr for the urban communist, and—the common framework—as the victim of a harsh bureaucracy for both. Anthropologists are all too easily led to assume a radical discontinuity between these segments of the national culture, but Andreas's admittedly idiosyncratic situation challenges such facile classifications.

Andreas thus draws on a rich vein of religious symbolism even as he rejects the explicit doctrines that it articulates. In this he exemplifies one extreme of what is a widespread stance toward the official religion in Greece (although his willingness to acknowledge the role of some rightist patriots is a more generous stance than one usually finds on either side of the ideological barrier). Andreas's view of Christ was not unusual among Greek intellectuals. The legendary struggles between the church and another and even more flamboyant atheist, the novelist Nikos Kazantzakis, are well-known outside Greece, and his *Christ Recrucified* (1954) expresses a perspective that is directly comparable to that of Andreas. Nor were these two self-consciously Cretan writers, steeped in local traditions of strong anticlericalism, alone among the wider community of Marxist intellectuals in Greece in their evocation of Christological imagery.

Moreover, Greek Marxists make no less energetic a claim on national sentiment than do the political conservatives. Like the latter, too, they often frame that claim, as we have seen, as the religiously grounded metaphor of resurrection. Here, too, Andreas is representative of his generation:

▮ Over the prison there fell an indescribable sadness. For us, ELAS and its leaders had resurrected (*anastísi*) '21 [that is, 1821, the year in which the Greek War of Independence broke out]. Every morning during drill, during parades, and in all our collective displays we began with a song. Pride of place belonged to "Olympus thunders." For all that we had fought the Nazis at sea, in the air, and in the desert, we felt that we were absent from our homeland and our admiration for the Resistance fighters was a form of worship. (*Tsingos*, p. 162)

The claim of moral equivalence to the religious nationalism of the Right is palpable.

Sometimes the link with revolutionary history was more immediate than metaphorical. Toward the end of *Tsingos,* Andreas describes the interaction between Tsingos and another prisoner, Pericles Soutsos by name, whose family originated in the Fanari district of Istanbul where the wealthy Greek burghers had actively opposed the 1821 revolution. Soutsos is teasing Tsingos about his long, thin legs:

▮ "Hey, Hadjimeleti [a kleftic name], you look like a doe!" he used to say; and Tsingos would reply with a single word: "Fanariot!"

And he called him Hadjimeleti after his great-grandfather who, as Tsingos had related to us, had given all his property to the 1821 revolution and remained destitute thereafter. And he, too, had told that story in order to tease Soutsos, who was descended from *the* Soutsos family and would sometimes tell us stories about his ancestors. (*Tsingos*, p. 167)

When political genealogies are literally embodied in people who know one another—and in Greece, a comparatively small country, they often do—the line between jest and conflict may be quite thin.

5 ▣

SENTENCE OF DEATH,
REBUILDING OF LIFE

After the collapse of the 1944 revolt, the prisoners were taken to the Mustafa Barracks jail in Alexandria, where an extremely polite British officer interrogated Andreas. Asked who had wanted him to volunteer for commando work in Crete a year earlier, Andreas replied, "The same person who brought me here: myself!" This was not what the officer wanted, however, since it told him nothing about communist infiltration, so "he did not offer me another cigarette" (*Tsingos*, p. 114) but, just as he was leaving and to make sure Andreas got the point of the interrogation, he formally introduced himself. He was Francis Noel-Baker, a British Intelligence officer whose family owned a huge estate on the Greek mainland and who later became a Labour Party member of the House of Commons.

From Alexandria, the prisoners were taken to the even less salubrious jail—the lunatic asylum of the Abassids, former rulers of Egypt, located in the Qasassin desert, not far from Cairo. Even while the siege of their camp was taking place, horrible rumors about torture and killing by the rebels in the Anglo-Egyptian press prepared the ground. At the Lebanon Conference, in which the Allies and the Greek government-in-exile began shaping the fortunes of postwar Greece, it was decided to put the rebels on trial; even the Government of the Mountains—the left-wing Resistance authority that had succeeded in controlling part of the Greek mainland—joined in the general cry of condemnation. In this atmosphere, the trials led to sentences of death for the thirteen alleged ringleaders—Andreas Nenedakis and Thanasis Tsingos among them.

Andreas has not spoken to me in detail about the time he was under sentence of death, and I did not feel comfortable trying to probe. He did once musingly recall the night after the sentence was passed:

● I remember the evening sentence was passed and they took us back to the cage, to a cage that was all barbed wire, and my friends there kept us company. So they talked to us, but I was *out* of the conversation, because they were going to shoot us in the morning. I heard, I could feel something, as it were, like . . . it was beyond the things of this earth. Well, they'd . . . in the morning. . . . That wasn't fear. But it was something I have never felt on any other occasion. And since the decision had been taken to shoot us, we were taken off to be shot in the morning.

This is Andreas at his most austere. He invites his interlocutor to imagine the sensation, which curiously resembles his description of the sense of soaring above earthly reality that he feels when he writes. Death is not a terrifying enemy: he accepts the idea of his own annihilation as a natural event, to be postponed as long as health permits but not as distressing as being maimed while still alive. Yet clearly he felt *some* kind of strong reaction to his predicament. The phrasing is formulaic, almost hermetic, and perhaps for that reason consistent with the dreamlike quality of an ultimately indescribable experience. So brief a description does not invite further elaboration except in the stillness of one's own thoughts.

In the ideological literature of many nation-states there is a long tradition of the brave last words of national martyrs. Greece is no exception: the plaint of the kleft Athanasios Diakos as he was led to his death by his Turkish captors—"see at what time death has chosen to take me, when the trees put forth green branches and the grass shoots forth"—is part of the national canon, famously recalled by Greece's "national poet" Dionisios Solomos in his *The Free Besieged* (Petronikolos 1975).

Such stories are not necessarily unfounded. Moreover, as we have already seen, they sustain a poetics of social drama that informs more recent and well-documented events; Janet Hart (1996: 253) has recorded memories of the Averoff women's prison in Athens during some of the most brutal days of the Civil War, when, each time a prisoner was condemned to die the following day, she would join her fellow inmates in a traditional dance—another device reminiscent of the War of Independence—and would remain resolutely defiant up to the moment when the jailers came to lead her to the firing squad. Defiance assured unity in the face of persecution. When Andreas's father was told of his son's death sentence, he retorted, "I too am . . . a communist!" As Andreas notes, his father did not really know what the word meant, but the divisive politics of the Greek leadership led the old man to despise the alternative and to rear up in a heroic pose of solidarity.

But Andreas chose neither dramatic gestures nor philosophical reflection on his predicament. Instead, he offers us insight through a description of Tsingos's response. The condemned have been marched back to their cells:

■   That first evening, Tsingos used to say afterwards, he felt strange. He would speak at length about the first night he spent [knowing he was] about to die and it is not possible to remember all of it. Nonetheless, since I found many of my own thoughts and many of the emotions I had experienced in his words I heard him out and did not speak. "When you're 25 or 30 years old and you've been sitting in the dock for days now, awaiting a decision having known right from the very first day what it would be. When you feel the presence of all your senses and life bubbling up from the very depths of your being. When you hear and feel people struggling to justify the act that deprives you of your life—being hypocritically sad, or fierce, according to their own reactions and to the instructions they've received from the services they work for, the laws, and to their rank. When you see around you even the people with whom you are sitting in the same dock looking at you as if you've been completely written off and as if they don't want to see a single hair left on your body. When you see that the people who are trussing your wrists with the handcuffs tighten them even more, showing their fear or their madness—or both at the same time. When you hear that they will grant you some final favor but they don't know, they say, whether you deserve it at all. When you look around you and you don't see anyone, or those who are dragging you off push you roughly into the back of a truck. When you want to breathe and they hide the very air from you with the excuse that those are their orders. When they start undressing you and take away your clothes and shoes and some of them look at these one by one to fit them on their own feet and bodies. When finally you're left totally on your own with a single pair of underpants in a cell in whose ceiling a blinding electric light burns night and day. When the walls have no ears, when they're thick, built of cement, ice-cold, right in the burning heat of Cairo in August. When you start to count back over the years of your life and the most improbable memories come to your mind: for example, a pair of felt slippers (*tsaroúkhia*[1]) your father brought you from Tripoli; or your grandfather Hadjimeletis who in '21 gave up all his property for the struggle. When you recall the manner of that royal commissioner who struggled to lay out whatever legalistic twaddle he could come up with in order to kill you—and we are, word of honor, old friends. . . . When you remember the presiding judge at the court-martial, a colonel who as a democrat would have been considered a 'putschist' had he not undertaken to try those of his own persuasion. . . . When the questions start, the answers, the half-words that come to your mouth along with the twitches

---

1. *Tsaroúkhia* are felt slippers with a curled toepiece; they are still part of the evzones' dress uniform.

that you unsuccessfully try to suppress. When you see light and discover it for the first time and the air is a body whose every particle has a distinct odor. When you open your mouth and timidly lick your lips with your tongue and suddenly start because they have a somewhat salty taste. When you open and close your eyelids in whatever way you can in order to moisten your eyeball and you think it's the first time in your life you've done such a thing. When you start to drown in thoughts that are empty, without meaning, without coherence. When everything starts to pass through your mind like a vision, even though you've closed your eyes. (You can't know that, they might also be open.) When everything around you acquires a special value and you figure out that all of that already existed but you paid it no attention. When you start to calculate, to count the days you've lived and the hours you have left. (And what proportion or percentage of eternity is that?) When, quite by chance, you discover that you aren't alone in your cell: there near your forefinger a gnat is fluttering, or it may be some other insect, and you can kill it if you want—kill it, and without a trial at that . . . or a court-martial, or a royal commissioner. But why do you stay your hand? Is it the first time that you discover that a bug has a life too? But if you don't kill it, it will drink your blood. And if these insects multiply they'll swallow you in your entirety. So you, too, are an insect, you whom they'll kill in order to protect themselves, their interests, their very existence."

"And now they don't want you even to think. They arrange your foot-steps, your sleep, your food. How many bedclothes are needed to cover your carcass, how long you are to breathe fresh air, just enough to be pre-served, so that they can dehydrate your soul and dissolve every bit of resis-tance that may be in you, any vitality you may possess. And they still can't understand who you are. And they imagine that they'll have killed your heart before they stand you up in front of the wall. And they can't appreci-ate that in spite of everything you are not alone." (*Tsingos*, pp. 124–27)

Such were the thoughts, then, of the condemned. They are a mixture of bitterness, defiance, a rush of disconnected thoughts and sensations, awareness of physical existence, contempt for the tormentors and their petty self-exoneration, bemusement at being betrayed by former friends, puzzled introspection. They return repeatedly to the physical reality of being a live, remembering person, known to none outside that embodied self. They express an austere disdain for those whose self-interest, wrapped up in bureaucratic falseness, cannot enjoy the final, rich, salty taste of life.

I could only quote this passage in full. Any attempt to truncate it, or to break the intense monotony of its reiteration of "when . . . when . . . when . . ." (which Andreas also uses for the dread days of numbing horror on the prison island of Youra in 1947 [*Prohibited*, p. 34], and which only gains in force from its appearance elsewhere in the Greek literary canon), would have taken too much away. It is not a startlingly original piece of writing—cliches and conventions abound—but it is perhaps relevant that the emotional charge of a song formula depends on familiarity as much as any conversational cliche. The impact of the passage, too, partly lies in the very ordinariness in which the author, whether Tsingos or Andreas himself, now finds a distillation of what matters about being alive. It is the most intensely everyday concerns, those that are socially and culturally taken for granted, that interest the sentiently dying man; that communicate the experience to others who share the same values as fellow-Greeks; and that give new meaning and immediacy to some of our more usual anthropological concerns—the body, memory, family, friendship, and all the destructive aspects of social form that here achieve a zenith at once of banality and of terror. The ability to discern a critical and personal response—an idiom of agency—in the conventions of everyday interaction supplies precisely the dynamic that finds anthropologists most at a loss for legitimate modes of description.

This is a sharpening of focus that gives specificity to half-submerged perceptions. I can no longer think about the petty bureaucratic betrayals that happen daily in the comfortable democratic polity that is Greece today—social strains that have long been the object of a rather sensationalist kind of fascination for me—without the chill of recall that this passage, constantly fed by my deep affection for Andreas, has implanted in my waking moments. The charges of betrayal that Rethemniots level at their neighbors when the tax official or the historic conservation inspector catch them out in some minor infraction echo—formulaically again—the fears of crueller years that some remember too well and others have heard their parents relate. In the banality of today's petty bureaucratic irritations lies the persistent germ of a far greater capacity for inhumanity.

And for some, like Andreas, that inhumanity did not end with the war. For them, the grim prison camps of the Civil War, the anticommunist "emergencies" of the 1950s, and the military juntas of the period from 1967 to 1974 became an agonizing treadmill from which death seemed a merciful escape. Pain and tedium were fused in the most malignant perversions of bureaucracy:

❚ All these things were part of the plan. Bouzakis [a senior camp officer] gives permission for us to get water from the wells outside [the perimeter], the captain of the guard agrees, but the gendarmes . . . know nothing about it. And the water jugs will be smashed on the prisoners' heads. And their only fault is that they are thirsty. (*Prohibited: The Diary of Youra*, p. 282)

Guards contradict one another's intentions:

> ▌ After mess—we had lima beans again today—we want to wash our plates
> or our mess-tins as well. We have no water and they tell us to wash them
> in the sea. But most times we are forbidden to approach there. If one guard
> permits it another one forbids it, and the difference between them is paid
> for with a number of smashed [prisoners'] heads. (*Prohibited*, p. 24)

Such caprice feeds off the rampant proliferation of bureaucracy in the
prison-camp, of "directorates that punch each other out" as each vies
with the rest to make the prisoners' lives end as soon and as horribly as
possible (*Prohibited*, p. 126).

Those awaiting execution in the grim Abbasid prison, of course, had
no expectation of anything else. Yet suddenly the war seemed to be ending. Prompted by threats from the communist forces operating throughout liberated Greece, the government of Prime Minister Voulgaris com-
muted all the death sentences. The EAM-ELAS leader Aris Velouchiotis
had threatened to take reprisals against the British if any of the prisoners
were executed. As Kostis Papakongos, the Greek writer and close friend
of Andreas from the time he was later to spend in Stockholm, bitterly
observed, "[Voulgaris's] soul ached more for the fate of the English in
Greece"—but not for that of his leftist compatriots. He was given little
choice. Nonetheless, the loud objections of the more hard-lining rightist
officers to his grudging clemency should have given clear warning of what
the prisoners could expect of this future that had suddenly, unexpectedly,
reappeared on their horizon.

None of the prisoners, including those serving milder sentences, secured immediate release. They were all moved to Port-Said, and thence to
another prison, this time at Kebeit in Anglo-Egyptian Sudan. Eventually,
however, they did begin to return to Greece. Andreas arrived back in
Athens in 1946. For the moment, the mutineers' offenses were officially
"removed from the record." The respite was to be all too brief, the erasure
of the past an illusion. It was not more than a matter of months before
the mutineers—and many others—were overtaken by a far more vindictive and sustained reign of terror.

Tsingos, too, returned to Athens and thereafter to long periods of jail,
exile, and torture. Once a promising architect and now better known as
a painter, he again took to drink. Both he and Andreas suffered many
moments of appalling physical and emotional pain, but they confronted
it in very different ways. In 1965, Tsingos died, his end as austere as his
life and as the final words of Andreas's memoir, published in that same
year:

▎When he died in February, 1965, nothing of value was found in his room.
Except for the military blankets from Kebeit, which he carried with him
until his last breath. And they kept him warm, as did the memories of our
life together, of war, and of prison. (*Tsingos*, p. 170)

For he—the Tsingos who speaks through Andreas—had indeed
known well how it would be. Despite everything, in death he was not
alone.

One of the most remarkable aspects of life in prison, and even during
the siege, was the democrats' capacity to organize a disciplined social life.
These desert-hardened soldiers had been willing to face death many times;
their social bonds meanwhile, perhaps like the more hypothetical community of the nation, offered a guarantee of life transcending individuals
and their immediate concerns.

The repeated history of political persecution in Greece is studded
with evidence of this extraordinary tendency to create collective life out
of loneliness and terror. This first became apparent during the 1936–40
Metaxas dictatorship, which developed the technique of isolating political opponents on remote islands only to find that leaving them to their
own devices created rich opportunities for organized cultural life and systematic political education (Kenna 1991). During and after the Civil War,
again, the most crushing isolation and numbing neglect could not prevent
the systematic maintenance of a political culture—not least among the
women prisoners, for whom participation in the Resistance held out
hope, unevenly sustained in practice, of eventual emancipation (Hart
1996). Even on Youra, where every waking moment and bodily function
was subject to viciously destructive surveillance, and where the authorities finally thought they had stamped out what they saw as sinister infiltration by communist "organizations," some ideas, information, and encouragement continually trickled through.

The mutinous Greek soldiers had little or no contact with the communist cells that were orchestrating a large part of the Resistance movement in Greece. Some, however, were already experienced in administrative matters, while others enjoyed a considerable range of intellectual
interests; all, moreover, knew from military life the practical advantages
of collective self-discipline. Long before the siege and eventual surrender,
and especially after their indefinite consignment to prison at Kebeit following the commutation of the death penalty, they had demonstrated
their capacity for creating and sustaining a true social life.

At Kebeit, in fact, the prisoners had some measure of freedom in such
matters as deciding who their cellmates were to be. As a result, Andreas,
Tsingos, and Pericles Soutsos ended up sharing a cell. It soon became

known as the "Psychiatric Clinic" because of the impassioned discussions that took place there. The three of them were impatient to bring some shape into their collective existence. After the bloody clash between the EAM-ELAS forces and British troops in Athens in December 1944, the British authorities at Kebeit became noticeably more distant and suspicious. Nevertheless, they still did not interfere in the prisoners' daily lives:

> Gradually, however, prison life took on a certain rhythm. The sailors along with the soldiers and officers did regular physical training in the mornings, then they began their lessons. Some books that had been saved from the flood [when the encampment was under siege] were copied. The old political prisoners from the Second Brigade had a small library. We ordered more from Khartoum, and reading, copying, and lectures on all subjects were activities that filled the days. (*Tsingos,* p. 153)

Kebeit probably represented the least constricting form of imprisonment many of them were to endure—the worst aspect that Andreas now recalls was the hyenas' howling at night—and they took full advantage of it. The loss of ordinary social life was itself a challenge:

> Prison did not seem like prison to us. One person was writing and learning a foreign language. Another was teaching or taking lessons; and we each had a job that kept us as busy as we would have been outside in "society," if not indeed more so.
>
> The [self-]organization of the prison was perfect. If the productivity and dedication in various kinds of work, in the factory, and even in private businesses and jobs outside the prison had been as great as ours during that time, then many of the problems that concern the world would have been solved. But of course we were a miniature portrait of an ideal world, one could say, despite the inadequacies, little differences of opinion, and minor squabbling. We all understood that the time we spent locked up here should not go to waste. We should gain something, learn something; and those who had more knowledge at their disposal or had learned more felt a need to transmit it. Tsingos taught architectural drawing to two or three groups, while he himself took lessons in English and political economy. A teacher one moment, at the next he took the position of a pupil in order to learn and to be instructed. He was a pupil and a little while later an illiterate fisherman whom he taught how to write waited for him in one of the cells. (*Tsingos,* p. 155)

Soon they were even producing a fortnightly literary review, "which may have been one of the best Greek periodicals of that time" (*Tsingos,* p. 160). And Tsingos used his organizational and technical skills to build a theater in a Classical Greek style.

Such organization required enormous self-discipline, and its frequent reappearance in the annals of political repression in Greece belies the common prejudice—as often enunciated by Greeks as by foreign observers—that Greeks are incapable of cooperation. Claims of Greek "individualism" serve the foreign-backed political Right well, providing a facile justification for authoritarian rule over an unruly people while, perversely, also extolling the same feature as heroic genius in opposition to the "collectivism" of communists and Slavs.

It is nevertheless clear that the self-organization of the prisoners at Kebeit, which probably owed more to the habits of military discipline than to ideological indoctrination of any stripe, needed no external control. Indeed, it flourished in its isolation, without, apparently, any suppression of free argument or open disagreement. In *Tsingos*, Andreas tells us that, while the Decembrist slaughter in Athens elicited quite varied responses from the ideologically heterogeneous prisoners, even this potential flashpoint failed to disturb the generally smooth conduct of daily business without any interference from the British camp authorities. Only among the three inmates of the "Psychiatric Clinic" did the arguments occasionally rage out of control.

These arguments nevertheless led to a temporary state of hostility, and did so in a manner decidedly reminiscent of the division of property among quarreling Greek siblings. Andreas prefaces his description of this event with an air of apologetic embarrassment that echoes more generic themes of Greek social rhetoric. Much as villagers often attribute their alleged divisiveness to living "far from God" (and from civilization), Andreas—although always with at least a hint of self-mockery—seeks empathy for the prisoners' loss of sociality in prison conditions, which necessarily cut one off from one's spouse, children, and all other kin. To a remarkable degree, however, the disputants replayed the key features of quarrels among kin—features reported in several ethnographies as intended to rescue social harmony from all but the bitterest of personal fights. Thus, the moment of greatest disarray shows that the complex social organization of the prisoners was not simply the result of some global idiom of modernity in a Weberian sense, whether military or communist-"collectivist." Rather, that organization exhibited some of the very features that are usually read as evidence for a tendency to social disintegration in which each individual follows the dictates of pure self-interest (*eghoïsmós*).

What happened was highly revealing:

▌ One day Soutsos and I came to blows and, since he did not manage to pull us apart, Tsingos called in Colonel Siotis, who gave us a scolding. He was older than all the other convicts, but, had he not also been a good human being, that would not have been enough to earn our respect and affection.

As soon as the colonel had left Soutsos and I set to dividing up our cell with chalk lines, and neither of us would let the other enter his space. Tsingos got the top end of the "T." But in order to go out through the door he had to pass through my space or Soutsos's. Thus, when he wanted to go out in the morning or came back at midday and found us there, he didn't know whose permission to ask in order to enter the room.

"May I set foot in here?" he would ask as, with a laugh, he came in through the door. Or else he'd come in on both feet, waddling like a duck as he straddled both sides. All these tricks had the effect of ensuring that the rules of movement and transportation in the "Psychiatric Clinic" were not carried out to perfection. Tsingos, always with a benign smile, tried to get us to understand that the cell did not belong to any one person; and that we would leave it behind one day to go back to Greece, where we could share out (*tha mirázame*) our fields—if we had any. The chalk marks on the floor took a while to fade away. Meanwhile, however, word of this business had spread around the whole prison and we had become a theater skit. (*Tsingos*, pp. 161–62)

Readers familiar with studies of Greek society will immediately recognize some key themes: the mediator whose superior social and moral standing provides the aggrieved parties with a dignified excuse for accepting a settlement; the gleeful disapprobation that internecine disputes—for these cellmates were virtually spiritual brothers—evoke in the larger community; and, perhaps most striking of all, the acceptance of an inconvenient division of property as a lesser evil than the continuation of a socially destructive quarrel. Andreas explicitly acknowledges the metaphor of property in the ironic aside about "dividing up" fields, the practice called *mirasiá*—often in the form of letting fate (*mira*) assume all responsibility through the casting of lots—that rural Greeks say is necessitated by the selfishness (*eghoismós*) of squabbling coheirs. And Andreas has indeed just remarked (p. 161) of the effects of the prisoners' isolation: "we had become so touchy and self-absorbed (*eghoïstés*) that we flared up at the slightest provocation."

It would be easy to dismiss these hints of rural society as the literary fancies of the openly traditionalist Andreas. What did Tsingos, the architect grandson of an urban entrepreneur, know of the inheritance practices of peasants? Perhaps Andreas, exercising a novelist's imaginative license, may have embroidered these details from his own intimate knowledge of rural practices. But the vast majority of Greece's urban population is of very recent rural origin, even today, and it is no less probable that Tsingos actually used this metaphor in the expectation—which, again, would still be widely shared—that its general import was clear to all.

Nor is the appearance of mockery and irony an intrusion of modern sensibilities. Shaming has a long history as a means of social control in Greece. The play of irony in local politics, gender relations, and the moral economy of respect emerges from close attention to linguistic nuance as constitutive of a wide range of social relations and reveals a flexibility that goes far beyond the formality of norms. Tsingos's elaborate courtesy toward the disputants, a more effective way of bringing them to their senses than either punitive sanctions or sanctimonious impugnings, is not unique to the educated urban elite. Both the appeal to higher moral authority in the person of Colonel Siotis and the mockery that followed the "division" were *recognizable* to all the actors, including the ill-educated foot soldiers who watched and understood the theatrical skits. Irony flourishes in reproach as an understated evocation of the traditional way of doing things.[2]

It is by means of such devices that conscientious members of Greek communities from remote villages to the prison-camp fellowship of Kebeit exact a measure of social responsibility from their less orderly associates. It is they, rather than some mechanistic feature of "society," who do this. And one could hardly characterize as endemically incapable of cooperation a national culture in which such effective actors seem to emerge with remarkable frequency. For Andreas, the self-organizing proclivities of democratically minded prisoners were far closer to the lived realities of Greek society than was the crudely overdetermined "order" that rightists sought to impose. His descriptions seem to confirm that assessment: they reproduce the ethnographically familiar lineaments of social experience.

In his account of "the painter Tsingos in war and in prison," Andreas does constantly emphasize the social. He makes the artist-architect's life a catalyst for the extraordinary birth of a social existence right out of the threatened final dissolution of physical life. At a very simplistic level, one might call the book a memoir rather than a biography. But that begs the question of Andreas's motives. For Andreas, this man, who met a lonely and alcoholic end and who resisted the temptations of becoming an agent of social control despite his doubly privileged status as an educated officer, embodied the independence of thought and action that paradoxically makes social life possible—and, less paradoxically, makes it bearable as well. The opposite state of being, which both Andreas and Tsingos were soon to experience, was the total usurpation of control over even the most private bodily functions on the bleak island prison of Yaros.

Because *Tsingos* is cast as a biography rather than as a novel, Andreas wisely does not try to describe his subject's innermost thoughts. In a culture where the conventional wisdom denies the possibility of penetrating

2. See also Maddox (1993: 192) on Andalusia.

others' minds, a realist idiom cannot sustain that kind of psychological speculation. (If *realities* are constructed, or at least pass through cultural filters, then presumably *realisms* must also be culture-specific.) The ironic, occasionally teasing, always deeply contemplative officer-turned-mutineer remains a somewhat impenetrable figure because that was the persona his taste dictated. Andreas captures the inscrutability with his own appropriately light touch. He presents Tsingos's thoughts under sentence of death as speech, externalizing the inner agonies in which Andreas can then recognize much of his own torment. We meet Tsingos in the only way that a Greek reader would find true to life. When Andreas wonders about Tsingos's inner mental life, he is plausible precisely because he does not claim greater penetration than any of his readers. It is only in works that announce themselves as fiction that Andreas dares to suggest what a culturally probable account of his characters' thoughts would be.

The one notable exception to his reticence in *Tsingos* concerns his recognition—but who "he" is, Tsingos or Andreas, remains artfully vague—of the ordinary soldiers' capacity for abstract thought and political sensibility. This again, however, was an area in which Andreas could reasonably assume an identity of perspectives: it was the basis of both his embrace of communism and his rejection of authoritarian leadership within the movement. Andreas seems to share my distaste for crudely heroic biography: perhaps he sees this book in terms closely related to his own affectionate but critical appraisal of Tsingos.

Although Andreas is himself an important actor in the account he gives of Tsingos's life, the portrait he draws of Tsingos occasionally blurs the boundary between the two. They were both sons of men who were ruined by the financial crash of 1929. The honesty of Tsingos's father "did not let him blow them into thin air with some scam (*kombína*)"—a wistful reminder of what had happened to Andreas's own father at the same time. Like Andreas, Tsingos distrusted professional politicians; like him, too, Tsingos felt repelled "by the quietude and security of the employee, the hunchback artisan, and even by the painless life of the bourgeois" (*Tsingos*, p. 26). Even Andreas's description of Tsingos's speaking style makes it sound remarkably like his own (p. 106): he "never stopped at a single thought, but within the last one others would spring up, to the point where you didn't know what to think about first among all the things he was saying, and you even started to wonder whether the fellow was in his right mind or whether you yourself were a person of lesser quality and ability but incapable of realizing it." I have only to cast my eye over the transcripts of his conversations with me to know exactly what he meant about Tsingos! "One could say that he was incapable of ever coming down to land" (*Tsingos*, p. 115).

At the end of the war, the long overdue return to Greece was not the joyous epiphany many had anticipated. By the time Andreas arrived in Athens, the variegated forces of the Resistance were regrouping for the major clashes still ahead. The right-wing officers who had conducted the military trials in Egypt were all members of an organization that was to gain enormous power in the years ahead. But for a few short weeks the leftists enjoyed comparative freedom from persecution.

Andreas even managed to quaff a brief but deliciously heady draught of vengeance:

● Those fellows who conducted our trial, the military judges and all that, were having a ball when we got back to Athens. I ran into one of the military judges drinking coffee in Constitution Square. I went down there with another friend of mine, Lefteris Mastorakakis, a good lad, he's dead now. "Mr. P——, how are you?" P——, that was the guy's name. A colonel. And now a general. "Ah," says he to me, "how are you? Er, who . . . ?" "I am Nenes," I tell him. "Don't you remember sentencing me to death? Where do you live," I ask him, "Mr. P——?" [*Imitating a whining voice:*] "I live near here, dear boy." He was afraid, he'll have said to himself, "He'll come and . . . [*Laughs.*] kill me, that guy, you see!" D'you see? [*In the weeping voice of one in abject fear:*] "Near here," says he, "is where I live."

And economic fortune, too, briefly smiled on Andreas. By chance he encountered the man from whom he had learned how to make butter before the war. This individual had set up a highly successful trading and real estate company; the minister of economic affairs was a director; and the entrepreneur put great pressure on Andreas—who was reluctant and had strong "tendencies," as he says, "toward escape"—to join in their venture. Andreas eventually succumbed to their blandishments. As a result, he became, for a short, gloriously ironic moment, a company director, shareholder, and respected member of the Athens Chamber of Commerce. He was living in grand style for those impoverished days and huge sums passed through his hands.

Soon, however, his foreboding proved well founded and his recent past came back to haunt him. In 1947, the Civil War was entering its second major phase and the authorities were demanding that all those whom they suspected of communist sympathies sign declarations of loyalty to the monarchy and the government. Those who refused were arrested, tortured, and shipped off to the same prison camps that many had endured during the previous phase of repression.

As we have seen, the supposed crimes of the Middle East mutineers had been "removed from the record"—that is, says Andreas, "as if they had not happened!" But a Greek proverb, as applicable to the inexorable blindness of an army-controlled bureaucracy as it is to fate, holds that "what is written cannot be unwritten." And an equally pervasive popular notion represents the nature of individuals as fixed and unchangeable—an attitude that makes Andreas's recognition of people's ability to change their ideas especially remarkable.

These twin determinisms of the popular imagination served the right-wing well. Acting on the premise that all those suspected of communism were irrevocably corrupted by its "foreign dogma," and faced with a real risk of defeat in the Civil War, the military-backed governments of that time "discovered" that the infamy of left-wing ideology could not in fact be unwritten. At most, one could exact declarations of loyalty to the state in which the apostates—of whom there were very few—rejected communism. Like the penitents of the Holy Inquisition, they were not released, although the harshness of their punishment was usually alleviated; their apostasy, or "repentance" (*metanoia*[3]) as the authorities sanctimoniously called it, served more to discredit their former comrades than to gain them mercy. Indeed, when in their despair they retracted their declarations, their act confirmed their tormentors' claim that their wickedness had indeed proved to be an ineradicable part of their nature.

In one short story about those terrible years, Andreas has a teacher fondly recall his pupils' curiosity: "'Sir, is it the earth that moves, or the sun?' his pupils would ask him. Poor old Galileo. . . . He'd remembered him in an appropriate place" (*Daisies*, p. 59). But Galileo had been one of those who broke under torture and retracted his ideas, only to mutter under his breath, so it is said, that he was right after all. Many of these victims of the latter-day secular inquisition in Greece, including Andreas, steadfastly refused to sign the humiliating declarations at all. For these hardier souls, too, Andreas found the Inquisition to be a horribly rich source of appropriate images.[4] In another short story, the guards have

---

3. *Metanoia* (modern pronunciation: *metánia*) is a term of canon law. Its use by the fascists gave an especially Inquisition-like cast to all their activities.

4. He is not unique among Greek writers in viewing the Inquisition as the historical model for present-day political repression; see Van Dyck's (1997: 36) discussion of Seferis, whose portrait of the Cretan painter El Greco's being forced to trim angels' wings to a standard size similarly uses the Inquisition as a model of vicious bureaucratic banality (Seferis and Tsatsos 1975: 77). But, as Van Dyck shows, Seferis's image was one of the poet's complicity in censorship; by contrast Andreas could not, and would not, be silenced. Religious metaphors are not absent from left-wing writers, but they were perhaps less persistent in some others: Calotychos (1993: 260) notes that in the poems of Manolis Anagnostakis, for example, the Christological themes of his earlier poems yielded to a bitter rejection of this and other idealist sources of metaphor. In Andreas's prose, the metaphors are, rather, of the Church as a repressive institution, and his use of the resurrection metaphor is an ironic appropriation entirely consistent with his view that Jesus was a great man whose ideals have been betrayed by the institutional church—also a widely shared view among left-wing intellectuals (see, for example, Kazantzakis's *Christ Recrucified* [1954]). Such analogies

taken four prisoners down to the seashore at Makronisi, tied each by a leg, and then threatened to burn them alive if they still refused to sign. One was doused with petrol:

■   Kothras then lit his lighter and, approaching him, asked him, "Will you sign, yes or no?"

The prisoner spat on him. Then Kothras threw the lighter at him and he burst into flame in a moment. A noise and something like a screech was heard. A voice from within the fire flung out curses and imprecations. And in a moment he flung himself just as he was into the sea.

"I'll burn you lot up on the mountain," shouted Kothras to the others, "and you won't be able to get into the sea in time."

The *alfamitis* [ex-communist now serving with the state security forces] held the rope firmly as it was dragged out to sea up to its final meter. The loudspeaker was at that moment broadcasting a talk [by one of the "penitents"]: "They told me that Makronisi was a Dachau, they told me it was hell, and I have found the opposite to be true. I have seen the officers' love [for us], the family warmth, the Christian behavior. . . ." (*Daisies*, pp. 39–40)

The state exploited Christian symbolism to the full and made especially cynical use of the ideal of self-sacrifice leading to collective immortality—a key feature of nationalist discourses everywhere. The military were able, in the Greek context, to draw additionally on both the popularity of resurrection as a metaphor for both political salvation (through the renunciation of communism) and the survival of one's line (through the system of baptismal names).

Indeed, in *Daisies of the Saint* (pp. 36, 39), Andreas recognizes one especially perverted variant of this logic in the declarations of loyalty to the state brutally forced, by means of Inquisition-like tortures, from political prisoners: now "resurrected," as he explicitly calls them, and told to inflict merciless beatings on their erstwhile fellow prisoners, they were relentlessly derided for their apostasy by an especially sadistic jailer who hoped to inflict on them a punishment fit for Sisyphus: if they talked back at him in anger, they would be cast back into the damnation of political heretics all over again. Any sign of mercy on their part toward those still so categorized had the same result. And those prisoners who still refused to sign would be kept standing in terror "until the Second Coming" (*Daisies of the Saint*, p. 51). This, truly, was a holy inquisition.

For Andreas the Inquisition was a reality: in the prison camps he had lived in its modern incarnation. The image always haunted him, some-

---

have popular resonance in Greece and elsewhere; for parallels in Andalusia, see Mintz 1982: 67.

times refracted through everyday encounters to produce absurdist parables of historical continuity. Two decades later, in Paris, he met a Frenchwoman whose skin cream had as its key ingredient mushrooms that had been fertilized with urine. Her lover had the brilliant idea of regularly inviting a group of their friends for generous amounts of beer, after which he collected their urine in a special container. The result was an increase in the production of the mushrooms, and hence of the skin cream:

█ This whole amusing affair was based on deep study over many years over numerous occult books, and the Frenchwoman knew that her colleagues had some knowledge of Solomonic cabbalism and had the innumerable recipes of the Middle Ages at their disposal. The witches, the holy women, and the Jewesses who were burned by the Holy Inquisition always left some secret in the hands of a priest who later marketed it to the greater profit of the faith and of the holy Catholic church. (*Seine*, p. 112)

Andreas surely read the dark side of this eccentric history through his knowledge of Makronisi and Youra. In writing of Youra, especially, he tells a bitter tale of the profiteering that allowed the camp guards to line their pockets by stealing goods and diverting food and other supplies from the prisoners, who were dying of starvation and despair—of the effects of their tormentors' efforts to make them repent.

And it is here that, while the guards "poured into the tents and indiscriminately, thrashing and blaspheming, were dragging the old, the sick, and the beaten to hear his speech, the oleaginous Father Prokopios spoke about [that is, against] materialism [a code name for communism as an attack on the spiritual], about various inconstant theories, about the flesh that is wearied and suffers in this transient life so that all we need to do is to save our souls. To ensure the return of Christ it is sufficient to admit and condemn our crimes. About the reward that awaits us IMMEDIATELY as well as in the future life if we DECLARE repentance" (*Prohibited*, p. 41). The convergence between political and religious repentance is here made complete. Like the Spanish Anarchists (Mintz 1982: 20, 67), Andreas is powerfully aware of the close parallel—in their case it was a direct genealogical link—between the penitentiary violences of church and state.

Andreas had a "file" (*fákelos*) on his political activities in the Middle East; inevitably, the anticommunist dragnet caught him. In early 1948, probably in the February of that year, he had gone to the engagement ceremony of a friend in Marousi. It was late at night when the festivities came to an end. Marousi, now a suburb of Athens, was at that time still separated from the city by open country and was a dangerous place during the Civil War, the lair of armed bands. Offered the simple hospitality of some mattresses, Andreas and some others decided to stay overnight. The police showed up:

● So someone betrayed (*kárfose*, literally: nailed) us. Because they wouldn't have come. . . . He went and "nailed" us, and they came and grabbed the lot of us! Including both bride and the groom and the rest of them. They all signed declarations, so to speak, and they were released. I would not sign a declaration. And they sent me into exile.

For leftists like Andreas, signing a declaration of loyalty—which would no more have guaranteed their freedom than confession saved the lives of those who were tortured by the Spanish Inquisition—was the ultimate betrayal. It gave the authorities power to undermine the determination of those who still endured by making a mockery of continuing resistance. Those who steadfastly refused to surrender mocked the power of the military instead.

Andreas was twenty-nine years old. A marked man, he was close to destitution, and had to live by his wits, already well honed in the fight for survival when he first lived in Athens just before the outbreak of war. As persecution intensified, he came to rely on the support of his kinsfolk from Asi-Gonia—who, like many of the shepherding families from Crete, had powerful allies in the police and army and access to basic foodstuffs that were hard to find in the starving capital. Not all were leftists, but kinship solidarity and localist sentiment usually came first.

For Andreas was about to face the grimmest torments of a life that has rarely been easy at the best of times. During the short respite following his release from prison, Andreas, back in Greece now, had been politically quiescent. Although a member of the United Democratic Left, a left-leaning party that managed to survive the banning of the official, pro-USSR Communist Party, and that had gathered virtually the entire left-wing intelligentsia under its aegis, he was characteristically reluctant to assume any active leadership role. Succumbing to pressure to head the Cretan regional organization, he resigned after just one week. "I was embarrassed (*drepómouna*)," he explains, using a term that gives an unfamiliar twist to the usual assumptions about "honor and shame (*dropí*)" in Greek society: usually associated in the literature with women's public self-presentation and sexual shame, the expression shows that Andreas saw in self-restraint and circumspection a mien that was perfectly compatible with his traditionalism. Faced with the daunting prospect of trying to lead such distinguished "personalities" (*prosopikótites*) as Lykourgos Kallergis—actor, fellow-Cretan, and a well-known socialist—he preferred to remain in the background. He preferred instead to engage in the cultural struggle and was interviewed at length by his friend Dimitris

Raftopoulos for the party's cultural journal, *I Dhrómi tis Irínis* ("The Paths of Peace").

His distaste for organizing roles, however, gave him no protection from harassment. The authorities were determined to compromise the weaker-willed of their opponents by forcing them to sign the infamous "declarations" and to isolate the rest from mainstream society by exiling them to remote island prisons. At the time Andreas was arrested, these prisons had already been functioning for many months.

Andreas was first sent off to "exile"—tightly supervised detention in a place far from home—on the island of Ikaria. After that, as one of the obdurately "unrepentant," he was transferred to the notorious forced labor camp on Makronisi. Then came Aï-Stratis (Ayios Efstratios), and finally the worst of them all: Youra (Yaros), once used by the Roman general Sulla as a safe dungeon for political undesirables and scarcely ever used again until the Civil War government in Athens saw fit to revive its minimalist survival conditions. These new prisoners seem in the course of forced labor to have found some remnants of their Roman predecessors. Virtually no human group had tried to live there, even under duress, during the nearly two millennia that had intervened.

While he was at Makronisi, Andreas received further bad news. A large consignment of American cloth goods had been delivered for the company of which Andreas was still not only a director but the only one available and empowered to sign. As a result, the merchandise sat in the custom-house, accruing overdraft charges on the original excise duty. Soon these charges passed the legal limit and Andreas, as the key signatory, was charged and tried for the company's delinquent tax situation. "I am sentenced in absentia, although they knew where I was, because, look: they sent my summons to Makronisi—I read it myself. But when the trial took place they didn't bring me in and they sentenced me in absentia. Do you understand? That shows that the whole business was a set-up." He was sentenced to three and one-half years in jail.

But this, as Andreas himself emphasizes, was the point at which Cretan solidarity began to play its customary role. First of all, the state prosecutor in Mytilene (Lesbos), under whose jurisdiction Ikaria fell, was a Rethemniot. He intervened to ensure that Andreas would be able to go to Athens, under guard, but in time to exercise his right of appeal. Meanwhile, aware of her son's increased peril, Andreas's mother came to Athens from Crete and contacted a liberal politician friend. This man, who was later elected to parliament for the region where I was to do fieldwork among Cretan shepherds (he is an anonymous presence in the discussion of patronage and politics in *The Poetics of Manhood*), was the scion of one of the wealthiest families in Greece and a native of Rethemnos. He had also been at school with Andreas; later he was to marry

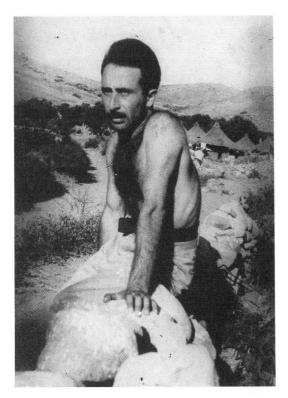

Lean years: at the Aï-Stratis
prison camp, 1951.

a descendant of one of the old imperial Byzantine families, a distant kins-
woman of Andreas's future wife (who claims descent from a different
Byzantine imperial family).

Fortunately, and with great prescience, Andreas's mother had made
a note of the names of the appeal judges. The politician telephoned the
presiding judge of the appellate court, who, by great good fortune, was
himself also a Rethemniot: if Andreas was genuinely guilty of a tax of-
fense, the politician declared, he did not wish to interfere, but he did
request that Andreas not be convicted on the basis of his political activities.

On the day of the trial, Andreas's case was one of several on the
docket. A judgment was expected at the end of the morning session.
Meanwhile, the court heard several other cases, including one matter of
currency smuggling. The presiding judge delayed announcing a decision
on Andreas's case until the afternoon:

● I had [a sentence of] three and a half years [for the tax offense], and
psou psou psou psou [the sound of lawyers whispering], without any-

thing happening, and: "He is acquitted because of [reasonable] doubts," he said something like that. And when I then came down from the dock, in shackles, because I was going into exile, they had brought me as an exile, to be taken back to prison, back again into exile, a lawyer asked me—[*Laughs*.]—the one who was trying [that is, representing the defendant in] the currency smuggling case—and the sentence there had remained the same—he asked me, "What became of you?" Say I, "I was acquitted." "Acquitted?" he asks me. "Yes!" "[After a sentence of] three and a half years?" "*Yes!* I was acquitted!" "But are we in our right minds?" says he. "We had eighteen months and [they left it] the same." Do you understand? Whereas [in my case] the *psou-psou* of [politician's name] had mediated.

It is perhaps not surprising that Greeks conventionally attribute others' successes in court to the use of political means. Andreas, like his father before him, expresses general distaste for such dealings—not, perhaps, on the grounds that they subvert normal judicial process, which was hardly available in those days of Civil War repression and emergency measures, but because they create compromising social obligations. In this case, however, the prospects of ever being called upon—and able—to repay the debt must have seemed remote indeed. The court proceedings were invested with all the trappings of due process, just as parliament continued to function and politicians maintained their networks of clients, but the simple fact that in this case it was necessary to make a distinction between the ostensible legal issue and the subtext of political persecution reveals a much more tightly controlled legal regime behind all the stage management.

Greek trial practices have not changed enormously in style, especially in the lower courts. Defendants are still routinely addressed as inferiors, and much of the negotiation is beautifully summed up as "*psou-psou*," all of it inaudible to the spectators. Justice takes second place to resolution: the lower courts still function largely as a form of social mediation when local channels have been exhausted or broken down.[5] At the time of Andreas's trial, the military-backed government could suffuse this weak legal tradition with its own idioms and goals of political regimentation. A politician's ability to bring off the kind of intervention that Andreas needed depended at this time on impeccable anticommunist credentials, a solid position within one of the legal political parties, and an equally solid local base grounded in an extensive network of patron-client relations that also included members of the judiciary and of the military establishment. All these advantages Andreas's protector possessed in ample measure.

5. See du Boulay 1974: 179; Herzfeld 1991a: 175–76.

A cynic would argue that the politician was willing to use his advantages in anticipation of political change, as an insurance policy against the day when people like Andreas would feel morally and politically obliged to repay the debt. It is true that in the elections of 1956, by which time Andreas was back in Athens as a (relatively) free man, his erstwhile protector was facing an extremely difficult election campaign on Crete as an independent candidate; Andreas was able to serve as liaison to the sole legal left-wing party (EDA or United Democratic Left) and could make sure that the local left-wingers supported this man. In 1948, however, the risk of letting the sentence stand must have seemed rather more substantial than any benefits in a hypothetical future. Also, Andreas's horror of political indebtedness had worked to his practical disadvantage on other occasions: it does not appear to have been a pose. Indeed, he remains mildly critical of his protector for having created such a powerful system of patronage in the entire electoral district that includes Rethemnos. When I began fieldwork in a highland village there some twenty-five years later, that network was still intimidatingly robust.

In such matters as Andreas's trial it is of course difficult to disentangle the rhetoric from the pragmatic aspects. The politician's pious instruction to the judge not to acquit Andreas if he was indeed guilty of real tax offenses, which doubtless also played on the judge's assumption of a righteously disinterested bearing with regard to anything except the ostensible business on hand, can be read in light of his own subsequent political actions. For by the time I was doing my fieldwork in the highland village, the post-1974 atmosphere of democratic reconstruction was projecting a bright critical spotlight on the entire range of influence-peddling. In highland Crete, this entailed close scrutiny of the alleged role of powerful politicians in the perpetuation of animal-theft, which was itself undergoing a major transformation into commercial brigandage. Andreas's erstwhile classmate and protector was among those widely suspected of cajoling prosecution witnesses who were his clients to retract their testimony. He retaliated to these charges by distributing printed fliers announcing that he did not want any animal-thief to vote for him—much to the amusement of some of his and others' alleged beneficiaries among the more active thieves. Again the disclaimer, again the lingering doubts (or, in some cases, snorts of disbelief): the politicians' dilemma in a patronal system is that they cannot afford to opt out of the game but soon find themselves on the defensive when that game is itself discredited by the processes of democratic reform that they may themselves have helped to initiate.

We cannot know what this man's true motives were in helping Andreas. At the time I met him, I did not yet know Andreas and would not have dared to quiz an active politician on so sensitive a topic, nor would his answers necessarily have revealed more than a diplomatic statement of principle. The politician is dead now, his memory zealously guarded—in true Cretan fashion—by a clan of powerful patrikin. In a study that deals in part with the issue of how motives and other aspects of the subjective self are represented, however, we should take Andreas's relatively benign view of this politician's activities seriously. Andreas—perhaps influenced by this experience, involving as it did a man he had liked since their shared childhood—also takes a truly Hegelian view of the mutual dependence of patron and client:

● Well, a parliamentary deputy these days isn't a [real] politician. But formerly we saw the same things, but less so, in my opinion. Now [the deputy] is the one who fixes his client's affairs, and he mostly tries to get things arranged for him in various ways, they keep pressuring him, they. . . . And these deputies themselves, that is, are . . . unhappy, how should I put it? they can't meet what we could call the clientelist demands of the people who vote for them.

It is not clear how ironic Andreas, a self-styled ironist, intends to be when he speaks in this way, but perhaps the ambiguity is itself instructive: patronage, which his father affected to despise even while allowing the so-called progressive leaders to exploit his enthusiasm for their cause, is clearly a source of great ambivalence in Greek society at large.

It is true that Andreas derived great benefit from his friend's intervention; and it is also true that presenting his own 1956 activity on the politician's behalf as the disinterested and voluntary reciprocation of past kindness works to his moral advantage as well. But there our ability to explain the dynamics of political obligation comes to a halt. In the flush of discovering the instrumental aspects of political friendship, anthropologists may have overemphasized a stereotypical image of southern European society, endorsing the cynical part of the local rhetoric while ignoring its expressions of affect—of whatever may not fall within the ambit of utilitarian rationalism. We cannot make sense of Andreas's own profound sufferings unless we are willing to make the implausible argument that his political actions—especially his refusal to sign a "declaration"—were driven by something other than purely self-interested calculation. Once we have reached that awareness and also noted that he is certainly not incapable of skepticism himself, should we not be warned by his guarded circumspection—generous though it may *also* be—into avoiding facile judgments about politicians' motives?

The earliest full-length study of political patronage in Greece, that of John Campbell (1964), is also a study of a culturally distinctive morality. Campbell scrupulously avoids passing judgment on what he found, but he also demonstrates that what outsiders would consider "corruption," a way of doing political business that seems extraordinarily resistant to reform (Kharalambous 1989), also depends on the maintenance of a sense of obligation that is to some extent unenforceable. We cannot know for sure how much risk Andreas's schoolmate-turned-patron was actually facing in helping a known leftist, but it must have been considerable. Andreas's portrait of the affect that made this help possible is a valuable counterweight (although not necessarily more than that) to the cynicism that could otherwise all too easily overwhelm our understanding of the relationship between the two men.

The politician returned to his business, and Andreas, under guard, to Makronisi. They were to meet again only after Andreas was released from Youra. After the politician's first successful election campaign, Andreas asked him how it felt to be in parliament. The politician's extremely powerful brother, supposedly the creator of the clan's entrepreneurial dynasty, scoffed at such a foolish question—perhaps mistaking this expression of intimacy for a literal attempt to probe another's mind—but the politician snarled back, "Andreas is an old friend. You keep your mouth shut!" Again, this suggests that loyalty and affect can not only surpass the ties of expediency, but may even—as Rethemniots insist is normal—take precedence over close kinship.

For Andreas, the vindication in Athens was merely a brief, minor interruption in the dreary career in jail that the authorities had laid down for him. Each prison was harsher than the previous one. Youra was indisputably the ultimate degradation. And still he did not "repent."

On Ikaria, Andreas and his fellow prisoners had at least enjoyed some freedom of movement. Placed in groups in a cluster of old houses, they could travel around the nearby villages and were subject only to a nighttime curfew, compulsory attendance for a few hours at the jail every noon, and the requirement that they check in at the local police station every day. Perhaps the most difficult restriction was that they were prohibited any contact with the locals. This did not prevent one young prisoner from getting sexually involved with a local woman; when the police got wind of the affair they grabbed the young man "and beat him for a week."

An imposed silence was insufficient as a barrier to romantic attachments, especially as a glance and a smile was the beginning of many premarital affairs in rural Greece in the days when an eligible young woman's parents was allowed no social interaction with unrelated men. Although it appears that this particular young woman did not face serious sanctions from her own kin, the incident nicely illustrates the state's assumption of the role of guardian of the *national* morality—a morality that communists were conventionally said not to share. Ironically, it seems that the police commander had only intervened because he had wanted the young woman for his own sexual enjoyment and had been rebuffed.

A glance from a young woman could indeed mean a great deal to these young male exiles, who were prohibited all contact with the local people among whom they lived and moved: "I flirted with a young girl of 15 or 16, and I'm sure she waited for me all her life. And at that time when we were exiles and so forth, a single glance, let's say, from a girl, played a great role." He could not speak to her, but that glance brought warmth and comfort into a life made bleak by stern isolation:

> The state's effort was to reduce us to nonexistence, as it were, they wanted to deprive us of our worth, they wanted. . . . You can't imagine what pressure there was on every side. When you live in such a place and a human being smiles at you, you feel better—you feel, in other words, that you are not *lost,* so to speak, that you haven't sunk into where they want to drown you, do you understand?

And this was only the relatively mild beginning.

For soon the order came to transfer the exiles to the much grimmer conditions of the correctional institution at Makronisi. This was not a haphazard decision. The authorities were determined to extract declarations of loyalty from as many of the political prisoners as possible. Their goal was to discredit them with their comrades as thoroughly as possible, and they forced some of them to write letters of repentance in which they entreated their kin in the villages to abandon the EAM-ELAS cause as well.

Andreas says he was never systematically beaten during his incarceration on Makronisi. To this day he has not been able to understand how he escaped the torturers' more ferocious ministrations. "I could have claimed the opposite, couldn't I?" he ruminates, in an ironic reflection on the thousands who have at last derived some benefit from their victimage at the hands of the Right. But in fact he was hung from a crossbar by his hair several times and was beaten on at least two occasions. On one of these, when he tried to get himself admitted to the prison hospital along with an old comrade who had been beaten almost senseless, some *Alfamites*—ex-leftists who were now forced to do the army's most brutal work—noticed that he was not himself injured in any way. They kicked him so hard they split his head open, so they had to drag him to the hospital after all. On another occasion, he was tortured in the hope of making him sign a declaration. A fellow Cretan with whom Andreas had served in the Middle East was now a powerful officer. First he tried gentle persuasion:

> So this fellow receives me—in the morning he offered me whisky. In the evening he meets me at the door: "Aha, so it's you who won't sign. . . . *I'll* fix you!" Well, so this cuckold and his gang were carrying some

Bureaucracy as repression: Andreas's government-issued identity card from Makronisi, 1950 (Andreas Nenedakis's personal archive).

wooden things, some spades, those thick pieces of wood, let's say, and they beat me as I've never been beaten before in my life. And it may have been the only time in my life, when they beat me then. I'd fallen down and they were beating me from on top—*bam!* on my back, you know. But it seems that I passed out, so they were afraid they would even kill me; so they left me.

By downplaying these incidents and thereby exempting himself from the victimology of the Left, Andreas was once again claiming the higher moral ground to which his anarchistic sense of restraint opens the way.

But there were other tortures. Music as well as the terrifying sounds of lamenting and keening were played at full volume through loudspeakers placed in the surrounding hills, in an attempt to break the prisoners' nerves. They were housed in tents with the latrines placed directly underneath. The food was rotten and teeming with insects.

> So many years of torment are no small matter. In the end the handcuffs do not wound you at all. They have worn through the bones and entered the heart. You keep wanting to weep all the time, and if you do not weep it's because hope is sucking up the tears. It's because everything is persecution and, amid the infinity of pain, your own pain looks like a game. (*Daisies*, p. 56)

In Makronisi and Youra alike, ordinary criminals were treated better than the political prisoners. In one of Andreas's short stories, when a guard objects vehemently to putting a political prisoner in the same cell as a group of crooks, a drug addict jeers at a car thief, "They are afraid of ruining your virtuous morals" (*Daisies*, pp. 118–19). The political prisoners were totally, deadeningly cut off even from the company of cheap criminals.

The utter dreariness of prison existence, the numbing of temporal experience, resists direct description. A third-person account might too easily seem clinically detached. Instead, with deep empathy for those whose sufferings were both more violent and more protracted than his own, and in order to portray a suffering subjectivity with the kind of conviction that his readers could be expected to share, Andreas twice adopts the medium of the diary to convey the dead weight of tedium. In one of the most economical pieces in his collection of "stories of prisoners," *The Daisies of the Saint* ("Twenty-two New Year's Days," pp. 120–24), the dull repetition of fugitive life under the Germans and the British, and then imprisonment under a long series of Greek authorities is given temporal depth—and a sharper pain that penetrates the ache of tedium—by the brief news the prisoner receives of the son he has never seen. As this minor hero of the Resistance is moved from jail to jail, his health deteriorating and his hopes dimming with it, his diary entries become ever more laconic, even banal, marking the attrition of the will by a weariness that gradually overwhelms everything.

Like most of the leftists who fought in the Middle East, Andreas—at least in his fiction—hints at feelings of envy for those who remained in Greece and fought in the Resistance. In many cases they languished far longer in the jails of the Greek rightists than did people like Andreas, who never had a chance to participate actively in the Resistance. Andreas met many such political prisoners during his own successive periods of exile and incarceration. He witnessed the petty, brutalizing harassment of Makronisi and its refinement as an instrument of total bodily control and disintegration on Youra. While he escaped all but relatively minor physical violence himself, his refusal to sign a declaration brought him sufficiently into the circle of the supposedly dangerous prisoners to appreciate the effects of the much more massive, sustained torment to which many were subjected. In the second chronicle-like tale of endless suffering, *Prohibited: The Diary of Youra*, he again uses the device of the personal diary to extend his understanding of that terrifying tedium far beyond the temporal extent of his own time on Youra, and even of his whole prison career. By thus portraying the thoughts of those who suffered the entire gamut of rightist persecution, he both submerges his own memories in the greater horror and achieves a culturally plausible degree of access to the inner thoughts of the Resistance heroes he both envies and admires.

If his suffering fell short of the extreme, it nonetheless lasted long enough to sharpen his awareness of the power of sheer time to magnify cruelty. The terrible strain between the grinding rhythms of prison life and the ordinary activities of a heedless world beyond is especially well illustrated by a detail in another tale of a prisoner whose son grows up in his absence. The little boy, his own child, is baptized with the name Stratis, which is also his own (*Daisies*, p. 116). This is unusual in Greece, where, although the godparent has the nominal right to choose the child's name, the parents usually manage to impose their own choice; for a male first child it is usually that of the father's father. On Crete, exceptionally, a boy may be named for his own father if previous children have died in infancy, apparently on the logic—said to be suggested by Gypsy fortune-tellers in such cases—that the new baby's chances of survival depend on its being associated with the very being of its vibrantly living father. Occasionally, too, also on Crete, a father will insist on giving his first son his own name as a demonstration of invincible self-regard. While Andreas cannot have been unaware of these practices when he wrote this short story, and while a Cretan might see in it a celebration of the prisoner's transcendent vitality, a more general Greek audience would always read this incident as a way of saying that the absent father was socially dead—for usually exceptions to the normative naming pattern commemorate dead kin. The practice of commemorative naming "resurrects" those who have gone before (often aging grandparents who are in fact still alive) but also effectively thereby submerges the commemorated person's individuality in a more generic and anonymous collectivity. In the tiny vignette of the baby's naming Andreas thus evokes all the tensions between self and society, present selfhood and historical collectivity, that serve to isolate the prisoner from the very sources of social existence while subtly reminding us also that for all the rightists' talk about a supposed national trait of individualism there is a strongly collective dynamic to Greek treatments of personal identity.

Both in *Prohibited: The Diary of Youra* and in the short stories in *The Daisies of the Saint*, Andreas certainly draws directly on his personal experiences. For example, in the story titled "An Unbearable Pain" (pp. 106–10), he tells the story of his mother's sacrifice of her gold teeth—of how he "ate her teeth" with the difference that now what moves the mother to this extraordinary gift is her son's letter saying that his friend and fellow prisoner Andonis's mother had just died. She has nothing left to offer Andonis in order to comfort him. Andonis, newly orphaned, has become "her new child." Finally she resolves on action: "In the morning she went to the same dentist [who had originally capped two of her teeth, the source of terrible pain in her youth]. She told him to remove the crowns because they were hurting her. She took the gold and when she returned home she already had a large parcel ready for it—so big that she couldn't lift it. And under the name of her son she also wrote the name of Andonis."

In the face of tyranny, all comrades are brothers—but it is their mothers who bring that to pass, because it is their mothers who brave the "unbearable pain" of bringing sons into a violently male world (see Caraveli 1986). In this simple tale personal memory, the funeral dirge theme of a mother's suffering, and the familial idiom of popular communism are fused together in four aching pages. But the community of motherhood also takes precedence over the global ideologies: "Children inevitably bring trouble and suffering; hence Marina's exclamation when told of the motorcycle accident [of an unrelated youth]: 'What mother cries?' Her own cry both identified here with the unknown woman and expressed her own suffering motherhood" (Dubisch 1995: 214).

Prohibited: The Diary of Youra lays out perhaps the most unrelieved horror that Andreas has described. Its diary format captures the relentless spiritual attrition of a torment that had no finite end. No prospect of release alleviated the unremitting beatings, kicking, and verbal abuse.

The book opens with many of its major themes already in place. A large group of political prisoners disembarks at Youra before dawn. They are immediately beaten and cursed by a whole group of guards—a scene they will have to witness many more times, with each new consignment of wretched human cargo. They are made to stand, motionless, on a little spit of land:

▌In a little while the sun came up over the sea. It started to rise, to climb high in the sky and to take away our last breath of air. The sentries changed places, drank water, urinated. We were forbidden all those things. We stood there, waiting.

The place was hard. Small stones winnowed out by the sea-spume and the wind glittered on the soil. And as soon as one tripped, at the first slip of a foot or of a bundle, the barren soil parted to reveal the dryness underneath—the rock, which was covered by a few fingers' thickness of powdered dust and sand.

Two meters away from us was the sea. How we longed to rest our tired bodies in the surf! To approach the line where the waves licked the ground. To wash our legs and arms and to let our parched mouths take in some moisture.

Every so often a regimental sergeant-major of the commissariat would come over with his assistants and beat us indiscriminately. He was seconded to Youra from the General Staff to supervise supplies.

"Are you married?" he would ask a prisoner.

If the prisoner was married, the sergeant-major would fall on him shouting and cursing: "And where did you leave your wife, you, where have you sold her?" If the prisoner was unmarried, so much the worse: "You didn't get married so you wouldn't have any obligations. . . . Did you marry the Party, then? Better that you didn't marry, that way you've not scattered your seed."

He was in his right mind. So it seemed. But [look at] the way that every so often he'd be seized with the need to run from his tent, shouting and asking the same questions all the time, ceaselessly from the morning on, you wanted to laugh: "Are you married? You aren't?" And he bashed away, beating without mercy.

No one felt either hunger or exhaustion. We wanted, however, to urinate. We wanted a drop of water to freshen our mouths even if it came from the sea. But the sentries were doubled along the foaming sea's edge with fixed bayonets at the ready. And the waves crashed on their boots and soaked our bundles. And you would have said that the very sea wished to subject us to tyranny.

At sunset one of the prisoners opened his trouser flies. We all followed his example. They couldn't button up our trousers as well. Another prisoner got up his courage and dipped his feet in the water. Two or three others went near him. That was the signal for the sentries to come pouring all over us. A terrible battle followed. They broke heads open. They beat bodies until they became tired. They were beating some until late into the evening. A silence settled, disturbed only by the moans of someone who had been beaten. And as soon as night came on the order was given for us to lie down.

It was the first night on Youra. (*Prohibited*, pp. 9–11)

The effectiveness of *Prohibited* lies largely in its incessant reiteration of certain themes: the savage, senseless beating of the new arrivals; the sadistic control of bodily functions; the indifference to an ordinary discomfort allowed to swell into numbing pain; the exaggerated performance of bureaucratic organization; and the sense of bleak isolation extending into infinity. Entry after entry rains down on the reader's consciousness with a calculated brutality that becomes physical in its sheer inevitability. Andreas's achievement is to hold our interest—largely through the indomitable voice of the narrator—throughout a long description of interminable boredom crafted as an instrument of torture. The graphic descriptions of special tortures such as the "fig-tree," from which prisoners were suspended upside-down for entire nights while being beaten to the point of paralysis (p. 131), come, if not as a relief, then at least as an affirmation of the possibility of a pain different from the everyday brutalities.

The inmates are stripped of their social and sexual being. Those questions about marriage are not coincidental: they express the logic of a pronatalist state (Andreas returns to this theme in *Ten Women* in his defense of abortion rights against the bourgeois state's appropriation of

women's bodies) that, by a converse logic, fears the fecundity of its enemies. The state tries to destroy the prisoners' marriages and to dismiss
their wives as virtual widows, with all the implications of whoredom and
frustrated hypersexuality that are associated with widowhood, especially
in rural Greece.[6] Since the state condemns many of the prisoners to
a physical as well as a social death, this is not a contrived interpretation: by asking each married prisoner where he has "sold" his wife, the
sergeant-major effectively unmans his victim by transforming him into
the pimp of his own wife—the ultimate degradation in a society where
generically "pimping" (roufiániá) is the usual metaphor of betrayal
from within.

This ritualistic separation of the prisoners from their wives had one
especially nasty corollary. At one point we learn of a camp commandant
who reinterprets the law to decide that henceforth correspondence will
only be permitted with those having the same surname as the prisoner
(p. 241): "Your brother/son-in-law,[7] your fiancée, your father-in-law,
your uncle are excluded." This limitation, whether fictional or otherwise,
recognizes the lurking traces of agnatic emphasis in the official ideology
of the family.[8] But its main effect, doubtless intentional, was to increase
the sense of isolation and to give the authorities more reasons for destroying letters—from which they first removed the stamps, to be sold back
later to the prisoners for sending another round of letters probably destined never to leave Youra (p. 147).

The control of bodily functions seems to have been an especially consistent feature of prison-camp life. It was also clearly much more than
simply an act of random cruelty. It impressed on the prisoners the full
reality of their physical as well as mental subjugation. Later, ruminating
on similar tortures inflicted by the military dictatorship of 1967–74, Andreas switches to a more analytical mode of description, full of dark humor. He describes how the bullying control of bodily functions increases
a prisoner's sense of uncertainty to the point where it becomes unbearable:

▌ All feeling is a weight in his guts. There where food and water gather and
demand an outlet after digestion. All of a person's existence craves an exit
after digestion. All a person's existence demands a toilet bowl. A place to

6. On widows, see especially du Boulay (1974: 123). A detailed case is also discussed in
Herzfeld 1985: 89.

7. Ghambrós is both sister's husband and daughter's husband (except in the mountain
villages of Crete, where the reciprocal term kouniádhos included sister's husband, wife's
brother [also kouniádhos in "standard" Greek], and some categories of cousin). See Herzfeld 1985: 54.

8. In official marriage announcements, required by law, a bride is described as belonging
to "the yénos [patriline] so-and-so."

dump the filth that has distilled within him. His whole existence. To empty out.

This is well-known to the people who hold the keys of the jail. They are well trained in these matters. Their thoughts, their lives, revolve around this cycle of the lavatory. To kill a person is an end (*télos*). If he has no work, shelter, food, he may find something. He moves around, walks, speaks, seeks. But if you lock him up in a small dark room and define the hour when he can relieve himself or refuse to let him do so, it is not just a deprivation to which he is subjected. Toiletology is a term unknown to psychology. However, psychologists are mere ciphers in comparison to gaolers and their terminology is deficient. (*Black April*, p. 196)

Although Andreas does not examine the torturers' practices with such a studied eye in *Prohibited*, preferring to let the dull thud of repeated brutalities speak for itself, it is clear that their habits and culture did not appreciably change from one period of their ascendancy to the next.

Their goal was to deprive the prisoners of the last scraps of autonomy that pride in their own resistance might have given them. The temptation of tiny acts of bodily relief set up a mocking echo of the prisoners' humiliation: it intensified the abject dependence to which the guards clearly intended to reduce them (see Aretxaga 1995). Thus, in much the same vein, cleaning the Youra latrines was an effective punishment because it showed how far the authorities had managed to make the cost of momentary relief the ultimate loss of dignity (p. 38):

▌ Those he [a particular guard] takes to the lavatory he obliges to clean it with their hands and many prisoners prefer this because the concession he makes to them is great: he permits them afterwards to wash in the sea without having to watch out for ways of evading a beating.

Of course, the punishment itself could be pushed to an even greater extreme, as when the guards shouted at a prisoner who was cleaning a latrine with his bare hands, "With your tongue! With your tongue!" (p. 50).

Illness was no protection; on the contrary, it was almost a provocation to further violence, usually prefaced by accusations of malingering. A doctor who supposedly had come to ensure the prisoners bearable medical conditions was interested only in vengeance, ranting (p. 308), "Here we have none of your own Bulgarian doctors who turned the hospital into a collective.[9] I'll turf the lot of you out of here as stiffs. You killed

9. In the language of the rightists, "collectivism" was an affront to the national ideal of "individualism." Anticommunist rhetoric in Greece and the United States shared many features during the Cold War period. Not merely the result of political expediency, this also reflects a long history of Eurocentric notions of individualism and perhaps also the shared ideological grounds of the American and Greek revolutions: in the eighteenth century, for example, Thomas Jefferson and Adamantios Koraes (the apostle of the neo-Classical or

my brother at Serres.[10] I shall take his blood back"—which is the standard phrase for exacting vengeance in a blood feud; for vengeance (*ákhti*, p. 310) was the personal goal of virtually all the torturers. By identifying all communists as "Bulgarians"—the presence of a Yugoslav as chief warder (p. 204) twists the knife in the wound by showing up the absurdity of the equation of ethnic identity or origins with political ideology—they denied their full humanity (p. 94):

▋ We awoke to the usual shouting: "Hurry, you Bulgars, or you're lost!"
   At the end nothing makes any impression on us. What does it mean to be Greeks (*Romií*) or Bulgarians? If you're Cretan you're of Turkish seed. If you're from the Morea [Peloponnese] it was Albanians who sowed your seed. The Macedonians are Bulgarians and the islanders Italians.

Andreas has perfectly captured the racist logic of the Right. Stripping prisoners' bodies and forcing them to engage with the filthiest tasks, moreover, forces them into a physical enactment of the same logic: they no longer control who or what they are, but dirt is clearly the ultimate expression of their alienation from the purified body politic the fascists claim to represent.

Andreas goes on to say that he certainly does not want to be the kind of Greek represented by his jailers. But they do, at some level, speak the same language: part of the horror lies in the fascists' ability to turn the familiar and banal into the demonic and inescapable (and to make vicious brutes out of heedless young village recruits). Thus, the fascists' language of collective revenge entails reconstructing ideological differences as both ethnic—which is how their Yugoslav colleague comes to be considered a virtual Greek, "thinking nationally" (*ethnikófron*)—and, ultimately, as grounded in agnatic kinship. The guards, using the segmentary logic of Greek blasphemy,[11] curse their prisoners' Virgin Mary as though she were not the same as their own. One commandant becomes absurd even to his own men, who (p. 101) "repeat his words in order to rag us but also to make fun of him: 'Our ancient ancestors (*i arkhéï imón*[12] *proghóni*), I screw your Virgin Mary. . . . You too have ancestors . . . Bulgarians!'"—which is precisely the point, since it allows the entire conflict to appear in the familiar guise of a kin-based dispute, in which each side denies a community of religious identity to the other.

---

katharévousa language) were in touch by correspondence. In the next century, Dora d'Istria made much of alleged contrasts between the "communistic" Slavs and the individualistic Greeks; see Herzfeld (1982a: 57–58).

10. Serres, in Macedonia, was the scene of heavy fighting during the Civil War.

11. On this, see Herzfeld 1984.

12. The form *imón* is extremely archaic and thus has clearly ironic resonance here.

Prohibited ends on an appropriately austere note: it seems that Youra, despite its temporary closure following a devastating official investigation, will open again. But that lies beyond the scope of Andreas's story. The "diary of Youra" ends (p. 319) with the ultimate bureaucratic cruelty: because the doctors and camp officers all agree that there are no sick people on Youra, this can only mean one thing: they are all dead. But vengeance was what they sought, and vengeance will one day be exacted again in return:

▌ However, the [grave] crosses of Youra and Syros, the blood of your innocent victims, the thousands of sick, crippled, and butchered, will pursue you your whole life long. To the end of the full century. (p. 319)

6 ▣

HAND TO MOUTH:
PORTRAIT OF THE ARTIST
AS A YOUNG WOMAN

The ingenuity that Andreas had exhibited when he first arrived in Athens continued to serve him well when he was finally given his freedom at the end of 1952. But now he had to face the economic circumscription that follows from political opposition in a repressive, if nominally democratic, army-controlled state. The authorities effectively blocked the communists' access to most kinds of office employment. Andreas despised such employment anyway, as we have seen. In taking this stance, however, he was not necessarily making a virtue out of necessity. Rather, his distaste for employment by others formed part of his existing set of values, while his father's disappointments remained an object lesson in relying for economic salvation on either kin or political patrons. His uncompromising stance in these areas produced, in any case, more or less the same degree of effective isolation as did his consistent refusal to sign the notorious declarations of loyalty to the state—the price his tormentors demanded for what would always, in their hands, be a highly precarious freedom of movement and work. He was truly on his own.

His isolation was further increased by his deafness—an element that also infuses his empathy with his mother's sense of loneliness resulting from her blindness. It was not until after a serious medical crisis in 1994, in which he lost virtually all auditory sensation, that he agreed to try using a hearing aid, one that was located in the frame of his eyeglasses and so did not expose his weakness. To his apparent surprise, this device actually worked, making interviews and all other conversation suddenly much easier for everyone concerned (including me). For decades, however, he had inhabited a muffled and often indecipherable noise, which only the truly determined made concerted efforts to penetrate.[1]

---

1. This isolation also evidently played a role in his inability to get a firm grasp of Swedish in Stockholm—his attendance at language class was brief and unproductive—or to improve his French significantly in Paris.

It is hard to know whether his deafness had protected Andreas from some of the worse abuses of his tormentors. They certainly had no interest in any kind of intellectual exchange with him and perhaps tired easily of arguing against his almost impenetrably impassive mask. All they wanted was to get him to sign away his political integrity. But this was a man already well used to coping with isolation and he met the threat of acute loneliness and deprivation with his own inner resources of calm indifference to their ugly methods. Similarly, faced with the threat of the dire poverty that easily befalls those whom no one dares hire, he readily found ways of making ends meet.

He had exhibited this hardy adaptability when he first arrived in Athens before the German invasion, with his home-based butter factory. Now, once again, he had to live by his wits alone. Thus it was, for example, that he improbably seems to have become the first producer of domestic detergent in Greece. A friend and former fellow exile had opened a cashmere factory in Athens and showed Andreas how they cleaned this delicate material using a solution of one part detergent to ten parts water. Much to his friend's puzzlement, Andreas demanded to buy some of this powerful fluid. He then added the appropriate amount of water, bottled the result, and put it on the market under the label "*Andreas Nenes: Saponol.*" He still recalls with great pleasure the astonishment of the wife of the poet Tasos Livaditis—yet another fellow exile—when, two years later, she saw for the first time how well it worked. Andreas's capacity for being hugely amused by such puckish triumphs was not the least of his inner resources during those testing times.

But those resources were especially tested by the petty harassment to which all the former political prisoners were continually subjected. As a writer, he could not rely on any of the few established publishing houses; like most writers of that time, he printed and published his books at his own expense. More surprisingly perhaps (and this is a source of pride to him), Andreas was able to cover his costs and even make a little profit on book sales. He also traded in fresh produce sent to him from Crete by his siblings. This gave him another advantage against the petty but repetitive harassment to which all suspected leftists were always subject. As was their wont, the authorities pulled him in one day to answer questions about his tax returns:

● So the police officer says to me, "Oh, so you're a tax-paying citizen, eh?"

"Yes," say I, "and what of it?"

He didn't expect that. He didn't expect that I'd be a tax-paying citizen, because those fellows thought that the Commies had nothing to do with that sort of thing. He was really surprised that I was a taxpayer.

This communist was a small-time merchant who never relied on the party to support him financially—except for the paltry sum of 150 drachmas the party newspaper (*Avyí*, "Dawn") would occasionally pay him for a short story in order to help him survive, much as it sometimes paid Livaditis a little money for one of his poems. What is more, Andreas had scrupulously attended to the paperwork for his business, to the chagrin of the authorities. There was little they legally could do—this time. Andreas had learned the lesson of his cloth retailing misadventures all too well: he knew that any minor infringement would suffice to return him to the clutches of the fascist police.

There was no respite from their baleful surveillance or the poison they spread through an entire national society. Even well-intentioned warnings intensified the ache of pervasive fear and uncertainty. One day in the street Andreas met a general who was serving in the notorious Greek secret service (KYP) but who was a kinsman and personally well disposed toward Andreas:

● "Look out," says he, "because there's . . . we've received a signal," says he, "in our Service. Someone has stabbed you in the back and we don't know what. . . . Your file, I'll get my hands just once on your file." Say I, "Tell me," I ask him, "why you're telling me about this?" "I'm telling you," says he, "so you will take care." "I *am* taking care," say I. "Why should I be taking care? The person who did this is ridiculous, because what can I do?"

Andreas figured out the informer's identity—he was an old schoolmate—especially when the same man, some thirty years later in Rethemnos, started boasting about his secret service connections, clearly hoping to impress and perhaps even terrify a few people. Andreas grabbed him and threatened to give him a public dousing in the nearby fountain but was prevailed upon to have mercy on him. And Andreas remarks, with his characteristic mix of irony and pity:

● He wasn't a bad lad [that is, when they were schoolboys together] but he was a failure . . . as a person, that is, in everything he did. I don't know how he ended up reduced to such a condition, and thought he . . . So he may even have been sick, perhaps he was. He thought that by maintaining he worked for KYP, as it were, it did him honor, it was something very important, and the rest of it. And that's how people consider it. In those days those things had value.

And he heeded his friend's advice to take pity on this sorry character and let him go.

A communist trader, a Cretan shepherd's son who could forego vengeance against his betrayer, a novelist who made money by publishing
his books privately, a singer of rhyming couplets who disclaimed their
authorship and yet has long despised the rhymes of bourgeois poetry in
favor of the freedom of fragmentary modern forms: Andreas stands dis-
concertingly athwart many of the chasms of our imagination. For this
reason it is tempting to view Andreas as a figure of transition between
"tradition" and "modernity." But what do these terms actually mean?
Their rhetorical play in a game of status makes the very notion of "transition" unclear.[2] I would prefer to view the uncertainty about what they
represent as one reason for the sense of ambivalence that pervades much
of Andreas's writing and talk.

It is not that Andreas is ambivalent because he is transitional but
that his ambivalence shows up the inadequacy of *any* categorical analytic
distinction between the traditional and the modern. The pride that led
his father to protect local Turks from the nationalistic killing frenzy of
his coreligionists sets the scene for the maverick communist who, after
facing a death sentence for his part in the uprising in the Allied army
in World War II, in 1966 renounces the party in protest against Soviet
repression of free speech. These are themes to which I shall return. For
Andreas, they are not disjunctures or contradictions. They are evidence
of the ever-present uncertainty of life—of the unpredictability that renders social life tangible and realizes formal structures through the aleatory
play of human action. War may be conducted in the name of peace, while
intolerance and prejudice may spring from egalitarian ideals (Kapferer
1988). Andreas has not allowed disillusionment to sour his personal commitments. He now knows, however, what was less obvious in his youth:
that every revolution has the capacity to betray itself, every brave new
principle to prove a changeling.

Even in his written discourse, his bemusement is evident: the premise
of orality ensures that it carries across from the spoken context to the
printed page of his own writings—that is, even without the obsessively
precise transcriptions in which the ethnographer tries to preserve every
vocal tic or nuance. Critics and friends noted this hesitant quality early
on, commenting over three decades ago on the almost aggressive rush
of assertions and the equally abrupt withdrawals and pauses. Thus Raftopoulos remembers first meeting Andreas as one of the few survivors of
the Foreign Legion troops, most of whom had been sent to the battle
of Bir Hakeim. It was not long before they met again, Andreas now face-
to-face with his sentence of death for participating in the communist

2. On the dialectic of tradition and modernity in Greek society, see Couroucli 1995, Deltsou 1995, Stewart 1991, and Sutton 1994; and, for Cyprus, Argyrou 1995.

revolt in the Allied forces, surrounded by a host of soldiers of many nationalities all smarting under the imperialist military discipline of the
British:

> At our next meeting, once again barbed wire, burning sun, and the pure-
> blooded bestiality of British colonialism. The "white fences" [a phrase An-
> dreas used as the title of one of his books] of the "last gentlemen" fell
> before a lyrical reaping fire. It forged a quiet, deep friendship, a certain
> intimacy among the races, the skin colors, the nationalities, without a lot
> of words, or with brusque straightforward words, or again with laden si-
> lences.
>   Somewhere in there I also got to know Andreas Nenedakis at close quar-
> ters. That's how he was. He speaks quietly and with restraint, leaving some
> phrases cut off in the middle, as if he's always afraid that he has already
> said too much. His whole stance, moreover, has something clumsy about
> it in the marketplace of daily relationships, like that of someone who lives
> very intensely and painfully in his world. His expression, his footstep—
> these have the bearing of proud isolation, almost an excess of humility. I
> don't know, but that's how I imagine someone like Alexandros Papadia-
> mantis [a nineteenth-century novelist and short-story writer] living among
> the events and ideas of our world. He understands the likes of you and me
> with great ease, I'd say he really does empathize with us. And he speaks
> very easily and with warm cheer. His enthusiasm erupts explosively. This
> is another, almost unexpected aspect of the man, that of the Cretan who
> within this gentle human being noisily gulps down the grappa (*rakí*) glass
> of his life, baring a row of strong, big teeth at death and at all the miseries
> of life. And this Nenedakis always has some [Cretan] rhyming couplets
> (*mandinádhes*) at the ready. (Raftopoulos 1963: 46)

This is the voice that Andreas represents in those of his characters
for whom he wants us to feel a particular empathy. And yet we also
recognize it from ethnographies: the parallel between the agonistic tensions of everyday social relations, the joke in the face of death, the constant struggle with nature. This Andreas resembles the Cretan villager
who, having just lost a beloved half-brother "boomed at a friend, 'To
yours too . . . !'—an ironic use of the traditional formula addressed to
unmarried youths at weddings" (Herzfeld 1985: 126). Ernestine Friedl,
one of the first anthropologists to do sustained fieldwork in Greece, reminds us that the ordinary response of villagers to the most casual expression of interest is *palévoume*, "we're struggling" (1962: 75). Such tension,
the constant demand for displays of self-confidence, cannot but generate
uncertainty as well; for what if one's all too real foibles and weaknesses
come to the surface? In this ambivalence, oscillating tautly between action
and bemusement (contemplation seems too deliberate a word), lie the

possibilities for change. Social beings walk a tightrope between daring and folly.

Andreas's voice and movements express this tension and so encapsulate the possibilities for a distinctive way of reading the present. The voice remains very much as Raftopoulos described it over three decades ago, sometimes accompanied by the noiseless drumming of Andreas's darting, emphatic hands—those hands that his wife Elli Komninou's drawings of our conversation have so immediately captured. The voice encapsulates passion and uncertainty; the hands, an urgency to explain, an occasional retreat into bafflement at life's vagaries. Many sentences remain incomplete. Ideas hurtle toward takeoff, then plow into the ground as new thoughts edge them brusquely aside. One of Andreas's Greek friends in Stockholm, where he fled from the military junta shortly after its coup in 1967, surmised that this was typical of those left-wing intellectuals who had suffered in the royalist prison camps. In Andreas's writings about those experiences, there is indeed a similar mixture of hesitancy and urgent pride that trembles in all his diction.

This, then, is truly a voice of experience. It is the voice of experience understood through the body, its torments, its discipline, and its opportunities. Ideology, for Andreas, is not only expressed through the mannerisms of the body, but is the result of the whole range of experience through which these mannerisms have been formed. He put this in blunt terms:

My ideological space, my ideological understanding, positioning (*topo-thétisi*), so to speak, was created by the reflections that I encountered in life, from whatever I took on board. Whether by sight or by hearing, or, when all's said and done, even the matter of food played a part, in my opinion it plays a part in this ideological [business].

As he explained, an austere diet of pulses and whatever other farm products were available, with meat a monthly luxury with additional feasts at Christmas and Easter, induced both a sense of class deprivation and a toughness of bodily discipline—so much so that his appetite is not a whit disturbed by grim memories of rotten pulses boiled and served with a thick layer of the dead insects that floated to the top of the prison-camp cauldron. In his own life, he continues to make a present virtue out of past necessity: his practiced cooking skills invert gender stereotypes, but, in parallel (although not as conspicuously ideological as the vegetarianism of the Spanish Anarchists [see Mintz 1982: 87–88, 161–62]), Andreas's pointed avoidance of rich sauces and of fatty foods in general is perhaps more of a demonstration of his fierce determination to keep his body both tough and pure. (He does in fact eat boiled mutton when he is alone; this is the definitive food of the Cretan shepherd, and he claims to feel a need for it occasionally.) He often expresses his determination to keep his body lean and fit in a conventionally masculinist language. In vaunting his austere culinary regime, he thus appears to clothe masculine pride in a partially, if not ostentatiously, nonmasculinist lifestyle.

Andreas talks often about food; he indulges himself less in its substance than in its ethical, historical, and social flavors. In his cooking he transforms produce into a fusion of some parts of his personal past—the celebration of his endurance—with the rejection of both the carnivorous masculinity of his father's environment and the bourgeois predilection for elaboration and excess. He also sees in it a consequence of the long illness of Elli, his wife—she was incapacitated by a weak back and muscular disease for several years—and thus a sign of his own partial domestication, but it appears that he had developed his kitchen skills even earlier as he also prepared the food when they were first together so that Elli could concentrate on her studies.

He does not argue that this makes him a feminist (and it seems clear that Elli would not see him as one either). On the contrary, he recalls with rueful amusement—rather than resentment—politician Virginia Tsouderou's observation that his writing in the female voice had nothing feminist about it.[3] Moreover, while he appreciates the power of the resistance to feminist ideas, perhaps he is too willing to identify the hegemonic force of that resistance as it operates among feminists themselves. Consider this description of a women's student organization in Paris in the 1960s:

▎ In the School [in Paris]—but outside it, too—the relationships I had were such that, without wanting to, I got involved in the various activities of the women's organizations whose goal was the dissolution of woman's social inequality. All of them spoke seriously then, took on every topic that came up heatedly and like true believers, and threw their efforts into the struggle right up to the moment when they got involved with some man. It struck me as strange and I always used to say, and believed, that women would never be able to do anything with their lives because something else always got in the way. What it was I myself hadn't yet figured out, but I noticed that the most dynamic of my fellow students became little lambs and dropped whatever task or activity they were engaged in, even their studies, as soon as they found a man. You might have thought that was the only purpose of their lives, as a person of the popular classes in my home town used to say. That is, self-perpetuation (*i dieónisi*). Or you might have thought that all these things that preoccupied us, equality and freedom,

3. Virginia Tsouderou was a parliamentary deputy of the New Democracy (conservative) party and has served as Foreign Minister.

were excuses for some other form of showing off, some other indulgence the purpose of which was, once again, to lure a male. (*Ten Women*, pp. 57–58)

And then, he relates (p. 59), they elected Mussolini to the honorary presidency of their society "because as they said he was the only man who could give women the freedom they needed." This led to a boycott of the society, with disastrous results:

▌ Only a short time later our numbers had thinned. All the girls were getting married and most married rich bridegrooms. Freedom was achieved by most of them through marriage and self-advertisement.

The scathing tone is not calculated to win admirers from among the ranks of dedicated feminists, even though Andreas clearly does sympathize with those whose plight it is to be valued in terms of their relations with others, in this case men. He remains puzzled to this day about the number of women who have failed to realize the chances they have had to escape from humiliation: again, he is clearly not a feminist but rather a man operating within a masculinist tradition that fails to satisfy his quest for insight.

Indeed, reading Judith Okely's appreciation of Simone de Beauvoir (Okely 1986), which (as perhaps especially befits an anthropologist's account) appraises the French writer's achievements and limitations in terms of her cultural and historical context, one can see how such labels may obscure our ability to understand local versions of global inequalities. Okely shows how de Beauvoir's cloistered bourgeois upbringing gave her writings a naïveté in regard to the condition of women living under different religious, social, and economic systems but points out that for her de Beauvoir's insights were indeed radically liberating. Achievement and relevance are always relative to particular contexts.

Instead of trying to accord him a feminist label that perhaps few would willingly accord him, least of all he himself, it may be both more useful and more accurate simply to say that Andreas has tried to understand the predicament of certain groups of women from his own perspective—that of a man who has suffered in ways that are analogous to, but quite distinct from, the pain of women in a sometimes ruthlessly masculinist social order. Moreover, Okely reminds us that in her own youth in Britain (and de Beauvoir's in France) higher education for women did little more than enhance the constraints of the dowry system (Okely 1986: 19, 28–29). This is exactly what happened among the Greek petite bourgeoisie and rural elite—a situation stripped of its exotic wonder by this comparison with the banalities of the Western European experience.

In these terms, Andreas is a perceptive analyst of the dynamics of grindingly petty oppression. While he sympathized with the plight of artistic and intellectual women he personally admired and while he sometimes helped particular individuals to achieve professional independence, he was less concerned with the emancipation of women than with class struggle and the freedom of political and artistic expression; his long bachelorhood during a time when he would in any case have been unable to support a family doubtless made him more receptive to women's concerns than were other leftists who, after the Civil War, settled back into the comfortable routines of bourgeois respectability and demanded that their wives and daughters give up the hard-earned freedoms they had achieved through participation in the struggle (see Hart 1996: 235)—a phenomenon that has been partially present in the aftermath of other social and political revolutions (see Lancaster 1992; Stephen 1995).

Indeed, what Andreas has to say about the condition of women comes through a filter of that same male pride, that exaltation of sovereignty, that also refuses the authority of the state. That pride, already transformed from the idiom of his father's village, is nevertheless still recognizably the pride of a Cretan male. His old friend of the days of exile in Paris in 1967–68, Yannis Angelopoulos, identifies his dominant characteristic as one of "chivalry." While this is grounded in ideas of mutual respect as the basis of all personal dignity, it is not feminism; it is not even necessarily conducive to a recognition of the social autonomy of women, although it sometimes takes this form. His conviction that women have never succeeded in seizing the opportunities offered them for self-emancipation may read distinctly like the fatalism attributed by conquerors to the oppressed—an expression as well as an instrument of their domination—and his peremptory tone, as he harangues his wife on these topics suggests, as indeed she perceives, that there are limits to his willingness to apply at home what he preaches in his writings.

But Andreas does oppose the dominant discourse on the reproductive role of women in his impassioned critique of the pronatalist state, which he accuses of reducing women to the role of demographic engines. In *Ten Women*, for example, he excoriates the dowry as a male-ordained channel of prostitution (p. 232); ironizes the state's pronatalism in two speeches in which female trial witnesses defend abortion as the solution to a whole series of social and even bureaucratic problems (pp. 96–107; 207–10); and comments on the imprinting of women's sexual shame on the body, producing the bent condition (p. 185) that is the analogue of the humble artisan's weariness decried by Tsingos and long viewed by Greek craft apprentices as the condition to which harsh masters and long hours reduced them.

Andreas also explicitly recognizes (p. 173) a phenomenon that I had found blithely ignored by Rethemniot men in general: the houses they claim as *patroghoniká*—inherited in the direct male line of descent—

were actually part of their mothers' dowries (Herzfeld 1991a: 136). In Andreas's account, a woman obsessed with her son so describes her own house; and it is her desire that "in her house her son [might] live, marry, and have children." Andreas draws an affecting and entirely recognizable portrait of the elderly woman, isolated and so afraid of challenging her son's autonomy that she ends by timorously participating in the discursive, economic, and moral expropriation of her own.

Andreas's access to the world of women both inspired and was developed through the art exhibit, devoted entirely to women painters, that he initiated in the mid-1950s. It was during this period that he met Elli Komninou, an adventurous young woman whose political leanings were very different from those of her *haute bourgeoisie* family but close to those of the intense Cretan writer and entrepreneur. Despite this ideological contrast, Andreas was able to find some resonances in Elli's family history with his own cultural and ideological predilections.

Elli's father's lineage bore the name of one of the great imperial dynasties of Byzantium. Andreas thinks that his great-grandfather, a doctor who went from the Russian Court to aid the cause of Greek emancipation at the outbreak of revolution, must have had papers documenting his imperial ancestry in order to win such favor in the new Byzantium of St. Petersburg. Whatever the reason, Catherine the Great, whose dreams of a pan-Orthodox sphere of Russian influence had led her to incite suicidal Christian revolts against the Ottomans in the Peloponnese and in Andreas's own ancestral region of Sfakia in 1770, sent Elli's great-great-grandfather to the famous old medical school of Padua—Galileo's university—to study medicine, thereby establishing a long line of doctors all the way down to Elli's father.

That same Komninos later came from St. Petersburg to the Peloponnese to participate in the more successful uprising of 1821 and the establishment of Greece as an independent nation-state. The splendors of the Byzantine court and of its self-appointed successor in St. Petersburg thus gave way to an unequivocally revolutionary identity in the crucible of nineteenth-century romantic nationalism, for Komninos became the personal doctor of the revolutionary hero Theodore Kolokotronis. This flamboyant guerrilla chieftain conducted a truculent campaign of attrition against the "pen-pusher" rulers of the state that he had done so much to create; their response was to canonize him as a national hero even as they attempted to silence him politically and even prosecuted him for sedition. He thus became an ideal-type model for those who thought that true Greekness lay in unremitting resistance to any—even Greek—authority. For Komninos to be associated with this quixotic emblem of all that is contradictory in modern Greek official history associated him with political tradition that led, three generations later, to the antimonarchist but passionately irredentist Eleftherios Venizelos. And indeed the medical tradition, too, was passed on in the male line, so that Elli's father found himself head of the medical corps with Venizelos's army in the ill-fated Asia Minor adventure of 1920–22.

Yet the Komnini, although not wealthy by the standards of nineteenth-century Europe, were comfortably established in possession of considerable tracts of farmland in the Tripoli district of the Peloponnese. Unlike the peasants, moreover, they seem to have been committed to a principle of nonpartible inheritance,[4] which, in conjunction with their care in each succeeding generation to ensure the professional education of their sons, virtually guaranteed the perpetuation of their high status as comfortable bourgeois citizens. Lacking neither money nor the right kinds of revolutionary association, they were perhaps unprepared for the lurch to the political Left and to social independence that came in the person of Elli. Even here, however, her defiant insistence on a career in art and her marriage to the irrepressible Andreas found their place in the scheme of things, and Andreas recalls with fondness and respect his father-in-law's rich repertoire of stories about the Asia Minor campaign.

Andreas and Elli met for the first time in 1957. Andreas was living a hand-to-mouth existence—he was, he says, a *clochard*, an allusion to the derelicts he came to know so well in Paris when he went into exile there after the 1967 coup. He needed urgently to make some money. He took work wherever he could find it; he particularly recalls working in a printer's shop. Later he also learned how to set up design proofs for car and other printed advertisements; this was profitable work, so that from a single commission he could sometimes make enough money to defray the entire costs of publishing a book—for he takes pride in that, unlike some other authors, he has never needed to depend on commercial publishers.[5]

In 1953, he and a friend had thought of selling old works of art and started combing the many junkshops that then existed in Athens. Paintings by now-famous artists of the nineteenth century could be bought for a song. One day, however, they came up with the idea of an exhibit devoted entirely to contemporary women artists. In those days, there were

---

4. Peasant systems of land inheritance in Greece vary widely across time and space. Equal partible inheritance without regard to gender is the general rule, although there are some exceptions (notably in the Dodecanese; see Sutton 1997; Vernier 1991) and the dowry represents a "compensation" to women for being, in the popular phrase, the "weak side" (*to adhínato méros*).

5. Kedros is the only major house with which Andreas has published. Many more publishers have recently entered the business, but poets and writers of fiction as well as local historians and folklorists continue to publish extensively on a private basis. No stigma attaches to this practice, although of late the imprimatur of some publishing houses seems to have acquired the status accorded to such establishments in Western Europe and North America.

virtually no true art galleries in Athens: Andreas claims, although not without a touch of his characteristically self-deprecating irony, that he deserves to be called the "father of the art-gallery managers (*galerístes*)." Even male artists had few outlets. And while artists of both sexes were known to the small circle of sophisticates, mostly by word of mouth, women were more isolated because of the severe restrictions that Athenian society generally placed on their ability to circulate in public. Andreas and his friend thus saw their chance.

They rented a space and invited 153 artists to exhibit. For the opening night the artists invited family members—"the father and mother, and maybe a brother"—for this was still an era of strict public chaperonage and, besides, there were few customers in the ill-educated, poverty-stricken Athens of the 1950s. The elevator became overloaded with all the artists' kith and kin and got stuck: another sign of the age, and not a harbinger of profits either. Andreas recalls that most artists relied on family and friends to buy their works because no one else understood that this was their means of making a living. Even Yannis Tsarouchis, later one of the most famous of all Greek artists in this century, was only able to survive thanks, Andreas believes, to the backing of the founding Director of the Commercial Bank of Greece. Tsarouchis, Manousakis (another well-known artist who has painted a fine portrait of Andreas), and several other painters went to see this patronal figure, and all assumed that when Manousakis, as the senior artist among them, was asked to name his price first, he would suggest 5,000 drachmas for his painting. But Manousakis asked for a mere 1,000 drachmas: "so the others were upset, because it meant they would have to set their price at 500 drachmas now!" Manousakis had misread the situation: impetuous in treating the banker generously as befitted a personal friend, he innocently cast his colleagues into despair. Money was scarce and artists had meager resources beyond these rare encounters with the affluent few.

But the exhibit of women's paintings and various other ventures in which Andreas worked with the artistic community in Athens were at least a start. Andreas learned about the economics of exhibiting and about the proper way to hang paintings. The Athenian public got one of its first tastes of an art world not confined to the European-educated elite, a world that Andreas soon thereafter also introduced to the general public in Crete. And Andreas plunged into a world of aesthetics and of artists that furnished his imagination with new possibilities and new insights. These were stringent times, full of political repression and financial hardship, but they were also times for invention and exploration. Andreas turned to the writing of a major book steeped in these vivid experiences.

Andreas Nenedakis, drawing by George Manousakis (Andreas Nenedakis's collection; reproduced by permission of the artist).

The Manuscript of the School of Fine Arts draws on Andreas's experience as an art gallery manager, his intimate acquaintance with the hothouse world of Greek art students, his marriage to Elli, and his direct presence during the student uprising of May 1968 in Paris. But the primary source was, in truth, a manuscript, a diary written by a friend and erstwhile fellow student of Elli's, a painter—Eleni Karayanni—who later achieved some local distinction before dying in miserable poverty. Andreas is quite open about the source of his insights: an act of textual expropriation, certainly, but evidently conducted with the full consent of the student. Andreas claims she was flattered by the revelations of her life and thought the result a significant literary improvement on her diary, but she agreed to keep silent about her authorship of the original diary so that Andreas would be free to let his imagination infuse the whole work as his own.[6]

6. A perhaps more cogent concern, that of gender-based inequality, must be set in the context of Andreas's defense—remarkable for the time and place—of women's interests.

The artist at home: Elli-
Maria Komninou (pho-
tograph by Cornelia
Mayer Herzfeld).

In fact it seems that she did reveal her involvement to a literary journalist, who then claimed that the book was really hers. Andreas was in
no position to deny this. But his use of the diary was not, I suggest, an
act of plagiarism in the strict sense of a work directed only to the greater
glory of its new author and without the diarist's consent. On the contrary,
he was very careful to point out to me how Dimitris Raftopoulos, in the
Paths of Peace interview with Andreas, had mistakenly attributed to him
the composition of traditional Cretan verses (*mandinádhes*) of a type that
it would have been locally acceptable for him to have claimed as his own
simply on the grounds that he had enunciated them in a new *context* and
so had given them new meaning.[7] It is ironic that Andreas, so scrupulous
about disclaiming this culturally unexceptionable attribution, should

For a striking contrast, see Okely (1986: 15) on John Stuart Mill's dependence on his wife
for a disquisition he claimed entirely for himself. Andreas is in any case completely frank
about his use of the diary, proclaiming it as evidence for the real-life basis of his novelistic
efforts, and it is unlikely that in Greece at that time there would have been serious disapproval of his action on the specific grounds of gender.

7. On the performance and content of *mandinádhes* and their interpretation in the context
of local ideas about meaning, see Herzfeld (1985: 141–47).

have faced criticism for basing his own, substantially different novel on a text that was made freely available to him.

The book retains the form of a diary, and its "author" is a provincial young woman who defies her family's matrimonial designs for her by attending art school in Athens. There she drifts from disaster to disaster—from near-rape by a glinty-eyed nun at the sanctuary lodging where her poverty and respectability had first led her to stay, to humiliation at school and exploitation by a conniving lover who is more interested in her pitiful savings than in her art or in her dreams of self-realization but who takes her sexual and emotional dependence on him for granted.

Andreas took the daily entries from the original diary, which for him lacked aesthetic direction, and shaped them into a parable about personal redemption through revolution. The art student decides one day to elude the watchful concern of both her parents back in their village and her jealously ambitious fellow students and slips off to Paris. There, in the student riots, she discovers true community and the liberation of her artistic passion.

Andreas no longer has the original manuscript in his possession. After he had assimilated its contents as fully as he could, he returned it to its author, who was quite uninterested, it seems, in what he chose to do with it. To him, by contrast, it offered an intimate insight into a woman's gendered dilemmas. As such, it also gave him a rare means to explore by analogy the sources of his personal animosity toward the cruelty of the banal—which he situates predominantly in the comforting certainties of the new bourgeois lifestyle and morality to which so many provincial Greeks aspire. It showed him at its rawest the pain of being a woman for whose more creative aspirations that bourgeois culture offered only cold incomprehension. In the novel, the family of the young woman's lover told her that her work as an artist, because unproductive, was immensely damaging to her marriage prospects and would therefore require an enlarged dowry in compensation.

She did not have even the empty comfort of seeing her training as a "cultural dowry" in its own right, as had recently begun to happen with university degrees in a few European societies (Okely 1986: 28). Among the Greek petite bourgeoisie, the purely economic dimensions of the dowry system were more rawly exposed—*timí* means both "price" and "chastity" in rural usage—and art, like literature, had not yet achieved the status of cultural capital among a people as yet unused to the luxury of sneering at mere utility.[8] Unlike de Beauvoir, whose well-educated fa-

---

8. *Timí* is one of the concepts usually glossed as "honor" in the anthropological literature. Disaggregating it in this fashion, however, exposes some of the calculations of cultural capital that it entails. For a more general discussion of the value of education as cultural and social capital, see Bourdieu 1984.

ther's declining fortunes gave her a good education of her own in place of a financial dowry (Okely 1986: 29), the art student faced only hostile incomprehension. When her lover demanded her miserable pittance of an art scholarship to prop up his faltering business, his family justified this as an advance on her dowry, saying that she could eat at home—their home—in exchange:

▌ That's why they were taking my scholarship away from me—like a loan—so that I could pay for my food at weekends. But, they kept saying, you're an artist—in other words, a worthless creature, without abilities, not producing anything, not earning anything. Who will feed you, who will clothe you, who will put shoes on you? This deficiency of yours—as though we were talking about being crazy or crippled—that is, this business of being an artist, your father will have to pay for that. (*Manuscript*, p. 147)

This is the gleeful response that Friedl (1962: 68) reports from a mainland rural community at the prospect of a wedding: "He [the father] will pay!" In Andreas's book, the trapped and despairing young woman notes:

▌ And his mama [an ironic observation about the real locus of authority] kept repeating that my parents weren't decent folks. Well, such are the prison bars of Paradise . . . and if he [her father] doesn't give it [the dowry], S. won't marry me. (*Manuscript*, p. 147)

Marriage remains the only conceivable goal for a young woman still trapped in the logic of her background. This is hardly surprising; Okely's account shows how radical Simone de Beauvoir's refusal of both formal marriage and childbearing, and her determination to enjoy a career and an identity of her own, had seemed to the relatively sophisticated young women of England and France in those years.

In that context, the dowry appeared to be an immutable institution in the Greek social landscape—and indeed recent Greek legislation that sought to "abolish" it seems only to have achieved a terminological adjustment that has had little practical effect even now. But the dowry was not oppressive only to women. It also created severe strains for entire families trying to swim upward through the viscous entanglements of class. Viewed in terms of nineteenth-century respectability as a means of assuring a woman's economic security and of announcing her family's status, the dowry became a terrible burden for fathers and daughters alike. For some women it might afford the only reasonable escape from a life of grinding poverty in the countryside, yet it was itself an oppressively demanding requirement to which few were immune. We have already seen how, in *Ten Women*, Andreas represents it as a goal for prostitutes, whose humiliation, he clearly recognizes, arises from the need for a dowry as the path to respectability in the first place.

The supporters of dowry as an institutionalized legal and social practice saw it as the repository of Greek tradition, and this view predominates—although without the romantic overtones—in ethnographic writing on Greece.[9] Even in these sources, however, there are hints that dowry has long appeared to those caught in its logic as a very different kind of institution. Far from being regarded as quintessentially Greek, it commonly possesses negative connotations of urban or even foreign origins— as a corruption of local values (see Herzfeld 1980c; 1983). The idea of paying a man to marry one's daughter dilutes the purity of motives that belongs to the idealized past of every Greek community; the practice, which in some places came to include the provision of a house where this had previously been the responsibility of the groom's father,[10] grew out of concerns with respectability and economic advancement that small local communities and poor families were ill equipped to resist. They were also the surest path to the life of the city (Sant Cassia and Bada 1992).

But even the faint hints of a less rosy view of the dowry may suggest that Andreas is less unusual in his recognition of the strain that this institution can inflict on a family's financial situation than he is in his empathy with the dilemma it creates for the woman who receives it. His concern is thus not a total reversal of conventional values but a reordering of priorities; for both father and daughter find that the institution of the dowry restricts their agency, albeit in different ways.

Whatever the reality of the history of the dowry as a social institution in Greece, its repressive dimensions have attracted considerable critical comment—particularly its implicit equation of a woman's worth with cash and with its categorical separation of men as active heirs from women as passively protected beings—(see Psikhoyos 1995; Skouteri-Didaskalou 1991: 155–84), and it was legally disestablished in 1983. For Andreas, it is one of the more objectionable aspects of bourgeois life, a way of reducing human—here, specifically female—value to a crude economic standard. The art student cared not a jot about her personal appearance; she swore freely and slept with her lover. But she had no financial independence. She saw in "S." the one male who showed some—limited—understanding of her passions and ambitions. She was utterly, miserably trapped.

Her own family had certainly not proved able or willing to understand. Andreas makes her articulate his own sense of the grievous continuity between traditional and modern life: "You see, fate is still the same for people today, however much humankind evolves." A Greek reader

9. Nevertheless, its practical disadvantages and the burden it places on families and individuals appear in that literature (for example, Friedl 1962) right from the start.

10. On Cyprus, see Loizos 1975; for comparable data from Rethemnos, see Herzfeld 1991a: 133–38.

would not fail to catch the irony here: Greeks supposedly do not *resign* themselves to fate, but the risk of failure bedevils a universe as bereft of security—and as thirsty for it—as ever before; "fate," the synonym for a woman's marriage, seems to invite resignation even as both the enormity of the repression and the range of resistance to it have both increased out of all recognition. Bourgeois ideals amplify older obsessions, while providing access to increasingly subversive visions of cultural redemption. In frustration and despair, she continues:

▍ When will people begin to understand someone different? Why can't I become what I want? They may be able to understand the meaning of each and every craft, but mine they can't fit into their little minds. "You're painting, or is that just to pass the time . . . ? Wow, darling, what a lot of bother, my dear . . . Hey, hadn't you better get married . . . That stuff is of no account . . . You should be making kids, live the way one ought . . ." Horrors! horrors! a thousand times over! Meatballs, potatoes, skirts, sluts, dessert cakes, visitors, money . . . garbage . . . shit! (*Manuscript*, p. 43)

And craft, while worthy of respect because it *includes* art—a reversal of the elitist perspective that Andreas deplores—is nevertheless not a *sufficient* description to convey to the ignorant what the artist actually does.

The heroine of *Manuscript* begins to internalize others' contempt for her lifestyle and ambitions and more generally for the increasingly marginal place of women in a bourgeois society that remains oriented to production but does not see art as productive; once respectability removes them from the workplace, all that is left to women, apparently, is the production of children—a restriction founded in the view that marriage without procreation is mere self-indulgence and further intensified by the official pronatalism of the state. Andreas shows us a woman involuntarily trapped by a bourgeois hegemony all the more ineluctable in that it utilizes the language, symbols, and values of "tradition."

Against this hegemony—which, as Jane Cowan (1990) vividly reminds us, is reproduced in myriad refractions of dominant ideologies through the glistening waters of twentieth-century consumerism—Andreas deploys the fierce iconoclasm of the dedicated revolutionary. The feminist critique of masculine religious models comes easily to him—first, because of his ideological scorn for religion generally and, second, because everyday speech refracts the unitary divine presence through the divisions and fissures of the experienced social world.

Other male Greek writers have adopted the first-person narrative stance of women—perhaps the best known example in English translation is that of Kostas Taktsis in *The Third Wedding* (1971)—but few have focused with so persuasively ethnographic an eye on the contradictions entailed in the social institutions of dowry and its negotiation, just as virtually no anthropologists—Panourgiá's (1995) account of illness, death, and family discord in Athens is the major exception here—have addressed the sometimes passionate displays of anger and grief that social norms generate *within* the family, behind the facade of kinship unity. Writers like Nenedakis and Taktsis can describe such internecine ruptures in ways that they clearly expect to be immediately familiar to their readers.

Both authors' scenes of bourgeois social life point up the extent to which specific social institutions make the Greek setting culturally distinctive and emphasize the absurdity of assuming that those institutions will overdetermine the conduct of individuals in sexual or other matters. In *Manuscript*, the art student mutinously considers her desire for a male lover. This is not what one would expect from a reading of Greek culture out of ethnographies, but in fact anecdotal evidence suggests that a socially disadvantaged woman might act precisely in this way in order to prove her worth in the face of a physical or other handicap. Elsewhere in southern Europe, notably among the Spanish anarchists (Mintz 1982: 91–99), free love became an effective way of challenging the entirety of authoritarian, patriarchal control, but in Greece such exceptions were usually episodic and highly personal, since even the communists frowned on sexual commitments (Hart 1996: 204). The student is musing:

> Perhaps I need a companion. That, however, is a matter of concern to me and to no one else. Because the way I am now, with so many worries, so much weakness, the way I've become exhausted by the unfamiliar work and the problems I have been facing, I find my mind slipping for hours at a time, and with a kind of condescension, into my family's way of thinking. About getting settled, and a woman's destiny.
>
> That's the trouble. Everything is constructed in such a way that you cannot escape. When I used to read the Gospel and the Old Testament, I kept discovering that those books were written to be read only by men. That's because, aside from the fact that they are well written, they are nothing more than a manual for the way of life imposed by men—the type of life they want—on people in general and women before all others. That is the point at which women must begin to overturn everything: at God himself, who is male. (*Manuscript*, pp. 24–25)

The art student rages at her emotional and sexual dependence on men. There is no paternal role model here such as Okely has perceptively identified in de Beauvoir's apparently uncritical acceptance of Sartre's paternalism toward her, a dependence that Okely herself decisively and self-consciously rejected as the allure of being "normal" in a world defined by male values (1986: 37, 49); but I can "ethnographically" recall at least one superficially liberated Greek woman who, with painful irony at her own expense, bemoaned a similar emotional dependence on men.[11] All this suggests that psychological and social effects of dominant gender norms become seriously distorted in any attempt at "structural" ethnographic representation, where the avoidance of personal feelings supports the dominance of those norms.

Andreas makes the student's emotional dependence on her lover, a psychological inner state described in terms that clearly were expected to be culturally plausible, the means of unveiling larger social and cultural inequalities. This is a rich illustration of how usefully the novelist complicates certain forms of ethnographic received wisdom through persuasive representations of an imagined mind.

Note especially how he moves from the student's sense of oppression to an indictment of religious orthodoxy in general. With a sociological lucidity worthy of a Durkheim or an Evans-Pritchard, he perceives that the elementary forms of the religious imagination reproduce the political and social order; while his scathing attack on a gendered deity articulates a view now commonplace among feminist theologians, he was more interested in emphasizing the role of religion in reinforcing *all* forms of inequality. It is also worth noting that this incendiary passage appeared in print only two years after the fall of the military regime, which had imposed blasphemy laws of legendary severity—perhaps because the colonels understood full well that attacks on the divine also impugned the temporal power that invoked it as the source of both identity and legitimacy—they had even commissioned churches dedicated to "their" saints (that is, those whose names they bore).[12]

In short, male control over the definition of the divine is emblematic of a larger and more encompassing hegemony, and Andreas uses the fe-

11. See the material in Herzfeld 1991b on "Khara." Note also that de Beauvoir's sense of dependence was accompanied by a humiliatingly persistent self-abnegation that Okely convincingly traces to Sartre's domination of their relationship and to the resulting naturalization of de Beauvoir's self-disgust as sexual in origin (Okely 1986: 76–77).

12. One such church was dedicated to St. George (for George Papadopoulos), St. Nicholas (for Nikolaos Makarezos), and the Archangels (*Taksíarkhe*) Michael and Gabriel (for Brigadier—that is, *taksíarkhos*—Stilianos Pattakos)—a combination the very oddity of which reveals its fundamentally political motivation. The idiom of blasphemy, which permits personal attacks to be expressed as attacks on one's own refracted segments of the supernatural world, might be thought to imply that this close personal association of religion and regime would have contributed to the discrediting of the Church in many segments of the population. That did not happen. First, even self-professed atheists continue to engage in religious practices as expressions of their cultural identity. Second, if these "refractions" of the divine world were indeed "personal," by the same token (and logic) they did not entail the discrediting of the fundamental images of divine and saintly figures on which they were predicated: *your* saints may be flawed, but *ours*—like "our women" (the idiom of blasphemy sexualizes the divine)—are perfect.

male voice to disconcert abuses of power in the broadest sense. Andreas tries to identify other inequalities through his understanding of the predicament of women. Although I am careful not to label him a "feminist," his position here does closely approximate to that of many feminists. In the following passage, for example, the chief juror in *Ten Women*, who is a beautician, describes her reactions after she had unexpectedly found herself called upon to serve in that role:

■ The judges were the way judges always are and the way they wish to appear: indifferent, unemotional, uninvolved. And it seems to me that, if the world were ever rebuilt, I would take away from men the right to try legal cases. I would put a woman minister in the Ministry of Justice. After that I would cut off the hands of Themis [the goddess of justice] and throw away the scales and sword that men have given her to hold—men, who out of hypocrisy and deceitfulness have made a woman the symbol of their deeds, without asking a single one of us. They've given her an air and a set of attitudes that no woman ever dreamed of. What right do men have to judge us? What do they know about us, and how can you judge another human being when you don't know how that person thinks? Even in matters where women are involved, it is impossible for a man to sort them out and pass judgment upon them. (*Ten Women*, p. 18)

In this passage, Andreas comments on the androcentrism of the Greek legal and bureaucratic establishment and explores the ramifications of its "survival of the fittest" atmosphere. It is a social club in which the devaluation of women sets the tone for what Kathy Ferguson (1984: 99–101) calls the "feminization" of all social relations—the justification of hierarchy in terms of an allegedly natural order grounded in the inequality of the sexes.[13] Moreover, Andreas has probed sharply beneath the formalism of establishment style, showing us that the stance of noninvolvement and indifference serves precisely the opposite goal from what it expresses: it is a disinterested pose that permits the pursuit of selfinterest—the paradoxical process I mean by the phrase "social production of indifference" (Herzfeld 1992)—in this case, in pursuit of the collective interests of men.

And again, as in *Manuscript*, the woman protagonist finds herself on the defensive in a classically hegemonic confrontation, in which she has internalized her subjection to a demeaning morality:

■ Now, however, I could not speak. In reality, I was myself the accused—accused by my conscience and by the attitude that male interests have created toward women. I too was in the dock because, at an earlier time, I

---

13. See also Okely (1986: 86, 112) for a similar appreciation of de Beauvoir.

had committed the same crime and, what's more, had done it with the accused himself. How much I would have liked him to recognize me! I would have liked him to stand up and start making fun of a court that could appoint *me* as head of the jury. It was just as well that he didn't realize anything either. (*Ten Women*, p. 18)

While Andreas's own language frequently reproduces the aggressive male competitiveness that perpetuates that process—a persistent concern with maintaining personal "sovereignty" (Faubion 1993: 125–26)—this may have seemed to him to be the only way to get people to listen. Certainly, as Andreas found in the prison camps, it is a way of maintaining a sense of personal worth in the face of brutally indifferent power. The price is continuing engagement in the game of sovereignty. To that extent, Andreas and his female protagonists are all caught up in the hegemonic processes that they are fighting. Given the cultural context, the very act of struggling traps them in its own demeaning logic.

This is especially clear in several passages in *Ten Women*. In the courtroom, for example, the prostitute compares the legal profession with her own. In another passage, a female lawyer lashes out at the ultimate hypocrisy legitimated by male power:

▌ You are hiding behind your finger if you think that your daughters, for example, are as pure as you would wish them to be and at the same moment you watch the next man's girl with a roving eye (*poniró máti*). You live with false feelings and dreams and you are surrounded by lies and hypocrisy and you are steeped in the sin of profit, lechery, and hypocrisy. So why do you act as if you didn't know that every girl from the age of twelve or fifteen has her boyfriend and has slept with him or, more commonly, with many. Why do you want not to know that most girls have visited a gynecologist and that abortion is a commonplace intervention in the clinics, without the parents knowing a thing, it's enough for the girl or her boyfriend to possess an insignificant sum of money? Which of you, gentlemen of the jury, can assure any of the others that the women on the jury, sitting on the jury bench, have not had abortions? A women has the right to interrupt her pregnancy. It is her business, it concerns her body, and, just as you cannot judge a woman who removes her womb or cuts off one of her fingers, so you cannot judge her for an abortion. Life does not begin, as some maintain, at the third or the fourth month. Life is a continuum and has existed in human beings from the first moment they appeared on earth. An abortion is nothing other than the cutting off of one branch of the tree of life. But you can't condemn the wind that blew it away or the hail that broke it off. What you can do is to support it, guard it, and help it. Only then will you have the right to protest, when you have exhausted all the means of helping it. (pp. 250–51)

This is hardly the demure picture of Greek maidenhood that emerges from some of the earlier anthropological portraits and from the idealizing nationalism of numerous folklorists. In *Manuscript*, the prototype of the art student appears to have led such a wild life that Andreas now ruefully says he would have written pornography had he adhered too closely to her original experiences. In the book, the open expression of her sexual desires clashes with the repressive institutionalization of bourgeois values to produce an ethnographic portrait in which agency, so to speak, only partially asserts its capacity to test or alter structure.

This had echoes in my own induction into matters Greek. As an undergraduate in England, I was amazed to hear a Greek-Cypriot male student asserting that nine out of ten female students at the University of Athens had lost their virginity by the time they graduated—and this during the rule of the military dictatorship, with its intense, comprehensive hostility to sexual freedom. Even allowing for male braggadocio and Cypriot disdain for the Greeks of Greece, this is an arresting assessment. It was only later that I came to see how the very rigidity of the moral code permitted considerable latitude of practice—especially in a culture in which dissembling had long been a highly treasured skill (Herzfeld 1983; see also Hirschon 1992). While it would be easy to attribute this difference to an urban-rural division, Margaret Alexiou (1991) and Renée Hirschon (1989), speaking for philology and anthropology respectively, have pointed out the violence that this dichotomy does to the long history of fluid relations between town and country in Greece. Besides, the art student came from the provinces, as indeed did a major proportion of the students at the University of Athens in those days.

Ten Women similarly undercuts the conventional image of chaste Greek maidenhood. In the courtroom, the mother of an accused man is being bullied by judge and jurors, whose refined respectability her bluntness offends. Her commentary plays back a sarcastic echo of her tormentors' hectoring contempt (p. 207):

▌   No, your honor, I have not been married. One child. Nor am I divorced No. But I got him with a man. Of course. . . . No, he was not my fiancé, he was simply a friend of mine. He wanted a child and I produced it, what do you see that's so strange in that? People get married in order to have children. That's what I used to be told, that's what I used to hear. I, however, found out that it was the opposite. That is, the last thing people getting married think about is kids. Children comes afterwards, without any thought or calculation on your part. Married people bring them into the world involuntarily. Of course . . . but they say so themselves! "We're getting married so we can get set up in life." Do you understand? They never say, we're marrying to have children. In the old days they said something nicer, but now they've forgotten it: "I will marry to resurrect my family." That, however, was the heroic age. Now people get married in order to get set up in life. There's another factor in the way. One of the two gains. Sometimes both. Certainly.

I found someone I liked and I had a child. I wanted it, and that was sufficient. Why didn't I get married to have a child? But, madam juror, why are you insisting? I have answered that one. In order to marry I had to have some self-interest, or someone other than me did. And such a thing was not possible because I have no money and because I didn't want to obtain it in that way.

The hectoring is all the louder for being indirectly represented here. And the speaker's remarks about the goals of marriage directly challenge, not so much the pronatalist state, as the equation of state power with the traditionalist male assertion of authority over women's bodies and reproductive capacities. Indeed, the idiom of "setting oneself up" (*apokatástasi*) is homonymous with the term for the restoration of public order, a concern of all conservative governments and especially of the military junta: it is the very reversal of revolution that signals the collapse of fervor (*Seine*, p. 234), although it can also mean a restoration of democratic order (and Andreas himself uses it to signify his intention of "restoring" the reputation of a local Renaissance poet, Marinos Tzane Bounialis, which he thinks has suffered undue indignities at the hands of bourgeois apologists and scholastic critics [*Cretan War,* p. 10]). In the context of providing for one's children, the term is specifically linked to marriage and the establishment of a respectable household.

The social act of marriage guarantees the "resurrection" of the family: the resulting respectability appears as the here-and-now sign and assurance of a collective eternity. This metaphor, not coincidentally, is also an allusion to Greek naming practices. The systematic repetition of baptismal names in alternating generations is linked to a concept of personal resurrection (*anástasi*) through the reproduction of the line of descent in the naming of its members. While this practice appears in many variants, all of them are directly linked to the local rules for property transmission, linking together the respective concerns of rural and bourgeois society; its basic logic is similar all over the Greek world. Andreas acknowledges this concern with the reproduction—or, as he more critically calls it, self-perpetuation (*dhieónisi*)—of the line of descent as part of a larger obsession with mortality. Unlike the bourgeois jurors whom the accused's mother rags so mercilessly from the witness stand, however, Andreas perceives it as human vanity further inflated by the technologies of modernity. This is why he makes the same concern with perpetuity a feature of *Manuscript,* but there as an artist's conceit. The connection is not itself unique to urban sophisticates: a close village friend in Crete, trying to make sense of my not having children, decided that my writing books would serve the same key purpose of ensuring a presence into the future—perhaps a modest echo of Thucydides and his wish to write history as a "possession for all time"?

That concern with collective self-perpetuation is also prominent in the ideology of the nationalist state. Indeed, David Sutton (1997) has recently pointed out the direct connection between naming practices and the concern with national place-names to which the Macedonia issue has given international visibility (if not, for most foreigners, much comprehensibility). More familiar yet is the constant harping on "our ancient ancestors," a proclivity that Andreas—who is quite susceptible to his own version of it—satirizes mercilessly in the rhetoric of the political Right. And one consequence of that concern has been a bureaucratic national historic conservation program that obliterates multiple local histories in order to build, quite literally, its own unilineal version of perpetuity (see Herzfeld 1991a). It is thus hardly surprising that as, only moments before, with studied clumsiness she forces her monologue back to the theme of the dowry, Andreas has the art student mutinously ruminating on the paradox of restoration (*anastílosi*):

▌ So this is what they tell us in the theory classes. They teach us the value of things, of the buildings, of the environment. And at the same time they introduce us to how they get destroyed. Everything seems like a machine that grinds up and destroys whatever falls into it. Mosaics are a case in point. The repairs and restorations are for the purpose of demonstrating and refurbishing the work, if possible, to its original state. Or at least to make it look something like the original. Well, everyone does what they want, according to ability and the instruction of the person who's directing the restoration. It would have been better to do nothing. No restoration at all. There should have been just preservation and conservation. As it is, a half-destroyed work has greater value, authenticity, than one that's been painted up and restored. (*Manuscript*, p. 145)

The student thus emphasizes the mortal uniqueness of the real world and its works. This is a conceptual heresy in the eyes of the bourgeois state, which is incessantly and increasingly driven to search for a time-obliterating renewal of material presence.

Andreas thus came to see the life of the prototype of the art student in *Manuscript* as mirroring a dominant aspect of Greek society: the transformation of peasant preoccupations with sheer survival into an obsessive lust for permanence and respectability, the latter being defined in the terms of a crass economism that leaves little room for self-expression. The agonistic ethos of rural life, expressed in the conventional view that life is a "struggle," does not lose its violence as it moves to the city and modernity. If anything, that violence becomes even more intense. The specific material forms may change as the shifts in the content of the dowry respond to the ever greater variety of available goods, but even these changes tend toward the intensification of what is fundamentally a familiar idiom of unceasing contest.

Notions of value are equally resistant to change, except again, perhaps, that of an inflation. It is within these parameters that social actors must still make their choices if they are not to be placed irrevocably beyond the pale—as happened to the prototype of the art student, whose parents disinherited her. In the novel, the student—caught between two sets of calculations, those of her lover ("S.") and those of his parents— finds herself succumbing to the same computation of measurable value, complicit in her own humiliation.[14] While she does not accept their dismissal of her art as an unproductive waste of labor, she finds herself drawn into a horrifyingly ineluctable empathy with the social and cultural myopia of her lover's parents.

Their son is short of money:

▌ S. told me that I would have to help him out with some of his business deals. The drowning man grasps at his own throat. It seems that he is in a tight corner in the trading he does. But what am I supposed to do? To give him my scholarship money and my wages from the summer workshop so he can put it all into his business. When I heard that, I was seized with dizziness. And he didn't think about how I was going to live, how I'd pay my rent, how I'd buy my pencils; he didn't think about the small amount I earn, because of which I have no work to exhibit because I even economize on the amount of turpentine I use. I would eat, says he, in his house. But how would I go to Piraeus for my food? And then again: what house of *his,* since his father calls me a ragamuffin and curses me while his mother behaves toward me in such a way that it's only because I'm sorry for him having to live with such parents that I pretend not to hear? Truly, what a fool I am. Has his guy so totally bewitched me that I have to sit and listen to him and put up with him and give him the right to talk to me like that?

I don't know how I came to tell him about a relative of mine who's a doctor, but he asks me to take him there for treatment. "Since he's a relative of ours . . ." So now he says he's a relative of his as well! But doctors want to be paid even when they are parlor pinks like my relative. And when, after so much insisting, we went to his medical office and I went to have a word with him in private, he only just stopped short of throwing us out.

Of course, he gave us some advice and a prescription for some pills, but we understood that he would not exactly be delighted to see us again. I sighed with relief because I would not be seeing *him* again.

I agreed to give him [S.] my scholarship plus the money I made in the summer from restoring mosaics. If you have so little and lose that as well, you don't get any poorer. I agreed to it because I wanted to make him happy. In fact, this man *must* love me. I have such ugly looks, I'm so untidy and badly dressed, that no one else would keep me company. No one else would take me into his home. And, to tell the truth, his folks have a point. His father is a small-time trader in the Vegetable Market, they have a little cubbyhole of an office, make ends meet and get by and their ambition is to marry off their son and to get hold of a spot of dowry. They do have a point. All their dreams have gone bust now that I've come into the picture. That's why they're nasty to me, that's why they don't want me. What can two old people hope to gain from me? They're losing out. I take away their precious only son. And they feel like old trees that have been torn up by the roots. (*Manuscript*, pp. 120–22)

Despite the aura of bourgeois modernity, there is much in this that we recognize from the ethnographic literature: the assumption, already seen in the mother's speech in *Ten Women,* that a woman's destiny is to be "set up" and marry; the hostility of the prospective mother-in-law; the "groom's" parents' avaricious dreams; and the assessment of a woman's value in terms of the balance between wealth and personal virtues and graces. Even the premarital sexual relationship is familiar: premarital sexual relations are sometimes even actively encouraged as a way of entrapping a good groom for a poor bride—which is precisely what the old parents seem to think has been done to their precious son.

Above all, there is the exigency of providing a dowry. But the art student's intense distaste for this institution, while in line with Greek feminist critiques, also accords with the longstanding Greek view of the dowry as an intrusive burden originating abroad or in the cities. If dowry is in any sense part of "traditional" Greek culture—and some form of dowry is well attested in both the Classical (Humphreys 1978) and the Byzantine period (Laiou-Thomadakis 1977; 1992)—so, too, is the view that rejects it as such.

The point is an important one in the present context, because it would be easy to view the scene just described as exemplifying a transition from traditional to modern values and practices and thus to cast Andreas as an observer and bearer of that transition. To some extent, certainly, his life spans a period of rapid material changes: what would have been an acceptable dowry even two decades earlier would have seemed laughably inadequate by this point. But disdaining the dowry is itself an element of continuity with earlier, rural practices. It is a stance as intrinsic to the social meaning of the dowry as is the more generic idea that in the old days young people were more chaste to the formulaic expression of Greek sexual morality. In that sense, Andreas is not so much the bearer of a new transition as the dramatic exponent of a deeply entrenched sense of transitoriness, and of nostalgia for a time of pure and disinterested reciprocity, in Greek culture. Moreover, he uses the argument about the dowry as a vehicle for revealing the workings of the gender hierarchy. It oppresses the student, desperate for both personal freedom and sexual gratification and caught between these desires, to the point of accepting what she knows to be her lover's craven (but also exploitative) traditionalism. The dowry she cannot bring to the relationship is the symbol of her humiliating dependence.

If a distinction is to hold between the traditional and the modern, it is thus not a transition from one culture to another but the reinforcement of an already acquisitive disposition by the overwhelming forces of capitalism and consumerism.[15] This amplifies the resentment of fathers and daughters against the institution of dowry and exposes it to critical discourses—notably feminism—of a novel kind. But when even the 1983 legislation has failed to abolish the substantive practice of dowry, thereby confirming both its persistence and its negative implications, Andreas's recognition of both these aspects belies any sudden transition to modernity.

Thus it is, too, with sexual morality itself. When Andreas makes his heroine swear, one can easily imagine the tut-tutting and headshaking of her carefully made-up kinswomen, as they complacently wonder what is going to become of her. But contestations of civility are not new to Greek society, and the image of the demure village virgin, at least in some parts of the country, is balanced by robust female sexual humor—a fact partially occluded, perhaps, by some male ethnographers' own inhibitions and social access (see Clark 1983). What *has* changed, and that dramatically, is the variety of ways with which ideals of propriety can be propagated and enforced, because the material stakes are more varied. Sometimes, one man discovers, even blunt directness has the appeal of novelty:

> ■ "Where would this have led, that is, if I'd continued to want her to love me? It's quite clear. In former times we used to add pepper, sauces, and all the rest. Flowers and all the various flourishes. The end (*télos*), however, is the same. Each era has its own way. Back then it was this way, now it's another way, do you see? The perpetuation (*dhieónisi*) of our kind." (*Ten Women*, p. 85)

15. See, for example, Argyrou 1996; Sant Cassia and Bada 1992; Sutton 1994.

The result of this proliferation is a deepening, almost cosmic sense of uncertainty, which perhaps also fuels the growing intensity of the agonistic quality in social relationships. Humans are still driven by the desperate search for resurrection, self-perpetuation, larger than the immediate, mortal world; and the modern bourgeois state, with its cheap chauvinism, feeds on that consuming desire and anxiety.

The range of decisions that ordinary people face is also enlarged as a result of this self-generating frenzy. Thus, the emergent bourgeois preoccupation with respectability that had led an intolerant brother to haul Andreas's mother out of school became increasingly unpredictable in its effects. What was now more valuable to a family that had forsaken farming for the city life: a fine house or a sophisticated education? Who was to judge?

More alternatives are available, it is true; but people do not necessarily have greater freedom to choose among them, and they may face a greater variety of sanctions for trying to make that choice independently. The author of the original manuscript was far less cooperative a victim of such repression than Andreas's mother had been, but her life was perhaps even more distressing: "truly she had lived a terrible life, a whole tragedy." Education, travel, personal development: these things may seem trivial in comparison with the very life that a sexually violated Sarakatsan girl might lose at the hands of her own outraged father, but the denial of control is no less absolute. It has, however, acquired a much broader field of play, amplified by the social, moral, and economic technology of international capital.

When he heard about the existence of the original diary manuscript, Andreas was quick to see the possibilities:

⬤ And she was a fellow student of my wife Elli. And she . . . she was telling me that she was writing this so. . . . this diary, and I told her, "Give it to me to read!" Many things, in fact, that exist in the book are unaltered from the diary. Of course, I made a novel out of it, as . . . because . . . in reality she didn't go to Paris. I made the heroine, so to speak, of this diary, I took her to Paris. I wanted to write someth— . . . well, that, that's why I somewhat changed the diary into a novel. Now, whether I succeeded or not, that I do not know.

That doubt seems to sit uncomfortably with the artisanal confidence with which Andreas sought—"of course"—to make a novel out of the raw material of the manuscript. But in Andreas the confidence of the artisanal chronicler or versifier is complicated by the awareness of unpredictability in oneself and in others that makes art out of craft. As he told me, he sees a close parallel between writing and painting. While a pedantic local historian accused him of "weakness" (*adhinamía,* here intended as indiscipline) for his serendipitous approach (see chapter 8), he argues that a painter does not work systematically from one corner of the canvas to the opposite side either. (I am more disposed to see writing, even of the academic sort, as a sculptural activity, but Andreas's point holds for that image too.) This painterly perspective gives Andreas license to invent: he drew heavily on his own experience, concedes that the first man the heroine sees doing his own cooking might have been modeled on himself, and emphatically announces, "*I* took her to Paris, novelistically (*mithistorimatiká*)!"

Confidence, on the other hand, infuses Andreas's peremptory demand to see the student's manuscript; hesitation comes with reflection on the result—although this, too, can be read as the appropriate performance of modesty in a truly strong, autonomous man. The abrupt switching between certainty and doubt marks the way Andreas writes and speaks. Andreas's sudden use of a formal word or phrase (such as *dhióti*) claims moral authority in a manner that in fact belongs to ordinary talk; at other moments, extreme self-deprecation supervenes.

Oscillation between hesitation and assertiveness is an inevitable effect of an ambition that seeks to create rather than merely to reproduce. Had Andreas been content to be a mere chronicler, for example, he would not have confronted the complications that a novelist's claims to originality entail; his originality would have lain, like that of the singer of rhyming couplets, in his ability to recontextualize what everyone already knew, rather than in some imagined region of pure, distilled significance. In a society in which the institutional invention of "literature" paradoxically represents both the attempt to conform to a Western European idiom of respectability and the search for a defining national genius, and in which Greekness is often symbolized by the self-conscious use of an oral mode, Andreas, an unabashed patriot, enacts in his personal uncertainties the dilemma of Greek letters in general.

His oscillations also allow Andreas to give depth to the portrait of the young woman. At the time of her prototype's studies, however, any woman of her background would have found serious conflicts between the larger resources created by the industrialization of Greece on the one hand and the powerful conformism that accompanied it on the other. This was the raw material on which Andreas set his creative imagination to work.

The gloomy self-accusations of a young woman who comes from an uncomprehending village background to study high art in Athens, and who accurately gauges both the fawning adulation of an overrated Parisian artistic scene by Greek artists and the real benefits that such a place can offer the unpretentious, transpose the dilemmas of Andreas the writer to the artist's canvas. The bitterly unhappy student's diary becomes a work of visual art—the "manuscript of the School of Fine Arts."

The parallel is striking. Andreas worries about how far his art is compromised by his realism but seeks to draw imagination from life where others would regard that as an oxymoron. The young woman, thirsting for her teachers' approbation but conscious of a "primitive" streak that nourishes in her the love of the bright colors of her sunny home village landscape or the desire to plant a definitely uncanonical tree in a formal portrait, is also the rebellious, contradictory Andreas, in a painterly and female mode. For such a person, transcendence means political revolution; without that release, the demands of a rigid bourgeois life reduce aesthetic enthusiasm to a self-defeating uncertainty and hesitation.

This apparent ambivalence masks a deep, political passion; indeed, it fuels that passion. The need for caution marks, not ethical or ideological uncertainty, but a deep awareness that any kind of commitment has dangerous and unpredictable consequences. This awareness, transposed from political to social criticism, similarly informs the self-lacerating hesitation of the protagonist of *The Manuscript of the School of Fine Arts*. With weary anger and bitter self-disgust, but also with ironic disdain for the powers that control her access to the means of self-realization, the frustrated young art student rages at her own persistent indecision, the painful deformity of conflict internalized:

▎ If only I could detach myself from the horrendous failing of ambition within myself! Because, at bottom, that's what it is. I would like to have everyone around me acknowledge me, have them believe in me and pay some attention to me. But that is not just ambition. Look, next to our house was Botonis's saddlery, in common parlance a saddler's shop. Well, no one ever doubted his mastery of his craft. When he told people, "You must buy this saddle for your donkey, that's the one for him," that was the one they bought. (*Manuscript*, p. 67)

This passage strengthens the sense that Andreas is writing about himself. Saddlemaker Botonis was a real person, an importation from Andreas's home town of Rethemnos, where this craftsman's reputation indeed appears to have been high. During my fieldwork, I came to know one of this man's sons, a leather merchant who was himself trained in the trade and recalls his father's mastery of it with solemn respect. Andreas, whose own life went from provincial merchant's son to city intellectual, shares—perhaps out of romantic nostalgia—that same respect for the solid artisanal pride of yesteryear, a pride that was not above indulging in minor pretentiousness. This was the point of Andreas's aside, "in common parlance a saddler's shop," in which he used a term (*saghmatopiío*) of neo-Classical resonance that Botonis's son had used to me in order to make sure that I, the inquisitive foreigner, fully understood, and respected, the traditional craft also conveyed by the colloquial equivalent, *samarádhiko*.

The point of this wry aside was certainly not to belittle artisans for some kind of ordinariness. On the contrary, the term *tekhni* (*technē*) means both "art" *and* "craft," as well as the more abstract "skill." But there is more than that to Andreas's evocation of artisanal competence. Rather, there is more than a hint of envy for the uncomplicated self-confidence of the artisan. Andreas wants us to understand how a creative artist might long for the freedom of constraint, for the liberty not to have to justify every experiment of which one is in any case desperately uncertain oneself.

The art student's perplexity is that of Andreas himself: ambition, something more than ambition, leads him to resent those who call him a chronicler rather than a novelist and to emphasize his own intervention in the young woman's diary, even while he deprecates any thought that his own recension might have achieved some measure of transcendent greatness.

"Whether I succeeded or not, that I do not know." This modest stance at least permits the possibility that, as a writer, he might have achieved a measure of success. His few attempts at painting offered no such consolation: "Silly things, actually. In reality, quite silly. But I want to tell you that I attempted . . . to do . . . those things because I think . . . it's always good to try your hand at what you judge"—the *galerístas*, exactly like the anthropologist, should be a participant observer, with all the slightly disingenuous self-effacement and direct involvement that this image conveys. In fact, Andreas, again like the anthropologist trying out the feel of an unfamiliar task in the field, knows that his painting is not an act of real commitment, unlike his writing—and unlike the artist's painting; he is a detached observer in a place at once strange and familiar. The sense of familiarity comes, not from a shared form, but from his recognition of a comparable passion. And so, cognizant of a common uncertainty and a common fragility, he transposes his experience as a writer to the visual idiom of the painter. This is indeed a portrait of the artist as a young woman.

The title of the book, *The Manuscript of the School of Fine Arts*, juxtaposes the verbal with the visual in a blunt display of this transposition. The title is syntactically odd: the construction—in Greek as much as in English—hints at multiple ambiguities. Who "owns" the manuscript— Andreas, the original diarist, the School? We are forced to wonder why it is not a *portrait* of that visualist institution (and yet, of course, Joyce's *Portrait* produces the same linkage although in reverse—of the verbal and the visual). And is Andreas's book to be read as a copy *of* the diary, or as a book *about* it? The term "manuscript," *khiróghrafo* in Greek, has overtones of "handicraft" (*erghókhiro*), an ontology to which the art student decidedly does *not* wish to be limited even though she recognizes that it too "calls for a sense of worth and careful execution." A stint trying to create letters for shopsigns, dramatized by the confining conditions under which she is expected to produce them, convinces her that there is a world of difference between artists and artisans. The form of this revelation reads like an allegory of Andreas's oscillation between art and craft, novel and chronicle. It is, after all, about letters. Bored by the routine before her, depressed by the drab Athenian life that seems to deaden everything, she slips into a daydream about the brightly glistening colors of the jars of sweets in the pastry shop opposite her father's house:

▌I came to. I had to get those letters done. But the letters that I had shaped were not what my employers expected of me. I was supposed to draw them from the style they had given me, but enlarging them to a height of ten centimeters. The kind of drawing I had learned at the School, however, was of another kind. I can do a face, a bust, the figure of a girl, of a boy. A tree, a house, a mountain, all those things I *can* draw, but the way a painter does. Freely, like a *painter!* What they asked me to do in that little cubbyhole of an office, in the tiny, unknown alleyway off Eolou Street, that we do *not* learn at the Superior School of Fine Arts. Not even the engravers do. And no one there knows how to do it. Not a single professor, not a student, not the rector. I was seized by terror. What would they say now, when they returned? How could I explain to them that the drawing we do as painters was one thing, what they were after from me quite another? But the most remarkable thing was that I didn't even know how to use the tools and pencils that were ranged before me. (*Manuscript,* pp. 135–36)

The student is struggling here between two sets of values. On the one side, she rejoices in the individuality of the artist and in the potential of careful training to set her free. On the other, she recognizes the kinship of her own nostalgia for bright colors with the more mechanical task she is unable to perform. Is there not a touch of glee in her observation that the learned are dumbfounded by the demands of practicality? In her malicious pleasure—"And no one there knows how to do it. Not a single professor, not a student, not the rector"—we hear the sardonic peasant who has little time for the pretensions of those who have acquired "letters" (see Meraklis 1984: 49). Yet she does not want to abandon what she has gleaned from the School; she has suffered too much to let it go without further heed. So, too, she can respect those who make picture frames, yet she fears what can be done to pictures by the people who order the frames and seem to regard them as more important than the art they encase: they are the embodiment of bureaucracy's victory over free and unconstrained expression—a bureaucracy that should have served the people but instead became its tyrant. Moreover, she considers such mechanical work irrelevant to her own capacities and dreams. The war within her, and within Andreas, is a war between contempt for arid academicism and the fear of ignorance, or, more positively, a deep respect for craftwork and a desire to produce something of far greater and more deeply individuated significance.

Andreas returns several times to the motif of the making and use of picture frames in order to highlight this dilemma. A frame is not a work of art like a painting, yet it requires its own artistry. Like Botonis's saddles, it is crafted rather than artistic. Unlike the saddles, however, which are made to control a natural *creature,* picture frames threaten and delimit another kind of freedom, that of artistic *creativity.* Precisely for that reason, a frame offers the comforting closure that the act and object of painting both lack. It delimits, defines, provides a sense of manageable limits, stanches the flow of disturbance from a painting to the social world of the nouveaux riches who can afford to buy it but would rather not confront its implications. When the art student tried to pay the doctor with a drawing, he contemptuously rejected it because it was unframed. This was a confrontation between the unthinking grid of defined spaces—also expressed by the gloomy and confining concrete boxes of the Athens cityscape—and the unruly nonconformism of the artist trying to break out. The motif returns in unexpected ways. Near the end of *Manuscript,* the student finds herself at the home of an especially well-known Greek expatriate painter in Paris. The luxurious apartment, she is assured, belongs to a Finnish baron (p. 173): "We couldn't figure out if there are any barons in democratic Finland; but since a Greek painter claimed it was so, perhaps he needed him as a picture frame. . . ." The frame appears frequently in this and other works by Andreas as the visual embodiment of bourgeois obsessions with tidiness and repressive classification.

It is because of her sardonic nonconformism that the art student can appreciate a rudeness in which she also discovers a total rejection of pretentiousness:

> On Sunday, in the bus, a woman sat opposite me. Sitting there the way she was with her hands folded on her apron she was an exceptional model for a mosaic. I drew her on a scrap of paper and wrote the colors down next to the drawing. I asked her to give me her address. I wanted to go to her house and have her pose for me. She turned me down rudely. I was delighted. You don't often meet people who don't want to have their faces immortalized. I told her that. She pretended not to understand, or perhaps she really didn't. (p. 142)

The passage reveals further layers of possibility: "I showed her the drawing I'd done and she began to give in." Now the student is torn between disappointment at this surrender and eager anticipation:

■ "I've got to ask my husband," she said. I found myself thinking she might be right. At the bus stop where we got off, she got off first. She pointed out to me where her husband was waiting for her. "Let her come." They had two children.

But even this retreat into conventional obedience—the wife asks her husband for permission—is not quite what it seems. The husband

■ took the saucepan off the stove. He was cooking something. That was the first time I ever saw a man doing housework. As the conversation went along, he explained why his wife had refused to pose for me. She was afraid, he said, that I might rob her. That what I'd said to her was an excuse to get into her house and grab things. People are ridiculous. (pp. 142–43)

The student returns the favor by presenting this appealing couple with the drawing. If the woman did not care to "immortalize her face," the student reciprocated by not caring about the loss of one of her best drawings. Her gesture was that of the poor person whose sense of social value is so high that she gives what little she has—like the poor old woman in village lore who proves her moral superiority by providing a glass of water and an olive for strangers, having nothing else to offer them (see Herzfeld 1980b: 342). In a similar mode, the student shows she does not care even about the last of her money from which her lover is studiously parting her: "If you have so little and lose that as well, you don't get any poorer. I agreed because I wanted to make him happy" (p. 121)—thereby turning the tables, as did the old woman in the village parable just mentioned, on those who regard men as the sole standard of social worth.

This is the self-restraint of internal strength. In the dismissive phrase with which the student turns her back on a good drawing she has only just executed, reciprocating her "model's" indifference to "immortalizing her face," we hear Andreas at his most self-deprecatory: pride in a work well executed, reluctance to glory in it lest he—or she—be reduced to the narcissism of those who can pay to commission works of art, and perhaps an uneasy awareness that the author of the original manuscript had also been indifferent to what Andreas intended to do with her writing. When we discuss the role of orality in Andreas's work, it will be useful to recall this evidence for a view of originality and authorship much closer to that of villagers talking about their improvisatory versifying than to the model implied in current intellectual property laws.

The student idolizes self-effacement. She ponders the contrast between the unaffected straightforwardness of the woman from the bus and the cosmetic artificiality of those who *do* wish to "immortalize their faces"—epitomized by a disdainful neighbor whose persona and little concrete box of an apartment are both redeemed only by the pot of basil she sniffs each day on the balcony. In this way, she is led to reflect on the irony of a creativity that can only be trained in dark places where it has little chance to flourish. The imagery is that of the ever-present picture frame:

▌ I could have asked the woman next door to pose for me. Our relations, however are of such a kind that I couldn't do that. She sees me as an old acquaintance, and not one she holds in great esteem either. Another kind of person. She puts on makeup like a varnished doll and goes out on the balcony with her pots of basil. That's what saves her. But she's like an old picture frame that's been thrown away, picked up, dusted off, varnished, and hung in the de luxe store along with the gold from Florence, the formica [furniture], and the concrete canopies. (p. 143)

Andreas has little respect for those who crave to be created by others, whether by having their faces "immortalized" or just "painted"—that is, with cosmetics—by others. Those others are another matter: they are the artists and artisans of this vanity. Even the beautician in *Ten Women* is a both highly trained and a creative soul:

▌ I created my own beauty clinic. All the top people in Athens pass through it. I am a more important factor of life than a government minister. More so, actually, since all these fine folks who supposedly direct the world and administer it must first pass through my office, so I can build their spirits, iron out their creases, and form them. The minister, for example, on whom our respected prosecutor, the court president, and the judges all depend, is my best customer. Truly, what a person he is. Very strong, very lively, very youthful—but only in his ministry and toward the people of lower rank who are in his service. In my clinic, on the other hand, he presents himself as he really is. Not a very pleasant type of guy at all. (pp. 16–17)

And this is the important personage for whose male chauvinist underlings the beautician evinces such loathing in court. As in a Cretan village, the moral hierarchy inverts that of officialdom, and indeed "englobes" it (Ardener 1975; see also Herzfeld 1985: 23, 25). The disdain for state functionaries recalls precisely that of men who consider themselves politically disenfranchised, but here it is transposed to an urban, professional, and, above all, female key.

These themes are central to *Manuscript*. A related aspect of the art student's persona through which Andreas explores his own preoccupations, as I have noted, is her hostility toward the excesses of a self-important academicism. That she cannot expect to survive as an artist without the benefit of formal instruction does nothing to improve either her temper or her self-confidence. Her hankering for the natural beauties of her home village—so much at odds with her family's pretensions of urbanity—struggles, as she explicitly remarks (pp. 141–45), with her equally strong desire for the approbation of her teachers in Athens. Here is the ambivalence yet again, this time in a form that calls on teachers to be accountable for their ideas to some human forum of experience.

These teachers impart discipline. Andreas does not contest the need for discipline, even for control. On the contrary, a gallery exhibit is the framing of a whole oeuvre, and Andreas today says that he often would not allow "his" artists to hang their own pictures, insisting on the auton-omy of his own kind of technical knowledge. But there is an inevitable tension between a formal knowledge that frames and delimits and a sen-sual understanding that constantly seeks flight from restraint. Andreas the technically expert *galleristas* is constantly struggling with Andreas the creative novelist.

This tension, so central (as we shall see in a moment) to what Andreas writes and thinks, seems to emerge from the logic of Greek social rela-tions. Social life is an area where excessive precision can be destructive. In the poorer segments of Rethemniot society—and perhaps in all of them before the advent of the consumerism that Andreas so bitterly decries— too much attention to punctuality, or to the exact measure or price of goods purchased, can only be gained at the cost of social capital. A repu-tation for stinginess, economic or social pedantry, or simply fussiness is inimical to everyday sociability (Herzfeld 1991a: 170). Andreas accords the same ethos of imprecision to the practice of true art: aesthetic disci-pline is not a matter of applying rules by the book, but a deliberately risky way of demonstrating mastery over the rules by playing with them, sometimes outrageously.

Social life is always balanced on the knife-edge separating convention from individual performance. An excess of conformity and unsuccessful attempts at panache are equally undesirable. Between these two unpro-ductive extremes, risky improvisations on the conventions of social life are sometimes elevated to a highly visible aesthetic. Thus, for example, verse exchanges among Cretan highland villagers turn insult into art by gently tickling the skin of violence, daring opponents to cross the line from verbal into physical abuse while making it clear than anyone who does so has thereby lost the game. In this way, too, some rural Greek populations seek through arranged marriages to establish tense but dura-ble resolutions of hostility between hitherto mutually hostile families (Campbell 1964: 50). The same logic allows Cretan shepherds to raid each other "to make friends," and makes even academic discussions a display of histrionic challenge that often seems to be the only legal cur-rency for obtaining eventual respect. As a Cretan villager once informed me, "If a man doesn't suffer torment, he doesn't find peace" (Herzfeld

1985: 45). Surprised many years ago by the insistence of a Greek writer and journalist that all worthwhile sexual relationships entail constant tension, I found considerable enlightenment in the treatment of this theme on *Ten Women,* where the tension is explicitly linked to a sense of cross-class voyeurism:

▌ "But from the beginning his behavior was such that our relationship had something tense about it, but that played no part. That is, so you can understand me, these situations possess both a certain attraction and a kind of exercise or if you will a continuous hypertension is created by an overheated state, and is precisely that [aspect] that preserves and increases one's interest. Despite all that, gentlemen, I must tell you that I have known many people and that my experience of life is great. In particular, of course, I have been concerned with our social problems, and because of my father and my own inclination I have been interested in the lower classes and I have dedicated quite a few hours on Sundays and holidays to helping and spiritually uplifting these people. Rarely, however, or never before have I encountered a case like that of the accused. Usually people who have received charity are attentive, humble, and grateful." (pp. 161–62)

This adds a distinctively agonistic tone to Andreas's Marxist variation on a *de haut en bas* theme of titillation and seduction reminiscent—unintentionally, I gather—of *Lady Chatterley's Lover.* It also brings images of sexuality into a specific conjunction with issues of class and psychological domination they do not possess in any of the ethnographies of Greek society published to date.

In many ways, Andreas's writings are variations on this theme of tension. In *The Manuscript of the School of Fine Arts,* this tension appears in a range of congruent dilemmas: discipline or freedom, social acceptability or art, precision or affect, the certainties of a bourgeois education in the technicalities of the artist's craft or the longing for aesthetic primitivism that brings to bursting pleasure all the satisfaction of the craftsperson's art.

Certainly the student of the *Manuscript* felt her life to be fraught with a tension that, while offering her intimations of an elusive meaningfulness, also threatened to overwhelm her with crushing weariness. Andreas thinks her prototype lived a "tragic life." This is perhaps the greatest difference between Andreas and the original diarist: he never appears to see himself as tragic, and, in the book, he uses his own perplexities to understand hers rather than, more exploitatively, the other way about. For protagonist and literary heroine alike, perhaps the greatest enemy was the sheer exhaustion that comes from battling the incomprehension of others. Anthropologists who have fought over and over against the terrible amusement that meets their tales from the field will easily recognize this grinding frustration. But Andreas's combative outlook will not allow him to treat such attitudes as a terminal barrier to his own dreams; in the book, he shows that he nevertheless understands why another individual—especially a woman trapped in the androcentric logic of her social environment—might be repeatedly tempted to surrender her hard-won autonomy.

At the end of the book, with its intimations of disappointment, the dispiriting conclusion appears inevitable: the struggle will *never* end. But that does not mean one should cease to engage it. On the contrary, ceaseless struggle is what gives meaning to life. These are the familiar lineaments of the agonistic society, cognizant of fate's outrages but never fatalistic in anticipation of them, precisely as it appears in so many ethnographic accounts.

Struggle in the face of implacable nature, the agony of a self-driven Sisyphus: in an ethnography of modernist Greece, these are the tension and frustration of rebellion against bourgeois formalism—the new merging of nature and culture, emblematically represented by the orderly pots of basil that appear on the concrete Athenian balconies of *The Manuscript of the School of Fine Arts*. The village-level struggles over personal autonomy live on in urban Greece, their forms transmuted but still a source of cultural distinctiveness (see Faubion 1993: 187). What makes Andreas's account different from the ethnographic reports of male pride in the face of both natural and social adversity is his understanding, lent particular piquancy by the female gender of his protagonist, that a person who succumbs to despair is not necessarily thereby diminished. Andreas does not admit to sharing this sense of grinding victimage, but he does want us to understand it, and to see that the only definitive escape from it lies in a revolution that, to the extent that it is political, must also be social.

He identifies much more directly with the sources of frustration in the creative process. One can decide not to care whether others appreciate or understand the meaning of one's work. It is harder to remain indifferent when this frustration is transposed to the actual creative act. Thus Andreas, a writer who has spent much of his life among painters, can immediately conceive of the experiential parallel. When a portrait is not succeeding, the despondent student notes:

> ▌ Work, work . . . And yet, at noon today when I could have painted, I didn't. This work isn't a handicraft. Which is also something that calls for a sense of worth and for careful execution. And yet, what was I supposed to do, then? Oh that wretched, ridiculous self of mine! (*Manuscript*, p. 62)

Note again the ambivalence about the relationship between art and craft.

Indeed, it might be useful here to return for a moment to *Bir Hakeim*, where Andreas seems more intent on exploring the "natural" human properties on which the self-conscious artifice of artistry, with its deliberate embrace of uncertainty and risk, then becomes a triumph over the anonymous obliteration of death. It is as though Andreas had anticipated the insight of Benedict Anderson (1983: 18–19) and Christopher Binns (1980: 180) that nationalism offers an encompassing sense of immortality and found it both apposite and yet also inadequate for the true artist— for whom the risk of eccentric invention goes hand in hand with deep skepticism. Here, too, we partially discern the grounds of his abiding discomfort with the totalitarianism of the communist states—"societies where belief in an afterlife must be refuted" and displaced by memorial monuments, but where in fact "many are forgotten, especially those deaths for which the state itself is responsible" (Watson 1994: 81). For this self-professed communist and atheist who left the party in protest against show trials in Moscow, the autonomy of the artisan and the artist offered freedom from such bureaucratic perversions of selfhood. Andreas claims not to be especially preoccupied by considerations of posterity. His writing offers him two benefits far more in keeping with his sense of personal independence: an escape from the stupidities of the present moment into memory and imagination; and a means of keeping body and soul together with the proceeds—a significant triumph especially at times when right-wing governments made sure he was debarred from many kinds of well-paid employment.

For those who do not seek to transcend craft to such precarious heights of independent creation and judgment as the writer, the technical certainty of the craftsperson—recall again Botonis the saddlemaker— shares in the predictability of nature, which in turn carries an animal's calm foreknowledge of death. For crafted objects live a useful life that ends in a peaceful, honorable death. Art, as a revitalization of memory, seeks—with all the uncertainty and trepidation that memory entails—to transcend that mortality. The disreputable characters in *Bir Hakeim* die with glorious anonymity on the field of battle; it is in his writerly portrait that they live again, their shattered individuality rebuilt in terms of the common humanity that in life they had been denied by their own actions and by others' contempt.

Thus, the motley crew of villains whose unlikely heroism forms the focus of the tale are all "natural men" in their exclusion from the ordinary range of the social. But Slateff, the big, silent, simpleminded Slav who seems most content when he is almost singlehandedly digging yet another set of foxholes for yet another Legion encampment, is the most innocently "animal"—so much so that he does not realize how negatively the others view his preference for the company of young boys. It is the night before he falls in battle:

▋ Tonight Slateff is different, neither wild in his ways nor peaceful. Tonight his work has something distinctive about it. Something choice and

strong simultaneously. He is like the master-builder who builds at all times with skill, with care and intelligence. Like the builder who with every stroke of his hammer places each stone, each pebble, in the place where it was missing, right where it is needed. And when he builds his house, then he feels inspiration billowing up in his heart and in his mind. Then every stone acquires for him a meaning that is invisible to the uninitiated—a meaning so specific for him, however, that you see him gaze at it, chip away at it, put it in its place, and see it as part of a completed house. It may be in the foundation, the ground floor, or the roof. It's all the same. He knows in advance where he's going to put it. He has measured it, he guards it, he puts it in place, there where he had previously thought to do so.

Tonight Slateff is building his house.

One often hears that some living things understand the approach of death.

Pigs about to have their throats slit shriek, they try to escape, they're restless. Rats jump overboard when the ship on which they were born and bred is sinking. Cats, dogs, horses. All have some premonition, something warns them. Is it instinct, premonition, or both at once?

Thus, too, human beings living closer to those creatures, closer to nature, feel something, have a sense of foreboding. Slateff is calm. Tonight his face shines with a light no one has seen before. His sheeplike eyes have lost their blank expression. On other occasions when Slateff dug he looked fine. As though his face was made out of some kind of metal and twinkled with light from work, from friction with the ground. That was a sight they all knew. Tonight, however, he is neither twinkling with light nor tired. He is aflame with brightness.

Tonight Slateff is not Slateff. (*Bir Hakeim,* pp. 114–15)

Slateff is the antithesis, within a range of characters for whom Andreas expresses both affection and admiration, of the art student in *Manuscript:* natural man as opposed to cultural woman. These are poles within Andreas himself, the Cretan shepherd's son who became a writer and *galerístas.* The student represents the desire for an *individualized* immortality—the artistic daring that, precisely because it is highly personal, lacks the technical and social props of the conventional world. Because it takes larger risks, it also hides a far greater fear of failure behind what others interpret as the arrogance of its self-regard.

This creative desire coexists with the terror that it might be misconstrued as greed for social success. For that very reason, Andreas seems content that this study should not present him in a heroic mode, that it is a cultural rather than a purely personal account. Similarly, he takes pleasure in a critic's praise of his personal modesty in *Bir Hakeim:* "And an author must be very satisfied when he manages this without having fashioned a personal style to increase a reader's interest or on its own to mislead the latter" (Paraskhos 1954). Thus, too, the art student despises anything that smacks of pure, social ambition even while her work inevitably suggests a fierce yearning for aesthetic individuality. She respects the signwriter, the saddlemaker, and the picture-framer, even envies them their certainties and satisfactions—but she needs more.

These tensions are not a privilege of the highly educated or of some rarified artistic temperament. They are also integral to the risk-fraught daily existence of the mountain shepherd, who must always balance a finely honed capacity for violence and warmth with the dignity of self-restraint. Andreas seems to separate out these two components of his own selfhood into the strongly contrasted characters of the self-cultivated art student and the amiably animal Slateff. But Andreas also shows that, for the art student, the disciplined aspect of social and artistic life, the control of the true artisan, is no less important than is the impetuous creativity that redeems it from routine.

For the art student—not an already formed artist, but one who is still learning the costs of the artist's independence—discipline indeed takes on frightening proportions. Art cannot thrive without a discipline of its own. Even for those who seek to transcend mere "verbalism," there is still no escape from technique. The student in the *Manuscript* struggles with the painfully elusive properties of color and line, torn between her "primitive" affection for the bright colors of her village and her scholastic desire to please teachers, between her contempt for professorial self-importance and her realization that her teachers in Athens knew their business better than their more famous counterparts in Paris and Berlin. These dilemmas transpose the political struggle for disciplined independence to the stuttering declamations of the author and the impulsive vacillations of the painter.

In these terrified glimpses of the ease with which she fears she could be lured into trivializing everything about which she cares, we can perhaps begin to appreciate the roots and the logic of Andreas's desire to write in a woman's voice—and, at the same time, his understanding that the social pressures are far fiercer for a woman painter than for a man who writes in a society which is androcentric and logocentric at the same time. This is, after all, a society where querulous male self-indulgence may still be far more widely tolerated than its female counterpart and where verbality is often a male prerogative (and where in women verbality is often dismissed as garrulousness). At the same time, Andreas himself regards—and makes his heroine regard—excessive logocentrism as the hallmark of both an authoritarian, foreign-imposed discipline and Greek intellectuals' undignified pandering to it. As a male writer, Andreas can logically only avoid the consequent contradiction by identifying his

political and cultural perplexities with the more acutely personal sufferings of a female painter.

For him, clearly, this woman's voice is that of a frightened but determined insubordination—the voice, at once hesitant and aggressive, of the
author. Fear is not, in fact, incompatible with aggressive Greek masculinity: according to the most swashbuckling Cretan sheep-thieves, it is fear
that creates the courage involved in their wilder exploits; in the prison
camps, too, Andreas knew that his uncompromising refusal to accept
humiliation was extremely dangerous but found that his fear of losing his
self-respect was more compelling. Moreover, the female voice epitomizes
Greek pride for Andreas's readers far more unambiguously than one
would expect from too literal a reading of Greek gender ideology, despite
the limiting case of folksongs about brave young women disguised as men
so that they could take part in the national struggle (Constantinides
1983). This association has less to do with stereotypical associations of
bravery with masculinity than with equally stereotypical assumptions
that make female domains—especially the domestic—the most accessible
metaphors for the intimate core of society.

This last point requires some elaboration. The dominant view has
long been that male and female spheres are categorically separate in
Greek life. Nor does the notion of "complementarity," introduced, at
least in part, to correct the impression that women were unimportant in
Greek life, dissolve the misapprehension that male and female attributes
are absolute and quite inflexible (for example, du Boulay 1986). What
all too often remains unexplored is the capacity of the stereotypes of male
and female to cross-dress, so to speak.

Greeks do in practice enunciate some superficially rigid stereotypes
of the "essential natures" of women and men, respectively (du Boulay
1974: 100–120). Since these apparently exhibit a rough correspondence
to actual social roles, anthropologists have tended to take them, if not as
precise representations of reality, then at least as patterns for emulation—
"models-for" rather than "models-of," in the idiom of Geertz (1973: 93–
94), but in any case as highly literal. These interpretations, as well as the
models themselves, are powerfully supported by the religious cosmology,
as they also were in the past, to some extent, by the legal system, with
its close ties to European ideas of propriety. In the long dominant cultural
ideology of the pro-Western Greek establishment, the public, political
domain is a thoroughly male place.

Surprisingly, however, there is also a considerable range of contexts
in which masculinity is indexed by the assumption of *female* attributes
(or at least feminine symbols). Less surprising, perhaps, is that such us-
ages are always found in *opposition* to the dominant code of respectability. They carry intimations of a rampant, perhaps illicit sexuality and
thus appropriately always seems to imply claims of intimacy, warmth,

or perhaps even amiable admiration for devious ways or uncontrolled sexual license—all attributes of the female stereotype. Thus, for example, a Rhodian male villager who had worked hard to establish a strong social position within his local community told a fable to illustrate the cunning of women, but then explained that he had used the same story to determine his own course of action (Herzfeld 1986: 230–31). Sometimes, the association is made through the alteration of grammatical gender, as with those huskily masculine Greek football teams (*Olimbiakára* for *Olimbiakós*, for example) by their adoring fans; more generally, speakers (especially on Crete) may "feminize" males in order to recognize their unusually impressive *masculinity* (for example, *papás*, priest; *papadhéla*, hulking huge priest). Moreover, a man may describe *himself* as *paliá poutána* ("old prostitute") to indicate his worldly experience in politics or more general dealings with people. While Greek Cypriot men delight in calling each other, with a revealing mixture of condescension and affection, *mána mou* ("my [dear] mother"); in some parts of Greece older women may reverse this pattern by addressing men and women alike as *yé m[ou]*, "my son." At the very least, it appears, some kinds of women can stand for some categories of men, a category reversal that is emblematically represented in folklore by the songs and legends about the brotherless young woman who goes off to fight with the guerrillas against the hated Turks, by a single dramatic instance of a female sheep-thief recounted to me with awe in Crete, and in the military annals of the Greek Revolution by the heroic female admiral, Bouboulina. While the rise of bourgeois culture has enormously increased the range and intensity of ambivalence, it has long been present in the Greek social imagination and experience, and—images of a rigid duality of gender roles to the contrary—is grounded in the understanding that gender itself is an ambivalent property.

The use of feminine symbols also reminds listeners of an imperfect world of human sociality. To be a socially attractive and benign person is to be, not a saint, but a sinner. In the androcentric social ideology I am describing, moreover, these moral flaws are explicitly feminized: the mark of intimacy is a sensuality mythologically traced to the sins of Eve and resulting in carnal and practical knowledge, in conflict, and in boasting and pride. And just as this makes exaggerated masculinity a consequence of corruption by women, so too the long years of subjection to Turkish rule are said to have engendered an "oriental" deviousness that has come to mark the intimate side of *Greek* "national character." Thus it is that socially benign humanity—as opposed to the ideal perfections enjoined by Enlightenment values—is symbolized by the base coarseness of "human nature," Greekness is marked by exaggerated Turkishness, and masculinity is predicated on the sexuality of women.

At the level of national self-characterization, one consequence of these symbolic assertions is that the left-wing, anti-Christian, and anti-bourgeois reading of Greek culture glories in the cultural ecumenicalism of the post-Byzantine era. Central to this ideology is *Romiossíni*, the exaltation of the Greek as defined by all the post-Classical accretions of national culture—Byzantine, Arab, Turkish—conveniently shorn, in the left-wing version, of their close associations with the history of Eastern Orthodox Christianity. This is a revolutionary Greekness, celebrated in the poetry of Yannis Ritsos and the music of Mikis Theodorakis, that stands in strong and mischievous opposition to the bureaucratic state.[16] (Andreas quarreled with Theodorakis over Andreas's disaffection with the Communist Party, only to see the composer experiment with the right-wing New Democracy a few years after the fall of the junta. Andreas wryly reflects that he may be the only true leftist to have remained consistent up to the present.) This is a vision of Greekness the diagnostic intelligence of which is not abstract ratiocination but the low cunning, or *poniriá*, that is also stereotypically attributed to women and that delights in subverting the pomposity and rigidity of officialdom of any kind.

Andreas resembles many Cretan men, from literati like Nikos Kazantzakis to the hill shepherds of his father's village, in seeing his own deeply felt patriotism as higher than that of the bureaucratic state. For him, as for them, attacking the pretensions of the powerful may be an act of patriotism in its own right. In this context, a female voice—especially one that continually challenges bourgeois notions of respectability and authority—is an apt trope for the intimate masculine challenge to formal values as foreign to an essential Greekness. In male contempt for the official establishment, much is made of the notion that the elite has little experience of real social life. This is a view that privileges low cunning over academic intelligence, passion over cultivated warmth, and sensuality over cold logic, inverting the binary hierarchy of the dominant gender ideology. Insubordination relies on intimacy; and the moral topology of intimacy, in the Greek imagination, is feminine ground.

Andreas can thus speak through the voice of the art student so many of whose problems and insights arise from predicaments of gender. The culmination of her story—the part of it he most freely acknowledges as fictional, the part that most effectively realizes his desire to transcend mere chronicle as a novelist—is her participation in the events of May

---

16. The title of Yannis Ritsos's poem and also of its musical incarnation by Mikis Theodorakis is *Romiossíni* (Ritsos 1974; Theodorakis 1987; see also Holst-Warhaft 1980), a term that encapsulates the Left's image of a Greekness more connected to its recent past—and its historical entailment in Byzantine and Ottoman culture—than the formality of neo-Classicism, although it did not exclude a populist and nativist reading of Classical influence in the modern culture (such as we find in Andreas himself, for example). Andreas greatly admires Ritsos, but split decisively with Theodorakis over the Moscow show trials.

1968 in Paris. But this segment of her story is not so much fictional as autobiographical. Unlike the live prototype of his heroine, Andreas *was* in Paris during the riots. The art student's joy at discovering the sudden appearance of public anti-junta sentiment among the expatriate Greeks and her subsequent disillusionment at how easily it crumbled again— these unquestionably mirror Andreas's own reactions and form the focal point of his parable of insubordination and self-discovery. For a brief, incandescent moment, as she designs posters for the revolution, the student ceases to be preoccupied by self-disgust. As she momentarily breaks free of the constraints of bourgeois morality and politics, she realizes every Greek's longingly imagined, autonomous self. Breaking the bonds of convention, she sees even the pretentious expatriates whose posturing had previously so angered her achieve a measure of dignity. At such moments, the internal contradictions of the formal, public order are exposed; and the ideal type of the Greek rebel, even for those who—like Andreas in some contexts—endorse the heroic values of masculinity, may become a woman.

But Andreas recognizes that such moments are in actuality tragically evanescent; bourgeois society all too easily restores and enforces a moral universe in which ambition must always vie with self-denigration: "Oh that wretched, ridiculous self of mine!" Then the picture returns to the confines of its frame, which determines its value and protects it from the conceptual pollution of uncertainty, indefinition, rebellion, art, femaleness. It is not clear whether the student will slip back into her former despondency, but the possibility looms large as, the riots rapidly fading into a hesitant memory, she prepares to return to the constricting proprieties of Athens.

And those proprieties were now truly constricting. On 21 April 1967, a military junta staged a ruthless coup. New daydreams succumbed to old nightmares once again. The picture frame had suddenly grown to monstrous proportions, choking the artistry and freedom within its inflexible clutch to a painful, asphyxiated death.

7 ▣

SORDID POWER:

COLONELS AND EXILES

When the military junta took power in 1967, I was an undergraduate in England. My Greek friends, who were already quite numerous, were, in varying degrees, hostile to this new development but certainly did not discourage my interest in going to Greece. As a result, that was the year of my first visit to Crete. Two years later, I was a scholarship student at the University of Athens, still largely insensitive to the full horror of what was taking place around me. I mention this because I do not want to gain unjustified admittance to the chorus, of foreigners and Greeks alike, who claim to have fought the junta throughout its existence. Some did so, and a few paid the highest price. The junta counted on the willingness of most people to compromise, however, and it was not disappointed. Especially for the Greeks themselves, the fragile gains made since the last round of repression were not only political: many clung to their new comforts and financial security and dreaded the prospect of renewed civil violence. Nor was it clear that the politicians had moved beyond the graft of earlier times, as the colonels were quick to point out once their coup had succeeded.

Andreas himself expresses discomfort at being among those who fled instead of fighting, a dilemma that appears to replay his predicament when the Germans invaded in 1941. Yet—once again—what could one person do alone? The politicians offered no solutions: *Black April* is partly an indictment of the political leadership whose nerve failed at the critical moment of the 1967 coup d'état and so reinforced the apathy of the populace. Were these leaders worth fighting for? What other alternatives existed? Others thought the braver course was to carry the fight to the streets and mountains of Greece. Similar dilemmas existed for foreigners: did their presence buttress the colonels or let some fresh air into the stifled country? For Andreas, as for many people, practical and personal considerations partially resolved these dilemmas.

When Andreas left Greece after the 1967 coup it was to escape a probable return to Youra, which would have plunged his wife into destitution. She joined him in Sweden but became pregnant and returned to Greece to ensure her child's right to Greek citizenship: a concern of many exiles was not to concede this precious right to the colonels' arbitrary decisions. When Andreas returned to Greece in 1968, it was, again, not to fight but to look after his family.

He, at least, had suffered exile and imprisonment in the earlier phases of Greece's painful groping for democracy, had proved his capacity for resistance and endurance, and had now tried to continue the struggle through his writing. *Black April* was possibly the first Greek book about the junta to appear in a foreign language. Andreas also had a pragmatic understanding of how deeply entrenched the horror and violence were, how ready to break out anew. Andreas's diary prose in *Prohibited* and in the short story "Twenty New Year's Days" materializes the deadening, drumlike, daily repetitions of pain, each entry a microcosm of decades of suffering. As he had shown by condemning the Moscow show trials of Yuli Daniel and Andrei Sinyavski in 1966, moreover, he did not consider repression a right-wing monopoly. But in an agonized land trapped by the tectonic plates of global ideological polarization, moderation is not a popular creed.

Indeed, such were the conditions for the creation of a self-fulfilling prophecy that the center would not hold. The self-stereotype of the Greeks as immoderate atomists, an image that has also permeated social-science writing about the country, provided a handful of rightist military officers with the excuse they sought for taking control of the country and resuscitating the persecution of the Left. Claiming that the unruly Greeks needed a firm hand and proclaiming themselves the surgeons who would mend this sick body politic and bring it back to civic health, the colonels struck down a fragile and hesitant democracy already sapped by an interventionist monarchy and by foreign subversion (see Clogg 1972; Van Dyck 1997).

That corrosion of the political process shows how deeply the several reactionary forces feared a popular mandate. It also illustrates how easily right-wing forces could exploit the stereotype of disparity between the supposedly unruly Greek and disciplined "European" in order to promote the interests of the western powers over the cause of Greek autonomy. A brief outline of these events will show how this self-fulfilling prophecy—so like those of the fatalistic oriental or the passive native of colonial imagination—was generated and sustained.

In the late 1950s, political repression began to falter. In Western Europe there were increasing protests against the continuing detention of political prisoners in Greece. When the aging prime minister, General

Pangalos, suddenly died, he was succeeded by his foreign minister. Constantine Karamanlis was a complex and subtle politician. He understood the importance of at least cosmetic concessions. He was also extremely resistant to control by the palace, with which his relations became increasingly testy as he gradually loosened the restraints on the opposition parties.

On 3 November 1963, for the first time since the Civil War, national elections led to the formation of a government of the political middle ground. Karamanlis, to his indignant astonishment, discovered that the ungrateful electorate was actually willing to make use of the political flexibility he had bestowed upon it. Suddenly out of office, he stormed off to Paris.

Substantive change seemed possible at last. Beholden neither to the palace nor to the military, buoyed by a popular mandate despite rightist attempts to suborn the electoral process, the liberal-Venizelist victors—the Center Union party under George Papandreou—were cautiously jubilant. Their optimism appeared to be justified when new elections on 16 February 1964 converted their plurality into a full working majority. Although at first a number of political prisoners remained in detention, most citizens were soon able to enjoy the pleasures of a free press, the partial restoration of the ordinary spoken (or demotic) language as the medium of the press and of education, and the gradual lessening of police surveillance over everyday life. Papandreou was no leftist—he had been the British authorities' choice for prime minister in exile during the earlier phases of the war and had refused to form a coalition with the procommunist United Democratic Left after his initial victory in 1963—but he did appear to espouse a more democratic approach to governing the country.

The palace was most displeased. Apparently under the thumb of his domineering mother, the recently widowed Queen Frideriki, the young King Constantine began to intrigue with various rightist parliamentary factions to buy the loyalty of one Center Union deputy after another. Matters came to a head over the prime minister's decision to install his own son, Andreas, as Minister of Defense—a move that surely presaged a thoroughly inconvenient democratization of the entire military establishment.[1] The young monarch was easily persuaded to install a series of caretaker governments, each falling victim in turn to his caprices and the

---

1. In May of 1965, a left-leaning plot involving an organization called Aspídha ("Shield") was uncovered in the military and Andreas Papandreou was accused of complicity; the public prosecutor subsequently tried to have his parliamentary immunity lifted so that he could be tried. Meanwhile, his suspected involvement had given the opposition the basis on which to charge that his father, the prime minister, should not also assume the defense portfolio, and this was a major contributory cause of the collapse of the elected government in 1965 and the eventual coup of 1967.

venality of its own members. These apostates allegedly accepted huge sums of money as the reward for their desertion; some became government ministers. Public disgust with the politicians meanwhile ate away at their moral authority. Rumors of an impending coup were everywhere. Indeed, both the king and the generals were plotting when a handful of more junior but ruthlessly decisive officers seized the initiative. Humiliating the king, emasculating their seniors' opposition, drawing NATO and the CIA into their anticommunist rhetoric, they laid plans for a regime to be distinguished by its cruel refinements of ignorance and repression.

On the night of 20–21 April 1967, there was an air of fearful anticipation. The date set for elections was less than a month away and the liberal Center Union, still led by George Papandreou, seemed certain to win again. The colonels struck.

Their sense of timing and their preparation were all too effective, and they met virtually no resistance from a political leadership that only days before had been noisily proclaiming its readiness to sacrifice everything for the salvation of democracy. Andreas has captured the frustrations of the time with devastating accuracy:

> Where are our leaders? A few days ago they were all shouting in the streets, at demonstrations, in the [entertainment] centers, in the newspapers, at political gatherings, that dictatorship would not pass. That the era of fascism was past. And that they would be the first to confront it head-on [literally: with their breasts], they'd set the example. They would sacrifice themselves, die for the political system, for the Constitution, for Freedom. . . . That they were the fighters of the E.D.A. [United Democratic Left] Party. The parliamentary deputies are most or all graduates of the jails and of exile. Many, of course, have been arrested. The military managed their plan well. They have addresses, they have names, residences. In the small hours they grabbed a few thousand people who had been convicted by military courts during the past two decades. They have the addresses of them all at the Ministry of Military Affairs. All the communists who have faced a military court since the Decembrist revolt of '44 have been picked up. But a few of them are walking about freely. No one knows how the degree of danger to public security has been defined. A few people say the arrests have been random. That the police, who have everyone's file, address, and place of residence, isn't showing much of a disposition to collaborate with the military. The police commanders want to establish whether the Palace is on the side of the putschists. Whether the Americans are supporting it, if it's a sure thing, whether the coup will succeed. They're all speculating. Many of them agree to collaborate right away. Some police stations are in on the game and are functioning within their jurisdictions. Others are idling. But everyone is awaiting developments.
>
> In the streets people who are well-known organizers with a history of

revolutionary activity are walking about. Why don't those people speak out? Why doesn't just one of them get up and fall in front of a tank? The people await a leader who will shout. Who'll resist . . .

And the silence descends. As the day goes on, exhaustion and disillusionment, indifference and a sense of abandonment affect people more and more. Most believe that the progressivist forces are getting ready to do something. The parties and political organizations. They can't let a whole people be gagged and chained. It's inconceivable that these same individuals would leave their fate in the hands of a few military officers.

Rumors start to circulate. In Crete there's been an uprising. Battles are going on in Thessaloniki. The air force is against the coup. The planes have been immobilized at the airfields. The navy has tied up its ships at the dock and the other bases. No one is with them.

No one is with them. . . . But who is against them?

Everyone says just that, but no one does a thing. No one takes a single step, lets off a single burst of gunfire, cries out a single time. There's not a single outburst. No one. . . . (*Black April*, pp. 57–58)

The colonels had made their plans with consummate care. They took over the radio network, arrested key politicians of all stripes (it soon became clear that outspoken democratic rightists were in as much disfavor as liberals and leftists), moved tanks into strategic positions, clamped down a curfew, prohibited gatherings of more than five people, announced that they had saved the country and nation from a dastardly communist plot, and forced the king to sign a series of edicts that progressively strengthened their nascent grip on total power. NATO averted its eyes; foreign capital seized the opportunity to suck the fragile economy dry; and the politicians' nerve failed those whose courage had sustained them.

▌ After so much self-sacrifice, enthusiasm, and abandonment of personal interests on behalf of the common good, we have politicians of the Center and Left who despised the intelligence of the people. They had acted, taken up politics, or behaved in such a manner as to show who—that you, o people of Greece—would be killed whenever "we" thought it fitting for you to be killed, and would go to jail or into exile when "we" thought you should. You'll vote, you'll demonstrate when *we* want you to and in the way *we* want. The slightest disagreement constitutes treason. We are the leaders, the wise ones, we are the bosses, no one has—or may have—an independent opinion. And when what happens, or is about to happen, is a mistake, we are not accountable to anyone. You are obliged to obey, to make sacrifices, to vote for us, to fight; and we'll arrange your fate. We who by the grace of God and of all progressive thought are the chosen ones, will decide, we will adjudicate, and we will remain, undamaged, on our thrones. . . . You are obliged to labor, to struggle, to die, and to put up with us. (*Black April*, p. 69)

Elderly communists suddenly found themselves back on Youra; youthful dissidents died under mysterious circumstances, their funerals undertaken by the military in sinister secrecy, their families charged for the burial expenses afterward; and the children of well-known leftists were tortured until they sang paeans of praise to their new "father"—George Papadopoulos, ringleader of the "revolution of 21 April."

The coup gave material form to the ultimate perversion of bureaucratic process. Greek civic institutions are compounded of three main traditions: the German legal positivism brought by the Bavarian monarchy in the first years of the state, a system that frames an individual's legal rights in terms of belonging to clearly defined categories rather than by virtue of being an independent social actor; the preceding Ottoman administrative system with its separate administration for each confessional community, and with its loose control over the system of favors and patronage through which the powerful prospered while the weak indentured themselves to those who could protect them from the worst ravages of the system; and a local value system which similarly recognizes a balance, or strain, between centripetal force of cultural and social ascription and the centrifugal imperatives of social agency embodied in notions of an individualizing self-regard.

These are the forces that have produced the powerful pattern whereby Greeks distinguish between categorical dislike for certain categories of people—Turks, Gypsies, Jews, and various religious groups, for example—and affection for particular members of those groups. The junta, like most totalitarian regimes, tried to obliterate any hint of agency that it had not sanctioned, reducing all individuality to mere categories. This was an ideological practice that fostered racism at the highest levels. It identified patriotism with hatred for those who did not completely fit the religious, linguistic, and political definitions by which the junta decided who was truly Greek. Its logic appears most compactly in the slogan "Hellas of the Hellenic Christians," a term that elided centuries of conflict between the Orthodox Church and the pre-Christian philosophy and religion of ancient Greece, placed communists (as atheists) beyond the ethnic pale and—once again—as "Bulgarians," treated claims to minority status as treason, and fueled a veritable industry devoted to the manufacture of subcategories within the overall classification. Writing of the torturers at the notorious jail on Bouboulinas Street in Athens, Andreas satirizes the taxonomic obsessions of the power-drunk military:

▌ They have studied anthropology, pathology, and, above all, psychology. They have worked for years to create archives just like those of psychiatric researchers. Every day they have in their hands hundreds of laboratory animals [the prisoners]. As soon as they set eyes on a person they know how long he can hold out, how much he can stand up to them (if he can stand up to them at all). And when occasionally they make an error in their assessment, they are not disappointed. On the contrary, they are full of joy. Exceptions fill them with enthusiasm and enrich their archive. Codification and systematization acquire new twists in interrogation methodology. (*Black April*, p. 167)

This is the vicious lunacy of Nazism, with which, as Andreas points out, the junta had historical as well as ideological links (see *Black April*, pp. 149–50). It is the metastasis of repressive routines to their most deadly extreme. It is, above all, a system that denies the very possibility of agency beyond that of the self-appointed guardians of the nation.

Its effectiveness lay to a significant degree in its ability to penetrate every moment of a person's life. The requirement that every citizen carry an identity card made control relatively easy. When the police make their predawn raid on the *boîte* (informal music bar) where the central character, a young woman named Loukia, and her friends are entertaining themselves, one man turned out not to have his card:

■   "What the devil, you go out of your houses without your identity cards?"

"Why? Is it the [German] Occupation, or are we going to the Bank? I went out to relax a bit and I didn't take it with me. It was in my other jacket."

"You have another jacket? We'll see about that!"

But the gentleman sitting there in the corner was an obstinate fellow: "I'm not carrying it on me, gentlemen, but here's my business card."

(K.P. Appellate Court Prosecutor)

"Where did you find that, eh? You're a tricky one, all right. We'll get you sorted out up at the station. I think we've hit the jackpot. Commander, sir, this gentleman says he's an appellate prosecutor. A fine place you've found to spend your evening. . . ."

"Watch yourself, my good sir, do you hear?"

"Come along now and don't make any trouble." (*Black April*, pp. 30–31)

Depression falls. As Loukia says (p. 31): "Why should a person depend on papers of this kind? In reality, not on those, but on the people who sign them, on the stamps, on the plastic covers, and on numbers. I, it says, am [number] 663479. . . ."

This passage rang all too true, although, as a foreigner, I fared rather better when an extremely youthful policeman stopped me for jaywalking during the junta years. Initially delighted, it seemed, to discover that I had no identity card on me, he then discovered to his consternation that I was a foreigner (although, he was quick to point out, I should have been carrying my passport). Perhaps anxious to avoid potential embarrassments with citizens of friendly powers, he finally puffed himself up and told me, "I'm letting you go because I like your sincerity. I could have turned you in at the station. But don't do it again!" True to the junta's claims of psychological omniscience, which flew in the face of Greek commonsense skepticism about knowing the minds of others, he used his assessment of my sincerity as the improbable means of preserving his threatened authority. Such actions are only plausible if all agree to the fiction on which they rest, in which the sincerity of the citizen becomes the coercive external mark of the government's authenticity.[2]

Andreas himself had a similar experience, although one that could have had far more serious consequences, several years before the junta came to power. Dragged into the security police office and asked whether he was a communist (which, of course, his tormentors knew full well he was), he retorted, "What do you want? I *am* a communist—do you want to discuss it?" And the policeman replied, "Well, sir, since you are one, I congratulate you on your sincerity!" Such pinpricks were the constant reminder of how a totalitarian state could become the judge of one's innermost thoughts, and hence, indeed, of one's sincerity. Trivial they may have been, but they served to reproduce with numbing frequency the denial of personal autonomy that reached its greatest intensity in the extraction of loyalty declarations.

Such a system penetrates the most humdrum areas of everyday life and turns external trivia into the apparatus of civic discipline. In one scene in the novel, the inhabitants of an apartment block are trying to decide what color their balcony awnings should be. Thus far they have not adhered to a single-color scheme, and this has created friction:

▎ The grocer downstairs had a green one, the *karamanlikós* [supporter of the exiled right-wing politician, Constantine Karamanlis] in the *rétiré* had red. And because this meeting needed more than five people in attendance, they had to get a permit—and a policeman in attendance—from an already overworked police station. Eventually the permit came through. (*Black April*, pp. 131–32)

---

2. In recent tax reforms, citizens are required to make "declarations of sincerity," which supposedly render them morally and legally more liable for their tax returns than was formerly the case. Precisely because this system introduces a new stringency in the application of the law, I doubt whether anyone in Greece seriously views these as a test of sincerity as such.

They soon realized that red was out for political reasons and scurried to conform (p. 133):

> ■   Green was supported by everyone, even the [*karamanlikós*] owner of the *retiré*. And the manager [*dhiakhiristís*], looking at the Junta's representative of "law and state" in the eyes, made a little speech "in support of the ideals of fellow-feeling, love, the citizen's obligations toward the authorities, the necessity of making religion and education the goal of all, especially religion." And thus he also "incidentally" mentioned "our ancient forefathers with whom we should have a special relationship because of the political system . . . because . . ."—and he stopped. That was a mistake, but the policeman didn't notice because at that moment he was staring at the manager's bookshelves . . .—"Because our apartment block is in the Doric style. . . ."
>   And the decision was taken "in favor of green."

The predisposition to uniformity and a respect for categories, as well as their willingness to be taken to absurdist extremes in the pursuit of Classical ancestry ("our apartment block is in the Doric style"), made bourgeois Athenians easy prey for the junta's taxonomic voraciousness. While Andreas is clearly enjoying himself at the junta's (and the bourgeoisie's) expense here, he nonetheless uses the scene to demonstrate how deeply and how easily the junta's predilection for total control could penetrate the most ordinary aspects of everyday life—right down to mundane matters of domestic space. Moreover, it was said that one in every four apartment block concierges was a police informer (*khafiés*) and that among the students a red line left by wearing a uniform cap betrayed the fact that many were policemen in disguise; in *Black April* (pp. 32, 134), Andreas mentions both these examples of the authorities' terrifying ubiquity.

Andreas Nenedakis recorded these horrors from exile in Sweden, where he had moved from his initial refuge in Paris soon after the coup. His *Black April*, first published in Swedish and widely acclaimed in that country, was the first major Greek indictment of the junta to appear in a foreign language. He also writes about the junta from the perspective of his subsequent exile in Paris in *The Seine, My Home*. The two works are very different from each other in content and tone, although both contain scathing accounts of the egotistical squabbling of the Greek politicians in exile.

Black April was also submitted for a possible French edition in Paris, but, as Andreas rather bitterly notes in the introductory matter to the Greek edition that finally appeared after the junta's collapse (p. 7), the jealousy of the Greek expatriate community was apparently the main impediment to that venture. (Something similar happened to his attempt to have an earlier book, *Prohibited*, published in Swedish.) For Andreas, such mishaps were simply further confirmation that politicians were more interested in settling personal and family scores than in restoring their country's freedom—a bitter fact of the Civil War years as well as the junta period, and one that provides a context for understanding the literary vendetta in which Andreas himself was later to become engaged.

Black April is largely written from the perspective of the fictional young woman, Loukia, this time in the third person. A scathing denunciation of the junta, it captures the tense mood of expectation on the night of the colonels' coup with the same laconic despair with which it describes the sudden return of harassment and torture into the lives of the victims of earlier persecutions. Occasionally parodic, especially when it lampoons the colonels' inept attempts to manage the syntactic contortions of the neo-Classical language (which they promoted with a zeal equalled only by their incompetence in it), it offers a spare but effective account of the brutality with which a truly banal regime, the embodiment of bourgeois respectability gone mad, attempted to lock creativity and criticism in an eternal iron cage. *The Seine, My Home* focuses instead on the life of the exiles after the coup. It is as critical of Greek politicians in exile as it is of the colonels themselves. A directly autobiographical account of Andreas's own quixotic tryst with poverty among the *clochards*, the Parisian derelicts, and of his growing disgust with the antics of his more fortunate fellow exiles in Paris, this work documents Andreas's own sense of despair—at his own desperate economic situation, at the political exiles' destructive self-importance, and at the long reach of the junta's power. Taken together, the two books are a personal testament to the helplessness that such a regime can sow among its opponents.

When the coup took place, Andreas and Elli had been married for a year and were living in a comfortable house in Ambelokipi, a suburb of Athens. The house had been part of Elli's dowry. The police arrested a cousin of Andreas, a communist and recent political prisoner who had just been released and had come to stay for a while with Andreas and Elli. Through him, the police tracked down Andreas as well. They woke him up in the night by knocking insistently on the door. Elli thought it was the concierge until their banging became violent. Barely allowing Andreas to throw on a pair of trousers, they dragged him off to the police station. There they proposed that he collaborate with them. His reply, predictably, was a contemptuous refusal: "Since I'm a leftist—I'm a Commie, I am—what kind of collaboration could we possibly have?" They kept him sitting there for a long time, forcing him to observe the beating of a long stream of younger detainees and compromising his reputation by making it appear as though he was in fact working with them.

In the end, however, true to their cat-and-mouse tactics (and no doubt because they considered him very small game), they let him return home. Soon they were back, rummaging and wrecking. They confiscated his personal library; one of his own books, *Prohibited,* was already on the junta's list of proscribed titles. Andreas was also aware that his having distributed pamphlets on behalf of one of the smaller resistance organizations in Athens was almost certainly well known to the police. Andreas recounts how the novelist Stratis Tsirkas asked to meet him over coffee and told him that PAM, the largest of the resistance groups, was demanding in the name of unity that the smaller ones close down. Andreas, furious, refused. Soon he discovered that people knew about his resistance work and, attributing the leaks to deliberate rumor-mongering by the PAM leadership, decided that Greece was no longer safe for him (*Policemen of Stockholm,* pp. 169–71).

He decided to go overseas. After a brief, disappointing stay in Rome, he tried his luck in Paris. At the Athens airport, where the authorities continued their sadistic toying with the harried would-be exiles, there were bad moments; but some of the officials, as Andreas is characteristically careful to recall, warned the exiles of trouble and pushed them through passport control too fast for their less sympathetic colleagues to have second thoughts. Thus Andreas found himself, almost penniless and bereft of his young wife's companionship, falling from the sky "like a meteorite" into an expensive, uncomprehending, and sometimes actively hostile world. Speaking no Italian and little French, isolated by deafness as his mother had been by her blindness, and prickly and forthright by turns, he soon grew as impatient of his fellow exiles' posturing as he was unmoved by his involuntary hosts' often grudging hospitality. His only constant companion was a brooding loneliness.

In those early days, the junta was usually willing to let the leftists they considered less dangerous depart—for Moscow, they derisively insisted—and in fact after one month in Paris Andreas did go on to Bucharest. There he met Dominique Eudès, a left-wing French journalist and author of *The Kapetanios* (1972), who was at work on that book by interviewing all the communist exiles he could find who had memories of the Civil War. In Bucharest, Andreas would have been able to live comfortably for a year off the royalties from two of his books which had been translated into Romanian. But Romania was a socially chilly place with no work for a new political refugee, and Andreas hastened back to Paris.

In Paris, however, his poverty made it all but impossible for him to rent lodgings on a regular basis. Indeed, his memoir of those days, *The Seine, My Home,* records his adventures living a vagabond existence with the homeless *clochards* underneath the spacious bridges that spanned the river and its embankments. His old friend in exile, Yannis Angelopoulos, thinks that the impression of virtually complete vagabondage during his entire sojourn in Paris could mislead an unwary reader: there were times when Andreas was able to earn a little money—hauling goods at the meat market of Les Halles, as Andreas himself records—and turn it into solid food and modest lodgings.

On one such occasion a substantial check suddenly came in the mail. It bore the perplexing legend, "*Antoniou C-nt. R.G.*," which it took Andreas some lengthy head-scratching to decipher—not least because of his relative unfamiliarity with the Latin alphabet. Suddenly he remembered that many months earlier in Athens a Major Antoniou, commander of the Royal Greek Police (French *commandant, Royale Gendarmerie*) had commissioned Andreas to do some research and organization for a massive police history he was writing (*Seine*, pp. 52–56). This episode perhaps belongs to the more "handicraft" and entrepreneurial side of Andreas's authorial career. As an author who finds no virtue in literary snobbery, moreover, he has some tolerance of such artisanal writers, even though many of them are among his categorical enemies—military, police, royalists. Some of these, as the Antoniou incident showed, could prove to be decent people with whom he could develop ties of warm affection. Antoniou had set out to write his history with very little idea of what such an undertaking would entail. He was fortunate in his choice of publisher, who was "perhaps the only one to admit he was a merchant" (*Seine*, p. 53)—thereby showing a sincerity of which Andreas clearly approved. Antoniou needed a researcher; the publisher put him in touch with Andreas, whose political convictions he was nevertheless careful to communicate to the police major just in order to cover himself:

> Major Antoniou and I became friends from the very first day. The poor man was quite out of his depth in the labyrinth of editorial work and the printers, publishers, and typesetters had led him to feel that he would never be able to get the job done. He seemed bewildered and dazed. He had worked for a number of years, and had gathered all those data about the activity of the *gendarmerie* since 1821, and indeed regarded General Makriyannis as its chief and founder.[3] And now that he had finished writing his History, he found himself confronted by these insurmountable obstacles. At first, of course, he had objections to my involvement because of who I was, but Ladias [the publisher] insisted that I was the only person who could really help him and that for the work that I would undertake to perform I had asked for half of what others would demand. My task was to hand over, each week, six-

---

3. General Makriyannis, a hero of the War of Independence, wrote his *Memoirs* (1992) in a simple demotic Greek that makes the work one of the key documents for the emergence of a demotic tradition.

teen color photographs of various police generals, chiefs, and heroes, and my pay represented 50 percent of the price that the printers were asking. He, however, wondered—and asked me to explain—why my prices were so low and how I would manage to do this work since I didn't have printing equipment, presses, or any of the tools of the trade.

So I explained to him that I was one of those intermediaries who nibbled away at small jobs simply in order to exist but who had both various abilities and kinds of knowledge; and that these jobs got finished fast and more cheaply. In the end he consented but I had to show him a sample of my work; and when I gave him the photograph of the police chief he had given me as a test, he was delighted.

I don't know—and didn't care—whether he checked up on my personal record. Then again my police file would have entertained him and he would perhaps have confirmed what I claimed when I told him that I found policemen appealing precisely because they have no connection with literature—he himself was an exception. As is well known, each file is a copy of the next and when you read one you can be certain that you've read them all—and you wonder how these people manage any degree of credibility, what with their pompous verbiage (*verbalismós*) and the verbal diarrhea that typifies their poisonous documents.

Antoniou even, eventually, took Andreas into the "hornets' nest" itself—the archives of the police headquarters. But Andreas was sorely disappointed in what he found there: "They all had round little bellies; they were all talking about their refrigerators, their apartments, or their bathwater-heaters. And I thought policemen never washed."

Andreas and Antoniou both found the experience hugely entertaining at another level:

● "If those with whom we were chatting in the junior officers' common room knew who you were, and particularly that I had taken you with me right into the archives, they would roast the two of us alive." To thank him I replied that these people had seemed decent and that he shouldn't have said what he had said. Perhaps to repay my ceremoniousness he replied, "If all communists are like you, I have committed great crimes." "I'm afraid I'm the worst," I replied to him. And it's true that my hair stood on end because the major had been the chief of the Traffic Police in Thessaloniki and I had heard of him by name before I ever met him.[4]

4. Gregory Lambrakis, a parliamentary deputy for EDA, was killed in a staged traffic accident in Thessaloniki in what was widely seen as a police-directed assault on the emergence of a strong progressive movement in Greek politics. The youth group named for him, the Lambrákidhes (note the "patrilineal" form of the name), was active in resistance to the Papadopoulos (1967–73) and Ioannides (1973–74) dictatorships.

This strange friendship celebrates reciprocity: the major pays his debts but also opens up his mind in an apparent response to Andreas's tolerant stance. In the end, his disaffection cost Antoniou dearly. A royalist, he presumably could not stomach the junta's abuse of the monarchy—and, after the king's disastrously ill-conceived countercoup in the December of 1967, its barely concealed contempt for the king. Andreas, attentive to even his friends' foibles, thought that the good major was probably indignant that the junta showed no interest in bringing his police history to publication. (He also attributes Antoniou's prompt payment not to feelings of penitence for his earlier persecution of communists but to his disgust with the colonels' indifference.) Whatever his motives, Antoniou joined the resistance but soon thereafter suffered a fatal heart attack. Andreas almost managed to survive on the money Antoniou sent him: "May God forgive your [sins], my dear friend Antoniou, major in the Royal Gendarmerie; the check that you sent me was almost salvation enough" (*Seine*, p. 56)—for Andreas's survival, that is, but also perhaps—Andreas admits to a playful sense of irony here, having been an atheist for virtually all his remembered years—for the major's immortal soul.

Antoniou's project excited Andreas's sympathies to a perhaps surprising degree. The major honestly wished to commemorate the gendarmerie—an institution with ideals for which Andreas had more respect than he entertained toward most of its members or their practices. He actually would have liked to find fierce warriors instead of banal fools down there in the archives. These would have been worthy enemies. Writing of the torturers on Youra in *Prohibited,* he is scathing about what he sees as their betrayal of the trust implied by their membership of a royal police force, regardless of his contempt for the monarchy itself. For Andreas, the paradox of friendship with a police officer was what gave it depth. His warm affection for Antoniou bears all the immense tension without which Andreas, like many Greeks and perhaps especially like many Cretans, would find friendship merely insipid. He was also notably responsive, as we have seen, to moments of personal growth: in his courteous reply to Antoniou as they were leaving the police archives, we hear the voice of the young Andreas/Xopateras discovering the folly of chauvinism and intolerance.

Nor did Andreas feel remotely uncomfortable about helping the author of a police history. Andreas has no illusions about writing as a profession. He does not set it off completely from more mundane ways of making money. In its more pretentious forms, it can at least be fairly harmless, and in Antoniou's case it was evidently not done for self-aggrandizement. Andreas was less charitable toward others. Musing on the ambitions of self-important military men bypassed by the more worldly colonels of the junta, for example, he draws a wickedly accurate portrait of the self-important minor author:

▌ Throughout his life an officer wants to arrive at the substance and rank of being a general. And when he gets there he plays politician or author. And when—of course—he writes his biography or a book about some great battle of the past the only harm it does is to his pocket. In any case, publishing a book is no big deal. With six months' salary or a part of his severance pay he achieves immortality. In the National Library his name will occasion a catalog card. And the first work of this new intellectual leader will await the second, third, and fourth books, to be shelved just as it was. The pages of the book will remain uncut,[5] uncreased, ironed smooth, as shiny as the boots of the general-turned-author, who drops in on the Library from time to time and asks to see his book so that he can check whether it has been opened by anyone. (*Black April*, p. 108)

Antoniou's project was different. Andreas's role in it was a humble one, that of a fixer taking pride in his cleverness. But Andreas also takes an amused and unpretentious view of his own status as an author and clearly saw nothing demeaning in his subordinate position in Antoniou's project. Like most of the known communists, he had long been forced to take whatever work he could find. In Antoniou, an unexpectedly sympathetic employer, he enjoyed the progressive opening of the major's mind. Perhaps he saw his chance in Antoniou's admiration for Makriyannis. As with Venizelos, who in death was to become the secular saint of political parties from the extreme Left to the extreme Right, so in Makriyannis—rebellious and culturally nativist general of the War of Independence—a royalist and a communist could discover the common ground of an admirable pride.

The *verbalismós* of the police files and that of assorted autobiographical generals was not Antoniou's language. Culturally, that alone placed this police historian more in alignment with the klefts than with his potbellied colleagues—or, for that matter, with the posturing political exiles Andreas came to detest in Paris.

With them, indeed, a familiar metaphor reappears in Andreas's discourse: the struggle between the suffering folk of revolutionary Greece and a petty and rapacious establishment that continued the repression of the foreign tyrants. The "relentless" youths who harangued the older leftists especially provoke his scorn:

▌ They badger us night and day about our mistakes without taking account of any mitigation, any justification. We should have won, we should have

---

5. Until recently, many books were published, as elsewhere in Europe, with their pages uncut so that readers had to perform this task for themselves.

brought the matter of the Resistance to pass and achieved its completion without being defeated—only those who vanquish are ever right—and we should have pulled it off even though three or four entire empires fell upon us. Our mistakes, they say, are the proximate cause, not the war waged against us by enemies, allies, and friends alike. That's it: had we won fairly and squarely, now that we've lost . . . we've lost affection, respect, and standing. Everything else is mere detail; we've become the whipping-post for all the compromisers, the devotees, the *décadents*⁶ who found this a chance to cure their complexes. On top of everything else they don't permit us—or in their own way turn their noses up in the air and disapprove or make fun of—the very slightest mention of those years or of our torment in jail and exile. In other words, it bothers them. They do not wish to hear about all that and don't even want *us* to speak about it; but the complex that has them in its grip is obvious. Of course, the same things happened to the fighters of the 1821 Revolution: the Fanariots who came to Greece to take the reins of administration treated them like whipping-posts and excluded them from power because they were bothered by the klefts' wounds, by their poverty and illiteracy, their way of dressing, their speech, and their demands for the recognition of their struggle and for a better life. (*Seine*, pp. 82–83)

Andreas soon became thoroughly disgusted with the self-styled resistance in Paris; but he was not much luckier in his attempts to rally support elsewhere. He sought help from the famous actress Melina Mercouri, a dynamic advocate of the antidictatorship movement abroad, and offered some of his books for publication in English as part of the struggle against the right-wing forces in Greece. She passed them on to a committee, informing him in a letter of 25 October 1967 that she was too busy to read them herself. Evidently the committee declined all interest, deciding that *Prohibited* was too "historical" and that *The Daisies of the Saint* merely had "many elements similar to what is happening today in our country." Instead, Mercouri suggested, Andreas should set himself the task of collecting useful information and impressions from Greece and from his sojourn in Western Europe. But that was not what he intended.

In the spring of 1968 Elli managed to leave Greece and come to Andreas in Paris together with their baby son Nikolas (an affectionate variant of Nikolaos, the formal name he was given, according to custom, in honor of Andreas's father):

█ A child of five months with big black eyes who smiles continually. My wife talks to him all the time and tells him I'm his father. I ask her if he under-

---

6. The word is in French in the original, but in Greek letters.

stands and she reassures me on that account. I feel reborn. I don't mind much if she sees what I've been reduced to. (*Seine*, p. 217)

But then, in May, the student revolution rocked Paris. Andreas, who had participated in the street riots, was suddenly suspect. France was no longer a friendly place: the police, who (as he notes in *Seine*) could be deliberately obtuse when they did not wish to take action, could no longer ignore him. He did not wish to be ignominiously—and dangerously— deported to Athens. So he left for Sweden, a land where he hoped to find the true benefits of practical socialism and a safer haven for himself and his ideas.

But there, too, his isolation from both the local elite—once again he failed to learn his host country's national language—and his fellow Greeks cost him dearly. True, his *Black April* was published in Swedish and to some critical acclaim. But his attempt to have *Prohibited* published by a Swedish house foundered on the usual petty jealousies: a Greek eval- uator made sure it was suppressed. Nor were all his problems with the Greeks. He found Swedish society impersonal, hypocritical, and unwel- coming—and, again with one or two notable exceptions, unwilling or unable to understand him. Elli joined him again for a while, but she even- tually returned to Greece to raise their child there. Even while she was in Stockholm, the silences between them were hard to bridge: he was filled with a sense of futility while she was focused on motherhood. He became increasingly despondent and irascible and—despite the moral support of a few good friends—came swiftly to the realization that this was not a setting in which he could expect to flourish.

But Andreas's disappointment in his Swedish experience was not con- fined to his personal misadventures or to the antics of his fellow exiles. It was also, or so it seemed to him, ideological. He had expected to find the smiling face of a more or less successful form of socialism in Scandina- via; perhaps inevitably, it failed him. He came face-to-face with some of the contradictions of socialist policies in practice and with the reality of bourgeois domination in a Swedish society in which the dominant values seemed the purest antithesis of what he considered valuable in being Greek.

He came to feel that the undeniable efficiency of the Swedish welfare state had left the citizenry doleful and listless. The irony was not lost on him: "You'll tell me, 'Since you're a socialist, a Commie and all that, how can you say that it has harmed them?'" At his most self-aware, Andreas realized the contradictoriness of his reaction: "there was that division inside me. . . . I knew what was right and what [wasn't], but I wish it could have been otherwise, do you understand?" He could not escape the feeling that the Swedes were suffocating in the deep security of a bureaucracy that—a detail that especially impressed him—required social security tax to be calculated even on a taxi receipt. (In Greece it was all but impossible to get a taxi receipt at all until very recently.) He found the resulting disposition of the Swedes dispiritingly "antipoetic."

But the anti-immigrant hostility of the Swedish police and their evident sympathy for rightist dictatorships in Greece and elsewhere upset him even more. These attitudes, embodied in ruthless policing of street activity, belied the much-vaunted liberalism of the Swedish state. "During the dictatorship I was in Sweden. And when I came back here I wanted to hug the police," he remarked. "Why? Because I saw Swedish policemen, while I was there, and they were killing a person in the [city] center. Why? Because he was running to get away." Andreas thought the Greek police were saints in comparison with their Swedish counterparts. Even allowing for the conventional flourishes of Greek speech, this is a surprising judgment, but it does seem to arise out of Andreas's own inner conflict about the effects of socialism on what he saw as the Swedish spirit.[7]

Andreas could see the humanity even in the most brutal of police thugs in Greece: he could understand their cruelty, much as he hated it, and he saw it as a perversion visited on often quite simple village lads by the bourgeois society they served. In his subtle awareness of his jailers' flawed humanity, he anticipates another hero of left-wing resistance fighters, the would-be assassin of the military dictator George Papadopoulos, Alekos Panagoulis (Fallaci 1980). One of Andreas's fictional characters, a man whose whole life is ground away in prison, year after year, remarks of his gaolers:

▌They are to be pitied. Deep down these people are not all bad. When you probe you find a bit of common humanity. It is fear, however, that forces them. Think of it: we are guarded and beaten by people who fear us. (*Daisies*, p. 123)

As we discover in his account of the Youra prison camp, they are also afraid of their officers and the other, more hardened and experienced guards, who are harangued and bullied until they go from being "numbed" to becoming callous. When one group of new guards arrives on the scene, Andreas even remarks, "They seem like good folks, even though it's clear they haven't yet entered into the spirit of Youra" (*Pro-*

---

7. For example, Greeks will sometimes tell an obviously foreign speaker of their language, "You speak Greek better than we do." This may be a discursive version of the power play entailed in hospitality (see note 6 to chapter 3 above), in which case we can read Andreas's comment on the police as being an ironic exaggeration (which does not preclude interpreting it as *also* an expression of cultural preference for the more direct personal style of Greeks in general).

hibited, p. 55; see also pp. 36, 56). Kostis Papakongos, in a novel about the Greek junta published in Swedish shortly after Andreas's *Black April* came out in the same language and reviewed together with it in some Swedish publications, begins with the following memorable phrase: "Andonis feared two things in his life: the policemen in Greece and the housewives in Sweden. The former used to shove him inside with a kick, while the latter shoved him out with their kicks" (1984 [1969]: 9). Andreas saw things the other way around.

The trouble with Andreas was that he could not abide what he saw as the impersonal violence of the Swedish police; and what he could not abide he could never resist provoking. He was always experimenting and probing and would not be warned off by friends with more local knowledge. Such a friend was Yannis Tsipras, who appears anecdotally in *The Policemen of Stockholm* as the same combination of host, friend, and guide as Yannis Angelopoulos in *The Seine, My Home.* On one occasion he went with Tsipras to hear a Swedish street orator who was attacking one of the secret services of the state. Getting the extremely reluctant Tsipras—who could foresee the outcome—to translate for him, he demanded to know whether these stories were true. Most of the crowd quickly melted away; the few people who remained turned on the two impertinent Greeks and bundled them off to Security headquarters. All that stood between Andreas and expulsion from the country was that, as the author of *Black April,* he was an "author" and therefore respectable. And all this, as Andreas ironically remarked, "in Sweden, a free state."

Andreas was in any case uncomfortable with the role of the recognized author, since he saw behind the respect that it secured for him personally a more general condescension toward—and sometimes contempt for—the exiles who had sought refuge from the Greek dictatorship among the supposedly socialist Swedes. Never happy with the idea of being treated as an honored artist, he saw in the respect it gained him in Sweden—it had never earned him the slightest social advantage in Greece—the confirmation of his worst suspicions: he was not valued for who he was but for the honorific title he could claim. In this context, his pride in being Greek grew apace along with skepticism about Swedish society. Yannis Tsipras, in whose home Andreas lived while he wrote *Black April,* recalls:

● He had a certain vision, which remains a vision . . . for everyone, so to speak, because in practice there are various ways of applying it and various outcomes. Once even Andreas, I remember, was looking at a dictionary of foreign words in the Swedish language . . . and he spotted a great many words that were Greek though the author may have presented them as French or Latin or German and so on. And he burst out about Swedish society—how it receives and deals with immigrants, about how there's a viewpoint that says, "Yes, we are sorry for you"— right?—and "We'll help you." Andreas's stance was that of a person with pride and dignity and he couldn't accept that. Here's a typical response: when Andreas's book *Black April* was published, some journalist—he too was an author, I think—he reviewed Andreas's book in a major newspaper here. Well, the position that this critic, this reviewer, took was as follows, as Andreas described it: Andreas said, "He brought me out onto the balcony, he presented me to the crowd, he made me famous, but at the same time he slapped me in the face in front of the people."

Tsipras, who continues to live in Sweden to this day, thought that Andreas had been too quick to judge the Swedes. But Andreas thought that the Swedes could never understand his deep distaste for playing the role of the bourgeois intellectual.

His dislike of Swedish ways also fed off his growing sense of political disenchantment. In Sweden, perhaps more than at any other time of his life, Andreas encountered troubling contradictions between the theory and practice of socialism. The Greek notion of personal autonomy often means *opposition* to the state, whether recast as the entrepreneurial individualism of the conniving petty capitalist or as the revolutionary ardor of the guerrilla and mutineer—and in Andreas both these self-images had already found fertile ground.[8] Such notions of autonomy clashed with the carefully inculcated Swedish obedience to a paternalistic bureaucracy. Sweden forced Andreas to confront the difficulties of reconciling the self-regard of a traditionalizing Greek with the true communist's respect for collective discipline.

That the Greek communists were capable of tremendous self-control and especially of social harmony is clear from the way they organized their lives collectively in the prison camps of successive right-wing regimes, and Andreas had—notably at Kebeit—participated in these efforts. Indeed, it was part of the rightist stereotype of communists that they were *only* capable of living communally and that, like the "Slavs" (especially the Bulgarians) who inspired them, they lacked the individuality of the true Hellene and European. But what Andreas confronted in Sweden was a culturally unfamiliar sense of how a socialist society should behave. Tsipras again:

8. James Faubion's (1993: 125–26 and passim) discussion of "sovereignty" usefully extends to the larger national and urban-based culture the analysis of Greek concepts of self-regard originally articulated by J. K. Campbell (1964) for a rural community. Especially valuable is Faubion's recognition that this concept can transcend such distinctions as gender, thus producing a variety of responses and forms according to the identity and ideology of each social actor. In the present context, see especially his treatment of one of the women writers also discussed by Karen Van Dyck (1997), Margharita Karapanou.

● He used to comment: "I'm not beholden to anyone. That is, I don't need the protection of some girl in the bureaucracy or some gentleman who works as an employee in some [government] agency or other, to give me instructions. There's your house, there's the toilet—you'll go on that side when you're going up after getting off the train, you'll go up on the right-hand side. . . ." Because, once, someone told Andreas off. That is, it isn't permitted to go up on the right-hand side, you have to go upstairs on the left . . . Now I don't remember how we go upstairs and downstairs because for years I've been traveling by car—that train's boring for me. Anyway. All that has to do with the details of everyday life, and this is something that shows up in Swedish society when they're going about their business. That is, the Swedish citizen is educated to point out to another citizen that he shouldn't park his car where it is not permitted. Right? Whereas none of that interests or bothers a Greek: let him demolish the houses next door if they don't belong to him! It's another mentality, let's say, that lets us have luxury apartment blocks in Greece, right? You admire what's inside, and the streets are appalling, because the streets belong to the municipality—they don't belong to him.

I have quoted this commentary at some length for several reasons. First, Tsipras, an anthropologist, is also a particularly well-adapted member of the expatriate community in Sweden, and his comments represent a more sympathetic version of the stereotypes than the usual European-bashing—a rhetoric in which Andreas, for political as well as cultural reasons, indulges with considerably greater passion. Second, it places the very different relationships between citizen and state that one finds in the two countries in a clear comparative perspective. While there are many individual exceptions, Greeks often explain—or excuse—their own actions and attitudes in terms of these generalizations: they engage in a strategic and practical form of self-essentializing that often allows them immediate tactical advantages even while it locks them in larger structures of power. Finally, what is most important for my present purposes, Tsipras's description provides a vivid account of Andreas's irritation from outside his own writings—for certainly that irritation also suffuses the bitter pages of *The Policemen of Stockholm*.

Andreas's discomfiture with the Swedish practice of socialism was not with its failure to carry out its promises, the practical problem that George Orwell summarized so succinctly: "For a left-wing party in power, its most serious antagonist is always its own past propaganda" (1970 [1968]: 579). On the contrary, in a sense Swedish socialism had effected its program almost too well, leaving the people not only demeaningly beholden to the state but also more interested in the petty details of bureaucratic regulation than in the gloriously messy interdependence of real social life. Andreas's bitterness in *Policemen* later led Lilika Nakou to tell him in a letter (29 June 1981), "It would have been better had you given it the title *The Demythologization of Sweden. . . .* A pity that you made my dream of Sweden disappear, demolished it." A more famous expatriate than Andreas, the American critic and filmmaker Susan Sontag, who was in Sweden at the same time, identified the frustration that underlay Andreas's disappointment: "The experience of any new country unfolds as a battle of cliches—especially if the country is, like Sweden, a rather famous one" (1969: 23). A brief comparison of their respective reactions, like the contrast between Andreas's and Yannis Tsipras's attitudes, reveals the enormous importance that cliches acquire for many expatriates as they attempt to achieve a sense of orientation. The cliches, grounded in the everyday experiences of locals and visitors alike, easily become self-fulfilling prophecies—which is why they cannot simply be dismissed as mere prejudice.

Sontag's description of Sweden and the Swedes explores some prominent cliches and their sources. Her description of "vast self-satisfaction" combined with defensiveness about alleged national failings sounds curiously like Greece. The defensiveness reveals a sense of geographical and political marginality, excused—just as in Greece—on the grounds of small size, and that leads to the identification of "Europe" as somewhere else—although as a place for vacations rather than as the broker of culture and power, as it is in resentful Greek eyes. And the Swedish propensity for self-disparagement in terms of "national character" differs from the Greek only in that Swedes place themselves on the inhibited and quiet end of the scale in opposition to Mediterranean peoples—a contrast with which most Greeks, including Andreas, heartily agree (Sontag 1969: 24).

Sontag compares the Swedes with a fairly wide range of cultures, including Danish, English, and southern European (she mentions Athens), and the fundamental difference she notes turns on the open engagement of passion—which she finds is rare among Swedes. But while Sontag found the Swedes to be as dangerously repressed and self-regulated as Andreas did, she also saw their fear of the police as rooted, not in the officers' capacity for unreasonable violence, but in the population's "level of guilt about infractions of the social code, such as being drunk in public"—the officers themselves "only deal with gross matters" (1969: 26). And while both locate Swedish reserve in a pervasive unwillingness to do anything that might place their security at risk—Sontag wryly observes that "genuine risk-taking (more exactly, the consciousness of taking a risk) is incompatible with the feeling that one is entirely safe" (1969: 34)—Andreas takes a much more sinister view of the specific role of the police in Swedish society.

That view is laid out in damning detail in *The Policemen of Stock-*

holm, a book that infuriated many Swedes precisely because it punctured that "vast self-satisfaction" and revealed the sources of gloomy self-discontent underneath—Sontag's "desolate psychic landscape" (1969: 38). As a Greek, and especially as a Greek with such a strong sense of traditionalism, Andreas seems to have been more forcibly struck even than Sontag by the contrast between Swedish conformism and Greek un-ruliness. But as Greek, too, he should have expected a hostile reaction to his invasion of the host culture's intimate spaces. Yet criticism has never deterred him; and, rather than locating his unease in a conflict between his own individualism and the imperatives of socialist discipline, he instead experienced a reaction akin to Sontag's observation: "Certainly, Sweden is not a socialist country, though . . . one hears many people here assert that it is" (1969: 34)—another cliche to provoke cultural critique. Matters were different for immigrants, some of whom did not dare express their political convictions too openly. An Armenian who had shouted his communist beliefs all over Paris was suddenly bashful, and Andreas observes: "The first socialist state in the world, and it's better not to have 'socialist-communist' desires" (*Policemen*, p. 146). So perhaps Sontag was more accurate in her characterization of the country as not truly socialist at all.

In any event, what both Sontag and Andreas found was a country rigidly controlled by its bourgeois establishment. For Andreas, the nearly penniless political exile, this was perhaps more immediately consequential than it was for the well-supported American filmmaker, particularly because the Swedish aversion to open conflict meant that political activism had to adhere to some irksome rules of etiquette. It was one thing for Swedes to object to the colonels' cruelties—as indeed some did to the point of assisting the exiles in the supply of munitions to the resistance movement. It was quite another for the exiles to question the motives of those benign-seeming policemen who strolled through Stockholm's streets like parochial warlords, or to insist on declaiming their political views in public spaces.

Sontag suggests a plausible explanation for the apparent split between Swedish left-liberal activism and the evidence of a repressed—and repressive—society at home: largely because Swedes were unwilling to engage in direct confrontation, she thought, their own political activism was largely directed toward overseas causes—including, she notes, that of the resistance in Greece, its local supporters galvanized by the presence in Sweden of Andreas Papandreou (Sontag 1969: 35–36).[9] But if Andreas

9. Andreas Papandreou, who in 1981 became the first socialist prime minister of Greece, was the son of veteran liberal politician George Papandreou. Andreas's alleged connections with the Aspídha group were an important factor in the 1963 political crisis that led to his

Nenedakis was right to see the Swedish police as complicit in the persecution of Greek political exiles, Susan Sontag and the Swedish leftists alike must have failed to perceive that complicity at all. On the other hand, as Tsipras noted, Andreas was never happy in Sweden, in a society whose language he did not speak; the junta, with all its evils, was at least familiar territory. And so the cliches became something more—a reason to return to the lair of the beast, once Andreas had convinced himself that even in Sweden he had not escaped the beast's tyranny.

Like other exiles, too, Andreas was struck by what he saw as hypocrisy in the Swedish state—a state that sold arms overseas, for example, even while it played a major role in mediating international conflict. (Sontag writes about this too. In fact, the convergence between her observations and those of Andreas and his friends suggests the strength of the cultural and social dissonance that all the expatriates experienced in Sweden. And, also like Sontag, Andreas did encounter Swedes who were prepared to be sympathetic and open. But those who were willing to make the effort to break the language barrier were few and far between.)

Ultimately, Andreas—a maverick at home and insulated from the Swedes by a language barrier he never managed to surmount—became the victim of his own wiles. A Greek friend in Sweden remembers accompanying him to some bureaucratic service, where Andreas quickly became bored with the even tone of the transaction. (Sontag offers a hilarious example of Swedish conflict avoidance: when two people in a car start to discuss the exact address of their destination, a third companion remarks, "Now, now, let's not quarrel" [1969: 26].) So he tells his friend to translate to the clerk his admiring remark: "You are very beautiful." Naturally the friend was reluctant but Andreas insisted, and the young woman blushed. The friend thinks that Andreas was not particularly interested in flirting with her; in his puckish way he simply wished to create a diversion, having sensed that this kind of behavior was appropriate neither for bureaucracies in general nor for Swedish encounters in particular: "he wanted to change the flow of the discussion, which for Andreas was completely boring and irrelevant!" In other words, he sought to create the tension that in Greece makes an entertainment of every social encounter. The longer he stayed in Sweden, thinks his friend, the more the grave silence of the Swedes oppressed him. Sontag again: "While . . . Swedes are among the most polite and amiable people I have ever met, their politeness contains so much anxiety—so much evident wish to appease, to head off real or imagined unpleasantness—it's hard fully to enjoy it"

---

father's ouster as prime minister and precipitated conditions favorable to the colonels' coup in 1967.

(1969: 28). And Sontag, like Andreas, is moved to be provocative—in her case, by ostentatiously lifting cigarettes from colleagues' packs in violation of the strict avoidance of even such trivial forms of debt.

In this dispiriting atmosphere Andreas found the greatest resonance among the exiles. Even his quarrels with them took culturally familiar forms: he knew how to deal with backstabbing enemies who spoke the same language. As appears to hold true even now for many Greeks in Sweden (Kodrou n.d.: 32–37), he found the local society alienating; his fractious compatriots were more immediately—more *understandably*—infuriating in their divisive politics and jealous backstabbing. The mutually opposed stereotypes of frosty Swede and fiery Greek seemed to reinforce each other's most aggravating proclivities. Andreas was especially incensed with the Greek reviewer who had caused the Swedish publisher to reject *Prohibited*. Through his association with the Lambrákidhes, a politically left-leaning youth group that was very active in resistance to the junta, he discovered the man's identity. One day he came over to Papakongos's home:

● "Look here," he says, "call this fellow." Because Andreas is a real man (*pallikári*), he didn't bow his head! And he talks to him on the telephone, telling him, "You did this dishonorable job," says he, "and you're a Greek," says he, "and you're a compatriot of mine. Well, *fthoúsou* [an expression of disgust, resembling spitting], he says, you ass (*ghaïdhoúri*[10])," says he, "so what should I do to you? Beat you? To beat you up, empty out your guts?" says he, "what should I do to you?" Well. "You're nothing," he tells him, "I'm leaving you right there in your decrepitude and your misery," he says, and puts down the phone. Those weren't Andreas's exact words, but that's the spirit of it as I recall. Andreas recovered right afterward. He recovered because he'd given battle: the guerrilla captain (*kapetánios*) in him quieted down as soon as it could.

In Greece it was still very unusual for books to pass through anything like a peer review, but the exiles clearly played the game for their own petty purposes and Andreas's fury took a form that they, if not their Swedish hosts, could easily grasp.

Andreas was often furious with the other Greeks. Once when he came to Papakongos's house in a state of obvious anger, his host's first thought was that he had been quarreling with other Greeks. And he was not far off the mark: Andreas had discovered some of the exiles berating a certain Vassilis who, once the "lion of Makronisi" who would not sign a declara-

---

10. This term of abuse especially alludes to the donkey's allegedly unpredictable, obdurate, and treacherous character.

tion of loyalty despite the most horrible tortures, had now become a pathetic alcoholic. "Those kids don't know who Vassilis is!" stormed the outraged Andreas.

Caught between the gloomy impersonality of the Swedes and the preening and quarreling of the Greek exiles, Andreas found few attractive diversions. There was no joy to be had from the Greeks (aside from a handful of tried and trusted intimates), let alone the Swedes. His wife and child were in Athens. Unsure of what awaited him, he returned to the lair of the beast.

For Andreas, the junta was an appalling reaffirmation of past tyranny. He was fortunate in being able to escape its worst excesses. He also retained his capacity to understand—if in no sense to condone—the desire of ordinary police officers to display zealous obedience to their new masters. In *Black April,* the half-crazed woman called Caryatid faces coarse threats of gang rape by the police (pp. 105–7):

▌ It wasn't the first time she had been hauled off to a police station. But the police had always acted seriously. Most of them, [anyway]. Sometimes they ragged her in a joking way; they were sorry for her. Others, again, left her alone, free to roam the Acropolis, and took no notice of her. But whatever the case, they had never behaved toward her like this before.

These men nervously competed for the favors of a vicious regime, and "whatever was repulsive in their souls came to the surface." The principal blame lay with those who unleashed it in them.

Andreas thus retained the mixture of biting anger and judicious self-restraint encompassed in the traditionalist vision that had enabled him to remain serene throughout his earlier privations. His is not a voice of forgiveness; but it does weigh and apportion responsibility. Moreover, he reinterprets the values of his adolescence to achieve his revenge through a more subtle range of devices. His weapon is his pen: "If I had not been a writer, I would have killed [by now]," as he was later to remark in a very different context. But the theme is still one of vengeance where his values dictated it, and its idiom remains that of blood and descent, transposed from physical violence to the more delicate plane of literary assassination. The junta inspired Andreas to his most explicit elaboration of these principles.

It is in his treatment of the junta's methods as a revival of the Spanish Inquisition that Andreas showed the most supple sense of connection between world history and the values of his father's village and his own upbringing. Anticlericalism is nothing new for the people of the Cretan hill villages, who view most priests as ruthlessly exploitative dealers in credulity and fear. The unctuous Father Prokopios, evil incubus of Youra, embodies all the venality the prisoners find in the official church: "Soon the priests sent by the 'revolution' will come to give us comfort again. Maybe Father Prokopios himself will come. The wolf delights in such comings and goings" (*Black April*, pp. 125–26). For readers of *Prohibited*, the prisoners' almost word-perfect recall of Prokopios's verbosely obscene call for "consciousness of our guilt" provokes an almost Pavlovian shriek of anger and pain.[11] His sanctimonious sermonizing, with its injunctions to repent and sign the odious declarations of loyalty, offers the ultimate proof of the distance between Church and faith: as I heard in Glendi time and again, formal religious devotions "were created by the priests" rather than the Higher Power whose existence even the most skeptical shepherd concedes. Andreas's dislike of clerics is at least as "traditional" as the piety they invoke.

To express that antipathy, Andreas draws frequently on the image of the Holy Inquisition (*Black April*, pp. 171, 198, 221, 230, 231, 233). The image was immediately recognizable: a reviewer for the Athens daily *Ta Nea* (Anonymous 1974) described the heroine as a "girl who falls into the clutches of the holy inquisitors of Bouboulinas Street," the address of the prison that by the end of the junta's reign of terror had become virtually synonymous with it. As in *Prohibited*, Andreas uses the figure of Galileo to suggest that open defiance may not be the most feasible or effective subversion: a victim of the junta's zeal for forcing declarations of loyalty out of prisoners faces that prospect with the nonchalant remark, "In that case I'll be a big name—remember what Galileo said" (p. 161). The principal torturer is the Grand Inquisitor (p. 198); police torturers are the confessors of this modern holy war (p. 221). In the junta we see another—and this time bitterly ironic—"resurrection," itself a play on the junta's claim to having created a revolution (*epanastasis*) that enshrined the resurrection (*anastasis*) both of Christ and of the Greek nation. In the Holy Inquisition incarnate (p. 221), Andreas offers a counter-resurrection, a vastly darker shadow of the religious past.

Andreas has a visceral understanding of resurrection, very far from the vanities of self-perpetuation with which he reproaches the bourgeoisie:

● A human life is multifaceted, full of variety, very, well. . . . Often, that is, I forget myself—I myself do this, at least—in the past, and . . . I think I've lived many lives. Since . . . exactly this life of mine, let's say, would stop on certain occasions . . . with court trials, a sentence . . . of death, and all the rest of it. Afterwards something else would start, so I thought I was being reborn.

11. Andreas explicitly links *Prohibited* with *Black April* in the latter, especially in his remembrance his wife's nephew; see *Black April*, p. 5.

In this perception, perhaps, lies the inspiration for his agile clambering across the multiple fissures between experience and imagination, fact and fiction, faction and figment. For him no Inquisition could threaten real extinction; and Galileo's moment of weakness was what allowed his truth to survive.

It is not only in his anticlericalism, however, that Andreas views the Inquisition through a prism formed in his father's village. He also draws on a local genealogy of evil. As we have already seen, the Inquisition is a source for some of his most bitter attacks on established religion. It may seem strange that in an Orthodox country this proud affine of a Byzantine noble line should find in the Catholic and Latin past the means of decrying the local religious hierarchy. Was it not the Latins who in 1204 sacked Byzantium and hastened its final decline? Were not various "Franks"—Catholic Western Europeans—the cynical occupiers of many Greek lands? Did they not exercise, as Andreas notes in another context, a rule so harsh that the suffering Greeks welcomed the infidel Turks as liberators?[12] Why does Andreas expect so obviously foreign an institution to convey the hatred and dread that many of his readers have experienced directly during the junta's harsh rule? In part, at least, it provided a means of denying the Greekness of the junta, just as the junta denied that of its opponents.

In *Black April*, the Inquisition appears more often and more explicitly than in earlier works. But it is here, too, that Andreas finally provides the key to the seeming paradox of what for Greek realities must otherwise seem an improbable metaphor. The answer lies in the use of a genealogical allegory that resuscitates the agnatic metaphor of the bloodline (*fléva*, literally "vein") and turns it back against its most eager users, the nationalists of the fascist Right. In a scathing diatribe, Andreas makes this explicit.

The relevant passage ostensibly concerns the junta's rhetoric. Papadopoulos had adopted a historically problematic slogan—"Hellas of the Hellenic Christians"—that recalls the mythopoetic contortions of the nineteenth-century historiography, in which the ideal of a confessional community encompassing all Greek Orthodox Christians confronted the awkward fact that the Byzantines had treated the term "Hellenes" as meaning "pagans"—a categorical embarrassment that was compounded by a popular memory (for by 1821 the name of Hellenes had been virtually forgotten in much of the countryside, being displaced by the vernacular *Romií*). The state needed urgently to sink such internal contradictions in the concept of a single bloodline or "race" (*Filí*). By 1967, however,

---

12. Indeed, Venetian rule was extremely harsh, but its "European" origin has made it less suitable as a symbol of past oppression than the Tourkokratía.

such mental gymnastics hardly seemed necessary; Greece could seek its sense of national unity on more immediate grounds. Andreas—never sympathetic to evocations of the official religion—derides the junta's intellectual pretentiousness throughout the book. Here his contempt is blunt. It is also phrased in terms that his most ill-educated reader could hardly fail to recognize:

▌ "We want Hellenic Christians. . . ."

What a fine motif, indeed. What a great intelligence is this artilleryman, this prime minister of the junta. He couldn't dig up anything better. Never before on this soil had a more hollow phrase been heard. The Byzantines were cleverer. The Turks were more diplomatic. The Franks were haughty, Metaxas wily, Kondylis a fine fighter (*palikarás*), Pangalos. . . .[13] All of them intoxicated with power and the various advantages it brings, concealed or otherwise. But no one like Papadopoulos ever set foot on this earth. Where did this bloodline (*fléva*) start from, fouling the twentieth century with its medieval mentality? Who knows what agent of the Holy Inquisition planted his seed in the Peloponnese during the time of the Franks, so that after a sleep of centuries some descendant of his would leap out and settle on the back of Greece's neck. Who knows . . . (*Black April*, p. 229)

This genealogy—Papadopoulos is a stereotypically Peloponnesian name, and the Frankish occupation of the region was one of the longest periods of Western European dominion in what is now Greece—justifies the metaphor of the Inquisition. Andreas thus provides a historical charter for the analogy, but he also takes care to do so in a lightly speculative manner that protects it from the absurdity of the literal-minded colonels' kinship metaphors. Yet his light touch does not mean that Andreas had no serious intent. His genealogical insult summons up the fighting language of the Cretan mountain villagers, with their warring patrilineal clans and their poetic aspersions on each other's ancestry.[14] This is an old idiom, also attested in the Byzantine epic poetry that the nationalists claimed for their cause but that on closer inspection turns into a riotous contestation of bloodlines in a world of bastards, dwarfs, warriors of mixed Byzantine and Arab ancestry, and even the sons of nuns—the chil-

13. Ioannis Metaxas was the right-wing dictator of Greece from 1936 to 1941. Generals Kondylis and Pangalos both played prominent roles in government, Pangalos as dictator in 1925–26, his overthrow being engineered in part by Kondylis; Kondylis headed a short-lived government in 1935 and this, too, was overthrown in a coup.

14. Although I have used the term "patrigroup" in *Poetics*, the term "clan"—especially for those familiar with Scots culture and history—may give a more immediate sense of this entity here. These groups practice preferential endogamy to the extent that it does not violate incest restrictions, however, and their mobilization for political purposes is increasingly a thing of the past.

dren of paradox, anomalous tricksters who embody the ever-unstable cultural ferment of the border marches (see especially Herzfeld 1980c).

Nationalists could not abide such ambiguities of descent. Instead, they transformed the tumultuous marginalities of an earlier age into a Manichaean struggle over the purity of blood, of descent. The right-wing regimes of the Civil War period had already revived this same idiom with all their talk of "Bulgarians" and of the bastardy of the communists' children. In portraying the junta's resuscitation of the same rhetoric, Andreas reminds us of the cultural context in which, with exquisite reciprocity, he seeks the tyrant's genealogy in the Inquisitors of the detested Franks—who, among other outrages, had sacked Byzantium in 1204. In the real social world in which Andreas grew up, those who hurled insults at another's patrilineal antecedents anticipated reciprocity with interest. In facing the fascists' genealogical hatred, Andreas was extremely well qualified to respond.

For the junta, like its predecessors, used precisely this kind of logic. The children of communists are "bastards," the offspring of atheists whose marriages are by definition unholy and therefore invalid. (Civil marriage was only legalized in Greece as late as 1983.) One widow was dragged away to Youra without seeing her small children again: "We are going to destroy your line (*tha sas kseklirísoume*)," the policeman [who arrested her] told her.[15] And an army officer shouted at her, "You'll break apart under our heels, and your bastard brats will die—you didn't take any account of them when you were carrying placards at [a demonstration at] Marathon" (*Black April*, p. 126). The state thus arrogates to itself the guardianship of children whose ancestry is stained with sin. In that process, it alchemically transforms blood into ideology and kinship into a coercive national unanimity.

Such forced conversions are usually doomed to failure, however, and *Black April* ends with the vicious punishment of the children of suspected communists. As had happened to the offspring of earlier exiles on Youra, these children, whose parents have been snatched into the junta's prisons, are told that they have been deserted by parents who preferred to devote their energies to their wicked ideology. They are forced to sing a prayer, over and over: "God of Hellas, help our father Papadopoulos to set our sick fatherland right and to put sense into our parents, who left us by the roadside" (*Black April*, p. 236). The children cannot understand what their parents have done wrong or who their invisible "father" is. A child

---

15. He was using the language of both the blood feud and the Civil War (see Hart 1996: 264–65). One sees here an aspect of the process whereby national and supranational movements define themselves in terms of local-level—and therefore immediately comprehensible—aspects of social organization.

who fails to sing is cursed as a "bastard" and beaten (p. 237); when he resumes the magical name of his "father" Papadopoulos, the torture stops abruptly, its threat still poised in midair above him. Especially on those who would not abjure their wicked parents or pray for their new "father," on those who obdurately longed for their own kith and kin, the sins of the fathers were to be visited without mercy. Such is the logic of genealogy turned against itself by a powerful state apparatus.

Elsewhere in the book, Andreas has an old communist tell the Civil War story of the government soldier who finds himself forced to participate in the execution of his own cousin ("an enemy of the fatherland," he is told). The cousin challenges that description and begs him to shoot him in the heart—"for the fatherland." The soldier heeds his cousin's plea for a merciful death, although he shoots him in the forehead instead. He then immediately blows his own brains out—"for the fatherland," Andreas sourly remarks (Black April, pp. 65–66). In that desperate final gesture, he has retrieved an intimate, familial selfhood from the infernal machinery of the fascist state.

Similarly, the junta's child prisoners did not entirely lose their autonomy either. Detached from their parents in a savage reversal of the "gathering of the children" (pedhomázoma) by the communists during the Civil War,[16] they neither understood nor believed the encompassing new genealogy that the state created for them. They knew that these soldiers who had suddenly invaded their lives and bodies were forcing them to live a lie. Their sufferings highlighted the stupidity that accompanied the junta's cruelty and made a mockery of its paternalistic pretensions. (An earlier version of the fascists' self-appointed parental role—and their denial of their victims' manhood and agnatic legitimacy—appears in Andreas's portrait of the old communist-turned-entrepreneur who had been hung from the Youra fig-tree and had been so mistreated that, three wives later, he still could not add "and Sons" to the name of his company: "they had made him useless as a man" [Seine, p. 116].)

In his perception of the colonels' expropriation of kinship and family, Andreas was certainly not alone, nor was it only intellectuals who found the dictators' imagery both culturally absurd and socially brutal. A popular joke about "father Papadopoulos" having sex with "mother Hellas" while "the people were hungry" soon began making the rounds; it was one of the first Greek jokes I ever learned.[17] A kinship idiom that serves

---

16. The capturing of Christian children for recruitment to the Ottoman palace guard of janissaries (who were reputedly Islamic zealots) provided one right-wing image of the process whereby communist forces retreating across Greece's northern borders would take children to be brought up in communist countries.

17. For the full joke, see Orso 1979: 3–4.

to express grand nationalist solidarities can also be the source of subversion; its very familiarity—the source of its propaganda appeal—opens it to the mordant dissection of everyday wit.

Events, however, were often more vile than any humor could express. The obscenity of the colonels' power is nowhere more poignantly described than in the closing scene of *Black April* (pp. 238–39). One boy suddenly decided to slip into the wood where adults were tortured by being suspended from pine trees and succeeded in cutting the prisoners free. The guards soon discovered the escapade and sounded the alarm, and the entire camp staff set upon the boy. The guards

▌ then woke up all the children of the camp and beat and thrashed them until morning.

Later there came a car full of officers with shiny buttons and golden stars on their shoulders, who walked around in the camp, inspected the tents and punishment quarters, and then all together went into the large block with the [radio] antennas on it; and as soon as they entered the motor started running and the screams of the boy who had taken down the hanged men began to rise to the very summit of Mount Penteli.

When the junta first struck there were those who did not take it seriously. They soon discovered their error. *Black April* contains many examples of the junta's total lack of humor. It also documents the deep weariness felt by the victims of former rightist regimes, people who had just begun to live more or less normal lives and suddenly found themselves the target of insensate hatred all over again. Andreas writes with deep compassion of an old Youra inmate who has been brought back to the hated prison island:

▌ A lifer, he had just been released two years before with a "pardon." The other day they grabbed him again. With the proceeds from selling a small field in his village he had bought a kiosk.[18] He had given all his money for the vertical space and entered it in order to earn his daily bread. He had spent his life in jail. He had been with ELAS, had fought the Nazis, and after liberation he had been sentenced to life imprisonment. He had remained in jail for seventeen years. Youra brought him to his knees. The rocks carried on his shoulders had left their marks on him. Isolation up there on the mountain, the "disciplinary punishment" of the great torturer Stratos, had crippled him. He walks as though he suffered from splayed feet.

And now they had brought him back to Youra. They had arrested him,

18. These kiosks (*períptera*), which sell an enormous range of small goods, from newspapers and candies to cigarettes and (in more recent years) contraceptives and small toilet items, are often reserved for renting by wounded war veterans and other needy people.

and all the others, on the dawn of the "Good Friday" of the "resurrection" of the nation. Of . . . Pattakos [one of the dictators], the CIA, and Papado-poulos. (pp. 121–22)

He was not alone. In *Black April,* Andreas describes one prematurely white-haired old fighter:

▌ Suddenly he sobs and his eyes filled with tears. He can't be as much as sixty. As though he was delirious.

"I survived but during the Occupation the Nazis killed my 18-year-old son. My only son. I was left with my two daughters and my wife, and in '48 I was sent into exile because I had fought the Nazis during the Occupation. I sat for eight years in Makronisi, in Aï-Stratis, in Ikaria. I grew old before my time. My wife brought up my children. A few years ago I came home and was helping to get the girls married, so we could live at home, and . . . My *curriculum vitae* . . . My *curriculum vitae*," he says over and over, because as soon as the service officer entered the police station he asked him for a *curriculum vitae* in order to let him go free. He told him his story and the officer packed him off to the basement cells. (p. 63)

He was *helping* to get his daughters married. The military had taken away his manhood: he is reduced here to a role secondary to that of his wife, herself emancipated by the revolution but ultimately trapped, like him, back in the drudgery and desperation of a life of Sisyphean privation (see Hart 1996: 243).

In many respects, the real horror of the junta was its appearance at precisely the moment when the aging former prisoners had finally relaxed into a semblance of ordinary life. The Nazis' collaborators had become the camp commanders of the post-Civil War years; their pupils, no less apt, returned in force with the colonels' coup on 21 April 1967 to thwart the hopes of the leftist ex-prisoners that democracy might gradually be emerging from the horrors of the past. And yet the fragility of those hopes—recorded by novelists like Stratis Tsirkas (*Lost Spring* [1976]) and Alki Zeï (*Achilles' Fiancée* [1987])—was everywhere in evidence. Lulled into passivity nonetheless, perhaps by the sheer repetitiveness of the squabbling politicians' incessant prophecies of doom right up to the coup, they were taken quite by surprise:

▌ In a little while the Plaka police station is bursting to capacity. Down below the basement isolation cells opened their doors wide to receive more prematurely awakened people, others beside themselves. Some are silent. They are familiars of the police stations, exile, Makronisi, and the jails. They have years and even decades of experience on their backs. The last pause has sent them to sleep. They had gotten married, had a child or two, a home. They'd bought a fridge by installments, some even an electric stove, a washing machine. What would happen now? How would their families live? How would they pay off their debts, the installment payments, the grocer, the rent. . . . It was enough to drive anyone crazy. (*Black April*, pp. 62–63)

The very banality of the bourgeois comforts to which these old fighters had grown accustomed provides the measure of the new agony.

The junta was an extraordinary combination of heedless stupidity and refined brutality. Nowhere was this oxymoronic condition more apparent than in its control of the news media. Andreas conveys this in *Black April* through a collage—actually more of a barrage—of headlines and lead stories that capture the absurdist quality of their style. The language is a particularly horrid form of the neo-Classical idiom (including a bevy of acronyms), and the quotations parody the junta's desire to prove democracy unworkable, communism "red dictatorship," and the junta's key values—including Orthodox Christianity and, at this point, adhesion to the principle of royal succession in the male line—vindicated by the flow of local and international events (see also Clogg 1972):

▌   Svetlana condemns the Soviet authorities for the conviction of Daniel, Sinyavski. Speaking to the representatives of the Press, the daughter of the red dictator, lord of the Kremlin, went on to confirm that five years earlier she had been officially baptized an Orthodox Christian.

The m. [that is, minister] of the Presidency G. Papadopoulos

A. Papandreou has been called to make a deposition regarding "Aspídha."

TRAFFIC UNRESTRICTED

The chief of the gen. staff has signed an edict ending the prohibition of movement of pedestrians and vehicles throughout the country.

The A.G.E. [Chief of the General Staff] has announced that the use of firecrackers is forbidden.[19] Violators will be tried before the permanent military courts.

It is rumored that the prime minister Mr. Kollias was "carpeted," criticized, by the "m." of the Presidency Mr. Papadopoulos because he used the term "counterrevolution" in his response to the King, whereas the situation is that of a "revolution." . . . Mr. Kollias has been forbidden to speak, to make public pronouncements, or to express his opinions in public, inasmuch as he lacks a suitable spirit appropriate to the goals of the . . . "counterrevolutionary" "revolution."

19. In many parts of Greece, firecrackers are set off during Easter and other times of celebration. Presumably their prohibition arose from the similarity between the noise they made and gunfire.

PARLIAMENTARY PRIVILEGES ARE REVOKED

A compulsory law will be signed through which deputies' privileges will be revoked.

MEMBERS OF PARLIAMENT WERE ASLEEP OR SOLVING CROSSWORD PUZZLE

Mr. Andrews Johns, 22, the youngest member of the Australian parliament, made a statement today declaring himself totally disgusted with the political life of Canberra. Members of parliament sleep during sessions, solve crossword puzzles, or read satirical magazines.

LANSING (MICHIGAN) 27 April

A brief bout of fisticuffs between two members of the state House of Representatives of Michigan was brought to an end last night when one of them was admitted to hospital with a fractured collarbone.

■   PARLIAMENTS AROUND THE WORLD SHOULD BE ABOLISHED

"M." of the Presidency G. Papadopoulos.

Interview with the "m." of the Presidency.

In Ano Liosia patrolmen of the rapid action squad arrested Dim. I. Katsiris, 37, resident of Zofriá, who had in his possession one .38 revolver and one Parabellum pistol with 14 bullets. The weapons were confiscated and Katsiris was sent before the His Majesty's Prosecutor.

"M." of Internal Affairs Pattakos clarified yesterday that . . . he had not "ordered" the ministry of Industry, as was reported in the newspapers, to attend to the regulation and effective disposition of the electricity supply problem . . . but "collaborated" with the minister of Industry, his colleague, in the search for a solution. . . .

"The slanderers of the 'Revolution' who nestle inside the censorship department will be crushed!" Public walk by the "m." of Internal Affairs.

The heir to the Dutch throne has given birth to a male child.

The Greek Authors' Society has been dissolved.

Upon the orders of the "m." of the Presidency G. Papadopoulos, officers visited the former president of the Society, Mr. Leon Koukoulas, who denied that during the sequestration and dissolution of the Society's offices the military committed any acts of violence and that the busts of the of the Society founders Sikelianos, Kazantzakis, and others were smashed.

"This cannot be investigated because Mr. Koukoulas died shortly afterward, as did K. Porfiris, who was buried in the presence of the Security Police of Athens and certain army officers. K. Porfiris worked with various newspapers and magazines, and was a member of the Society of Greek Authors."

It has also been denied that, during the removal of the one thousand book titles prohibited by the "revolutionary counterrevolution" by the National Library, volumes of ancient authors, books by foreigners, and manuscripts of the Revolution of '21 were removed. All these stories are the work of rumor-mongers who will be prosecuted and sent before the military courts.

DENIED: ALL DENIERS OF THE UNDENIABLE DENIALS of the "m." of the Presidency G. Papadopoulos. THE SEVENTY TRUCKLOADS OF ARMS WILL UNQUESTIONABLY BE LOCATED. "m." of the Presidency.

PROOF

At the three-judge Criminal Court R. Paskhalis, 38, coffee merchant, was sentenced to 8 months' imprisonment for violating laws 22)8)52 and 286)14 concerning the illegal possession and bearing of weapons. (*Black April*, pp. 117–20)

This passage, which concludes a considerably longer fusillade of military communiques and censored headlines, accurately depicts the tone of the times. The unceasing rattle of stereotypical announcements and predictable outcomes projected the sense of hopelessness beyond the torturers' offices and prisoners' cells; for ordinary people, too, felt powerless before the informational juggernaut to offer any explicit alternatives to what was being presented to them as the state of the world. Those with little knowledge of what lay outside the immediate confines of Greece found it both morally hard and politically unwise to resist the colonels' smug portrayal of Greek moral superiority; those with access to other perspectives found their knowledge useless (and indeed highly suspect) in the colonels' brave new world.

Collage is a minimalist descriptive technique. Andreas is especially severe with his language when he describes deep emotion and its sources. The dull crash of headlines and communiques, like the deadened consciousnesses that infuse his account of Youra, does far more to excite a reader's horror than a string of hyperbolic adjectives, and all the more so when Andreas impishly allows the parodic to provide a hint of climax. Note, however, that the absurdist denial of the deniers of the undeniable is not the final entry; by closing with an ordinary announcement of a police action, Andreas reminds us that there seemed to be no end to the constant police surveillance, that the moments of comic relief that the Papadopoulos regime provided through its clumsy neo-Classical Greek and political ineptness were in fact the measure of the success of its repressive tactics: failures of style made no difference to its actual grip on the country. On the contrary, as Achille Mbembe (1992) has argued for dictatorial postcolonial regimes in West Africa, this very fact effectively confirmed the reality of the buffoons' power.

Like many intellectuals, Andreas was both horrified and fascinated by the colonels' use of language, an area in which their cultural gracelessness was especially evident. (Listening to the speeches of Papadopoulos allowed some, I recall, to seem quite obedient to the regime while privately amusing themselves at the dictator's expense.) For those of us who lived in Greece during those years, his newspaper collage is a horrifyingly precise reconstruction. For a moment I was not even sure, at first reading, whether the parodic eruption at the end was from the author's pen or the colonels'. When one reads *Black April* now, so many years after the regime's passing, Andreas's words still conjure up anew an atmosphere in which it was not always easy to distinguish between farce and tragedy.

The toughest prisoners on Youra never signed the hated declarations of repentance, and they were denied a place in the rightist vision of eternal resurrection. For themselves, however, their refusal to sign became the ultimate act of resistance to those whose power spelled eternal death to the country and its people.

During the colonels' dictatorship, the same confrontation was revived, the tortures refined and intensified. In a country where the very idea of penetrating another's mind is treated as absurd even though everyone tries to do it, the statements of penitence that the junta demanded were well understood—and this only enhanced the effectiveness of the technique—as a way of compromising those who surrendered and thereby of further sapping the strength of the resistance. This was a game over reputation and power, not, in any realistic sense, over hearts and minds. The junta did not expect love; it demanded obedience. In this it was fully consistent with the social theory of ordinary people—a major factor in its success.

Andreas, as we have already seen, shares the general Greek skepticism about knowing the innermost thoughts and character of others. He also has no time for literal-mindedness. Much as elsewhere he plays with orthographic conventions to make fun of the powerful, in *Black April* he tackles the junta's pretensions by mischievously taking their extraction of loyalty statements at face value. The old ex-prisoners from Youra and Aï-Sratis are hauled back into jail:

▐ The householders, the workers, the scholars, and the chosen representatives of the people come back to the prison cells after so many years. A few white hairs on their heads, a wrinkle in the face, the bare gums—these can better tell you about their life and past than the files stacked up there on the shelves. There you have the dead letter, the inanimate paper which tells its own tale; and which presents people through a prism of hatred and intensity. If you open a file to read it, if you believe what's written there, you can sit down with the same person it describes—if you don't already know him—and discuss and think along with him about how you would deal with this criminal, how you could protect yourself from him. And when your interlocutor confesses that he himself is the "criminal" described in the file, you could go mad. How could it be thus? There go all your psychological abilities, your knack of reading a face, your instinctive sensitivity, your experience of life—they all go to pieces. You discover that you don't know people, that you're either blind and deaf or entirely insane. You discover that what was written in those papers either possess a power that sees things differently—the eye, so to speak, of a new kind of X-ray machine—or that these are people from another world. People who see what is right as bad, what is straight as crooked, the honorable as dishonorable, patriotism as betrayal, betrayal as love of fatherland and so on. (*Black April*, p. 70)

And this is the rub: those who deceive themselves into thinking that they can read others' minds (with "a new kind of X-ray machine") are also incapable of understanding what is morally right—and if they are aware of their own tactics, their guilt is all the greater; for indeed they know full well what they do.

In this passage, Andreas recognizes the common device of claiming to be able to read others' character even while, in a more generic sense, denying the very possibility of doing so. He also articulates aspects of his own philosophy of representation here: rather than attributing thoughts and personality traits to individuals, he prefers descriptions that move his readers to their own subjective assessments. In the words of one review of *White Fences*, his collection of short stories about the soldier who fought at El Alamein:

The book thus becomes a terrible denunciation of the enemies of humanity and freedom. Of the imperialists. But this does not happen through curses and maledictions, nor with the words of manifestos; it emerges like a fiery conclusion, a fiery sword, from the actions of people in motion. (Porfiris 1959)

In a word, Andreas restores agency to the victims of a brutal overdetermination. And that move entails rejecting any pretensions of knowing its victims' minds. The colonels' claims to such knowledge furthered their exercise of tyranny. Andreas's mockery of these claims shows that the psychology of terror can strip people of their agency even—indeed, especially—when it is based on total ignorance of who and what the victims are. It reduced their personalities and desires to total irrelevance, and it generalized the terror by reversing the commonsense view so prevalent in everyday Greek social thought: the torturers *could* know a prisoner's mind, and it did not even matter if they were wrong.

Only those who refused to sign declarations of loyalty to the regime were able to resist this annihilation of the autonomous, private, sovereign self celebrated in almost every ethnographic study of Greek society. These few, Andreas among them, could even exploit the bullies' thirst for triumph to reverse roles and assert their own agency over that of their tormentors: the notorious torturer of Youra, Glastras, "did whatever he wanted to the prisoners' bodies, but their souls he could not tame. And the more he became aware of this the angrier he got and the more he was consumed with frenzy" (*Black April*, p. 124). Lack of self-control was the definitive, final humiliation that the torturers tried to induce in their victims, and to which one of their leaders had now succumbed instead. Moreover, the resisters' determination mocked the torturers' claims to psychological omniscience. For, under such conditions, there could only be one motive for refusing to sign a declaration of loyalty to the regime. Virtually the only situation in which motive could never be in serious doubt was thus the one that the regime could least afford to acknowledge: defiance of its control over the minds of all Greeks.

The metaphor of resurrection, expropriated by the junta to legitimize its power grab and reappropriated by Andreas as a leitmotif of ironic disappointment, was not always bitter. On the contrary, resurrection—key to the ideology of Greek naming and personal identity, as we have seen, and the dominant metaphor of the struggle for independence in 1821—was the one symbol that the junta undeniably shared with its foes. It was the key to the ownership of the past, the ultimate source of legitimacy in the present. The hope for redemption, for an end to the junta and its cheap cruelty, never faded; and in the rich notion of *kaïmós* the Greeks turned pain into fierce decision.

Kaïmós is usually translated into English as "grief." It does mean that, but it also conveys the focused passion that brooks no interference—the desire of the aesthete, the longing for lost love. Emotional terms present a particularly tough challenge to translation (see Abu-Lughod and Lutz 1990). Among the speakers of a language, too, they provoke the imagination to leap across the chasm that separates individuals from one another. Such concepts clearly do mobilize tremendous energy, in precisely the sense of Durkheim's image of the "effervescence" of the crowd. Andreas, always unwilling to play mind-reader, portrays such effects and makes them credible, not by dwelling deliberately on how they work, but by showing us how the key emotional concepts are evoked by those involved in dramatic moments of popular political response. The technique is thus analytically parsimonious but descriptively both rich in detail and austere in tone. As a result, it satisfies the most rigorous objectivism of formal ethnographic description while simultaneously allowing us to weep and cheer with the characters of his tale.

His handling of the concept of *kaïmós* nicely illustrates this effect. In Greek, words for intense emotion more easily encapsulate extremes of both sorrow and joy than they do in English: *ékstasi*, for example, from which the English "ecstasy" is derived, can mean a gripping fury as much as an intense pleasure, while *lakhtára* denotes both the deep longing of the lovelorn and the terror of impending death. Similarly, *kaïmós* encapsulates contradictions of intense emotion that otherwise are only graspable through such complex ritual enactments as the Greek (and wider Balkan) parallelism between death and marriage (see Alexiou 1974; Herzfeld 1981). When a writer like Andreas uses the idea of *kaïmós*, he conjures its intensity out of the vivid description of its use. *Kaïmós* is consuming sadness, but it is also concentrated desire—such as that of the dedicated hobbyist, for example.

Realized as song—specifically, in Andreas's story, the left-wing composer Mikis Theodorakis's song *Kaïmós* (a setting of a poem by Dimitris Christodoulou), banned like all his works as political by virtue of his authorship alone—it gave tangible form to the indomitable refusal of the Greeks to succumb to their tormentors. It is the promise of an eventual redemption, beyond anguish. It is the hope of spiritual and political resurrection, indefinitely deferred. The object of desire is democracy, its name a slogan secretly painted on a wall:

■ "DEMOCRACY" appeared, scratched out down to a faded shadow, on the wall of the royal garden. It had been written in red at night; at dawn it was erased, washed off; but in the morning it greeted the trams and buses. The morning passengers sat up sharply. They sat bolt upright in their seats and the buses moved on more slowly—as if by braking they were honoring a great man who had died, or resurrecting him in this way. The drivers began softly whistling a song. Each one of them a different song. People had heard on the radio the decree banning certain songs. And it had been published in banner type in the newspapers: ON THE BASIS OF VOTE 9/20/60 SONGS WITH POLITICAL CONTENT ARE PROHIBITED. But everyone was quietly murmuring these songs. From every window came a wind bearing griefs (*kaïmí*) "of political character." The phonographs were blaring at full blast: "Barren rock, barren rock, my grief (*kaïmós*), [I measure it, and am filled with pain]. . . ."

Out there in the Aegean, on the dry islets, human beings measured their griefs once again in a "disciplinary mode of life." The salty spray of the sea, the unceasing wind, the thirst, the shackles of prison. The very perimeter—the entire Aegean Sea. The finest world in the universe had suddenly become a hell. The sun beating down on stone, enforced confinement, life without motion. A desert that becomes more intense when, from where you are sitting and unable to move, there appears on the far horizon a sail, a rowboat, and it is lost beyond the promontory. A knife-thrust in the heart. An unbearable pain.

"Barren rock, barren rock, my grief (*kaïmós*). . . ."

On all the walls of Athens appeared the same slogans. In Pangrati, Metaxourgeio, Kallithea [Athens districts]. In Kallithea one evening the "rapid action squad" plastered a youth across the half-finished slogan "Long live DEMOCRAC. . . ." They stitched his body with a machine-gun. They picked him up and took him away with them. His pockets were full of fliers: DOWN WITH FASCISM. In death the lad gazed at the cemetery. Nude and laid out on the marble as he was, he looked like a Kouros [a pre-Classical statue of a youthful male] disinterred from the soil of Attica and waiting to be hauled into an upright position.

■   What is death, when you achieve something? Whether you are twenty years old or eighty, it is all the same. "LONG LIVE DEMOCRAC . . ." was written there on that wall in Kallithea and dyed with his blood. It was as though he had built a palace, created a family, planted trees and arrived at his end. It was for this that he was destined.

LONG LIVE DEMOCRAC. . . .

Others will complete the slogan. Just as some began the building of the Acropolis and others finished it. Others will set Democracy back on its feet. His colleagues, his friends, the young people yet to come. It is all the same: life, and we ourselves—we are so . . . insignificant. We must do something, be it just a slogan on a wall. Everything counts. (*Black April*, pp. 144–45)

Or, as Andreas says in the preface to the Greek edition, dedicated to the memory of Elli's brother's son, killed in the 1973 uprising of the Polytechnic students that was to precipitate the junta's eventual demise— the boy who, years earlier, had wonderingly asked his uncle Andreas to explain what his book about Youra (*Prohibited*) was all about:

■ But what is death, when you achieve something? Whether you are seventeen years old or eighty, it is all the same. It was as though he had built a palace, created a family, planted trees and arrived at his end. It was far more. . . .

Like a folksong motif that links chronologically separate events in a common historical significance, Andreas's refrainlike prose indexes the transcendent sameness of certain key events. It shows us that, for him, every youth who stood up to the tyranny of the junta was embodied in his nephew. As in a funeral lament, moreover, death is a wedding—here, because to rebuild democracy is as creative, as generative of the nation, as the building of a family.

This is Andreas's answer to the junta's violent appropriation of familial metaphor to express its vision of the nation-state. The "destination" of young people, according to local social values, is to marry; and the purpose of marriage, we have seen, is the perpetuation of the line, its "resurrection." When they die prematurely, destiny is projected onto other defining moments of the ideal life—in villages often onto the wedding they did not live to achieve.[20] The passive *kaïmós* of the prisoners abandoned to measure out their grief on a barren rock in the Aegean Sea becomes the active *kaïmós* of the youthful, whose collective destiny is to turn that tragic longing into incrementally decisive change.

In July of 1974 I had come to Athens from fieldwork on the island of Rhodes, trying without success to secure the reversal of an expulsion order against me—one of the junta's last internal acts as it came crashing down in the debacle of its interference in Cyprus and the resulting Turkish invasion of the island republic. It was dusk. I had wanted to celebrate with Greek friends over their new-found freedom, although I was also brooding on the price the Cypriots were paying at that very moment. But I could not celebrate even this partial joy with anyone: the banning order meant that I was no longer legally in the country and would have to leave at least for a while. No one knew what was going to happen. (A friend, Th.D. Frangopoulos,[21] was picked up by police one of those nights and asked whether he approved of the changes taking place; when he refused to answer on the grounds that his innermost thoughts were his own business, he was thrown repeatedly against a wall in a final vindictive act.) The junta's bureaucrats were still clinging to their desks; the future was uncertain.

So I sat pensively with my wife in the gathering night, on an English friend's balcony. Suddenly a soft sound plucked at the fading light. It was a low, tuneful whistle, that seemed in its hesitant rise and fall to test the air for lingering danger—and the words came on their own:

> Barren rock, barren rock, my grief,
> I measure it, and am filled with pain.
> And it is my plaint:
> "Mother, when will I see you again?"

I froze, my eyes stinging.

The last time I had heard the songs of Theodorakis in the open air, two years earlier, had been in Cyprus, where there were no harsh restrictions on songs "with political content." Now the Cypriots had ceased to sing; it was their turn to lament the violence of the junta's passage; and the whistling borne on the warm evening air was quiet, hesitant, not the

---

20. This practice is described in my *Poetics of Manhood*, (1985: 126).

21. A well-known poet, Th.D. Frangopoulos is also one of the authors in *Eighteen Texts* (1972; see also pp. **295**).

brave blast of a few years earlier. No one knew what was going to happen. The future of the new era was in the hands of the wily old rightist, Constantine Karamanlis, recalled from his haughty self-exile in Paris to fill the complete political vacuum that the junta's ignominious collapse had created. The junta's bureaucrats were still clinging to their desks (I know that because they were able to have me turned back at the border the first time I tried to re-enter the country); the future was uncertain.

But at least one Athenian that night could whistle the song of *kaïmós:* "Barren rock, barren rock, my grief. . . ." And the grief had found its destiny; truly, others had completed the slogan.

8 ▣

FROM THE CRETAN WAR
TO A BATTLE OF BOOKS

The restoration of democracy in 1974 was decisive. In short order, understanding that times had changed and that old methods of repression could no longer prevail, the conservative government of Constantine Karamanlis took firm steps: the restoration of representative parliamentary process and the writing of a new constitution, the legalization of the Communist Party in Greece for the first time in more than four decades, and the establishment of the ordinary spoken language as the official language of education, law, the media, and all official business. In 1981, the Panhellenic Socialist Movement (PASOK) won a clear parliamentary majority that some have held as the cleanest elections in Greek history and as an unambiguous affirmation of the political Left's unprecedented freedom of access to power.

During these years and up to the present, Andreas Nenedakis has continued to write actively, free at last from the stifling constraint of state censorship. Although he has been extremely productive during this period, I focus on two areas, both deeply associated with his native Rethemnos. The first of these is his edition of the seventeenth-century poem, *The Cretan War*, in which his efforts of several decades culminated. The poem itself was written by a Rethemniot Greek refugee from the Turkish invasion of Crete in 1645–69, Marinos Tzane Bounialis, and takes the form of an extended verse lament that documents in considerable detail the inexorable advance of the victors and the plight of the vanquished. The second and more complex achievement is his novel *Voukéfali*, which is set in Rethemnos during the period immediately preceding the 1922 collapse of the Greek forces in Asia Minor and the enforced departure of all Muslims ("Turks") from Crete. The contemporary meanings this work has acquired appear most clearly in the context of the literary vendetta it has provoked.

These two authorial projects complicate, in different but mutually illuminating ways, the definition of Andreas's role as a writer. On the one hand, in *The Cretan War*, he undertook a task normally and straightforwardly associated with academic philology and turned it into an exercise in critical social history. He makes no claims to the kinds of academic expertise normally deemed essential for such a project, preferring instead to claim the special knowledge of a cultural insider—and indeed to accuse his academic predecessors of localist bias, since none of them were from Rethemnos. (For those readers who are unfamiliar with localist politics on Crete, the best context for understanding these passions is the surge of demonstrations that greeted the news that the University of Crete would be located in Rethemnos, and that eventually led to its division, by schools, among the *three* largest Cretan towns.) Andreas undertook his edition of Bounialis as a labor of love, believing that his childhood memories of his family's archaic-sounding village speech gave him a privileged insider's right to correct the false emendations of academic editors who lacked such knowledge. Both his nativism and the academic establishment's dismissal of his efforts recall similar arguments in anthropology about the relative knowledge of the "natural" insider and the "objective" outsider. Andreas paid for this edition out of his own funds, a relatively common practice in Greece even after the sudden efflorescence of publishing houses in the 1970s. But the irritated indifference of most of the academic community, which Andreas reciprocated in generous measure, has never altered his perception of this project as one of scholarly and above all of *factual* intent.

With regard to *Voukéfali*, by contrast, he neither seeks nor offers any concessions, but instead aggressively defends its novelistic character. The only claim he makes here for special local knowledge is that it afforded him possibilities of realism in his depiction of character and of universal aspects of class struggle. Such a work, he argues, should not be mistaken for a chronicle of historical fact: its truth is both more conditional and more transcendent—a product, not of literal reporting, but of life's lessons.

His concern with class struggle, however, infuses both books with a common ideological focus. This comes into focus with the novelist's version of what Sally Falk Moore (1987), writing about ethnography, has called a "diagnostic event"—an occurrence that encapsulates recurrent aspects of the local cultural, political, and social logic. The event that most fully satisfies this definition is mentioned in both works: the famous moment when Andreas's father defended the Rethemnos Turks against the bloodlust of his covillagers. That such an event takes on significant dimensions in *Voukéfali*, a novel about the precise period in which it occurred, makes obvious sense; but why would Andreas even mention it in his critical edition of a Renaissance poem?

This puzzle holds the key to larger questions: how social knowledge is apprehended in Greece, how the historical past is filtered through present-day politics, and how battles over the definition of genres and professional identities—not to speak of aesthetic standards—may be embedded in the immediate social realities of kinship, alliance, and locality. It is thus in these two more recent works that the ethnographic implications of Andreas's writing take on a particularly critical interest. This is as true of the contrast as of the similarity between them. For, whereas Andreas is prepared to concede (and even to revel in the fact) that in *The Cretan War* he is venturing into unknown waters, tweaking academic noses with his local knowledge of dialect usage but recognizing that the scholars' technical skills may supply other insights, in the debates about *Voukéfali* he insists that the novelistic nature of his undertaking gives him full license to write as he wishes and to do with the historical raw materials whatever he deems aesthetically appropriate.

Andreas first read *The Cretan War* as a youth, in the Vlastos archive, and the stirring lament for the fall of Crete to the Turkish invaders remained a vital presence within him. For Andreas, as for many Greeks, memories of an earlier age were not museological curios but a source of inspiration in confronting the tragedies of the present. (Once again, there are rich precedents for such intellectual analogizing among the rural population from which Andreas draws inspiration. Cretan shepherds invoke national history as the very justification for their unruliness and to represent the central government—especially when in the hands of conservatives—as the heirs of the Turks [Herzfeld 1985: 19].) Thus, when he reached Stockholm, Andreas was induced to revisit *The Cretan War* by his friend Mistakidis, philologist and editor of a series of semischolarly booklets under the name—redolent with associations of the 1821 War of Independence—Rigas Ferreos.[1] These booklets were published in Sweden and Cyprus, the former as Mistakidis's place of residence, the latter as the single Greek-speaking territory that was free from the beastly rule of the colonels.

In his preface to Andreas's booklet, Mistakidis, writing under his pen name of "Mesevrinos," pointed out the parallel between the Renaissance poet's experiences and those of today's Greeks under the colonels (Mesevrinos 1969: 7): "in its totality this historical event presents striking analogies of historical determination with the complex tangle of problems that the Greek people must today confront in order to survive, victim

---

1. Rigas Ferreos (or Velestinlis) led an unsuccessful revolt against the Ottoman empire; as a result, he was executed in 1798. His combination of pan-Hellenism and democratic idealism has made him something of a cult figure for left-wing groups in Greece, and his name was especially appropriated by one of the most active resistance groups during the dictatorships of 1967–74. On his historical trajectory, see Douglas Dakin (1973: 27–30).

of its 'fate,' at this moment an unwilling pawn caught between two all-powerful, mutually inimical alliances on the verge of clashing with one another." Once it was the Crescent and the Cross; now the bastions of capitalism stared down the hammer and sickle.

Mistakidis uses with deliberate irony—his quotation marks follow the more conventional Greek usage—the image of fate with which Greeks have thought about the impersonal forces limiting their ability to chart their own course. Here, clearly, the philologist is hinting at a point I have tried to develop more analytically in my own work (Herzfeld 1992): that attributions of fatalism are part of a larger pattern in which the powerful deny any agency to the disenfranchised—a pattern that in Greece appears in a wide range of situations from petty bureaucratic encounters to international relations. It is in the latter sphere that Mistakidis, like Andreas Nenedakis, perceives the important analogies between past and present humiliations, although Andreas—whose 1969 essay as well as his 1979 introduction to the full critical edition of Bounialis's poem considerably enlarged the discussion of social history on which Mistakidis touched in his 1969 preface—also goes further than the more austerely academic Mistakidis in seeing both conflicts as thoroughly enmeshed in global confrontations among social classes. In this he is in close accord with the Greek Marxist social historian Nikos Svoronos, whom he quotes in his 1979 edition of *The Cretan War* (pp. 31, 62) with unequivocal approval. Indeed, Andreas makes the poet, Marinos Tzane Bounialis, the voice of an oppressed indigenous class of artisans, the perfect historical model for a self disinclined to claim special privileges for the author over the craftsperson and determined to make common cause with workers and peasants. This attitude also surfaces, subtly transmuted, in his disputes with the critics of *Voukéfali*.

Andreas's passion was to rehabilitate Bounialis against what he saw as unjust criticism of the work's poetic qualities by non-Rethemniots (or by those who found his dislike of the privileged and wealthy discomfiting) (see, for example, *Cretan War*, p. 170). This was a task that, as a native son himself, he felt especially qualified to perform. The link is a virtually ancestral one, for, as he points out, his father's mother was born around the beginning of the nineteenth century; given a high degree of longevity among the highland villagers from whose vernacular Andreas derives the language of Bounialis, relatively few decades separated her from the poet:

▌ Then, I know that there they speak the language of Bounialis. What the "specialist" philologists claim, that apparently the language of the Cretan texts was the language only of the towns of Crete at that time, is proof of how little they know Crete. We of course know that these "specialists" are petty bourgeois who have never been outside the town[s] and shudder at the very idea that they might sleep for a night in some village. And they certainly would not spend time with people like the Asi-Goniots. A ride in a private car does not suffice. In any case, the villagers retreat inside themselves or try to speak their [best] "Greek." All the towns of Crete had up to 25,000 inhabitants in the sixteenth century and many of these were not Greeks. Whatever dignity and ingenuity may be shown by those who claim that the inhabitants of the towns created this culture on their own, they will not be able to persuade many people.

For how could Chortatsis [another Renaissance poet from Rethemnos] know the words used in agricultural tasks, the names of plants or trees, foods, and also even words heard only in the villages for reasons having to do with the economy, special relationships with nature and animals and even understandings brought into being by contact with the mountainside and with fields? The lives of the "bourgeois" were even more closed than they are today, and only someone who had direct contact—that is, someone who lived in the countryside—could know and feel the way its inhabitants did. (*Cretan War*, pp. 12–13)

The nativism of this passage does not prevent Andreas from recognizing the philologists' technical skills, but he demands comparable respect from them.

The vital link is his father, also a key figure in *Voukéfali*, and—again as in that work—class is to a significant degree a battle over the meaning of authenticity:

▌I must explain a few things that concern my feeling for the language and my desire to restore Bounialis's reputation and text as far as possible. I remember the last descendants of certain families named in the various lists [of Venetian nobles], some are still alive. I remember their down-at-heel dignity, their tailcoats, some had horses and went for a walk in the afternoons. The petty descendants of the "grandees" who wandered around, poor, some were so odd that the children followed along in their wake. Rethimno was a closed society (*politía*) for outsiders, but certain houses were a great mystery for the locals too. Elderly ladies spoke quietly and melted away behind their lace curtains, and aged, worn-out gentlemen walked with an otherworldly air, unapproachable. What they were thinking about, what family crest narrowed their brains and forced them to live as they did off the bit of income they could get from an olive grove or a house they could rent out, was the subject of many discussions that I heard and that made my imagination flare up so I could not calm down.

However, I was brought up by a very different person. My father's shop—he had some merchandise then—later he fell on hard times, he was not adaptable—was at Bounialis's Porta Gora, the Great Gate as the road is [now] called. There lots of people came inside, all of them villagers. I

knew them by their first names, many were my relatives. I used to go their
houses, their villages, I knew the work they did. Our family was growing,
we were five or six children. We all went to school. The Old Man, as we
called my father, wanted us to learn letters, "Greek." He sent us to a private
school to learn French.

He was approaching eighty. He had been born during the 1866 revolution and his mother suckled him in the Madhára. He kept many of the
experiences that he had in his childhood years. Soon he became a thief, a
rebel (khaínis), one of the best-known of western Crete. In the guerrilla
warfare of 1889 he was twenty-three years old and his activity great in
Apokoronas and in western Rethimno. He had gained a name . . . "He
didn't fear any Turk," I used to hear the old men say. I also understood
it from their behavior. I used to see it in their eyes when they were talking.
But what I remember well is that ALONE he prevented the Asi-Goniots
and the deserters from the '22 campaign [who had fled to Crete] from
slaughtering the Turkish women and children, when Asia Minor fell. "If
you want to go and slaughter Turks, go to Smyrna," he told them. "And
if you want to enter Rethemnos you will have to slaughter me first. . . ."

And the next day Ali Vafis, the leading Turkish burgher, came to our
house. And he begged him to accept his mansion in Petaládhika [the blacksmiths' street], he would give it to him for that great liberation, with a
contract—many such "sales" had taken place at that time and many "patriótes"[2] found themselves in possession of properties. . . .

And the Old Man would not speak to him. He just looked at him, un-
smiling and hard, until the red-headed Turk—he must have been the descendant of Venetian apostates—left bowed down as if he had received a
gunshot to his proud head.

So this "Old Man"—he had married at age fifty, after his return from
Epirus, where he fought together with Mavilis—he spoke to me about him,
and with Romas—spoke another language. And it bothered me and I didn't
want to listen to him and I felt badly, because as a Rethemniot, child of
the town, I used to hear my fellow students' parents, the petty bourgeois
and small merchants of the town, using different words, or, if they were
the same, my father's emphasis of certain consonants, especially lamvdha,
his verb endings, the use of "tsi,"[3] archaisms, or words that were unknown

2. Patriótis (plural, patriótes) means "patriot" and a series of concentric identities from
"fellow villager" to "fellow citizen."
3. The retroflex l (lamvdha) and the use of tsi (instead of "standard" tous and tis for,
respectively, the masculine and feminine accusative plural pronouns/definitive article) are
stereotypically regarded as two of the diagnostic features of Cretan speech.
   The most formidable critic Andreas had to face was Nikolaos Tomadakis, a professor
of philology at the University of Athens and a Cretan himself, whose critique (1979) of
Andreas's edition attempted to score cheap shots (p. 401): "a contemporary and rustic,

in the town, infuriated me, and the worst was that I was forced to learn their meaning, because there where I wandered around, at the broad well that is at Bounialis's "Porta Gora," they all spoke that language. In any case they couldn't speak any better. And I made fun of them . . . I, and everyone in Rethimno, made fun of those who used "the most perfectly organized language that medieval and modern Hellenism has heard," as Seferis says in his introduction to the *Erotókritos*.[4] (*Cretan War*, pp. 10–11)

Andreas did not only learn respect for his father's language and for the attitudes that led him to protect his Muslim fellow townspeople from the Christian Asi-Goniots' rage but to refuse Ali Vafis's offer; he also came to see these cultural and personal traits as repositories of all that was best in the Greeks. Lest anyone doubt his father's patriotism or the historical bond that connected the Nenes clan to the Cretans of Bounialis's day, he prefaced the 1979 critical edition with a photograph of his father, in full Cretan dress, standing atop the Turkish flag that he and his mates had captured at Metsovo in the Balkan Wars—the self-same flag that he was to keep for so many years in his house. The legend accompanying the photograph is revealing (*Cretan War*, pp. 8–9): "The flag of which Bounialis bemoans its flying high in the sky above the island of Crete was captured by the kapetánios at Metsovo during the liberation wars of 12–13."

Andreas's own style in the preface and introduction to his 1979 edi-

---

genuinely Rethemniot dress had to be devised (in the editor's view) for the presentation of the new edition. But then why should it be called, not a 'Nenedakian' edition, but a critical one?" Andreas wrote an extensive reply, never published, but on this point he merely commented, "Absurd and jesting. Mr. T's ironic jibes are matters of underhandedness," although he also noted, in connection with the specific matter of the language, "These [comments] about the Asi-Gonia language are a joke, although the Asi-Goniots should be proud that they have their own language . . . despite Tomadakis . . ." (ellipses in original). In fact, Tomadakis's separation of the rural from the urban was presumably a more ideological than analytic perspective: on the unsustainability of the rural-urban dichotomy, see (for historical philology) M. Alexiou 1991 and (for anthropology) Hirschon 1989. The reaction of S. Alexiou was infinitely more generous, and Andreas responded with mutual respect. Andreas also has in his possession a warm note from Pandelis Prevelakis congratulating him "for having performed the useful work of republication" (letter of 24 December 1979). Evidently Tomadakis felt he could condescend to the nonacademic Andreas. Indeed, in 1974 he wrote to Andreas to congratulate him on *Manuscript*: "One thing I do not forgive in you: you are very much a local patriot and very *Rethemniot* . . . whereas you are in every respect a *better* writer of literature than your fellow-villager [*sic*: the term is *khorianós*] and Academician [Pandelis Prevelakis]." But this bantering tone, which perhaps foreshadows his criticism of Andreas's edition of Bounialis in its rejection of "village" culture, nevertheless left Andreas ill prepared for the vitriolic tone of the 1979 review.
4. See Seferis 1946.

tion of *The Cretan War* reserves a slightly apologetic version of this extreme patriotism. In a tradition that harkens to the nineteenth-century historians Konstantinos Paparigopoulos (1853) and Spiridon Zambelios (1852), who argued that the common people preserved the true Hellenic spirit despite the foreign ("Roman") character of the Byzantine state bureaucracy and Church hierarchy, he conceded that, when the Greeks were faced with cultural and demographic annihilation by the Catholic Venetians and later by the Muslim Turks, it was ordinary people's devotion to their religion that sustained their sense of identity—possibly an embarrassing admission for a self-styled atheist. In a similar vein, he recalled his father's determination that no Nenes should ever admit to weakness and his exhortation to remember that the Asi-Goniots, in whose village supposedly (and according to local songs) no Turk had ever settled, had gold in their blood—a statement that he was later to quote also against his principal local critic when the latter, scion of a lowland family, attacked the memory of Nikolaos Nenes:

> ■ Chauvinistic perceptions, certainly, but this way of looking at things maintained the lineage (*yénos*) of the Greeks for so many years during the time of slavery, ready at any moment for revolution, and led it to freedom. And it is certain that this was the most important feature of modern Hellenism, which managed to free itself of its Byzantine and theological features, believing that all who live in that space we call Greece were Greeks (*Éllines*), and to acquire the consciousness that enabled it to arrive at the realization of the Greek nation (*ethnos*). (*The Cretan War* [1979], p. 14)

For Andreas, Bounialis was a perfect vehicle for the promotion of a class-based reading of Greek history. At the turn of the present century, Yannis Psicharis, the apostle of linguistic demoticism, had counted Bounialis as one of the great sources of the capacity of the ordinary language to survive so many centuries of purist repression (*Cretan War*, pp. 108–9). Andreas was thus able to construct an intellectual genealogy that connected Bounialis to the class identity, ideology, and language of the modern Greek Left as well as to Andreas's own local cultural background. (It is noteworthy that Stylianos Alexiou, who published his own edition of the poem, instead recognizes as ideological the Christian conviction that links the fate of the vanquished to their prior sins [Alexiou and Aposkiti 1995: 92]—a valid observation that links Bounialis's poem with a huge number of laments in Greek and other languages, but that does not give emphasis to the class resentment that this symbolically Christian argument may well have masked.)

In this apparent reversion to a more folkloristic sense of genealogy, one can see how richly the genealogical metaphor, from Nietzsche to Foucault, has linked the construction of intellectual identities to often highly local politics and even to the literal demands of kinship. Andreas makes it abundantly clear that his relationship with Bounialis is not to be read as a literal line of descent. But his invocation of his father's line and the bickering over clan histories that followed the publication of *Voukéfali* recall our attention to the extent to which the idea of an intellectual lineage is embedded in the immediacy of a local social context. In Greece, where the nation is often represented as a vast clan, and especially in agnatic feud-prone Crete, the overtones of kinship ideology and its claims are far from subtle. Just as local supporters of the socialist party would claim a kind of "descent" from Venizelos on the grounds that ex-Prime Minister Papandreou's father had served the great man as his personal secretary, so Andreas—with considerably more persuasive logic—hints that he himself is truly close to the Renaissance poet Bounialis in terms of the modesty of the true poet who lets others call him by that name (p. 109), of social class, of cultural identity and ideology, and, virtually, of descent itself.

This powerful claim becomes especially important in the arguments about language. Andreas draws on his intimate memories of Asi-Goniot speech—to which he scornfully compares the fake Cretan of the modern media—to suggest that the typesetter of the original Venetian edition of the poem must have been from the eastern part of the island. But his attempts to restore western Cretan verb endings, possessive pronouns, and tense markers sometimes ran afoul of the exigencies of meter and euphonics, as he himself admits (*Cretan War*, pp. 165–66). His philological work is, he himself says quite clearly, that of a rank amateur and secondary to what he sees as his main task.

We should nevertheless note that the archaeologist and philologist Stylianos Alexiou, who felt compelled to hold up his own edition of Bounialis for sixteen years in order to take account of Andreas's work on the text, and who was clearly irked by Andreas's charges of localist bias, has responded with a characteristically generous acknowledgment of Andreas's real contribution even in those areas in which his technical knowledge was deficient. Alexiou shares with Andreas a respect for scholarly passion no matter what its source may be; at a time (during the junta years) when professors barely deigned to speak with students, he received me graciously in his office in Iraklio (where he was director of the Archaeological Museum). With Andreas, there was a longer history of mutual engagement. Nevertheless, one of the most gratifying responses to Andreas's hard work on Bounialis was Alexiou's warm acknowledgment that his local background *had* enabled him to spot some serious errors in earlier editions, and to praise the love of Bounialis's poetry that had led Andreas, before anyone else, to appreciate its true qualities.

Alexiou wrote in the personal copy of his own edition that he gave

The writer engaged: Andreas at home (photographs by Cornelia Mayer Herzfeld).

Andreas that it was "a reciprocal gift for his great contribution to the understanding and assessment of Tzane." For, as Alexiou (Alexiou and Aposkiti 1995: 38) remarks, "Nenedakis, being a Rethemniot, loved the text as few have loved it" and, against the philological errors with which he charges Andreas, notes, "He is among the few who have seen that this was a poet of significance" (Alexiou and Aposkiti 1995: 39). Alexiou and Nenedakis also agree in rejecting the view that Bounialis was merely a hack who copied another poet's style in order to produce a factual chronicle (*Cretan War*, p. 77–81; Alexiou and Aposkiti 1995: 110). As Andreas remarks (p. 172), ultimately the question revolves around assertions about what constitutes real history—the central debate in my study of Rethemnos and in this book.

"Had I not been an author I would have killed." We now turn to a climactic debate (and the context of this remark), one that is still continuing as I write, about the veracity, morality, and aesthetics of *Voukéfali*. Here, in many respects, Andreas comes full circle back to his social context on Crete—not only because *Voukéfali* is set in his native Rethemnos but also because a large part of the debate concerns clan reputations rather than aesthetic judgment.

I emphasize this at the outset because I wish to avoid two traps. One is to overemphasize the intellectual importance, for the Rethemnos intelligentsia as much as for the larger Greek readership, of a mean-spirited attack on Andreas's family as well as his own good name. The other is the reverse danger: that of forgetting that literature is never produced in a social vacuum. By insisting on the ethnographic focus of this account of the confrontation, I can at least avoid giving undue scholarly legitimacy to an attack that used all the paraphernalia of scholarship to pursue a family feud—which is precisely the basis of the interest that it does offer.

Yannis Tsouderos, local scholar and representative of a politically prominent local family, responded to the publication of *Voukéfali* by producing an entire history of Crete since Venetian times, the sole purpose of which was to rebut some of the historical claims of Andreas's novel. Andreas has somewhat alleviated the difficulty of knowing how to assess this outburst by responding with a new book of his own. Anthropological readers will perhaps be struck by parallels with the Sahlins-Obeyesekere debate, while others—especially those with a specifically Greek interest—may find more profit in comparing the Rethemnos situation with the debate over *Black Athena* between Martin Bernal and Mary Lefkowitz. In all three cases, despite enormous differences in audience and range of topic, the arguments are about the nature of history. While it is clear that the battle of books is more demonstrably embedded in social particularities in Rethemnos than it is among the members of the American anthropological and philological communities, such comparisons may all the more effectively illustrate the effects of oppositional rhetoric and social context on the logic of intellectual disagreement wherever it occurs.[5]

What, then, is this novel that has angered a local critic to the point of writing an entire book in turn in an attempt to refute its contents? The story is the tale of the town elite, men who held consular rank representing various foreign powers and who wielded the overwhelming political and economic power within the town. The year is 1922: the Greek armies in Asia Minor are about to be routed, and the Cretan Turks and Asia Minor Greeks will shortly be driven from their homes by the Treaty of Lausanne (1924) that, with the exchange of populations, formally brought the hostilities to a close. Andreas documents the economic decline of the Turkish community in Rethemnos, the subtly shifting relations between Turks and Greeks, and the profiteering and pretentiousness of an elite of little education but immense local authority.

This is a novel of vignettes, deftly interwoven so that we see how the everyday humiliations and triumphs of the principals reflect the inexorable tide of events—the impending departure of the Turks (many of whom were in fact Greek-speaking descendants of apostate Christians), the economic absorption of Rethemnos into the larger economy, and the fading of the local dignitaries' importance in a world growing steadily wider and more open. It ends with the departure of some of the most prominent Turks:

> From the rowing-deck of the ferry launch, the travelers watched the boats half floating, half sinking in the foamy sea, and as they move further away from the shore they see their houses being lost, stripped of their color by the mist, rusty, so that only the citadel looms over the sea like a barren rock, deserted and uninhabitable.
>
> "The decaying town" is now what they call our town. . . . (*Voukéfali*, p. 319)

This is a picture that Pandelis Prevelakis also acknowledges in *The Tale of a Town* (1961); M. N. Elliadi (1933) also movingly describes the deep sadness with which the Turks departed from their homes. But it is Andreas who captures the subtlety of Greek-Turkish—or, rather, Christian-Muslim—relations in Rethemnos during this era of endings. These are relationships in which the usual tension between categorical hatreds and personal affections acquires a rare intensity, and Andreas observes this with the wide-eyed wonderment of the child he then was:

5. See Obeyesekere 1992; Sahlins 1985 and 1995; Bernal 1987; Lefkowitz 1996. For useful assessments of the former debate, see Borofsky 1997; Parmentier 1996.

▌ We're friends with the Turkish children who live on the Üzün Yol, as the Turks call the Makrí-Stenó [that is, the Long, Narrow Street]. And when they wander around outside their house we lay together, we chase each other around; and Ali is the child of a family that's involved in some of my father's work. Sometimes his mother sends us little baking-pans of *kataïfi* and other sweets.[6] Those are the days when they are celebrating a festival, and my mother says they're good people. (*Voukéfali*, p. 158)

But there were mysteries too:

▌ Ali's mother loved mine very much and one day she came and told her that I should not come to their house as they were celebrating. I did not understand why I should not go to their house, since indeed they were celebrating. But my mother didn't let me go outside so my mind was on this and I didn't know how I could give her the slip so I could get outside and go to see Ali. I didn't manage to do it, however, and the next day in the morning his mother came and brought us a big tray of *kataïfi*. She said something to my mother, who let me go back with her.

Ali's younger brother was in bed and, as he told me, ill—but as far as I could see the only thing wrong with him was that he wasn't up and about. When Ali and I were alone he told me that the day before they'd had the *sünet bayram* (circumcision ceremony), and that this was why his brother was in bed. So I thought he must have overeaten at this *sünet bayram* business, and that calmed me down.

I often used to hear people talking about the *sünet bayram* ceremonies, and they spoke of them with disdain and laughed about the matter. Everyone talked about the Turks and expressed views about them in the same way in every regard. It may be that my mother was the only person from whose mouth I never heard a bad word or a negative judgment against anyone, even the Turks. She always used to say that all people were good— Turks or Greeks, Gypsies or Blacks, as she used to put it. In fact, there was only one black person living in our own, but he was a Christian; indeed people said he was an Abyssinian, the son of a local person who'd lived for years in Abyssinia and returned with lots of money and a little black child who spoke Greek, and I never heard anyone refuse to be in his company or avoid him because, as he said, his father was one of our own.[7]

One of the things that I found incomprehensible, however, was the fact that while we lived side-by-side with the Turks, so that our houses and

---

6. This is the Turkish *kadayıf*, for which the distinctive dough—somewhat like shredded wheat in consistency and appearance—is still handmade by one family in Rethemnos; these were my landlords for much of the time while I was completing my fieldwork there.

7. House sale contracts from the turn of the century record at least one former "Ethiopian" (that is, black) female slave as a seller. Her name is clearly Muslim.

theirs were jammed right up against each other with only a wall between them, and while in the patios and gardens within the town one could sometimes go into the Turkish houses unimpeded, when they held their Ramadan celebrations not only did we not join in, but I would hear people talking about them in an inexplicable way which nonetheless left in my thoughts and in the depths of my soul something indefinable. If I hadn't known Ali and been friends with him, I don't know where that feeling would have led me.

We often used to laugh at home when people said the Turks were fasting and we were eating; or, when the reverse happened, they may have made fun of us, as they did when we ate pork. In our house we kept a little clay pot that was full of pork, preserved in fat and salt; our mother used to give us a bit every day, and it was very tasty. In fact, as I wanted to give them something whenever Ali came to our house, and to make even better friends with him, I used to tell my mother to give him some sweetmeats, *ommatés*, as we called them: they were made from the guts of the pig we slaughtered for Christmas and filled with rice, raisins, and almonds. But she wouldn't give him any, saying that it was a sin and that the Turks didn't eat pork. There was something concealed behind all that business that I couldn't understand. "You mean," I told my mother, "that by eating pork we're committing a sin; well then, I won't eat any more pig." No indeed. And for a while I really didn't eat any; but I then I forget it by the time winter and Christmas arrived. (*Voukéfali*, pp. 159–61)

But these innocent puzzlements were only part of the story. Among the children fights broke out across religious lines. The Turks became exceedingly nervous; Andreas cites some newspaper entries showing that—significantly unlike the wealthy local Christians—the wealthier Muslims were buying a measure of tolerance by contributing to the Red Cross fund for the incoming refugees. (It was this discovery that was the topic of my first conversation with Andreas at the Rethemnos public library, when I naively decried the idea of consigning these data to a fictional work.) The sense of impending confrontation grew; the conceptual gap between clan battles and ethnic warfare narrowed:

▌My father would take my older brother and me by the hand and we would walk along in front of the hodjas of the Valide mosque as they sat and drew on their hubble-bubble pipes there at the Pigada coffeehouse, next to the Great Gate. We would walk slowly along and the hodjas watched us without expression; my father, as though doing it on purpose, walked slowly and with dragging steps, letting us stare at the hodjas with the tactlessness that children display when they are looking at something that makes a great impression on them. His stance almost showed disdain, as though there was nothing in front of him, or he looked at them in such a way, as he stroked his mustaches into shape and letting us watch them, as to show no respect or the slightest trace of esteem. It was clear that he was making a show of strength. I used to hear from then on that "for every male child you have in the house, you are pointing another gun." And that was directly related to how matters stood with the Turks and with the numerical superiority of the Greeks. But it seems to me that this was also a necessity in relationships among the Christians, and that the production of male children played an important part in the life of any family in relation to the others. (*Voukéfali*, pp. 168–69)

Indeed it did, and still does, particularly in the highland Cretan villages where animal-theft and the vendetta define the tenor of clan relations. It is instructive here, in *Voukéfali*, to see how Andreas suggests the implicit concentricity between clan and national levels of identity, and he even implicitly connects the agnatic strength of clans with the official pronatalism of the state. These analogies, which reflect a larger pattern in Greek social and national discourse, played an important role in the reception of *Voukéfali*.

One direct link with the interests Andreas pursues in *The Cretan War* lies in his respect for the ordinary language of the local people and his contempt for the pretentiousness of the local establishment. Invitations went out to attend the biggest society wedding of the year:

▌All the most select people, with, in pride of place, the consuls, the big merchants, Turks and Christians alike and those who were descended from families of Latin and Byzantine nobles, and the. . . . They almost included the intellectuals, but there weren't any in the city of letters and arts aside from the general ancestor obsession (*proghonopliksía*) and the sense that they were really all intellectuals themselves since they lived in the city where the Cretan Renaissance arose and Chortatses was born.[8] And that was the reason for the war against the man from [the mountain village of] Axos. "It is a matter for wonderment why those gentlemen who are concerned with the language do not wish gradually to impose the language of the cities on the village, but instead wish to transplant that of the most uncouth peasants into the cities. Is it not indeed a matter for wonderment and condemnation?" wrote one newspaper, bothered because the teacher Dafermos from Axos taught demotic Greek in the primary [that is, "demotic"] school. (*Voukéfali*, p. 37)

Or, as one should have to express it in English to make its sheer lunacy more easily accessible, it was because he taught the children in the ordi-

---

8. George Chortatses, a Rethemniot vernacular playwright who flourished between 1600 and 1637.

nary standard language of the country. (Admittedly this was not the everyday Greek that the Cretan schoolchildren spoke at home, but the national standard is nevertheless closely related to the Cretan dialect—a
point that, as we have seen, Psicharis recognized, and that Andreas and
others saw as the special significance of the vernacular literature of the
Cretan Renaissance.) In Greek, the lunacy comes across with cutting clarity in Andreas's words, not only in the pompous archaism of the newspaper quotation, but in his own devastating pun "taught demotic Greek in
the primary school" (*dhidháski ti dhimotikí sto dhimotikó*). To Greeks,
primary school is the place of "popular" education where a child's formation begins.

Andreas delights in poking fun at the self-designated high and mighty
of Rethemnos society. His crack about "ancestor obsession" exploits a
phrase more commonly associated with the national establishment's slavish devotion to Classical prototypes; by associating it both with the ridiculous verbiage of the neo-Classical language and the Frankish and Byzantine domination of medieval Crete, he exposes the pretensions that he
later satirizes when he leads us to realize that many of these grand associations are historical accidents and that, in any case, the good burghers
are painfully ignorant of the history that these names actually represent.
Hence, too, his merciless swipe at the noble families with Latin and Byzantine names, whose authority he then attributes to their recent acquisition of wealth (*Voukéfali*, p. 41). Indeed, he suggests that the only true
Greeks on Crete were probably the villagers, and, still more daringly,
adds that their hatred for the Venetians seems to have led them to help
the Turkish invaders (p. 98). This completely unsettles the image of a
European heritage posed in absolute opposition to the Turkish aspects
of local heritage. A century after the Turkish conquest, a local poet remarked that Cretans could not tell "if the Turks or the Franks [that is,
Venetians] were better" (text in Papagrigorakis 1964–65: 27). Andreas
thus manages, once again, to reclaim the language and culture of the
Cretan Renaissance for the Cretan rural and working-class population
and, in so doing, to pour icy water on the self-satisfaction of the town
aristocrats with their Europeanizing and neo-Classical pretensions.

Like other working-class Rethemniots of his generation, Andreas still
clearly remembers the stiff mien and measured gait of these haughtily
self-important citizens. While he concedes that not all of them were fundamentally bad people, he treats their self-absorption and pomposity as
symptomatic of the faded feudalism to which they feebly still clung. And
this is what their present-day descendants find it hardest to forgive.

The characters who serve his goal of exposing such pretensions are,
predictably perhaps, almost all drawn from very different backgrounds.
Andreas, who in such books as *Bir Hakeim* and *White Fences* demon-

strated his ability to empathize with colonized peoples of vastly different social and cultural backgrounds from his own, here returns with passion to the same theme in his hometown. Here his concern is with people the local elite contemptuously dismisses as "characters." His respect for popular wisdom leads him to recognize what several anthropologists have noted in other contexts (for example, Balshem [1993] in suburban Pittsburgh and Badone [1991] in rural Brittany)—namely, that formal medicine, as well as its self-satisfied practitioners, can become the focus of resentment and resistance on the part of marginalized populations. It is thus with delightful malice that Andreas has a *komboyannítis*, or folk doctor, disrupt the wedding feast that has just been announced with such grandeur. The folk doctor was invited by accident:

▌ And the *komboyannítis* showed up at the wedding ceremony at the Theatre and later, when he sat down at the table with the other professionals— the two doctors, the lawyers, and the high school principal, who in their annoyance avoided talking to him—and tried to open up a discussion of the topics that were dear to him, the seahorse [which he used, dried, in his medicaments] and the various mountain herbs, their special properties and their profusion, giving each one its Latin name, everyone, even the "well brought up" bride, led by the regional and town aristocracy, followed his speech with surprise and terror.

The fake doctor had stood upright and in an official manner had begun to talk about how the curative properties of the seahorse were known from antiquity when the town was just a village of fishermen and when the local doctors used to collect seahorses and cured many diseases, but especially those of the skin and particularly smallpox and syphilis, which were the scourge of that time.

All admired his knowledge and his fluency, but especially his impudence. But even though they were disposed to applaud him—those, that is, who thought that his presence was a fine idea of the bride's father, to invite this "type" to create a pleasant and amusing atmosphere—they were in for a disappointment because Mr. Triphyllis whispered in the ears of the mansion guards to drag him, still standing, out of the hall. This produced a general sense of relief, especially among those of more serious mien, despite the protests of the "doctor"—who, coming down to earth, castigated the entire company for the illiteracy and disrespect of the town aristocracy for the curers in the science of Hippocrates, who, of course, just like the folk doctor himself, had no piece of paper from "Athens" (*Athinisi*[9]). (*Voukéfali*, pp. 38–39)

To this day, the battle between folk curers (who are often called *praktikí*,

---

9. A Classical Greek locative, often used in the nineteenth century.

or "practical" curers) and the official medical establishment continues, in Greece as elsewhere. It still has the larger implications of confrontation between local or class pride and centralized authority; and Andreas uses it here for the admitted purpose of mocking petty bourgeois values. Note especially that the folk doctor attacks the assembled notables for their "illiteracy," thereby not only deflating their airs and graces but suggesting that their cultural pretensions are in fact entirely hollow—that they are more ignorant in their context than he is in his. The prototype of the folk doctor was an Asi-Goniot by origin, a poor man for whose intelligence and ingenuity Andreas had considerable respect. In this sly vignette drawn from life, Andreas satirically intimates the play of power, fear, and force that an ethnographer would more probably feel required to spell out in order to reveal the particular social pressures at work.

Andreas does not preach; his books, although politically and socially alert, are not political tracts. This is consistent with his tactic of not spelling out the motives of his characters but instead leading his readers to derive them from the narrative—a favorite device of the Greek village gossip reported by ethnographers (for example, du Boulay 1974: 195). Innuendo is central to gossip, and Andreas's writing builds on that tradition.

The consul of France has announced a huge feast to celebrate Bastille Day. A local newspaper, remarking favorably on the event, promises to publish a list of all the names of the town notables, so that there would be a public documentation of their ancestry and their present civic contributions:

▌ But what made a great impression was the fact . . . that the list began with the consuls and indeed with Lardotiros [the consul of France]. Many said that he had had previous disputes with the consul of England,[10] who should have appeared first because England and her consul always had the first word about anything concerning the island. Others again thought that because of the feast Lardotiros was preparing they were doing him the favor of presenting him and his family first, and some down-at-heel fake grandees with the well-known Byzantine and Venetian names who were jealous of Lardotiros and Vous [the consul of Britain] gave it out that it was all a ruse of the newspaper to set them up for a quarrel. (*Voukéfali*, p. 114)

Without for a moment attributing motives himself (except for the minimalist mention of jealousy), Andreas delicately draws together some favorite themes of everyday conversation: the quarrels of the mighty, the self-seeking of the media, and, above all, the strong preference for any explanation of events that depends on a conspiracy. The narrator would not dream of suggesting anything so dishonorable, but he has, of course,

10. Namely, Great Britain; everyday Greek speech rarely makes the distinction.

heard what others have said. The gossip's delicately insistent whisper does its work twice over, in the event described, and in the narration, and so it lends itself to the projection of these speculations about motive to a readership far larger than the small society of Rethemnos then and now: this is a canyon of echoes stretching into posterity. Small wonder, then, that it has made the consuls' modern heirs anxious.

Despite these wickedly accurate appropriations of talk for his own purposes, Andreas does also allow his characters some moments of introspection. Perhaps the most charged, since it speaks to the very self-deception of power, is his depiction of Alatsas's contemplation of the end of his control of the salt (Cretan *alátsi*) monopoly:

▌In reality this colossus felt very weak, and the idea of the end—any end—terrified him. If he lost his stroll around town, the polished atmosphere with which the consuls and the Street of the Czars [today's Arkadiou] preserved the vanity of success, he would fall apart.

And as he thought about all these matters and doubt spoiled his mood, he discovered that the wheeling and dealing at the Monopoly amused him, satisfied him, and made him feel happy, because he was begged for a single oke of salt, or because he was able to impose an obligation on someone who was not entitled to any but who, thanks to his intervention, could load up his donkey. (*Voukéfali,* pp. 58–59)

Although these thoughts are represented as private musings, their form is that of open gossip. Motives grounded in conspiracy and power-lust and based on tangible signs such as the malice-laden glances with which the bishop and Alatsas challenge each other in church (*Voukéfali,* pp. 135–36) have a plausible ring. They are like excuses: to be effective, to have some actual effect on the course of events, they need not be convincing (since we cannot know whether anyone really believes them) but they must be socially acceptable (since then everyone has the same interest in not challenging them). Andreas captures the formulaic character of gossip with a nicely sardonic eye for the externals that legitimate it, so that we are drawn into the cultural logic by which people infer each other's motives in a society that explicitly denies that possibility.

Most commonly, such scenes revolve around issues of status and kinship. Andreas reminds us that these seemingly fixed properties of individuals are highly contingent and negotiable, thereby challenging the rhetoric of descent. While anthropologists have similarly argued that these social forms are more supple than their formal rhetoric would concede (for example, Karp 1980), Andreas is interested in the motives behind their management because he himself, openly and for ideologically explicit reasons, has reasons for wanting to expose the conditionality of the leading citizens' status.

Many of these worthies claimed to belong to true *tzákia* ("hearths"), families of noble, landowning origin. Andreas does not accept these claims. We have already heard his mockery of those who base them on surnames of Byzantine or Venetian origin; much of the social message of *Voukéfali* is that the real measure of status among these families is money—new money. While their appointment to consular positions gave the heads of these families grand airs in public and led them to affect the mannerisms thought most likely to sustain a cultivated and above all "European" image, their situation was actually quite precarious, since it depended more on the fluctuations of the international market than on their family backgrounds. (In the 1960s, when the demand for Rethemnos soap suddenly vanished because detergents and mass-produced soaps from elsewhere had flooded the market, those who had not managed to move to larger cities were ruined.)

But in the period of which Andreas writes in *Voukéfali*, it was easier for them to bury their heads in the sand. They were able, and inclined, to invest considerable energy in the construction of fine pedigrees, hoping that these would shore up their fortunes. On an island where patrilineal kinship is still a dominant idiom, moreover, all the talk of lineages and blood was immediately comprehensible to the plebs they hoped to impress, while their European patrons all still boasted royal families and aristocracies similarly organized in terms of agnatic bloodlines. It was not impossible for a wealthy burgher of recent village origin and some education to adopt the rhetoric of aristocratic status.

Rethemniots were perfectly aware of this: they were, after all, as astute as the members of any society in calculating the malleability of their own social rules. It is thus quite plausible for Andreas to represent the ruminations of the wife of the English consul in church in these terms:

▌ Her eye is a sharp razor blade. It doesn't just look. Nothing escapes her, but she literally strips her fellow citizens bare. And these are matters of great moment. The impressions she'll bring away with her will one day be used at the Ladies' Society on one of the women in church today, and you might think she was a Circe:[11] when she touches a plebeian woman she transforms her, if she wants her as a member of the Society, into, so to speak, a thoroughbred Arabian mare. (*Voukéfali*, p. 136)

Superficially, however, clan membership remained immutable. It could be invoked for all sorts of political intrigues, as the legitimate basis for loyalty and the public expression of affect. Even though today the patriline plays only a muted role in the Rethemniots' electoral decisions, being

---

11. Circe transformed all of Odysseus's men into pigs when they arrived at her enchanted isle.

mainly a rhetorical device for cajoling those of a candidate's supporters to whom it happens to apply, it is certainly not irrelevant in tight races or neighborhood political contests. In 1922, it was more directly in tune with the leading citizens' European pretensions—something analogous could be discerned among the dynastic habits of the great houses—while it still also made sense to the workers and peasants who were supposed to be impressed by the consuls' pedigrees.

Alatsas thought about running for mayor:

> ▌ And thus as hour after hour and night after night he sits on the highest balcony of the Paradise [the hotel he had built], he thinks about becoming mayor of the town, even if his rival is from the same clan and has the same name [not Alatsas, which is a personal nickname]. Of course the other fellow with the same name is deeply respected, is very learned, and enjoys great esteem in the town because of the letters he sends the king on the anniversary of his coronation, on his name day, on his birthday, and even on the occasion of his convalescence from some form of constipation that left His Majesty bedridden for a fortnight. What are the parvenus in the other towns to think, with their vineyards, their olive groves, and all the noise they make? In this town, nobility and rank have taken firm root. Proof of it lies in the letters that his kinsman the mayor receives from the king. These flatter him for a moment because some reflected glory emitted by those letters falls on him as well as because he has the same name as the mayor, but he thinks he's more able and intelligent and has the Paradise as proof, and he must push the other fellow aside so that he can take his place and so bring honor on their name, on their surname. And his homonymous fellow citizen (*sinonómatos*[12]) the mayor, learning that Alatsas, his own flesh and blood, wants him out of the mayoralty, came to the brink of apoplexy, and for a long time he doesn't go to the town hall or walk around in the streets, and if all their agnatic kin in town hadn't fallen on Alatsas it is questionable whether he would ever have gone for a walk in the streets again. It hurt him so much—especially the ingratitude of Alatsas, who had held the Monopoly for so many years with his support and connivance. (*Voukéfali*, p. 151)

How does Andreas know what these two identically named characters actually think? In fact, he makes few claims of doing so, but he describes their reactions in terms of the actions from which any townsperson would draw much the same conclusions: Alatsas's endless nights on the balcony of his hotel, the pride of Rethemnos; the mayor's sulking and

---

12. There is no satisfactory way of translating this term. In rural Crete, two people who share a baptismal name also thereby share a social bond, signaled by the use of the reciprocal address term *sínome*.

seclusion; and the sudden eruption of excited activity within the clan, which would be impossible to hide from the town at large for any length of time.

In his treatment of Greek-Turkish relations in town, he adopts a similar tactic. He can reasonably assume that the Turks are hoping that Kemal's victorious rout of the Greek forces in Asia Minor will bring the Turkish army back to Crete, not because he knows it for a fact, but because this is a widely shared assumption among the Greeks. He describes the local Turks' mien as sweet-natured and polite, constrained by fear that an unguarded word or action might provoke disastrous short-term violence. The Turks, he suggests, feel they can afford to wait. That, after all, is presumably the fear that the Greeks openly express among themselves and to which his kin and their Greek friends would have been privy; as he points out, the Greeks harbored analogous thoughts of eventual victory. In this way, he is able to breach the wall of mutual inscrutability, not only among individuals of the same faith, but also in interreligious relations (*Voukéfali*, pp. 262–63). Andreas neatly reverses the balance of thought and action: "Everyone's bearing and behavior were indeterminable" (p. 263)—a phrase that immediately resonates with the recognition of indeterminacy in recent social theory (for example, Giddens 1984).[13] People are hard to read, especially at the very times when others try hardest to read them. Andreas has turned this simple paradox into an interesting reflection on the social discourse of motive and character.

His technique is to take the conventions that everyone takes for granted and ask why people would adhere to them. Thus, for example, he has the English consul reflecting on the satirical attack on him that had been launched during the Carnival celebrations and thinking that his position demanded a show of tolerance and unaffectedness. The ideal of "simplicity" is still particularly strong among relatively wealthy Rethemniots.[14] Like the secretiveness that must be performed in a very public way or the modesty that must be blazoned across some individuals' acts, this kind of simplicity is only possible for those who can afford a return to humble roots. The gambler boasts only of losses, never of gains, in this society; and all social life is a gamble requiring the smiling of the skilled player. Andreas knows this well. He also knows that such displays of simplicity take much elaborate preparation—besides, as we learn elsewhere in the book (*Voukéfali*, p. 183), Alatsas is a compulsive accountant and measurer.

13. The Greek terms are *aprosdhióristi* (indeterminate) and *aprosdhioristía* (indeterminacy).

14. On this affectation of simplicity in Rethemnos, see *A Place in History* (Herzfeld 1991a: 60–61).

This is a personal characteristic that violates the equally elaborate display of disregard for precision in commercial relations that allows Rethemniots to forge social bonds through displays of warm personal generosity rather than on the basis of open calculation (see Herzfeld 1991a: 168–74). Andreas is also aware of Marx's observations on the fetishization of money and the commoditization of goods, theoretical constructs that are not far from the social perspective of many poorer Rethemniots. From these insights, ironic decoctions of the pretensions of simplicity and disinterestedness, Andreas builds a familiar picture of how motive is constructed in gossip: he presents the consul's ponderous ruminations as an internalization of exactly the kind of intrigue that collectively the townsfolk either adopt for themselves or attribute to others.

Andreas is also an actor himself in this account, at least through the figure of his father. Old Nenes has a cameo role in *Voukéfali*. Not only do we hear in full the story of his defense of the Turks against the furious Christians from Asi-Gonia, but he is also accused of killing Reçep, the Turk who confessed to the murder of a Turkish notable, the event with which the book begins.

Serif-bey, the assassinated notable, was not, Andreas tells us, like other Turks. In appearance blond and blue-eyed, so that Andreas assumes he must be the descendant of Greek or, more probably, Venetian apostates, he refused to engage in the divisive politics of the other leading Rethemniots. He was also cordial toward the Christians. This is not the first time that Andreas associates a tall, blond appearance with values of which he approves. He follows local convention—some of which has passed into scholarly writing of the more nationalistic variety (for example, Poulianos 1971)—in associating that physical type with the proud Sfakians from whom he himself claims descent and, through them, the Dorians with whom he and others connect the language of the west Cretan highland villages (for example, *The Cretan War*, p. 14). Once, describing a Turk he remembered from his childhood, he told me:

> ● I remember one. A fine fellow. The one who was right across from our shop, a milk merchant. Who looked as if he was an Asi-Goniot, for instance. *A Greek!* And he was pale; and he had a long head, he had.

This was the shape that Andreas remembered when he exhumed his mother's skull before burying one of his brothers: a mark of beauty, which he also associates with her blue eyes, and which he could contemplate with affectionate equanimity even while his relatives recoiled in horror. Perhaps these genetic images owe something to the popular work of the Soviet-trained physical anthropologist, Aris Poulianos, at least indirectly. Be that as it may, they reproduce a popular hierarchy. His own brother George was relatively light-haired, and Andreas frequently mentions this fact. Such matters become significant in the context of the historical argument in which *Voukéfali* is currently enmeshed.

It may seem strange, even discomfiting, to readers who are accustomed to embarrassment at the very mention of skin or hair color that so determinedly antiracist an author as Andreas should retain explicitly genetic views of descent and character. But it must be remembered that in Greece, a small country that has been culturally homogeneous for most of this century, even quite small differences of manner are immediately noticeable; and, as Konstandinos Tsoukalas (1996, vol. 1:145) notes, Greece is no less prone than other countries, its past reputation notwithstanding, to the global pest of racist responses to disintegrating national borders (see Panourgiá 1992; Seremetakis 1996). Indeed, the prerequisites for racism are already well in place. Physical differences have commonly been associated with differences of character, and this, in the face of an influx of immigrants, very easily transmutes into discrimination, a process that also rests on the cultural and legal patterns of stereotyping already mentioned. It is not a far cry from a system that associates personal names and character with inherited characteristics to racist generalizations about "others."

Those who, like Andreas, have opted to stand against racism may nonetheless do so in terms that paradoxically retain this cultural ideology of inherited traits. That much is clear in the assessment of *White Fences* by Dimitris Raftopoulos (1959a):

> Reading books with humanitarian, antiwar intentions, we have rarely sensed so strongly and so naturally the absurdity of war, the leveling of the ego and the cruelty that takes place in military camps, the militaristic corruption, the racial prejudice. And we have rarely made such a close acquaintance or become so familiar—in Greek literature, at least—with people of a different color. Saad, Kirí, Lau, Khuri, Sind among the "natives"[15] and Tzanis and Mr. Ilias among the Greeks (*Romií*) are multiply illuminated characters with authentic humanity, and with their weaknesses uncovered and with their greatness concealed by the insignificance of their everyday appearance. (Raftopoulos 1959b: 150–51)

While this passage suggests part of the appeal of Andreas's writing for anthropologists—his delicate understanding of the balance between everyday appearance and personal capacities—it also shows that at the level of generalization it was still necessary to argue for the common humanity of those who looked different.

Moreover, notions about heredity die hard. Here we can best recall again the experiences of Neni Panourgiá, the Greek anthropologist who

---

15. The term appears in English (and in Latin letters) within quotes in the original.

dared to open up the intimacy of her family and recounts how her dark, "Gypsy" appearance was compared to her sister's fairness. Through her professional and personal odyssey, she brings into critical focus what might have been dismissed as a trivial jest, showing that the attitudes that today surface as a more dangerously generalized racism have their roots in deeply entrenched local theories of heredity. (The Glendiots, too, many of whom are darker in appearance than the people of nearby villages, are sometimes derided by the latter as Gypsies or Arabs—and seem as ironically aware of this as Panourgiá.) For Panourgiá, the play of racial stereotypes is diagnostic of the family tensions that, as my student at the time, she had told me were a central feature of Greek social relations but that were also curiously absent from the existing ethnographic record; as a family member rather than simply as a Greek, she could enter and describe this privileged space of discord.[16]

But she writes primarily as an anthropologist: she offers her readers an analysis that recognizes the interest for them of being able to see such intimacies from within. The novelist Andreas, by contrast, is engaged in a feud in *defense* of that space and of larger spaces concentric with it. Even before the feud erupted, moreover, he wrote as a defender of Cretan virtue and purity of descent before an audience of often contemptuous urban Greeks. For him the point to emphasize was a blondness at once immanent in Europeans, Greeks, Cretans, and the people of Asi-Gonia in general and the Nenes patriline in particular. And at times, at least, he concedes that such claims are strategic rather than literal: "We say we're the descendants of the Ancients, whereas we are not, but that too plays a creative role in reinforcing our internal resistance"—that is, to any threat against personal or collective autonomy.

Indeed, Andreas's association of blondness with a certain kind of descent—with the Sfakians, with the "good families" (*kalósiri*) among them especially, and with a glorious western origin (whether Doric or Venetian)—initially appears to sit uneasily with his dislike of chauvinism. In this sense, he is indeed not a relativist. Rather, in a perspective that fits better with some anthropological *critiques* of relativism (notably Fabian 1983), he seeks the common ground of all human beings even while noting what is special about his own cultural heritage. It is here that we meet one of the most interesting contradictions in Andreas's demeanor. For it is true that he believes Greek culture to be superior in some sense, and that

---

16. Panourgiá has also commented to me (personal communication) that even family membership is no guarantee of access, so that she learned important things about her family from the comments of outsiders. Both social entities, the nation and the family, enjoin their members to act defensively against any unwarranted prying or other invasion of a collective intimacy.

he saw in the decline of the Turkish community of Crete a predetermined turning-point that owed something, at least, to a depleted stock. By the same token, in his irritation with the smugness of the Swedes he remarked that the Greeks should stop trying to be "European," while the "Europeans" should be proud of "being Greek"—a thought that then led him to reflect with some bitterness that such thinking would get him called a "[right-wing] nationalist" (*ethnikófron*),[17] a term for which he has only the most profound hatred (*Policemen*, p. 27). His nationalism is tough and uncompromising, and he yields to no colonels or police thugs in his national pride.

And yet—and yet: his is the nationalism that views any act of discrimination as a disgrace. His model is his father's protection of the Muslims in 1922. His friendship with a left-wing Turkish family in Stockholm, lovingly described in *Policemen*, prompts thoughts of common ancestry—blood and light hair appear again:

▌ Now we're two thousand miles from the Aegean and the enmities and passions are wiped out and far away. There is of course some caution on our part, but they are more spontaneous. Laughing, brown-haired, benign and generous. They looked like Peloponnesians or Greek islanders. And that's what they may have been [by origin]. Who knows. . . . (*Policemen*, p. 122)

They were from Istanbul: they must have been "of . . . mixed Turkish and Greek descent" (pp. 145–46)[18]—an ironic comment, as the ellipsis signifies (a standard Greek convention). It leads Andreas to a wry aside: "In Europe we have ended up as nationalists." (It is apparently harder to be socialists in socialist Sweden: irony reinforces irony.) So even as he turns to the language of blood and loyalty he is aware that its significance is very much a matter of context—like the Glendiot villager who informed me that as a guest worker in Germany he found his Turkish fellow immigrants much more congenial than their German hosts even though he knew that in a war with Turkey he would be among the first to fight; or like the villager who drily commented that his clan segment had apparently been turned from socialists into liberals by its leaders' personal loyalty to certain patrons (Herzfeld 1985: 113).

Like many Greeks, he has no illusions about his compatriots themselves, especially about those who confuse chauvinism with patriotism.

---

17. This term has exclusively right-wing implications.

18. He describes these people as being "Turko-Greeks" (*apo tous . . . Tourkoromious*), an expression that implies recognition of the extensive intermarriage as well as cultural mingling among Greeks and Turks over many centuries, a phenomenon that the more chauvinist elements of the political Right have been particularly determined either to ignore or to deny.

In *Voukéfali,* he rails against the upstart Greek merchants whose greed and indiscipline led them to harass the remaining Turkish population amid the misery of its lowest ebb; he describes with barely restrained emotion the last encounters between the two communities, as neighbors and friends were rent from one another by the machinations of politicians and commercial interests; and he satirizes the foretaste of his own humiliation at the hands of the fascists:

> And one day a poor fellow who didn't mind his own miserable business but wished to get mixed up in public matters—it seems that this right belongs only to the well-to-do—shouted out at a rally just as the army's arrival was announced, right into the speaker's face: "Down with war, no more war!" What happened next had never happened before. One fellow slugged him in the head with his cane and all the bystanders fell upon him.
>
> The crowd became a dense mass and no one knew any more who was hitting whom. The big retail grocers and the smallest fry of the Great Gate, the beggars, alike became agitated, and the very saints in the icon-stands lost their tempers. With all the shouting and screaming, and because the row spread widely and everyone was blinded with agitation and patriotism, the little chap managed to slip out of the melee, dash away, and take to his heels. That same day, however, the gendarmerie managed to capture him and locked him up in the jail. And when the police chief arrived he discovered to his dismay that the man's son had been killed in Ukraine. He cursed him, he called him all kinds of humiliating names, and he told him he should be proud that his son had been killed and that he himself should request to be sent to the front line in order to avenge his child and not shout "down with war" and get in the way of those who wanted to go and take the blood of his child back.
>
> "But the army is not fighting in Ukraine, Chief, sir."
>
> "Yes, we're fighting the Turks; but behind the Turks are hidden the Bolsheviks, didn't you know that the Bolsheviks are supporting the Turks?"
>
> "And when we went to Ukraine, were we fighting Turks?"
>
> "Look, you, are you a Bolshevik?" (*Voukéfali,* pp. 226–27)

At the conclusion, the poor fellow ends up in a psychiatric ward, which protected the Rethemniots from being infected by his dangerous ideas.

Andreas is alive to the various ways in which ethnic and political categories can be interchanged, commingled, and reversed. He has seen too many Greek communists dismissed as Bulgarians while a Yugoslav rightist became a Greek. For him, however, these are false ascriptions: he does believe in the existence of real national identities, durable forms of consciousness that have survived the oppressions of the centuries. He does not accept the negotiability of identity that anthropologists usually take for granted. There is more than a hint of essentialism in his thinking about culture, race, and nationality; and it is an essentialism symbolically grounded in the language of heredity that was an integral part of his formative background.

It is this that enables him to be a nationalist without being a chauvinist. Indeed, he sees chauvinism as a betrayal of national standards. Again, the basis of this logic, with all its obvious internal traps, lies in his upbringing, with its emphasis on haughty restraint as the mark of moral superiority but also on the presumed natural inferiority of certain categories of people. (He recognizes the negative side of these connections—for example, when he notes that when he discovered that the heroic poet Yannis Ritsos, unbreakable enemy of fascism, was homosexual, it was his deeply inculcated Cretan perceptions that made him regret this even though it would not have bothered him in any friend for whose manliness he had less regard.) Chauvinism is a violation of the rules of hospitality, writ large. It demeans those who express it, for, in failing to recognize common humanity across national or racial lines, they are denying their own humanity.

For Andreas, the embodiment of this understanding was, again, his father's defense of the Rethemnos Turks against the Asi-Goniots. It was more than the recognition of a common cultural idiom such as the Glendiots' experience of Turks in Germany. It was more than a grand expression of the superior position of the host over the guest. It went even beyond the Greeks' proclivity to distinguish between categories and personal relationships. It expressed, Andreas believes, his father's conviction that a massacre at that point would have terrible consequences in a war of revenge later—a clear extension of the deterrent logic of feuding to interethnic relations. But it *also* encapsulated the claims to the Greeks' moral superiority that Andreas suggests are destroyed by acts and attitudes of chauvinism. Claims to moral superiority must rest on morally superior acts.

Andreas suggests that chauvinism was perhaps, like Orthodox Christianity, a necessary evil in that it provided an incentive for the survival of a Greek consciousness. The successive occupiers of Greek lands, whether themselves claiming Greek cultural identity or not, were unable to quench the more popular consciousness of that heritage. Here, in fact, Andreas's Marxist orientation is completely in accord with a strand of Greek historiographical thinking that leads from early nationalists like Spiridon Zambelios and Konstantinos Paparigopoulos to Marxist-inspired historians of the present century such as Yanis Kordatos, who wrote in the years around the Asia Minor disaster and after, and the more recent social historians Nikos Svoronos and Spiros Asdrachas (see, for example, Asdrachas 1953; Svoronos 1983). Andreas expresses through his writing a perspective on ethnic identity that insists on the integrity and durability of the Greek—and hence on its tried and tested virtues in this sense—while acknowledging the fundamental respect owed to all human beings irrespective of race, culture, or ideology.

It is this ability to respect Turks as people while claiming such respect as part of his vision of Greekness that presumably inspired the award of the Greco-Turkish Peace Committee's İpekçi Prize to Andreas for *Vouké-fali*. But some of his critics were less impressed. To those who continued to operate with the positivistic assumptions that Andreas calls chauvinistic, his stand is unacceptable and his portrait of his father an act of betrayal. Furthermore, as a Cretan from a small society that compels a response to insult, he found himself in a position in which he felt so compelled by a local critic. Let us now turn to that dispute.

It was put about that Old Nenes, Andreas's father, had killed Reçep. But why? Once again we are back in the steamy world of small-town gossip, attributions of motive, reputation—and social class. Andreas writes for a national audience, but he is locally read for quite parochial reasons that ensure—for such is social life—that "the past is never quite past but reverberates in the present" (K. Stewart 1996: 75); anecdote, novel, and ethnography live in each other. Andreas reminds the reader that he is present in these events, his father is a social presence also:

> Now who said it was Nenes, my father, who had killed Reçep, so it was put about throughout the city and talked about by Turks and Greeks alike, it's not difficult to guess. The consuls and the ağas would have killed him first had they been able to do so, but my father was not one of those people who are easily made to disappear.
>
> The consuls and ağas reckoned that since my father was friendly with Serif-bey and since such friendships reach the point where each one feels obliged to avenge whatever evil may befall his friend, the rumor would be credible and they'd be able to relax. My father was out of town the day Reçep was killed and those worthies said that he was away right after the murder on purpose, so that they wouldn't be able to get him involved. (*Voukéfali*, p. 53)

This description of Greek small-town gossip carries conviction because it is ethnographically precise. Andreas does not fully avoid attributing motives himself in this instance. Through his father, and by inserting himself in the text, he has become an active participant in the social process he is describing. His voice is that of someone who is actually talking about who did what, when, and why. And in the process he has raised the stakes. If this is a historical novel, as he claims, why do we hear his voice so clearly? Why does his declaration of class war take the form of a vindication of his father? And why, given that the principal attack on the novel is viewed even by some of those who dislike it as excessive and unscholarly, has he taken the step of responding with a similarly substantial volume?

A quick perusal of the two books reveals the answer in all its simplicity: this is not a true literary debate, as Andreas rightly told me, but a feud initiated on the grounds of a highly literalist, historicist reading of Andreas's novel. At stake, once again, is a central concern of this study: to what extent is realism a representation of the real? For the principals, this is both an aesthetic and, in the broadest sense, a political question. Yannis Tsouderos considers the book a libel against his mother's clan; Andreas responds because Tsouderos doubts the Greekness of his name (a common device of what Wace and Thompson [1914] called "political philology"), calls his representation of his father an insult and Old Nenes himself pro-Turkish, and—the strangest thrust of all—denies that Andreas's deceased brother George ever existed. In the feuding villages of the hill country, such charges have led to vendettas of long duration. Indeed, Tsouderos finds the phrase "my father was not one of those people who are easily made to disappear" [literally, who are easily lost] (*Voukéfali*, p. 53; Tsouderos 1995: 8) to be a threat in precisely this idiom: he explicitly finds the idiom of violence among clans in the text and responds in kind. Both prefer to wield the weapons of the writer than of the armed shepherds; but the battle is joined in the clan terms that both antagonists as well as their audience understand perfectly.

But why respond at all? Here Andreas cites the logic of the small society—a place where reputations center on precisely such matters of clan-based importance. Rethemnos is well known in Greek literature as a gossipy, inbred place. Lilika Nakou's semi-autobiographical description in *Madame Do-Re-Mi* infuriated many of the same, mostly conservative, right-wing citizens as did Andreas's *Voukéfali*. In that book he gives us a description of this society that deserves to be placed alongside Robert Redfield's famous account of *The Little Community* (1960).

Andreas thus argues that he has little choice but to defend his family in the way he knows best. The personal slurs—Tsouderos uses terms like *skilovrízi* ("swears like a dog")—he addresses calmly enough, mostly by poking fun at the small-town academicism of an author who in all seriousness can place the legend "philologist, etc." under his name on the title page. This is irony in combat with a self-important academicism. From time to time, there emerges a note of incredulity: how can a serious scholar think that any harm to personal or family reputations could come from a novel, even a historical novel? But Tsouderos has chosen to stake his forces on ostensibly academic grounds, producing instead a battle about truth claims, and Andreas responds on those grounds instead.

The mudslinging is impressive by any standards. No one with any connections to the principals is entirely safe from at least a spattering, but the heavy fire is reserved for the agnatic clans of the principals, their wives, and their mothers. The major accusations concern historical charges of betrayal of the national cause—to the Venetians, the Turks, or the Germans: it matters not who the beneficiaries are because the capacity for treason is considered to be constant throughout history—a hereditary taint in the male line.

Tsouderos's point of departure appears to be the highly unflattering representation of Alatsas, the salt monopolist and hotel owner, whose prototype was a member of the clan of Tsouderos's mother. But the families of the other principals, notably the consuls, belonged to the same social class. This is the main objective of the satire: Andreas does not disguise his class antagonism, which is one of the reasons for which he inserts his father—the proud shepherd who never learned to use the citified speech of the local elite—into the narrative. Thus, for example, he openly affirms that he killed Alatsas off—from apoplexy, surrounded by prostitutes—ten years earlier than the man's peaceful death at home, for reasons that went beyond the mere license of a fictional writer. When I asked him why he did this, he responded with a wicked touch of wit:

● Because it had to fit with the times, that is, when the times were *changing*. And indeed he came down in the world after. . . . In fact I really did him a favor. Because he, after the Asia Minor catastrophe, the salt trade fell into the hands of the state, it was no longer in the jurisdiction of the foreigners and the Consuls, and so forth. They created the monopoly, not exactly for the state, it was the International Economic Commission. I.E.C. Matches, alcohol, all those things had a seal, a band, on which was written "I.E.C." They got huge profits from it, let's say. He carried on there as an employee (*ipálilos*[19]), as director or whatever, but he did not have unrestricted jurisdiction or managerial control. Do you understand? He had come down in the world by now. Really I made him die in order to get him off the hook. I was bored with . . . well, that's novel-writing for you!

But it was precisely these acts of poetic license that, in a literal reading of the text, provided the grounds for complaints about historical distortion.

In his zeal to prove Andreas a liar and an incompetent, Tsouderos took the unwise step of challenging statements that Andreas has made

---

19. An *ipálilos* is literally "one who serves *under* someone else." In a culture that accords high value to personal autonomy, this is clearly a demeaning situation by definition, and it is in ideological resistance to the idea of employment so conceived that leftists like Andreas are able to reconcile their Marxist emphasis on the common good with the cultural imperatives of sovereignty.

about his own family. The denial of brother George's existence is the strangest element in this strategy, but its logic becomes more apparent when we shift perspective from the literary to the social. The emphasis of the Greek naming system, as we have seen, is on "resurrection": the embodied commemoration of close kin, whether because they are in the generation now passing or because they have already died. To deny that a beloved close agnate, especially a brother, ever existed—which Tsouderos does on the grounds that he was unable to locate George's birth certificate in the state registry—is tantamount to denying the entire clan. Under Greek law, it would in fact be possible for Andreas to sue on the grounds of "undermining his family's standing," but this option appears to be of little interest. If one purpose of legal process is to dispose rapidly of family disputes and to ensure that the administration of justice remains in official hands, these sons of Cretan clans want none of it.

If there were any doubts about the social character of Tsouderos's attack, it is easily dispelled by his assertion that "Nenes" is a Turkish name. This charge generalizes to an entire clan his criticism of Andreas for daring to suggest that Old Nenes had actually done anything so unpatriotic as defending unarmed Turkish civilians against a horde of blood-lusting Cretan shepherds. Andreas agrees that even possession of a Turkish name does not make one a Turk—but he is adamant that the name is Indo-European, quoting similar names from as far afield as Spain and Sweden and arguing that the village name of Nenedes (plural form of Nenes) on the island of Samos—now replaced by "Ambelos" ("Vine") because again some official mistakenly assumed that Nenedes must be a Turkish toponym—is further evidence of its Greekness. In ancient Greek, there is an almost identical kinship term (*ninnē*, grandmother; cf. *nennos*, father's brother, mother's brother), and this provides a perfect counterweight to Tsouderos's argument that *Nenes* is nothing but a *Turkish* kinship term (*nine*, "grandmother") (*George Nenedakis*, pp. 27–28; cf. Tsouderos 1995: 13).

In fact, Andreas admits, there are other possibilities. One that he seemed to consider plausible when I suggested it was that some antecedent had been given the nickname of Nenes because of a habit of saying "yes, yes, yes, yes" (*ne, ne, ne, ne*) all the time, a not uncommon habit with some impatient individuals. This, he said, was acceptable too, because, after all, *ne* is a Greek word. Indeed, such an explanation is suggested by his first encounter with Thanasis Tsingos, in which his monosyllabic answers of "*ne . . . ne*" to the latter's questioning—Tsingos was an officer of the military police—led to a good-humored exchange:

> ■ "Are you in the antitank unit (*andiarmatistís*)?" he asked next.
> "Yes (*né*)," I told him, keeping the binoculars to my eyes.

"Did you come up here today?"

"*Né.*"

"Are you an NCO?"

"*Né.*"

"Hey, Nené . . .," he said with a laugh, "what's your name?"

"Even if you weren't a prophet," I tell him, "lieutenant, sir . . . that *is* my name."

He laughed. It is rare for an ordinary soldier to become friends right from the start with an officer. But I felt so comfortable and his tone was so friendly that had I realized at that moment that I was talking with the commander of the military police—as Tsingos was—I would not have felt differently. (*Tsingos*, p. 12)

Tsingos became a close friend from that moment. But with Tsouderos, a former friend and beneficiary of Andreas's kindly concern who has now turned against him,[20] Andreas prefers a derivation of the clan name that offers a more perfect polar opposite to Tsouderos's calumny.

Note that what matters is less the accuracy of the derivation—hopelessly beyond certainty in any case—than its appropriate symmetry in a fight about essential Greekness. This is the logic of the vendetta once again—which is how one local journalist in Rethemnos (Petridis 1996) has perceptively dubbed the confrontation. Indeed, Andreas himself, like many of the Rethemniots with whom I talked about this latest *cause célèbre* in the literary topos they inhabit, recognizes the aspect of agnatic vindication as the key to understanding it.

Andreas's Greek and Cretan identities are extensions of selfhood and family pride. They are neither negotiable nor vulnerable; they require neither unprovoked aggression nor undue self-congratulation for their defense. Andreas's contempt for the nationalistic revision of the past is, by the same token, an outgrowth of his refusal to boast of his personal achievements or to consider them "important" (*spoudhéo*). The logic in which both sides have engaged is that of a system in which clan, regional, and national identities are like concentric rings, easily fused into a single notion of collective being. In this system, an attack on one level is an attack on all. Their best defense lies in the manly virtue of subordination of the self to the pride of the clan—the linchpin of what Andreas calls the Asi-Goniot self-regard (*asighoniótikos eghoïsmós*) that sustains him in this confrontation. This subordination of authorial self to clan collectivity mocks his main critic's posturings in a fashion that the latter cannot answer without further exposing himself to ridicule: such is the strength of ironic modesty in a world of literal-minded penpushers.

---

20. This personal history is spelled out in an appendix to *George Nenedakis*.

That Tsouderos has interpreted *Voukéfali* as a challenge to the historical claims of his social class is as clear as is his transmutation of the entire argument into a clan dispute. Andreas has certainly read his opponent in this way. Indeed, Elli's reaction to a story that Tsouderos had stormed out of the office of a local newspaper that refused to publish his first response to Andreas's most recent contribution to the debate, and to the flurry of charges and countercharges about who would be allowed to publish what, was to comment wryly, "And then we talk about the production of male children!" But Andreas was displeased with this analogy, arguing that it did not make sense because his own defense of his father's and brother's memory was not directly related to collective activity—which, as Elli had noted on another occasion, was precisely what Tsouderos had tried to make of his own personal anger.

Siring many sons was certainly, as Andreas mentions in *Voukéfali*, an important aspect of both clan and national disputes. Elli had, I suggest, perceived this analogy in a way that was sensitive to Tsouderos's tactics, even if Andreas was reluctant to play exactly the same game: Tsouderos wished to appear as the defender of his own and of his affines' clans. But he also attempted to elevate that defense into a defense of national honor, identifying these clans' histories with the cause of national liberation. In the process, he slips from nationalism to chauvinism, to use Andreas's distinction, and is unable to see that Andreas's father's defense of the unarmed Rethemnos Turks was not a betrayal of national honor. Above all, he inadvertently shows that the management of fact is intimately engaged with the defense of household and clan: having doubted the existence of Andreas's brother George, he is confronted by a book whose title includes George's name, whose cover sports a photograph of both brother George himself and of Tsouderos engaged in amicable conversation with Andreas, and whose subtitle is an explicit attack on the entire Tsouderos clan—an attack, moreover, that with subtle historical allusion (if not the most chivalrous implications) likens them to women.[21] Note, finally, that Andreas's increasingly insistent mentioning of George's fair skin also reiterates a genetic claim about the non-Turkish derivation of the patrilineal blood, structurally analogous to his emphasis on the fair appearance—and therefore "Venetian" ancestry—of the most attractive of the Muslim characters in *Voukéfali*. This is truly a blood feud—it is a feud about blood.

Andreas has accepted the challenge of the feud: in the context of

---

21. The original saying was that of the Byzantine emperor Justinian, whose aside about the power of women is parodied here to produce a parallel slight against the Tsouderos clan. Although highly literary, the device reproduces the usual form of interclan insults—that is, by feminization; this confirms the vendettalike properties of the dispute as a whole.

Rethemniot society, he clearly felt that he had little choice. In any event, Tsouderos's decision to launch this attack may have been a tactical as well as a substantive error. Kostas Petridis, the local journalist who reviewed the new Nenedakis book in one of the Rethemnos newspapers and noted its clan-based animosities, has suggested an aspect of the confrontation that was additionally confirmed for me by another local scholar—Mikhalis Troulis, a historical archivist and philologist whose own admiring review of *Voukéfali* also drew Tsouderos's fire (see Petridis 1996; Troulis 1992; Tsouderos 1995: 9–10). Tsouderos chose to make his stand on historical accuracy. As a result, he has opened a veritable Pandora's Box, not necessarily to the delight of those close to him: Andreas, drawn into the role of reluctant historian by Tsouderos's own insistence on judging the novel *Voukéfali* by the standards of academic history, has paid embarrassingly close attention to the officially recorded history of the Tsouderos clan. Perhaps most damaging is his challenge to the clan's alleged (and much vaunted) descent from the Kalleryides, one of the illustrious families with which the Byzantine emperor Nikiforos Fokas repopulated Crete after his massacre of its Saracen occupiers in 961. He has also contested its claims to a past of unalloyed devotion to the patriotic cause, suggesting instead a significant record of collaboration and betrayal—surely a direct riposte to Tsouderos's charge that Nenes was a Turkish name and that Andreas had represented his father as pro-Turkish, not to speak of the implicit smear against his winning the İpekçi Prize. Beyond their local interest or their relevance for this biography, the consequences of such revelations, as both Petridis and Troulis have pointed out, may actually be significant for the interpretation of Greece's national history. And that, especially for those who dislike the chauvinistic and self-serving jingoism of the old order, would be no small benefit.

The Tsouderos clan has certainly played an active and well-documented part in Greek politics. In earlier years, this clan and others with which it intermarried achieved various forms of fame and, sometimes, notoriety. Before World War II, a history of the leading families of Crete gave great prominence to the clan (Mourellos 1931). By provoking Andreas's own family and class pride, Yannis Tsouderos has now effectively placed that history under a searching and critical light—and many of his closest associates evidently wish he had never put pen to paper. For now the clan's national claims are exposed to a new and unflattering critique.

Thus, what might have seemed a purely parochial dispute is proving to have far wider implications. In Greece it potentially embarrasses one of the best-known political lineages. But I would also like to emphasize that it permits some salutary comparisons with major cultural debates about, in effect, the ownership of the past—the topic that I originally went to Rethemnos to study, and that underlies many contemporary "culture wars" of more global significance. Here, in fact, I return specifically to the debate over whether the Hawaiians had considered Captain Cook to be a deity, which became an argument about what kind of cultural or ethnic positioning confers the right to attribute particular modes of thought to Third World peoples ("natives"). And I also return to the *Black Athena* dispute, which escalated into a mirror image of the debate about Captain Cook: it turned a scholarly disagreement about cultural influence in the ancient world into a clash between African and European claims to the right to represent—and, by extension, to own—the roots of "Western civilization." Scholarly disputations of fact have now been transformed into arguments about ethnocentrism and racism.

Black Athena offers a conceptual bridge between the global culture wars and the *Voukéfali* dispute, because it ostensibly threatens the neo-Classical view—axiomatic for Greeks of politically conservative bent as well as many others—that the origins of Greek culture are autochthonous and, above all, European. To judge impressionistically from conversations I have heard, it is a far more widely known work among educated Greeks than *Voukéfali*. Nevertheless, the comparison between the *Voukéfali* dispute and the more famous debates is suggestive. The *Voukéfali* dispute is a relatively local refraction of the same identity politics that we find in the more celebrated debates, so that the comparison highlights key connections among local, national, and transnational arenas in the politics of knowledge.

The fault lines of confrontation between an essentialized East and an equally essentialized West run right through modern Greek society and culture. Pre-1922 Rethemnos, with the uneasy coexistence of Christians and Muslims that Andreas describes in *Voukéfali*, appears there as both an example and an allegory of the hardening lines of ethnic and religious conflict. The encompassing atmosphere of regional politics remains painfully strained to this day. Competing cultural ideologies respectively acknowledge and deny the shared cultural kinship of Greece and Turkey. Small wonder, then, that such crudely essentialist allegations of Turkish origins, identity, and sympathies should have angered both the militant antichauvinist and the warrior-patriot who coalesce with such complex incandescence in the person of Andreas.

The attack on Andreas represents neither a serious professional threat to him nor an intellectually engaging position in its own right. Andreas's taunting dismissals of the self-styled "philologist, etc." are probably a better answer to Tsouderos's pretensions than some of the angrier epithets that he also uses, and they lend an almost festive air to the way in which Andreas turns the historiographic tables on the would-be historian. As a result of that tactic, the major contribution of Tsouderos's book lies less in his own arguments than in the new lines of inquiry to which he has provoked Andreas and others. The dispute also merits attention for the way in which it discursively enacts the politics of clan identity. This local refraction of global issues, in turn, instructively allows us to examine some of the most widely reported cultural tempests as though in a distorting mirror or under a microscope. And it shows clearly that questions of genre, especially when they pit historical against fictional realism, may have substantial consequences for the politics of meaning, truth, and the past.

9 ▣

PAINTING AN
ETHNOGRAPHIC PORTRAIT

Andreas has spent most of his adult life engaged with the visual arts, so it seems appropriate to start bringing this account to its necessarily provisional close by turning back to his interest in painting. For it is in the balance of light, color, proportion—all the arcane matters that still make him feel ignorant when Elli speaks—that he finds the closest analogy to his writing. In this he is completely unlike Sartre, who rejects the very idea of such an analogy, and with it the literary claims of realism (1949: 7–37). He shares Sartre's insistence on the importance of the author's political integrity and would presumably not have been averse to Orwell's conclusion: "it is invariably where I lacked a *political* purpose that I wrote lifeless books and was betrayed into purple passages, sentences without meaning, decorative adjectives and humbug generally" (1970 [1968]: 30). But his instrument is a visual sense that rescues the poetic from the banal—that is, precisely, its political mission.

All writers, even academic ones, have—I suppose—some kind of figurative understanding of how they write. Andreas does not confuse prose with painting, but he recognizes the artisanal and aesthetic dimensions—art, skill, and craft, all conflated in the Greek term *tékhni* in both of these media—and finds guidance in the resulting analogy between them: it is a means to his ends. It was the *tékhni* of the saddlemaker Botonis that at once expressed his self-confidence and inspired the confidence of others (*Manuscript*, p. 67); that of the painter complicates the artisan's competence and pride with the self-doubt that bourgeois society engenders in those whose work is not obviously a means to security and wealth—a "cultural dowry," in Judith Okely's telling phrase.

While my own sense of writing is more that of sculpture, with its shapes and surfaces, Andreas embraces the imagery of light and line. For both of us, the satisfaction lies in a craft that transports us into affective worlds that, while they offer an escape from the mundane pressures of the moment, nonetheless distill aspects—very different aspects for each of us—of the worlds that we have experienced, our *viómata*—our *expériences vécues*—regardless of our respective professional identities. As Andreas feels himself transported outside earthly irritations, for example, I have often found in my imaginative revisitings of Glendi and Rethemnos a refuge from the bureaucratic drudgery that often accompanies the real pleasures of academic life.

The products of these pleasurable hours also have crass material consequences, be it said: for Andreas, a livelihood; for me, a means to professional survival and recognition. Andreas has taught me to fight the hypocrisy of suppressing this simple truth (and in fact I was open to his lesson, having told Glendiot friends how much they had helped me build a career—a point that, after the fact, made my presence in their village more comprehensible to them). There is no point in pretending:

> ▌And the woman painter who was using tempera to depict the faces of the guests [at a fashionable party that had just been disrupted by a huge quarrel] from the moment she entered the house could not carry on with her work, and her colors became ever darker. "What we needed here was a photographer with flash, not me . . . ," she thought contemptuously to herself, but the 1,000-drachma note she'd stuffed in her bra consoled her. And she might even have found the situation amusing had she not feared that her admirers in the singing clubs of the Plaka (which is what they all were), who would do anything to greet her, apparently to show that they were cultured people and lovers of art, would think she'd turned into a laboratory animal. (*Ten Women*, p. 142)

For Andreas, it would have been silly and dishonest to insist on a hard-and-fast demarcation between art and artisanship, as crass in its own way as the reduction of aesthetic value to economic terms that he satirizes in *Manuscript* and *Ten Women*. The difference is one of social context. Andreas knew the artisans in Rethemnos in his childhood, and he has intimate knowledge of the life of artists in Athens (see especially *In Parallel with R*). He is thus able to link the metaphor of writing as painting with his personal *viómata* and, through them, with the inner lives of others—of people whose motives he does not directly claim to read but whose self-expression he can skillfully recapture in the language of satirical empathy. And since he mocks himself, he sees no reason to spare the obvious pretensions of those he has observed.

In painting, he finds an escape from the bureaucratic and commercial calculation, which, his pragmatism notwithstanding, often disgusts him because of its sheer pettiness. His ire is in any case directed more at bureaucratic small-mindedness than at people's sometimes unavoidable concern with their economic needs. This is why he expressed such amazement at Tsouderos's tidy vision of the writer as someone who works systematically and in order from one end of his project to the other—a character like the flirtatious bystander in *Manuscript* who advises the art student on her color scheme. Perhaps some scholars do think in this mechanistic fashion; but Andreas has no great respect for arid academicism at the best of times and will not play the scholarly game of classifying facts to which arguments about his historical accuracy beckon. (His refusal to split art from artisanship is a further illustration of his distrust of grand schemes of classification.) Andreas compares the notion of the lineal, methodical writer to that of a painter who works only in one direction across the canvas: to him both are absurd, banal.

The parallel of writing with painting is not an immodest claim to intellectual privilege, placing the artist above the demands of scholarship. On the contrary, it is of a piece with Andreas's respect for artisanal work, a mode in which the craftsperson's individuality resists the standardization of industrial production (as well as the deadening cruelty with which Marx's *Capital* impressed him when he first read it in prison in Sudan). His respect for artisanship is, in turn, consistent with his deep dislike of educational and class snobbery. And it also harmonizes with his enjoyment of activities that affect the discipline of the body, such as cooking and gardening:

● Every kind of work has this *meráki,*[1] this. . . . It has a beauty, a . . . creativity, how can I describe this to you? it's. . . . Even the cook, when he makes a good meal. . . . I, when I cook (*psíno*[2]), I know that . . . the pot's on the fire, and I can't read, I keep getting up all the time, *tak!* to go and see, you know, that's how I do it, to see. . . . As the painter paints his canvas, let us say, so is the cooking of food. And that is no easy task. The same goes for a bakery, exactly the same. Even more important and special is the work of the gardener or horticulturalist. Very interesting work. . . . Watering, pruning. . . . I can tell you that he influences the plant, he does, the gardener himself. That is, they even say, and I've heard, that he even influences the *taste* [of a plant]. . . . That's the way it is with food. Eh, there are some cooks who can make a tasty meal. A person *gives*—how should I put it?—something of himself. I can't explain it any other way. Well, all those professions, all those activities as it were, offer a great deal of interest. It's not just . . . to sit down and write a novel is also a wearying task, and often, in my opinion, as a

1. *Meráki* (Turkish *merak*) is the intense enthusiasm of the person focused on a particular activity (see Herzfeld 1981).

2. The verbs for cooking are significant here: *psíno* (literally "roast") denotes a specifically *male* activity, especially among Cretan shepherds, who leave all other forms of cooking to women (see Herzfeld 1985: 223).

task in its own right has no special attraction. Of course, there are moments when you escape from yourself. The writing leads you away and
you write two pages and you get away from this filthy real world. . . .

But in this, too, Andreas does not claim a special grace for his own avoca-
tion over those of others. He recognizes the specific demands and responsibilities of writing but does not allow these to constitute the grounds for
a claim to intellectual superiority. In this we are close, for I have argued
(in *The Poetics of Manhood*) that anthropological theory may derive as
fully from our informants' social perspectives as from our professional
reading; that was certainly my own experience. The professional goals
and audiences of a novelist and an anthropologist may be more specialized and specific than those of a cook and a shepherd, or they simply
address a different audience, but this, we both argue, does not justify a
social hierarchy of intellectual (or artistic) labor.

Hierarchies do abound socially, however, in the contexts in which artists
and artisans learn their tasks. In *Manuscript*, Andreas paints a portrait
of harsh indifference and crass academicism in the artist's training and
links these, in their worst incarnations, both to the bland Bavarian neo-
Classicism that neutralized the social realities of the War of Independence
and to the more recent bourgeois conformism that has a casual bystander
advising the art student to arrange her colors in deadly symmetry. In
Voukéfali, it is the turn of the artisanal apprentices whose training is in
so many ways less dully formal but whose subordination to their masters
is a harbinger of other social hierarchies that are just beginning to affect
their lives. Andreas describes the blacksmith's gentleness with the animals
he shoes and contrasts it with his rough speech toward his apprentices,
mitigating it in a way that would be impossible in an urban academic:
"'This animal has more sense that you do,' he used to tell his apprentice.
'Than all of us,' he'd blurt out; and he'd caress the creature" (*Voukéfali*,
p. 212). This blacksmith had a son who went to school with Andreas:

> He wanted Thodorís to learn letters, as the latter told me. He wanted to
> become a teacher. And I thought it likely because he was the best pupil.
> He wrote the best essays in our class and once, when our teacher had us
> describe the school, he sat down and wrote three pages describing all our
> fellow pupils. He had painted them and described them as his father could
> do with mules. (pp. 212–13)

Here, explicitly, is the analogy between painting and writing, framed by
Andreas's respect for the artisan and, in turn, by the artist's respect for
animals. Authority and hierarchy may be productive when they are combined with love and respect—Andreas appreciates the importance of dis-

cipline, especially self-discipline—but they become perverted by the soulless automatism of mediocrity and, most of all, by what Andreas sees as its dominant social expression, the bureaucratic values of the bourgeoisie.

But whereas the artisan is supremely self-confident—the blacksmith and the saddler, for example, do not hesitate to show an animal's owner that they know its needs better than he does—the artist is hesitant and self-doubting. The artisan is producing something for practical use and knows—indeed, must know—its requirements exactly, as well as the social and economic context in which its uses will be unambiguous. The artist and the writer, by contrast, must grapple with the uncertainties of social life and interpretation, complicated by the expansion of relevance beyond the face-to-face society of the small town. Andreas describes their socialization into this vastly enlarged world in *Manuscript,* where the art student is forced to move beyond the explicit tasks of an artisan in order to reach out to a larger audience—yet still an audience that reads, thinks, and speaks in Greek—and, at the same time, to transcend the unimaginative bourgeois society around her.

Is it modest uncertainty that we see in the painter and the author? Representing the self of a Greek artist—a self that both is, and (in a literal sense) is not, his own—allows Andreas to reach an audience in a way that its members can understand and with which they can subjectively identify. The uncertainties of social relations in Greece, especially, are such that the existential dilemmas of a nonconformist belong to the mainstream of experience: formalism and revolution, forever locked in their mutual tension. Thus, Andreas's (and the art student's) self-doubts are immediately recognizable to Greek readers and generate the sense of having entered his subjects' innermost thoughts through the superficially artisanal device of straightforward, austere descriptions of externals.

Much as Sartre adopted a "utilitarian" perspective on writing (1949: 19), Andreas views it as more closely analogous to the craft of the saddlemaker. He knows how he wants his imagined reader to interpret what he writes; he is like—or at least envies—Botonis, who told his customers which saddle to buy because he knew better than they which would fit their animals best. So, too, for Andreas the writer is a self-assured artisan: "The reader . . . progresses in security. However far he may go, the author has gone further" (Sartre 1949: 54). Andreas is a confident guide, and his contempt for critics—so like Sartre's, and despite his obvious and very human pleasure with those who do praise his work—derives from his conviction that they are deluded by the bright lights of Paris and London. And he makes us laugh at them. Much as Constantine Cavafy articulates an implicit theory of literary criticism through his ironic poetic depictions of artists who suppress their own originality (Jusdanis 1987: 42–

48), although to very different effect, Andreas's merciless lampooning of the pretentiousness of those trained in Paris and elsewhere illuminates his view that Greek artists should stop sacrificing their originality to an ideology of derivation—an ideology that only finds cultural value in "Europe" (*tas Evropas*[3]).

Andreas, who grew up among artisans and small traders and made butter at home to sell on the streets of Athens, certainly has no time for such pretensions, which would deem artisanship a second-rate activity. What he crafts as an author has a purpose beyond precious self-reference: he is not a conscious stylist (although he is certainly capable of retrospective self-assessment), nor does he have much patience with those dry critics and drier academics who argue endlessly about the virtues and demerits of particular ways of writing. For him, beauty lies in use, for, as Sartre remarks, "in prose the aesthetic pleasure is pure only if it is thrown into the bargain"—that is, rather than made the sole, and solipsistic, goal of creativity (1949: 25–26). Unlike Sartre, however, Andreas does not draw a hard-and-fast line between prose and poetry. Indeed, like Eco and Orwell (although with much greater pleasure than the latter in the act of writing), and with a sensibility that more closely resembles Jakobson's view of the poetic in virtually all speech than it does Sartre's purism,[4] Andreas links the poetic qualities of prose to the moment of production:

⬤ When I write I am beside myself and I feel, I can tell you, that these are the happiest moments of my life. I feel something that [excites] me . . . and afterward I can't correct it [the text] because the discourse loses what you might call its poeticity. Certain pages were corrected by this woman, the philologist [who worked as his copy editor at Kedros—the publishing house where *Voukéfali* was published], and it had lost. . . . but I couldn't do anything because it had already been written on the typewriter and so forth. I mean, prose has poeticity, even though it has

---

3. This is an artificial plural form, from neo-Classical usage; Andreas uses it to mock the pretentiousness with which some bourgeois pretended to a knowledge of both syntax and art that they did not possess.

4. See especially Roman Jakobson (1960). Andreas's recognition of the poetic qualities of prose, while informal, constitutes a theory of textual aesthetics. This is especially significant in conjunction with his realism. Andreas's recognition of the poeticity of prose and of the everyday produces an aesthetic corollary to the poetry of disillusioned intellectuals of the Greek Left in the 1950s and 1960s (see Calotychos 1993), in which writers "resort to a 'defamiliarization' of seemingly unpoetic words in a poetic context" (Calotychos 1993: 265). (On defamiliarization, see Stacy 1977.) Many of these poets—notably Manolis Anagnostakis—were friends of Andreas, but his suspicion of anything that smacked of intellectualism makes it difficult to assess the degree and direction of actual influence, especially as he insists on his intellectual independence from these writers.

no rhymes, therefore rhyme neither benefits nor adds to the poeticity [of a text].

For Sartre, among verbal discourses it was only poetry that resembled painting. Perhaps it is because he does not oppose prose to poetry that Andreas can embrace the idea of a direct analogy between painting and prose. Moreover, unable to privilege any intellectual activity over manual artistry, he sees both painting and writing as fundamentally artisanal. In a bourgeois social environment where culture vultures (*koultouriáridhes*) often exhibit a crassly derivative snobbery of style, moreover, Andreas has never felt constrained to confess to the embarrassment that Sartre experienced at finding such rude pragmatism in himself. On the contrary, he seems to delight in the freedom it gives him from the judgment of people he despises. And he has been truly free in this respect, for his early industry made him the money to pay for the publication of his work, which in turn earned him enough to keep going—we must always bear in mind that private publication is a common phenomenon in Greece, where no opprobrium attaches to what in the United States and Western Europe would be seen as "vanity presses." It is only in the post-junta era that the publishing industry in Greece has emerged as a distinct entity from the riot of cheap, private printing that still serves all but the most successful writers, and that has provided the first opportunities for many who later became famous as "authors."

Given such freedom from academic criticism, Andreas has been able to remain openly unrepentant about his commitment to themes that others dismiss as mere folklore—themes that are also consistent with his artisanal view of his own work. Those criticisms encourage him, if anything, since they affirm the distance that separates him from the studied pretentiousness of the cultured *nouveaux riches*. For the same reason, while warmly appreciating the support that such academics as Stylianos Alexiou have accorded him, he finds in that support evidence that he was right to dare to publish his edition of Bounialis's *The Cretan War* in the face of academic skepticism; he expresses only an ironic repentance for his brazen invasion of academic privilege—which he views, rather, as an academic intrusion into his own Cretan heritage.

In like fashion, too, he can always claim the moral high ground in a country where refusal to accept authority remains a mark of national identity—even, paradoxically, in the eyes of the state. Although he writes for a national audience and transforms local Cretan values into allegories of more transcendent virtues, Andreas remains in some performative sense the traditional Cretan artisan plying his craft because he knows that for him it is the right thing to do—and it is a self-image that offers considerable security in Greek society, where such protestations of autonomy—what James D. Faubion (1993) calls "sovereignty"—are a trademark of cultural authenticity.

In that setting especially, the confidence of the artisan and the pomposity of the critic are poles apart. The artisan derives personal autonomy from a technique that is rarely made the object of self-conscious contemplation. The critic, by contrast, for Andreas as for Sartre, is a hack—representing what Nikos Kazantzakis in particular pilloried as the antithesis of the glorious unpredictability of the truly free Cretan man. Such people are pen-pushers (*kalamarádhes,* a generic term of opprobrium for mainlanders on Crete), bureaucrats, drudges who "get excited only about classified matters" and "never bet on uncertain issues" (Sartre 1949: 30). In both Andreas Nenedakis and Nikos Kazantzakis, resistance to such representatives of bourgeois stagnation is cast specifically in terms of the rejection of foreign-imposed formality—hence Andreas's constant railing against Bavarian academicism, in opposition to which he makes his native identity the repository of true freedom.

If this identification of liberty with national character seems limiting to a non-Greek audience, it does take Andreas significantly beyond Sartre in one important respect. The French existentialist, in explaining that a writer cannot but be corrupted by any ideology that denies freedom to others, remarks, "A blacksmith can be affected by fascism in his life as a man, but not necessarily in his craft; a writer will be affected in both, and even more in his craft than in his life" (1949: 64). Andreas, ever attentive to the image of Greekness that he articulates, is more comfortable with an artisanal definition of his calling, which becomes a way of challenging its privileged status without denying its specific responsibilities. I suspect that this difference has a cultural and social basis. In the Greek setting, artisanship is always evaluated in terms of its fidelity to personal autonomy: those who craft objects also craft themselves, and they do so in a public, culturally coded space (see Kondo 1990). Not to have stood up for his own values—to have condoned the Moscow show trials, for example—would have been a betrayal of Andreas's craft as a writer as well as of his principles; indeed, craft and ideals merge at this point. Such an act of betrayal would have been more directly analogous to slipshod craftwork than Sartre was evidently prepared to perceive, not only because any act of creation is in some sense necessarily political, but also because Andreas knows from direct experience how central the concept of a spontaneously expressed *meráki,* of a dedicated finesse that arises from the act of crafting rather than from studied premeditation, is to the Greek artisan's sense of self.

Richard Handler (1988) has extended the insights of novelist Lionel Trilling (1972) and historian C. B. Macpherson (1962) to argue that the production of a carefully constructed authenticity is central to the cultural claims of modern nationalism in Europe and elsewhere. In this sense, Andreas is a true modernist, for he finds the writerly self not only in the Sartrean refusal to compromise freedom and personal autonomy but especially in the authenticity best exemplified by the artisan. This, for Andreas, is also a more locally cultural project: to be truly Greek, the writer must model selfhood on the unmediated authenticity of the artisan—a studied spontaneity, as it were, that lends a self-consciously Greek cast to the performance of sincerity that Trilling identifies as a distinctive product of European modernity (1972: 11).

Thus, in Andreas's world, any idea of style for style's sake is not simply antithetical to the author's calling, as it was for Sartre; it is also obtrusively alien to local ideals of spontaneity. Hence the paradox of Andreas's stance, which grants a parity of respect to the artisan's intellect—a congenial move analogous to my insistence on acknowledging my shepherd informants as theory-makers (in *The Poetics of Manhood*)—but does so by parochializing artisan and writer as refractions of a national self-stereotype. We should not forget that the Greek term from which we get the English "authenticity" (*authentēs*) still has immediate connotations of authority, self-sufficiency, and the personal sense of autonomy that connects Greek modernity with its antecedent traditions.[5]

Andreas thus does not make the surprisingly absolute distinction between artisan and writer that we find in Sartre. He does acknowledge that modern artists may not enjoy the luxury of total self-confidence of artisans invested, like Botonis, with complete authority by the communities in which the latter ply their trade; but this difference derives precisely from a social breakdown that confronts everyone with increasingly difficult and lonely choices. Blacksmiths or saddlemakers might in fact be nominal fascists in Andreas's world, and some of them surely were—but only because fascism's populist message had blinded them to what it ultimately portended for their personal autonomy as artisans and as Greeks. For Andreas, any surrender to fascism would have undercut artisanal integrity precisely because it would have disrupted the *social* world to which the artisans belonged and from which they derived their identity. That traditional artisans, being less experienced in the ways of the larger world, might perhaps be more easily deceived was another matter: their focus was all on their work, which did not directly force political choices upon them as it did upon writers. But the eventual consequences of participation in a repressive state would be spiritually corrosive for all, and its effects would pass through the flawed crafting of subjective selves and material or textual objects alike.

That is why, in *Bir Hakeim*, Kitsos, the peasant lad from Thessaly,

---

5. *Afendikó*, another derivative of this root (possibly via Turkish *effendi*), is the term Zorba uses for "boss" in *Zorba the Greek* (Kazantzakis 1952).

wants to stand in the breach against the Nazis: it is the very basis of sociality as he knows it that the Nazis will steal in the form of land. This is the same reason for which his friend Xopateras meanwhile starts to rethink the patriotic platitudes on which he has been raised. Regardless of our occupations, Andreas tells us, what we do is the fullest expression of who we are, and the true author—like the self-confident artisan or the quiet man of power in a shepherding Cretan village—has the autonomy to draw strength from his very flaws. Andreas—son of a shepherd, animal-thief, and warrior—explicitly grounds this perspective in his ancestral culture:

> Some people have great ideas about themselves because they are authors, they're painters, or whatever, and we light lamps in their honor and swing the censer over their heads. These things are ridiculous. It's a matter for each individual, let us say, as to whether he is pleased with his work, whether he is productive in the way he wants, and so forth—not for others. Now, whether others achieve anything or not—that's not a matter I'm interested in investigating. *Why* don't they achieve anything? I don't. . . . Then, something else: a person is created. That is to say, a person is the outcome of a process that has taken place, generation after generation. And so it arrives at a particular result: my own personality, so to speak, which becomes an author. That isn't only the result of whether you read continually, or of whether you write. There is a certain heredity—not heredity, exactly, but a process, from the ancestors, and so on. You can see what I'm talking about, I owe a great deal—others say it too—to my father. I believe that my father, although he was a warrior, a man of the gun, so to speak, and a thief in those times, an animal-thief, nevertheless had a certain cultivatedness, let us say. Well, now, you'll say, "What of it? Why?" Genet, the Frenchman, was—what is it they say—a rogue, but still he turned out to be an artist. *Tss!* Do you understand what I'm saying? It's irrelevant that he's had some bad habits, done certain bad things; because that's one thing, and his ability to create a work of art is quite another. So quite simply, the one thing gives way to the other, and the evil gets left behind, the bad things disappear . . . and the good gets developed. . . .

Pretending to be other than oneself is not simply hypocritical; it is a complete surrender of the self, of sovereignty—precisely what both fascist regimes and bourgeois lifestyles demand. And the refusal to bow before the current gods of imported fashion is, for Andreas, the most valuable meaning of the patriotism that he so greatly cherishes: his is an identification, entirely consonant with the perspective of a highland Cretan villager in this regard, of self with bloodline, island, and nation, realized through acts of performance and creation in an idiom that is self-consciously spontaneous and therefore, in his logic, Greek.

From the rough courtesies of highland Cretan shepherds' masculinity to the genteel provinciality of Rethemnos and thence to the harsh brutality of Cold War confrontation—Andreas had experienced in full the genesis of a distinctively Greek modernity. Certainty had never been part of his world. The ambivalence his voice expresses is that of a man brought up to a heritage of aggressive masculinity in which strength could only be shown by those willing to risk losing it—in a fight, in a raid on other shepherds' flocks, in gambling, in verbal duels. It is a voice schooled in the adversity of displacement and prepared for it by a social ideology that had always placed a high value on the capacity to improvise and take risks, coupled with contempt for, in Sartre's phrase, "those who never bet on uncertain issues." In such a place, strong men do not necessarily vaunt their strength, for that is the ultimate risk: it threatens to expose their weakness, their powerlessness to "fix" power for all time, or to stand up to its incursions from the state and other official tyrannies. Certainly there is no place here for a *profession* of authorship, with its bourgeois laurels and security of status. Andreas's explicit distaste for the title of "author" is congruent with this intellectual rendition of the social poetics of rural manhood.

His distaste for authorial pretensions is grounded in a view of society in which human beings do not fall into easy moral categories and in which a different mixture of creativity and evil appears—partly through the determination of heredity—in each. His father was a sheep-thief, yet he was also a man of sensibility; his Foreign Legion comrades were petty crooks and convicted murderers in whom he nevertheless discovered true humanity and affection. In this vision, there is no room for the categorical virtues of "authorship."

Indeed, he projects the same distaste for privileging the artist back through time, especially on precursors he admires and with whom he identifies. Writing of Marinos Tzane Bounialis, the poet of the seventeenth-century fall of Crete to the Turks, Andreas declares:

The real, true poet never writes, "I am a poet . . ." [but] waits for others to tell him so. That has value: acceptance by the public. Besides poets always—the true ones—doubt the value and quality of their work. And because this phrase—*oudhé poté penoúme* ("nor have I ever so boasted")—comes along, he assures us about his previous occupation, but also about his talent. Bounialis will have heard it [said] often in Rethimno: "Bounialis is a respectful person, and despite his worth or his work he's never been heard to boast." And he repeats it without fear, because after all for a creative artist these are all familiar matters, and they may be worth giving up one's life to them, but they lose their value when you try to extort praise or applause. (*The Cretan War,* p. 109)

By the evidence of his own writing (in *Tsingos*), Andreas knew very little about the visual arts when he left Greece in flight from the German invasion. (He also only read Marx's *Capital* even later, in prison in Sudan.) When Tsingos alluded to the name of Van Gogh, Andreas "thought he was swearing in *Arvanítika* [a form of Albanian spoken in some parts of Greece]" (and certainly missed the point of the allusion [p. 133])! This humiliating discovery of Andreas's own ignorance left a permanent mark on their relationship: when Tsingos, after some success as an architect in Brazil and Paris, finally abandoned architecture altogether for painting, Andreas could not bring himself to judge Tsingos's work (p. 169).

But the association with Tsingos awoke an interest that was cultivated by other friendships born in the midst of the prison-camp grimness. Fasianos, Manousakis, Tsarouchis: some of the most important names in the Greek art world educated his willing, thirsty sensibility, while his own practical sense often helped him to advise them on hanging their work against the dictates of their own idiosyncratic judgment. Another painter, Fotakis, was his cousin (see *In Parallel with R.*, pp. 93–94). And Elli's artistry has continue to provide a primary point of reference.

Art, for Andreas, is an act of resistance to institutional control. It is the means of expressing a personal identity that can never be reduced to the dry classifications that are both symbol and instrument of bureaucracy. But whereas the verbal art of the writer always risks tangling directly with the authoritarian verbalism of state institutions, Andreas sees in representational art an ideal space for placing a subversive irreverence well out of the bureaucracy's vindictive reach. By extension, this both protects and marginalizes Andreas himself. It is partly because his own restlessly exploratory oeuvre defies classification; as his old friend Yannis Angelopoulos argued as he thought over Andreas's life in Paris and later, he has not found it easy to gain recognition from the literary and academic establishment in Greece. But that determined disobedience to every sort of categorical control, reaching as it does into the deepest recesses of his work and life, gives both a distinctive message that appeals especially to the professional self-deracination of anthropologists.

He explores these issues in quite a deliberate manner and relates them to central issues of national identity as well. The art student in *Manuscript*, for example, experiences as both a personal and a professional tension what is arguably the defining predicament of modern Greek statehood: how to impose discipline on a nature—a "national character"[6]—defined by its indiscipline? The dilemmas of women and artists subvert

6. See my discussion of the concept of national character in *Cultural Intimacy*, especially in the context of ideas about European identity (1997a: 89–108).

by metaphor and example the confident claims that the state makes to the authority to speak for all Greeks. This creates a surprising parallelism between expressions of aggressive masculinity and the female voice—surprising, that is, only until we recall that the most powerful metaphors are precisely those that can draw similarity out of difference.

To many readers, possibly including some sophisticated urban Greeks, the idea that the swashbuckling banditry of sheep-thieves and national heroes could have anything in common with the modernist image of an almost pathologically insecure female art student will seem very strange. At one level, the parallel works as a key metaphor just because it *does* seem so improbable, an electric spark of revelation jumping between opposite poles: Andreas, writing both about and to a self-consciously modernist culture, produces a shock of recognition. It is modernity, especially an occidentalizing modernity, that makes the parallel improbable; consequently, the modernist sensibility is also at once shocked and intrigued by it.

What Andreas documents so well is the multiplicity of ways in which women are forced to internalize a sense of being inadequate human beings. And this, he suggests, holds also for men as they confront the foreign-imposed and unrealistically formal machinery of the bureaucratic state, successors to a series of foreign—and often Western—oppressors. In the prison camps to which he was sent, Andreas had ample opportunity to witness the process whereby male domination becomes a dominant metaphor for the internal subjugation of those placed lower in the hierarchy. He saw it in an unusually brutal form, moreover, a systematic humiliation of proud men designed to cast doubt on their human value forever in their own as well as others' eyes through the implication that the state was displacing them as the fathers of their own children and masters of their wives and daughters.

Art is the site of a complex response to all these forms of repression. It can bring into unexpected and embarrassing focus the conditionality of bureaucratic and other forms of power. The state is grounded in the contradictions engendered by the circumstances of its own foundation. While it may deploy art to propagate a normative reading of that past, unruly artists can no less easily play in subversive ways with the same themes, calling its claims of representational realism into question. In the official determination to repaint Greece in the terms of a doggedly neo-Classical aesthetic, virtually any other idiom can challenge this vision from within, and in ways that, because they are often not made verbally explicit, are much harder to suppress than are political diatribes and irreverent textual revampings of the nation's glorious history. Andreas's view of his writing as a painterly art thus supports one critic's shrewd assessment of *The Seine, My Home:*

Nenedakis makes depositions of History. That "little History" that often illuminates the great variety. He writes carelessly, heedlessly, just as he speaks. (Stamatiou 1985)

The voice is real in its very imperfections—although, as another critic has intimated, these rough edges—again as with painting—may not be unintended (Dokas 1993).

Moreover, Andreas himself dislikes correcting his texts or letting a copy editor do so: "I can't correct it because it loses its poetic quality, the discourse does. (. . .) I want to say that prose discourse has poetic qualities, and yet it has no rhymes, so rhyme is of no benefit nor does it help make something poetic." Part of that quality, for Andreas, is a deliberately approximate and unfinished tone, alternating, like his speaking voice, between confidence and doubt. Indeed, his attitude toward rhyme exemplifies this ambivalence. He despises its bourgeois incarnations, likening them to the rings and other baubles worn by elderly urban ladies—"they remind me of prison" in the way that they subject hands and faces to the hypocritical discipline of fashion. But he also sees the ability to improvise rhyming couplets as one of the marks of Asi-Goniot manhood: here the discipline of form becomes the grounds for showing a truly poetic imagination. Yet again, however, whether from compulsive honesty or from masculine perversity, he would not accept Raftopoulos's attribution to him of some improvisatory verses in precisely this genre. Through this ambivalence, grounded in his image of what it means to be an Asi-Goniot, he resists the banality of bourgeois culture—in painting the idiocy of coloring by rote lampooned in *Manuscript,* in writing the facile assumption that "whatever is written in rhyme must be poetic," and in all things the routinization of spontaneity and risk.

Subversion of the official idiom of representation also provides an incentive to discovering alternative possibilities in the received facts about the national past. For Andreas, ever the political rebel, patriotism does not mean passive acceptance of the official line. On the contrary, it requires a critical resistance that for a person of his social formation is truer to Greek tradition than the imported neo-Classical posturings of the elite. This is especially important for the actual creation of the Greek nation-state, a cultural as well as a social event the significance of which has long been hotly contested by competing political forces.

The official historiography of the War of Independence (1821–33) gives pride of place to the role of the "klefts" (Greek *kleftes,* "thieves"). These supposedly freedom-loving guerrillas who swept down from their mountain eyries to harass the Turkish armies form the centerpiece of school texts, commemorative rituals, and officially sponsored art. Yet their very name reveals a contradiction. The violent actions that made them central to the Greek achievement of independent statehood exemplified the kind of insubordination that no newly established state authority could tolerate for long. If the klefts who fought the Ottoman armies exemplified virtues of independent masculine courage for whom the official historiography could claim an ancient lineage, these very qualities ensured that their successors under Greek rule would become both political and conceptual outlaws—no longer heroes but bandits.[7] In the same spirit, these hardy rebels contemptuously dismissed the authorities as "Turks"—a conceit that persists among the Cretan shepherds, who also characteristically turn the tables on officialdom by justifying endemic theft: wasn't it thieves—*kleftes*—we all heard about at school?

Those original heroes of 1821 were as hostile to the values and laws of the Bavarian monarchy with which their efforts were rewarded as they had been to the Turks, if indeed not more so. The monarchy stood for a modernist rationality of state that undercut all their dreams of creating personal armies and fiefdoms (Dakin 1973: 309–16). Today's sheepthieves value silence as the best defense of their privacy but love to boast about their exploits in self-glorifying detail (and in this bifurcation resemble the dual stereotype of women as oscillating between quietly demure embodiments of the Mother of God and gossipy agents of the Devil). The nineteenth-century klefts similarly appear to have set little store by the formal language of officialdom—the neo-Classical Greek they often could not understand without interpreters!—or the orotundities of the foreign-imposed royal court. Yet it was this court that effectively suppressed their antiauthoritarian message by canonizing them as national heroes. In conversation, Andreas often traces the persecution of the communists at the close of World War II and later to the original power struggles between the guerrilla chieftains on the one hand and the monarchy as well as successive governments on the other. And again, like many leftists, he attacks the Right with its own favored insult: they are, he says, "unworthy of being called Greeks."

The official portrayal of women, in parallel fashion, placed them on a fine neo-Classical pedestal and so attempted to protect them from the temptations of exercising their own agency. Andreas shows, especially in *Manuscript,* that he fully appreciates and resents the power of representation to overwhelm its object. He is especially scathing about nineteenth-century court style in his allusions to the aridities of its academic successors, and he also actively appreciates the implications of the parallel between gender and other social hierarchies. Here the female student's voice seems peculiarly well suited to the task of resisting such regimentation, its painterly scorn withering in its precise embedding of personal

7. Herzfeld 1982a; Koliopoulos 1987; Politis 1983.

experience in the historical circumstances that give it shape and meaning. Here, too, the parallel between gender and cultural hierarchies becomes explicit. The previous generation of Greek painters had learned everything by rote:

▌ Each pupil had to paint the way his teacher painted. All that talk about initiative, talent, and all the rest was fine, but only when the teacher deemed them acceptable and when they "smelled something on his breath." Then there was Munich, which did not let us see the world in any other way. That king, Otho [Greek: Othon], did not just bring his thugs, who really tyrannized our people and changed the path of our Nation for it. He also forced us to see as his lieutenants wanted us to. Up to this very day, our painters see as Otho wanted them to see back then. . . . The braves of 1821 dressed in Bavarian costume in their biographies and heroic portraits are a sorry joke. So much verbalism—in the use of color, in the gestures, in the draftsmanship, in composition—is unbearable. I can imagine Makriyannis and his grimaces. And his joy, when the Painter painted his icons. Makriyannis, now, he could see the way a painter does. Which shows that he had the right kind of feeling. He shows that in his *Memoirs*. I keep that book by my pillow and refuse to be separated from it. (*Manuscript*, p. 139)

No less than a painter, a writer of words can aspire to freedom from verbalism.

General Makriyannis has become a symbol of a Greekness quashed and ignored by the forces of political conservatism and foreign domination. At the opposite end of the spectrum stands the imported king: Otho, the second son of Ludwig II of Bavaria, who arrived at the end of 1833 to assume the throne of Greece. Initially popular as the symbol of Greek aspirations to full European nationhood, he and his petulant German advisers, with their disappointed neo-Classical ideals, soon frittered away the support and interest of ordinary people. Their bureaucratic rigidity fed the Greeks' aggrieved sense of a distinction between nation (*éthnos*) and state (*krátos*), as did their espousal of a Hellenic culture imported from the architecture and art schools of Munich. Even at the linguistic level, the stilted formalism of Greek official discourse discouraged literary styles that were obviously close to everyday speech, eventually creating, in turn, a demoticist backlash no less artificial or essentialist than what it sought to displace (see Tziovas 1986). In this context, "Bavarian" has become the expression of an insipid formalism backed by authoritarian control. It is the artistic equivalent of the romantic bourgeois morality that kept women in a formally educated version of their "traditional" domesticity but could not, as Alexandra Bakalaki (1994) has pointed out, suppress their own expropriation of the paraphernalia of a "European" identity. Andreas recognizes that he, too, as a schoolboy had fully absorbed this stultifying aesthetic, exemplified in his successful exercise in poetic pomposity, and doubtless that early skill provides much of the technical mastery that allows him to parody the sanctimonious religiosity of Father Prokopios, the absurdity of the colonels' fake purism, and the pretensions of Rethemniot town dignitaries and jumped-up art students who looked to Paris for their legitimation and said so in neo-Classical phrases of emetic artificiality.

To Andreas, as a Cretan, Bavarian "verbalism" has always seemed especially repellent. It represents, in the cultural domain, the stultifying effects of a conservative, foreign-dominated, oppressively bureaucratic order. To this rebellious son of a former shepherd from Asi-Gonia, a man whose own family was steeped in the ideology of reciprocal raiding and the ideals of silence and powerful self-control, one whose political convictions were forged in his resistance to the foreign-dominated royalists of the mid-twentieth century, the pompous yet insipid Bavarian court culture was a noxious imposition on Greek life—especially when applied to the "thieves" (*kléftes*) to whose daring guerrilla mode of warfare Greeks commonly attribute the real achievement of national independence. For Andreas, as for many others, the compromised independence of Otto's time was the precursor of the rightist repression of the Civil War and later. Art thus became a primary metaphor for the grounds of a struggle between a tyrannical bureaucratic pedantry and the freedom to experiment, to take risks, and to embrace ambiguity as necessary to any kind of social existence.

It may now seem strange that Andreas—after the deep horrors of exile and torture, and the cosmopolitan pleasures of the art world—should engage the pettier unpleasantnesses of his home town. But—like Cavafy's city, or like the Paris that in similar vein (though he denies any "influence") Andreas feels one can never leave behind despite its cold hostility and his own despair—Rethemnos is always with him. Its inhabitants' very fractiousness over matters of culture demonstrates, he once claimed in a concert review, their "aesthetic superiority" (Nenedakis 1955). Surely, ineluctably, it has drawn him in—not back, because he has never left. Bitterness is not a reason to run away; and true Asi-Goniots and Sfakians, Andreas will tell you, never run away. Besides, bitterness is not the dominant emotion that springs from the pages of *Voukéfali*. The impish humor, the love of place and people (with some notable exceptions, of course), and the tender admiration for artisanal skills and the dignity of the poor are the main colors with which he paints his admittedly mischievous portrait.

The bitterness and the dislike are reserved for those whose seemingly harmless self-indulgence can so easily become transformed into unthinking brutality and viciousness. Here the real enemies are ignorance (and especially failure to acknowledge one's own lack of knowledge) and its twin, pretentiousness. These deficiencies, sometimes even amusing as personal foibles, become extremely dangerous and violent when they infuse a whole system of political control. From the consuls to Makronisi and Youra—and now back: this is the trajectory through which Andreas's painterly pen works—as he says, *not* in a straight line, but back and forth, back and forth, probing, dodging, hesitating, plunging into the riot of light and dark that is human life.

His methods are broad brush strokes:

> In his narrative he uses a method that is characteristic of all good authors: he paints momentary scenes. Very frequently, indeed, these scenes are chronologically, geographically, and even conceptually distant from those that immediately follow them. But these scattered brush strokes eventually put together a story with a beginning and an end: the history of a town, but also many partial histories [of specific characters]. . . . (Dokas 1993: xv)

He incorporates large tracts of textual collage—from the art student's manuscript to the parodic newspaper headlines in *Black April* and the period-piece newspaper extracts quoted in *Voukéfali*. Here the same critic is less kind, arguing that these turns to "chronicle" cause a loss of pace. But the vision is unmistakably both his own and one that speaks to Greek audiences. True to his political commitments, moreover, it acknowledges and incorporates the social problems of the country, especially the production of a false discipline that is either brutalizing (as on Youra or under the junta) or, simply but not necessarily more benignly, demoralizing and banal. Another critic specifically notes this quality in *Manuscript*:

> Dozens of easels set up one next to the other in the meanest of spaces. Work with a model. Each youth is influenced by the next. As soon as anyone utters a word, away goes that valuable concentration that neutralizes the hostile external conditions. In this context the student tries honestly to learn how to paint, overcoming the successive disappointments, misunderstandings, rejecting all the elements that cloud her painterly vision.
>
> The internal monologue, which has lost none of the warmth of a confession, describes quite pointedly the problems of the Greek world. These are basic problems of education, not just in painting. . . . Economic and social problems that affect even aesthetic judgment and constitute the context of the manuscript.
>
> Thus, the spontaneous confessional text becomes representative of educational conditions in Greece and a witness to the heroism that accompanies virtually every student in the wholly antiheroic context of everyday life. (Spiliadi 1977: 4)

The critic captures here some of Andreas's appeal, not only to a Greek audience, but also for anthropologists. For it is above all his sense of the creation of a context of habitual practice (Bourdieu 1977), the inculcation of adherence to the dull taxonomies of banal authority, that he describes with such disturbing, defamiliarizing, *dehabituating* clarity. From the minor harassment of the artisanal apprentice to the machinery of industrial conformism that so appalled him when he first read Marx's *Capital* and to the drudgery of an educational system mired in rote and run by hacks, he sharpens our awareness of the dullness that we have come to treat as a necessary part of life.

His writing exudes this urgent impudence. In the words of the art student in *The Manuscript of the School of Fine Arts* when confronted by a well-meaning onlooker who offers her advice about which colors to use:

> I started and turned round, laughed, and thanked him. And it was as though I told him to leave me in peace, because, if a painter did what passers-by told him to do, then what he'd paint would be a work of plural production. (p. 137)

The nuisance obediently departed, producing his one memorable moment: "He took his shadow and left." He is a fictional antecedent of Tsouderos, a model from art for one of life's inconveniences: for inasmuch as Tsouderos wants writers to write in a straight line, he ironically (if inadvertently) confirms Andreas's depiction of the pedant and the bureaucrat. The student's testy reflection had for a moment become a genuinely effective instrument of both her individuality and her agency, as well as a succinct expression of Andreas's aesthetic. Her scorn is devastatingly conveyed in the phrase "work of plural production"[8]—painting by the numbers, as we might say, or on the factory line. In an inspired moment, agency can undermine the most banal convention and rout the most crass conformist—the presence whose very emptiness is a burden on everyday sensibility and an impediment to creative thought but that easily retreats in the face of moral strength: "He took his shadow and left."

Andreas thinks I will be criticized for writing this biography about someone who is not considered one of the "summits" (*korifés*) of Greek literature today. (Possibly making a virtue out of necessity, but possibly just recognizing political realities, Andreas attributes the comparative scarcity of reviews of his work to his refusal to play the game of the *koultouriáridhes*, the in-crowd of culture vultures.) When I telephoned to tell him that this book had been accepted for publication, he again said that I would be criticized for writing about so minor an author—so I told him

---

8. The Greek phrase *ergho plithindikós* is an ungrammatical construction (neuter noun plus masculine noun/adjective) that yokes the term for the polite form of address (modeled on the French "polite plural," *vous*) with a fleeting image of consumerist art.

that I had already mentioned this prediction of his in my text. He was clearly delighted to hear it! Like him, moreover, I face the prospect of such a reaction with equanimity (if not perhaps with quite his glee). The book grew out of a particular encounter, a particular friendship, and a particular set of overlapping interests and passions: I could not have written it about anyone else.

Andreas's attributions of motive and desire clearly elicit recognition from his Greek readers; even when he is praised for entering the mental world of non-Greeks, it is as a writer who through his nuanced descriptions of the palpable world can transform the seeming inscrutability of exotic people into differentiated personalities and attitudes that Greek readers, often more accustomed to thinking about non-Europeans in categorical rather than individual terms, can acknowledge as akin to their own—an especially poignant illustration of the pervasive tendency that Greeks so often claim as characteristic of their culture: to make sweeping generalizations about the world's "races" while warmly embracing specific members of such groups. In that cultural setting, realistic fiction sometimes proves more persuasive than the necessarily composite and intentionally nonintuitive idiom of ethnographic description.

In this sense, Andreas quite literally "gets under the skin" of racial prejudice. Editorializing of the varieties practiced by scholars and journalists, or given dramatic form by Brecht and others, would only draw attention to his narrative wiles and so defeat their purpose. Instead, he achieves his effect by the indirect parables of his fiction—not through abstractions about common humanity, but through respectful attention to the idiosyncrasies and dignity of individual human beings. It is an especially persuasive strategy for Greek readers because it forces them to deal with credible portraits of people instead of confronting received ideas about "race" in the abstract.

Andreas's intensely personal framing of the issue of racism plays on individual personalities rather than on categorical ascription—in other words, on everyday Greek social practice rather than on the legalistic rhetoric of broad and often racist generalization. He achieves this effect in part by playing on the Greeks' conventional recognition that one cannot know another person's thoughts and on their equally conventional assumption that fathoming those thoughts is integral to daily social existence. He thus produces an ethnographically convincing and anthropologically attractive argument, and he does so through a determinedly nonacademic mode of expression—a way of presenting his ideas that is consistent with his distaste for establishment pedantry.

Andreas lures his readers toward an individually grounded, interpersonal understanding of cultural difference. Large segments of his writing share this habit of deepening portraits that appear initially to be drawn from widely accepted stereotypes, transforming them into more complex characters in which Greek readers feel they can discern something of themselves. The Greeks and Turks of *Bir Hakeim,* the torturers and the tortured of his prison-island tales, and the pompous burghers as well as the folksy town "characters" of *Voukéfali* all appear initially as stereotypical marionettes, only to develop complex personalities that incrementally complicate the reader's easy generalizations.

This is also all of a piece with Andreas's insistence that he has "never" written a chronicle: he only writes novels, grounded in a reality that initially disarms the reader by its familiarity. This is the process that, according to Wolfgang Iser (1993: 3–4), fundamentally distinguishes fiction from expository prose. The text pleasurably backgrounds Andreas's didactic goal of laying bare the pretensions of the provincial high and mighty and of finding the sublime in ordinariness. He is interested in a different kind of reality—one that resists the bureaucratic representation of knowledge in historical periods and dry facts:

▌ Many of the episodes that I relate may not be placed in their correct chronological sequence. Nevertheless, they are true. Besides, my effort is to give a picture of Tsingos's life during that period. It may be, however, that all I have managed to do is to separate the events of the Middle East—"those heroic events . . ." as he used to say as if he wanted to say that he was [now] continuing that "tradition" in another way—from the last years of his life (*Tsingos,* p. 11)

—sad years of the gradual drowning of creative energy in alcoholic decay. Andreas shows far more interest in the brute realities of social existence than in generating the "folklorism" with which his detractors so facilely charge him.

His critics, both literary analysts and local readers in Rethemnos with a special interest in Andreas as a native son, also transform an aesthetic debate about the quality of his writing into an argument about the precise interpretation of the past. In so doing, they enter a picture—an ethnographic view—of the politics of culture and knowledge. It is in fact they who enable us to move discussion from purely aesthetic judgments to a field that is at once broader and more susceptible of contextualization.

By dismissing him as a mere chronicler, for example, his foes at once deny his artistry and create grounds on which they can then also challenge his competence. What is more, they can turn his probings of fictional minds into libels against actual people: what a stereotypical character might have been expected to think and feel—a culturally convincing fiction—becomes an ill-intentioned imputation of the basest motives to specific individuals. A novelist can imagine a whole range of subjectivities with impunity; a chronicler does so only at great risk.

Methodologically, this recalls the ethnographer's reliance on gossip and the local politics of reputation, here transcribed onto the larger canvas of literary debate. What is more, Andreas is never free of the watchful eye of his native Rethemnos. He recognizes that Rethemnos is a "small society"—a common local cliche of rueful self-recognition—so that what he has to say about the town will almost inevitably offend as many of his fellow citizens as it will please. He also knows that in such an intense emotional arena there is no easy line to be drawn between the real and the imaginary, the literal and the metaphorical, or the dispassionate and the partisan.

He understands this intensity from direct experience. In describing an unpopular arrest, he observes—just as I have done—that local officials cannot act as though they were independent of complex social relations with those over whom they exercise their authority. They must act as fellow members of a small community even when they are police making a spectacular arrest (cf. Herzfeld 1991a: 96–98):

▌ The gendarmes were locals, so people greeted them and they smiled and were full of pleasure at their achievement. Here everyone knows everyone else—the thief the next thief, and the householder the person who is about to seize everything he owns if he doesn't watch out; and the police know and are known by all. Each person bids the next good day, they all greet each other, and all smile. All think about—and know—who the person who's just offered a greeting is, how much and what kind of property he owns, how he eats, how he sleeps, and with whom he has dealings for better or for worse. That's what a small place is like. At the instant anyone looks at you, your whole family tree passes across his brain in a flash, along with your property, your trees, your fields, and the animals you raise. Whether you're a good person, whether you have a sense of decency (*bésa*), whether you are doing any business with the high and mighty, with the police. Who's on your side, who you're fond of, who you'd slaughter, and for whom you'd be prepared to give your life. They're no better than people in other places, but woe betide you if you do anything to annoy them. All smile, all want to have friends, to make friends with everyone else, but the way life is today it's become quite hard, it's easier to acquire enemies and easier still to fall by the wayside and become their plaything and laughing-stock if you are just a bit too good for your own safety. (*Voukéfali*, p. 191)

These proved prophetic words in the very novel that outraged some of Andreas's fellow Rethemniots, and it is the smallness of the place—the wholeness of the social context—by which he justifies his decision to retaliate in kind against the attacks of his local critics. It is a small place with clear expectations of retaliation: his standing requires such a response, for he has never entirely left Rethemnos behind—indeed, he probably could not otherwise have painted such a dangerously evocative portrait of it.

For the same reason, Andreas recognizes that—no matter how passionately he defends the fictional character of his writing—its vivid use of local detail culled from oral and archival sources will provoke strong reactions in those who see their families or their social class lampooned in his work. Andreas rejects the standard Greek convention of announcing explicitly when he wishes not to be taken literally; in his most controversial novel, moreover, he makes liberal use of journalistic sources that are the particular domain of that convention. As a result, his ironic teasing at the boundaries between reportage and imagination often provokes fury; but he is a self-aware social actor in the places and times of which he writes, sometimes even a kinsman of those he describes, and many of these reactions serve to confirm the acuity of his *social* insights, playing out the long-term political and ideological conflicts of which they are at times both the vital expression and an effective tool.

Much of the petty gossip described by ethnographers of modern Greece concerns the delicious secrecy of others' motives and desires—topics for excited speculation precisely to the degree that they are ultimately unfathomable. I suggest that the work of critics exhibits decided similarities with gossip in this regard. Classifying authors is a way of guessing (or alleging) their intentions; because these intentions are always open to speculation, the critical industry, like village gossip, never lacks for raw material. The debates that swirl around Andreas's work concern what he says Greeks do, or what particular types of Greeks might have said and done. What is more, they echo current anthropological preoccupations with questions of "ethnographic realism."[9] Andreas calls most of his major writings "novels." Moreover, he thoroughly resents all attempts—of which there have been many—to treat them as historical chronicles. He also insists, however, that he dislikes the idea of calling himself an "author," opposing this term to a self-deprecating description of his writing as simply a way of making a living. This is not necessarily disingenuous: writing has been one of a number of creative ways in which he fought against real privation. At least a part of the disbelief that this modest self-view elicits is politically motivated, and Andreas's devotion to realistic historical representation feeds that skeptical response—especially in reaction to his use of photographs and of finely honed circumstantial details gleaned from old newspapers and other documentary sources.

---

9. See Clifford 1983, Clifford and Marcus 1986, Manganaro 1990; for a sustained critique of the second of these works, see especially Behar and Gordon 1995; Cohen, Mascia-Lees, and Sharpe 1989.

He describes his reasons for providing such realistic touches:

● It is rare for the pages . . . I write to be what I really want to do. . . .
That is . . . in my opinion this is something that concerns everyone who
works in these areas, even painters, musicians, and so forth. They aim
for . . . the best, the Perfect, so to speak, and never reach that goal. I,
well, let's say the last book (*Voukéfali*), that . . . I wanted to give it another form . . . and yet something else emerged. Why? I can't understand it. That is: I didn't at all want it to have bits of chronicle in it,
dates and so on, I wanted it to become pure novel. But . . . later . . .
I thought that perhaps it would be . . . not an original idea, that is . . .
but a sort of modernism, if I can characterize it thus . . . a novelty. To
put in . . . facts that have the character of a chronicle. Eh, well, so
whereas I didn't want to put them in, in the end—in they went. So what
was the result? Some people called it a "chronicle," others a "novel."
Whereas I . . . for me it is a novel, pure and simple. That is, regardless
of whether I have . . . facts and dates in there, which I do, so to speak,
or extracts from newspapers. That doesn't bother *me*! Because Tolstoy
wrote *War and Peace*—have you read it, or do you know about it?—he
describes the campaign of Napoleon the Great in . . . there, and he says
things about the Battle of Borodino, let's say, this, that, and the other.
Well—is *that* a chronicle? Tolstoy's book? [*I responded negatively, and
he continued:*] So why should mine be considered a chronicle, let's say,
just because I have some things which are, so speak, historical facts?

He was not allowed to avoid the social consequences of using "real"
names and events in *Voukéfali*. Like Cavafy's city or the Paris of his own
imagination, his hometown follows him always, demanding its price for
his license. To this demand he has some spirited answers that compel
him, as he concedes, to deal with his erstwhile fellow townsfolk on home
ground.

He also defends his choices by pointing out that he has placed all the
real quotations from contemporary sources (such as newspapers) inside
quotation marks, thereby freeing the rest of his text to the world of the
imaginary. He uses quotation marks in his novels much as I do in my
ethnographic writing: to signal that what lies between them is attributable
to a specific person in precisely the same words. Everything else is analysis, imagination, or synopsis.

My usage springs from a scholastic concern for precision: I want to
be sure my readers know that whatever is demarcated by quotation marks
or block quotes in my ethnographic studies is a faithful rendition (although usually in translation) of what I actually heard. For Andreas,
however, the usage is much more playful. In the early years of the Greek
state, massive efforts were invested in making the neo-Classical language,
an invented idiom rarely used for everyday speech, the standard for all

official and educational purposes. Such an arid language policy was deeply inimical to poetic fantasy, perhaps in part because it was so closely associated with practices of bureaucratic control and the humorless exercise of power, and it left its mark on ordinary speech and writing as well.

In this context, quotation marks often have more to do with marking off the poetic and figurative from the literal than with accuracy as such. Peter Mackridge (1985: 348) has observed that modern Greek orthography, inculcated through schooling in the importance of "literalness" (*kirioleksía*) and "exhortations to avoid figurative language," is especially prone to placing quotation marks around anything that might seem "colloquial or metaphorical." And Karen Van Dyck has explored the absurd extremes of this proclivity under the military regime of 1967–74, when dictator George Papadopoulos "wanted the word and the thing to be exactly the same" (1997: 19; see also Van Dyck 1994). But the phenomenon was both older and deeper than the junta, for it sprang from a bourgeois antipathy to risk and disorder that was already deeply rooted in Greek society when the colonels seized power. Figurative language was "matter out of place" (Douglas 1966) in a world governed by Eurocentric ideals of linguistic, racial, and moral purity.

Such is the neo-Classical aesthetic that Andreas has always so detested. It called for the repression, not only of the pollution of foreign-derived words, but also of the semantic pollution, from a rationalist perspective, of ambiguity. Deliberately or not, Andreas has turned this arid tradition on its head: he uses quotation marks to encase documentary extracts that even his enemies must accept as true by the logic of their own insistence that he is a chronicler rather than a novelist. Andreas's parodic play is a trap for the self-appointed realists who must read his work in a literal way in order to justify their own anger, for irony is most effective when it succeeds in inviting its unwitting targets to attack it as untrue.

This is a device that quietly avenges everything he detests. Andreas is well aware that putting on a show of precise literality can actually be a way of obfuscating disinformation and ideological bias in the media and of denying access to resources in the bureaucracy. During the Greek Civil War and the military-controlled governments that persisted after its conclusion, he saw both these deployments of literality at an extreme that strained the suspension of disbelief to the breaking point. He was prepared to use a wide range of parodic devices to push it beyond that point. In *Black April,* for example, the absurdist crescendo of newspaper headlines and communiques shows how excessive displays of precision tend to incite the disbelief they are intended to suppress. Collage of this sort is a creative trap for literal-minded readers: when they dismiss Andreas as a chronicler, they reveal that they have missed the deliberate irony of his juxtapositions and occasional moments of parody. Struck by the extraordinary closeness between the beginning of *Bir Hakeim* and his conversational account of escaping from the German occupation of Greece, I asked whether this was not straightforward reporting of facts:

● Yes! Yes, but excuse me: yes, but [I did it] in a way that was novelistically placed. . . . It was I who fled to Turkey. But did I write it down like diary entries? *No!* It was just that I could remember certain things.

By that token, the barrage of newspaper headlines in *Black April*, his account of the 1967 military coup, is all the more alluringly deceptive and reminds us that realism—which may be rooted in experience—is not necessarily intended to provide the neutral factuality of a railway timetable, to use the closest approximation to pure referentiality recognized by George Orwell (1970 [1968]: 26). In this writing, satire reaches out beyond its narrative object to menace the too-serious reader as well.

Such traps for the unwary abound. Thus, by reversing conventional orthographic practice, Andreas appears to reproduce everyday reality, whereas in practice he is calling the bureaucrats' bluff. Note, for example, *his* use of quotation marks in a passage about a prisoner in the notorious Youra camp, who after torture is being shipped off to the nearby island of Syros for terminal hospitalization, as was usual at that time:

▌ Yangas, however, expired before the caïque could set off. And when someone said they should get him off the boat and bury him here, the guards responded that he was considered to have been "credited" to Syros and had to go there. The bureaucracy's involved, you see. . . . (*Prohibited*, p. 50)

This is not the unorthodox punctuation through which women writers under the junta challenged the comforting certainties of referentiality, as Van Dyck has demonstrated (1997: 133). It is, rather, a usage so orthodox as to be unquestionably parodic. A Greek reader would easily recognize the mockery of bureaucratic language here. Like the poetic devices described by Van Dyck, but through dramatic ordinariness rather than exotically poetic usage, it has the effect of mocking the authorities' implicit claim to have instituted exact and literal meanings for every word in the language, and it also raises awkward questions about the authority of those so mocked. For "words in quotation marks, much like proper names, have a certain weight that other language does not carry; quoting is one of the main textual practices by which writing is authorized" (Van Dyck 1997: 132). If what is authorized suddenly looks ridiculous, the entire edifice of authority is suddenly at risk.

Other flashes of parody abound. In *Ten Women*, again (pp. 211–12), Andreas casually exposes the absurdity of a national census that considers people to live at the domicile where they slept on the night the census was taken—a system that blithely ignored countless nocturnal assignations that violated the prevailing official morality, to some extent mandated by law, in all matters of sex. Official facts, the epitome of literalness, suddenly look much less sturdy.

This is important, not only as an insight into the deep skepticism with which Andreas has always confronted the civil service and the profession of journalism whenever they were under any degree of military control, but also because it grounds his perspective on questions of fact and fiction in a social and historical context. The issue of genre—is Andreas a novelist or a chronicler, and what are the implications of asking?—defines his ambiguous authorial relationship to the society in which he lives and on which he comments.

On the one hand, he insists that he is a novelist; on the other, he rejects the title of "author." This is less contradictory in Greek than it would be in English. In Greek, whereas the novel—as a species of narrative—occupies a somewhat vague space between literate and oral models, the term *singraféas* (author) has all the implications of that formalist academicism that Andreas so heartily detests. Denying that he is a "significant literary personality" and rather coyly insisting that he simply "happened to be born in a very interesting era," he consequently represents his writing as the reshaping of "lived experiences" (*viómata*) through the narrative form of the novel: "I am, as it were, the pulse of all this, it shows itself in a certain fashion in me."

This partial denial of writerly authority has to be seen in the larger context of Greek literary concerns with orality as the hallmark of authentic Greekness. Scoff as he may, Andreas's insouciance in matters of self-advertisement will probably be read by most of his compatriots as the urbane equivalent of the Cretan shepherd's disclaimer of interest in self-regard: "not that I wish to boast, but. . . ." (It is clearly an old formula: recall the seventeenth-century poet Bounialis's claim of authorial modesty: "nor have I ever so boasted.") In Greece, as elsewhere (see Bauman 1992), this kind of disclaimer is a hallmark of oral discourse, and so, in Andreas's everyday commentary on his career, it serves as a way of affirming his commitment to the oral idiom that is appropriate to portraying life's experiences. In his refusal of honorifics—recall his irritation when he was hailed as an "author" in Stockholm—he rejects bourgeois and fascist conceptualizations of the literal, much as, like the women authors of the junta period (Van Dyck 1997), he does with his handling of language and punctuation. In each of these arenas, moreover, he opposes Greekness to the creeping international sclerosis of bourgeois routines. In this way—in a move directly analogous to my own use of marginality here and especially in my discussion of the position of Greece in the history of anthropology and colonialism (in *Anthropology through the*

Looking-Glass)—he turns the apparent parochiality of his Helleno-centrism into a means of exposing the parochiality of a world grown bourgeois, banal, and beastly.

This context gives meaning to his assumption of a female narrator's voice. The association of orality with female—and hence politically weak—narrators is a well-known device in Greek male-authored litera-ture, at least from the time of the nineteenth-century writer of short sto-ries George Vizyenos (see Syrimis 1995). Andreas's use of the first-person female voice is an effective challenge to the formalism of the bourgeois state, with its banal routines and conventions and its cheap masculinism, although it represents a much more explicit challenge than the indirect ironies of women writers who had to brave the colonels' heavy-handed demand for literal language.

In oral discourse, ambiguity and irony have relatively free play, corre-sponding to the uncertainties of social existence rather than to the predict-able formulae of official business; they represent creativity rather than conformity. The evanescence of the oral converges with the spontaneity of the unofficial and the mortality of the oppressed. Given that for most Greeks the act of writing has deep symbolic implications of official power and permanence, moreover, a style that presents itself as oral also thereby distances itself from the deadening terrorism of the police state and the more benign dullness of its successors. It recuperates ideas about the free-dom of self-expression from the heavy academicism that for decades sub-jected both the ancient authors and modern writing to conformism, cen-sorship, and the ideals of a presumed standard of "European" excellence. If writing is the instrument of power, intimations of orality suggest the friable basis of that power.

The other association of the written word is permanence: what is written cannot be unwritten, the adage goes, and this is as true of police and bureaucratic "filing" as it is of the hand of fate itself. But it is also true of literary production. In a 1946 essay, George Orwell wrote that "sheer egoism" was a major motive for writers: "Desire to seem clever, to be talked about, to be remembered after death, to get your own back on grown-ups who snubbed you in childhood, etc. etc. It is humbug to pretend that this is not a motive, and a strong one" (1970 [1968]: 25). While Andreas expresses only contempt, significantly in the voice of a female narrator in *Ten Women*, about the desire for self-perpetuation through one's progeny and the resurrection of names, he cannot entirely escape the circumstance that he does write—that he is making his own posterity, however reluctant he may be to contemplate that concern. Dis-claimers that to English-speakers might sound contrived nevertheless have the ring of authenticity—in Trilling's terms, Andreas is a true mod-ern; and, like so many moderns, he demonstrates his modernity through his explicit engagement in traditionalizing talk—talk that emphasizes its own orality even when it is written.

However powerfully Andreas may despise the motive of self-perpetuation, moreover, he is aware that his writings may play a role in creating a posterity—if not his own, then at least that of his patriline, including the brother whose existence he now finds himself obliged to assert. But I would like to place this aspect of Greek writing in a still larger context. Reading modest disclaimers as the conventional trope of astute social performers, we can assume most Greeks will perceive that Andreas—whatever his actual, innermost intentions may be—knows he will be understood to be making a claim on, precisely, posterity. He, too, knows that others will so interpret him:

> Now, you've often said to me, "You're an old man." Excuse me, but when you say those things, I say, "Look, Michael's thinking that I am thinking about. . . . [that is, death and posterity]." Well, as long as I can, I'll stay alive. After that, it's all over. Nor am I interested in posterity and all the rest of it. The books I write—I don't think about whether they'll be read after my death one way or the other. . . . And that's just fine.

In that reflection, Andreas is constructing me as an imaginary interlocutor to whom he can reply convincingly because, again in the imaginary space created by this fiction, his thoughts are completely transparent. Perhaps there is also something of an affirmation of our own friendship, in which pretense becomes untenable.

But Andreas knows that the Greek readers for whom he writes will largely treat his disclaimers as rhetorical. This is in part because the act of writing is so fundamentally associated with permanence in Greek culture. The Cretan village friend I mentioned earlier finally felt he had made sense of my obstinate childlessness when he told me that writing books was like having children and exposed a motive for my own writing that was certainly plausible in *cultural* terms. Besides, the idea of *eghoïsmós*, a more positive notion than its English-language cognate (having many male children is one of its components for most rural Cretans), extends to such culturally familiar and patrilineally inflected constructions of desire as the thirst for revenge—if not exactly on "grown-ups who snubbed you in childhood," then on those who have allegedly insulted your close kin and defamed their memory. In a society with a strong valuation of descent in the male line, such matters are to be taken seriously.

Mention of names raises issues of anonymity and libel—further offshoots of a concern with posterity. As an anthropologist, I have almost always felt constrained to use pseudonyms for my local sources because so much of what they told me could have landed them in trouble had it been directly attibrutable to them: the admittedly permeable screen of the pseudonym deflects the more substantial dangers. A novelist may not feel such devices to be imperative: after all, this is fictional writing. On the other hand, by his own avowal, it is grounded in life's experiences. As a result, Andreas oscillates: he uses both pseudonyms and real names. Recognizing that his use of real names in at least one novel, *Manuscript,* created some social difficulties for him, he nonetheless vehemently defends his strategy:

❶ Why should you change a name, given that such things are significant? Just because it's a novel? Besides, in a manner of speaking they will live on, *if* the book lives on too, into *eternity*—you're promoting their fame, as it were. That displeasure is not justified, rather, it's fakery. That is to say: certain people have gotten a particular view of themselves just because they've become very famous of late, you're supposed to pay them respect. . . .

Here he does acknowledge the power of the printed word to secure posterity. While he has expressed some distress about this permanence as it relates to the most scurrilous attacks on him, however, he—unlike most ethnographers, who avoid the problem by using pseudonyms—expresses surprise when others object to being named. The fictional anonymity of ethnographic writing yields, in Andreas, to the fictional specificity of fact.

The printed word provides the means of expanding the local beyond its immediate social boundaries. In a country where official ethnology treats oral traditions as "monuments of the word" by converting them into printed form, orality, like other forms of spontaneity frozen by the action of a writer, is an important component of Greek claims to authenticity—to the Greekness of *Zorba,* for example. Assumptions about what constitutes the distinctiveness of oral as opposed to written texts are fraught with cultural politics. Thus, for example, during the Civil War and its immediate aftermath left-wing scholars insisted that most medieval and Renaissance texts were derived from oral ("popular") sources, while their rightist counterparts sneered at the folk as degenerate heirs to a literate Great Tradition.[10] In Andreas's novels, it is sometimes the most obtrusively "oral" moments that entail the most self-conscious textual management. The cries of the storm-tossed refugees with which *Bir Hakeim* opens, for example, are presented as living speech, yet they barely appear in Andreas's *spoken* recollection of the personal experience on which he based that passage. The spontaneity of oral discourse, like the realism of which it partakes, is a literary device. In Andreas's writings,

---

10. See my discussion of these debates about the relationship in Herzfeld 1982a.

it is tied to the Greekness that also—somewhat paradoxically—infuses his image of authorship as an artisan's careful work.

Through his use of an oral style, Andreas particularly reminds us that ambiguities are part of lived experience: oral utterances defy the certainties of the dictionary and upset the programmed semantics through which petty functionaries have justified torture, denied access to bureaucratic services, and straitjacketed culture in the name of an arid sense of public order. He also explicitly speaks of his own enjoyment, and use, of irony. His attacks on literality are all of a piece with the critical labor of his writing, which strips away the layers of hypocrisy that protect the special interests of the privileged and the pretensions of the self-important. In this he resembles George Orwell, whose contempt for "humbug"— whether in politics or in art—was equally scathing, albeit in the face of often subtler and more diffuse forms of tyranny. Andreas's mockery of those who claim absolute knowledge, from inflated academics to vicious torturers and their ecclesiastical sycophants, springs from direct experience. That experience, bodily and psychological alike, has recorded the violence that keeps the mask of literality in place.

The most consistent celebration of the literal in the bourgeois Greek state is centered on the aesthetic and historiographic ideology usually, if perhaps simplistically, summarized as "neo-Classical." This is the view of Greek culture as the damaged fragment left by a glorious past which is now to be recreated in the modern age. For Andreas, as for other Greek writers, there is certainly no contradiction between respect for the ancient heritage and disdain for its exploitation by slavish academic hacks and ignorant military dictators who invoke "our ancient ancestors" at every turn but do so in terms largely formulated in the political and academic centers of Western Europe. It is entirely consistent with Andreas's outlook that Constantine Cavafy, the ironic Alexandrian Greek commentator on the self-deceptions of the Hellenistic age, is perhaps the single Greek poet for whom he expresses unqualified respect—far more, it appears, than for his friends and fellow sufferers in the political concentration camps: Manolis Anagnostakis, Tasos Livaditis, and Yannis Ritsos. And Andreas, illustrating his delicate appreciation of irony, told me that it was precisely in Cavafy's native Alexandria that he found embodied in a local dignitary the pompous disregard for Cavafy's vision that Cavafy himself so often satirized in his verses about Hellenistic personages.

A social scientist and a sworn foe of the military junta (like Andreas, he lived as an exile in Paris during the military dictatorship), Konstandinos Tsoukalas has given us a precise view of Cavafy's ironic vision:

It is not an accident that it fell to the Greek worshipper of the ancients, Cavafy, to seek the truth of History in irony. For Hegel had already spoken, himself perhaps ironically . . . of the cunning of History, which tends to overturn and reconceptualize all the schemes of mortals, concluding that the only thing anyone ever learned from the study of History was that no one ever learned anything from the study of History.

The Greek Cavafy, however, did learn; and he offers us another proposition—that one can broaden Hegel's irony, which becomes deflated before his absolute certainty about the role of the observer himself, [by] drawing on the very work of exercising judgment and philosophical thought: that an observer and a poet can draw inspiration from their very contradictions, uncertainties, and self-deceptions; that nostalgia for the lost or unfeasible requires no apologetics or repentance; that beyond deceptive truth and falsifiable transparency a person's—but also a poet's—stance toward the fluid and unstable things of life can be judged by that individual's dignity, courage, and internal consistency. (Tsoukalas 1996: 332–33)

This passage accurately depicts a perspective to which, despite obvious differences, Andreas also adheres.

Perhaps no genuinely serious writer can afford to take the literal at face value. But Andreas confronted, in the Greece of the military Right, the most destructive consequences of too massive a dose of the literal. He also confronted one of its most absurd conclusions in that context: that the ordinary (demotic) language of everyday life lacked the semantic stability of the lifeless neo-Classical (purist) language and was fundamentally subversive because it was communist-inspired, contaminated by Slavic ideas and Turkish forms, and antithetical to everything truly Hellenic. Writing a demotic Greek that poked fun at the pretensions of the colonels' heavy-handed and ill-informed purism, Andreas was also, during such difficult periods of his life, deeply concerned with questions of the uses of linguistic form to monopolize and define truth, for which he preferred the mordantly selective use of direct quotation to the more indirect, allegorical tactics preferred by several of his contemporaries—including most of the contributors to perhaps the best-known literary attack on the military junta, *Eighteen Texts*.[11] Andreas's writing thus offers an exemplary antidote to the social and political uses of literality.

He does loosely use the term for "novel" (*mithistórima*) to mean a "faked tale" or something that could not have happened in real life, in the same way as Greeks also often use *paramíthi*, "fairy tale" and sometimes with the same sense of disapproval (*Tsingos*, p. 119; *Prohibited*, p. 53). Nor is he averse to adopting the device of presenting a novel as drily factual reporting. His account of Youra, for example, is written in

11. The title of *Eighteen Texts*, as Van Dyck (1997: 19–20) has pointed out, nonetheless itself mocks the junta's literal-minded order that book titles should be precise descriptions of the contents, so terrified were they of the subversive power of figurative language.

the form of a diary, and, while it is undoubtedly based in part on his own direct experiences, it is clear that he has borrowed extensively from stories he heard from other inmates as well as from his resources of imagination. Yet he elaborately disclaims intervention in the text; at the beginning, in an epigraph, he announces (in the terms of a metaphor for suffering then widely current in leftist poetry and, at least in Andreas's native Crete, used in working-class speech for the exhaustion of manual toil[12]), "This book the political prisoners of Youra signed with their blood; I just copied it." He adds his initials for further verisimilitude. At the end, he signs off as "the editor/publisher"—the term (o *ekdhótis*) is in fact usefully ambiguous, and all the more so as Andreas, as usual, published the book privately.[13] In this way, too, he constitutes the book as an act of memorialization, a response to the "colonization of public and private space" (Watson 1994: 19) that characterizes totalitarian regimes of either camp, and reminds his readers that the most deadening oppression can provide the means of commemorating its victims.

But it is in Andreas's biographical writing that we see these ambiguities most directly confronted (and perhaps where I remain most directly forced to reflect on the problems of writing a biographical account of Andreas himself even as I bring it to a close). It seems fitting to end this book with his own meditation on the nature of the exercise with which, in its turn, his life has confronted me.

The key moment comes in his rather scolding but affectionate memoir of Thanassis Tsingos, the architect and artist with whom he faced execution for mutiny. That book is perhaps the fullest expression of Andreas's capacity for conveying a sense of his empathy with another human being, his ability to naturalize his exploration of another's innermost thoughts and emotions. For they had faced annihilation together, he and Tsingos, and this gives the biographical exercise on which Andreas embarks some of the most realistic "feel" we encounter anywhere in his writings.

Yet it is here, at the very moment that a reader is made to feel that all academic discussions of style and fictionality are the merest froth on the surface of lives profoundly lived, that Andreas turns the tables. The biography of Tsingos is also an autobiography; and, like most autobiog-

---

12. See my *A Place in History* (1991a: 13). For a similar metaphor and ideology in Galicia, see Roseman 1996.

13. This is a not uncommon literary device—see, for example, Pushkin's *Belkin Tales* and the figure of Dr. Watson in Arthur Conan Doyle's Sherlock Holmes stories and novels— but Andreas uses it here with a brusque finality that itself is part of the realist effect that he achieves.

raphy, it is more *obviously* fictional (though not necessarily *more fictional*) than a straightforwardly third-person narrative. The story grows in the telling, as Andreas merges with his subject, and as the narrated event merges with the narration itself.[14] Like the shepherds of the Cretan highland villages, who do not always distinguish between exciting events and the equally exciting tales they tell about those events, Andreas—here and in all his works—challenges the rigid distinction between imagination and life. In so doing, he allows me to step beyond the conventional limits of ethnography as a description of a society and culture bereft, to a large extent, of speculations about motive and desire. In describing his imagination as he renders it accessible, he helps me to break free of the localized boundaries—the village, the suburb, the institution—of normative ethnography. But he does not thereby show me that, in conducting such research, I have merely indulged in self-referential games, fiction masquerading as fact. For the problematic distinction is not that between fact and fiction, or between ethnography and novels: these are discriminations based on the implied intentions of authors and readers. It is between a desiccated, mechanistic, bureaucratic reductionism and the recognition that a lived reality defies prediction—that the idea of the literal is a denial of experience itself. And while—as an ethnographer—I have always tried to pursue the richness of that ambiguity, Andreas has taken me much further than I would have dared, holding the handrail of my profession, to venture on my own.

It is in his literary portrait of the painter Tsingos that Andreas reveals, as Cavafy describes his poetics and as ordinary people everywhere articulate the social visions by which they live, that Andreas describes the paradox of lived experience. It is not that art imitates life. It is that our knowl-

---

14. On narrated and narrative events, see Bauman 1986. Paul John Eakin comments usefully on the links among fiction, selfhood, and autobiography (1985: 3–6); he also notes Sartre's recognition that the category of autobiography cannot be sharply separated from that of the novel (Eakin 1985: 7–8). Vincent Crapanzano (1980) places similar concerns in the context of an ethnography far less obviously rejectionist of its intellectual underpinnings in anthropology than that of his fellow Moroccanist, Kevin Dwyer (1982). (Note, too, that the recognition of Crapanzano's book as "experimental" has obscured antecedent works by women writing about women [Behar 1995: 26, n. 10]. The perhaps inevitable partiality of ethnographic work must also, and for related reasons, be made explicit: the present work is a book by a man about another man and makes this apparent; in that respect it is like *The Poetics of Manhood*, although I hope I have learned to be even more explicit now. Such a recognition of authorial intention can only benefit the clarity of reading—hence my reluctance in chapter 1 to call the book experimental. Even though I note such devices in Andreas's own discourse [see also Bauman 1996], I do claim that this is *merely*, at least, a performative disclaimer!) For an especially cogent critique of positivistic approaches to these issues, see Okely (1992: 3–4); see also Herzfeld (1987a: 1) on the relationship among experience (Classical Greek *empeiría*), the empirical, and empiricism.

edge of life is inseparable from the social art through which we make life recognizable to ourselves:

█ I do not know what name to give all these things I am writing about Thanasis Tsingos. In any event, it is not a biography. As I rummage about in my memory at every hour, every moment, I recall conversations or actions of his and try to put them in order. But it is obvious that I am not succeeding. And if I try to link each up with the next what will come out in the end is a novel (*mithistorima*).

But wasn't his life, and weren't the lives of all us at that time, a novel? (*Tsingos*, p. 10)

REFERENCES

Abu-Lughod, Lila, and Catherine A. Lutz. 1990. "Introduction: Emotion, Discourse, and the Politics of Everyday Life." In Catherine A. Lutz and Lila Abu-Lughod, eds., *Language and the Politics of Emotion*, pp. 1–23. Cambridge: Cambridge University Press.

Alexiou, Margaret. 1991. "Literature and Popular Tradition." In David Holton, ed., *Literature and Society in Renaissance Crete*, pp. 239–274. Cambridge: Cambridge University Press.

Alexiou, S. 1965. "To Kastro tis Kritis ke i zoi tou ston 16' ke 17' eona." *Kritika Khronika* 19: 146–78.

Alexiou, Stylianos, and Martha Aposkiti. 1995. *Marínou Tzáne Bounialí O Kritikós Pólemos (1645–1669)*. Athens: Stigmi.

Anderson, Benedict. 1983. *Imagined Communities: Reflections on the Origin and Spread of Nationalism*. London: Verso.

Anonymous. 1974. "Kiklofórise O *Mávros Aprílis* tou Andréa Nenedáki." *Néa*, 10 September.

Ardener, Edwin. 1975. "The 'Problem' Revisited." In Shirley Ardener, ed., *Perceiving Women*, pp. 19–27. London: J. M. Dent.

Aretxaga, Begoña. 1995. "Dirty Protest: Symbolic Overdetermination and Gender in Northern Ireland Ethnic Violence." *Ethos* 23: 123–48.

———. 1997. *Shattering Violence: Women, Nationalism, and Political Subjectivity in Northern Ireland*. Princeton: Princeton University Press.

Argyrou, Vassos. 1996. *Tradition and Modernity in Mediterranean Society: The Wedding as Cultural Symbol*. Cambridge: Cambridge University Press.

Asdrachas, Spyros I. 1983. *Zitímata Istorías*. Athens: Themelio.

Badone, Ellen. 1991. "Ethnography, Fiction, and the Meanings of the Past in Brittany." *American Ethnologist* 18: 518–45.

Bakalaki, Alexandra. 1993. "Anthropoloyikés prosengísis tis sínkhronis ellinikís kinonías." *Dhiavázo* 323: 52–58.

299

————. 1994. "Gender-Related Discourses and Representations of Cultural Specificity in Nineteenth-Century and Twentieth-Century Greece." *Journal of Modern Greek Studies* 12: 75–112.

Balshem, Martha. 1993. *Cancer in the Community: Class and Medical Authority.* Washington: Smithsonian Institution Press.

Bauman, Richard. 1986. *Story, Performance, and Event: Contextual Studies of Oral Narrative.* Cambridge: Cambridge University Press.

————. 1992. "Disclaimers of Performance." In Jane H. Hill and Judith T. Irvine, eds., *Responsibility and Evidence in Oral Discourse,* pp. 182–96. Cambridge: Cambridge University Press.

Behar, Ruth. 1995. "Introduction: Out of Exile." In Behar and Gordon, eds., *Women Writing Culture,* pp. 1–29. Berkeley: University of California Press.

Behar, Ruth, and Deborah A. Gordon, eds. 1995. *Women Writing Culture.* Berkeley: University of California Press.

Bernal, Martin. 1987. *Black Athena: The Afroasiatic Roots of Classical Civilization.* New Brunswick, NJ: Rutgers University Press.

Binns, Christopher A. P. 1980. "The Changing Face of Power: Revolution and Development of the Soviet Ceremonial System." [Part 2 of 2.] *Man* (n.s.) 15: 170–87.

Borofsky, Robert. 1997. "Cook, Lono, Obeyesekere, and Sahlins." *Current Anthropology* 38: 255–82.

Bounialis, Marinos Tzane. 1979. *O Kritikós Pólemos.* Edited with an introduction by Andreas Nenedakis. Athens: n.p.

Bourdieu, Pierre. 1977. *Outline of a Theory of Practice.* Translated by Richard Nice.

————. 1984. *Distinction: A Social Critique of the Judgement of Taste.* Translated by Richard Nice. Cambridge, MA: Harvard University Press.

Calotychos, Vangelis. 1993. "Realizing and Resisting 'Self-Colonization': Ideology and Form in Modern Greek Poetics (1790–1960)." Ph.D. diss. Harvard University.

Campbell, J. K. 1964. *Honour, Family, and Patronage: A Study of Institutions and Moral Values in a Greek Mountain Community.* Oxford: Clarendon Press.

Caraveli, Anna. 1986. "The Bitter Wounding: The Lament as Social Protest in Rural Greece." In Jill Dubisch, ed., *Gender and Power in Rural Greece,* pp. 169–94. Princeton: Princeton University Press.

Clark, Mari H. 1983. "Variations on Themes of Male and Female (Reflections on Gender Bias in Fieldwork in Rural Greece)." *Women's Studies* 10: 117–33.

Clifford, James. 1983. "On Ethnographic Authority." *Representations* 2 (Spring 1983): 118–46.

Clifford, James, and George E. Marcus, eds. 1986. *Writing Culture: The Poetics and Politics of Ethnography.* Berkeley: University of California Press.

Clogg, Richard. 1972. "The Ideology of the Revolution of 21 April 1967." In Richard Clogg and George Yannopoulos, eds., *Greece under Military Rule*, pp. 36–58. New York: Basic Books/ London: Secker & Warburg.

Cohen, Anthony P. 1994. *Self Consciousness: An Alternative Anthropology of Identity.* London: Routledge.

Cohen, Colleen Ballerino, Frances E. Mascia-Lees, and Patricia Sharpe. 1989. "The Post-Modernist Turn in Anthropology: Cautions from a Feminist Perspective." *Signs* 15: 7–33.

Constantinides, Elizabeth. 1983. "Andreiomeni: The Female Warrior in Greek Folk Songs." *Journal of Modern Greek Studies* 1: 63–72.

Couroucli, Maria. 1993. "Heroes and Their Shadows: The Hungry, the Humble and the Powerful." *Journal of Mediterranean Studies* 3: 99–116.

———. 1995. "Le *lalein* et le *grafein*: Parler et écrire en grec." *Revue du Monde Musulman et de la Méditerranée* 75–76: 257–71.

———. 1996. "Silence et mépris de la stratégie de l'araignée dans la société urbaine." In Odile Cavalier, ed., *La femme et le mariage en Grèce: Les antiquités du Musée Calvet*, pp. 499–511. Avignon: Editions de la Fondation du Muséum Calvet.

Cowan, Jane K. 1990. *Dance and the Body Politic in Northern Greece.* Princeton: Princeton University Press.

Crapanzano, Vincent. 1980. *Tuhami: Portrait of a Moroccan.* Chicago: University of Chicago Press.

Dakin, Douglas. 1972. *The Unification of Greece 1770–1923.* London: Ernest Benn.

———. 1973. *The Greek Struggle for Independence 1821–1833.* London: B. T. Batsford.

Damer, Seán. 1988. "Legless in Sfakia: Drinking and Social Practice in Western Crete." *Journal of Modern Greek Studies* 6: 291–310.

Danforth, Loring M. 1976. "Humour and Status Reversal in Greek Shadow Theatre." *Byzantine and Modern Greek Studies* 2: 99–111.

Deltsou, Eleftheria. 1995. "O 'istorikós tópos' ke i simasia tis 'parádhosis' ya to éthnos-krátos." *Ethnoloyía* 4: 107–26.

Dokas, Nikos. 1993. "Stis arkhés tou eóna." *Kiriakátiki Eleftherotipía*, 2 May, p. xv.

Douglas, Mary. 1966. *Purity and Danger: An Analysis of Concepts of Pollution and Taboo.* London: Routledge & Kegan Paul.

Dubisch, Jill. 1995. *In a Different Place: Pilgrimage, Gender, and Politics at a Greek Island Shrine.* Princeton: Princeton University Press.

du Boulay, Juliet. 1974. *Portrait of a Greek Mountain Village.* Oxford: Clarendon Press.

————. 1986. "Women—Images of Their Nature and Destiny in Rural Greece." In Jill Dubisch, ed., *Gender and Power in Rural Greece*, pp. 139–68. Princeton: Princeton University Press.

Dwyer, Kevin. 1982. *Moroccan Dialogues: Anthropology in Question*. Baltimore: Johns Hopkins University Press.

Eakin, Paul John. 1985. *Fictions in Autobiography: Studies in the Art of Self-Invention*. Princeton: Princeton University Press.

Eco, Umberto. 1979. *The Role of the Reader: Explorations in the Semiotics of Texts*. Bloomington: Indiana University Press.

Eighteen Texts. 1972. *Writings by Contemporary Greek Authors*. Cambridge, MA: Harvard University Press.

Elliadi, M. N. 1933. *Crete, Past and Present*. London: Heath, Cranton.

Eudès, Dominique. 1972. *The Kapetanios: Partisans and Civil War in Greece, 1943–1949*. New York: Monthly Review Press.

Fabian, Johannes. 1983. *Time and the Other: How Anthropology Makes Its Object*. New York: Columbia University Press.

Fallaci, Oriana. 1980. *A Man*. Translated by William Weaver. New York: Simon and Schuster.

Faubion, James D. 1993. *Modern Greek Lessons: A Primer in Historical Constructivism*. Princeton: Princeton University Press.

Ferguson, Kathy E. 1984. *The Feminist Case against Bureaucracy*. Philadelphia: Temple University Press.

Friedl, Ernestine. 1962. *Vasilika: A Village in Modern Greece*. New York: Holt, Rinehart, and Winston.

Geertz, Clifford. 1973. *The Interpretation of Cultures: Selected Essays*. New York: Basic Books.

Gefou-Madianou, Dimitra. 1993. "Mirroring Ourselves through Western Texts: The Limits of an Indigenous Anthropology." In Henk Driessen, ed., *The Politics of Ethnographic Reading and Writing: Confrontation of Western and Indigenous Views*, pp. 160–81. Saarbrucken: Breitenbach.

Giddens, Anthony. 1984. *The Constitution of Society: Outline of the Theory of Structuration*. Cambridge: Polity Press.

Gokalp, Altan. 1997. "Lire Yachar Kemal." *Anka: Revue d'art et de littérature de Turquie* 29/30: 13–41.

Gudeman, Stephen, and Michael Herzfeld. 1996. "When an Academic Press Bows to a Threat." *Chronicle of Higher Education*, 12 April 1996, p. A56.

Handler, Richard. 1985. "On Dialogue and Destructive Analysis: Narrating Nationalism and Ethnicity." *Journal of Anthropological Research* 41: 171–82.

————. 1988. *Nationalism and the Politics of Culture in Quebec*. Madison: University of Wisconsin Press.

Handler, Richard, and Daniel Segal. 1990. *Jane Austen and the Fiction of Cul-*

ture: An Essay on the Narration of Social Realities. Tucson: University of Arizona Press.

Hart, Janet. 1996. *New Voices in the Nation: Women and the Greek Resistance, 1941–1964.* Ithaca, NY: Cornell University Press.

Hauschild, Thomas, ed. 1995. *Ethnologie und Literatur.* Bremen: Kea, *Zeitschrift für Kuturwissenschaft,* 1.

Herzfeld, Michael. 1980a. "On the Ethnography of 'Prejudice' in an Exclusive Community." *Ethnic Groups* 2: 283–305.

————. 1980b. "Honor and Shame: Some Problems in the Comparative Analysis of Moral Systems." *Man* (n.s.) 15: 339–51.

————. 1980c. "Social Borderers: Themes of Conflict and Ambiguity in Greek Folk Song." *Byzantine and Modern Greek Studies* 6: 61–80.

————. 1981. "Performative Categories and Symbols of Passage in Rural Greece." *Journal of American Folklore* 94: 44–57.

————. 1982a. *Ours Once More: Folklore, Ideology, and the Making of Modern Greece.* Austin: University of Texas Press.

————. 1982b. "When Exceptions Define the Rules: Greek Baptismal Names and the Negotiation of Identity." *Journal of Anthropological Research* 38: 288–303.

————. 1983. "Semantic Slippage and Moral Fall: The Rhetoric of Chastity in Rural Greek Society." *Journal of Modern Greek Studies* 1: 161–72.

————. 1984. "The Significance of the Insignificant: Blasphemy as Ideology." *Man* (n.s.) 19: 653–64.

————. 1985. *The Poetics of Manhood: Contest and Identity in a Cretan Mountain Village.* Princeton: Princeton University Press.

————. 1986. "Within and Without: The Category of 'Female' in the Ethnography of Modern Greece." In Jill Dubisch, ed., *Gender and Power in Rural Greece,* pp. 215–33. Princeton: Princeton University Press.

————. 1987a. *Anthropology through the Looking-Glass: Critical Ethnography in the Margins of Europe.* Cambridge: Cambridge University Press.

————. 1987b. "'As in Your Own House': Hospitality, Ethnography, and the Stereotype of Mediterranean Society." In David D. Gilmore, ed., *Honor and Shame and the Unity of the Mediterranean,* pp. 75–89. Washington, DC: American Anthropological Association, Special Publication # 22.

————. 1991a. *A Place in History: Social and Monumental Time in a Cretan Town.* Princeton: Princeton University Press.

————. 1991b. "Silence, Submission, and Subversion: Toward a Poetics of Womanhood." In Peter Loizos and Evthymios Papataxiarchis, eds., *Contested Identities: Gender and Kinship in Modern Greece,* pp. 79–97. Princeton: Princeton University Press.

————. 1992. *The Social Production of Indifference: Exploring the Symbolic Roots of Western Bureaucracy.* Oxford: Berg.

―――. 1997a. *Cultural Intimacy: Social Poetics in the Nation-State*. New York: Routledge.

―――. 1997b. "The Taming of Revolution: Intense Paradoxes of the Self." In Deborah E. Reed-Danahay, ed., *Auto/Ethnography: Rewriting the Self and the Social*, pp. 169–94. Oxford: Berg.

Hirschon, Renée. 1989. *Heirs of the Greek Catastrophe: The Social Life of Asia Minor Refugees in Piraeus*. Oxford: Clarendon Press.

―――. 1992. "Greek Adults' Play, or, How to Train for Caution." *Journal of Modern Greek Studies* 10: 35–56.

Holst-Warhaft, Gail. 1980. *Theodorakis, Myth and Politics in Modern Greek Music*. Amsterdam: Hakkert.

Holton, David, ed. 1991a. *Literature and Society in Renaissance Crete*. Cambridge: Cambridge University Press.

―――. 1991b. "The Cretan Renaissance." In Holton, *Literature and Society in Renaissance Crete*, 1–16. Cambridge: Cambridge University Press.

Hondros, John Louis. 1983. *Occupation and Resistance: The Greek Agony, 1941–44*. New York: Pella.

Hsu, Francis L. K. 1979. "The Cultural Problem of the Cultural Anthropologist." *American Anthropologist* 81: 517–32.

Humphreys, S. C. 1978. *Anthropology and the Greeks*. London: Routledge & Kegan Paul.

Iser, Wolfgang. 1980. "The Reading Process: A Phenomenological Approach." In Jane P. Tompkins, ed., *Reader-Response Criticism: From Formalism to Post-Structuralism*, pp. 50–69. Baltimore, MD: Johns Hopkins University Press.

―――. 1987. *Prospecting: From Reader Response to Literary Anthropology*. Baltimore, MD: Johns Hopkins University Press.

―――. 1993. *The Fictive and the Imaginary: Charting Literary Anthropology*. Baltimore, MD: Johns Hopkins University Press.

Jackson, Michael. 1986. *Barawa and the Ways Birds Fly in the Sky*. Washington, DC: Smithsonian Institution Press.

―――. 1995. *At Home in the World*. Durham, NC: Duke University Press.

Jakobson, Roman. 1960. "Linguistics and Poetics." In Thomas A. Sebeok, ed., *Style in Language*, pp. 350–77. Cambridge, MA: The MIT Press.

Jelinek, Estelle C. 1980. "Introduction." In Estelle C. Jelinek, ed., *Women's Autobiography: Essays in Criticism*, pp. 1–20. Bloomington: Indiana University Press.

―――. 1986. *The Tradition of Women's Autobiography: From Antiquity to the Present*. Boston: Twayne.

Jusdanis, Gregory. 1987. *The Poetics of Cavafy: Textuality, Eroticism, History*. Princeton: Princeton University Press.

———. 1991. *Belated Modernity and Aesthetic Culture: Inventing National Literature*. Minneapolis: University of Minnesota Press.

Just, Roger. 1992. "Triumph of the Ethnos." In Elizabeth Tonkin, Malcolm Chapman, and Maryon McDonald, eds., *History and Ethnicity*, pp. 71–88. *Association of Social Anthropologists, Monographs*, no. 27. London: Routledge.

Kapferer, Bruce. 1988. *Legends of People, Myths of State: Violence, Intolerance, and Political Culture in Sri Lanka and Australia*. Washington, DC: Smithsonian Institution Press.

Karp, Ivan. 1980. "New Guinea Models in the African Savannah." *Africa* 48: 1–17.

———. 1986. "Agency and Social Theory: A Review of Giddens." *American Ethnologist* 13: 131–37.

Kayalis, Takis. 1994. "O ekseftelismós tis loghotekhnías." *Víma*, 20 February 1994, pp. 40–41 (B6-7).

Kazantzakis, Nikos. 1952. *Zorba the Greek*. Translated by Carl Wildman. London: Lehmann.

———. 1954. *Christ Recrucified*. Translated by Jonathan Griffin. Oxford: Cassirer.

———. 1956. *Freedom or Death*. Translated by Jonathan Griffin. New York: Simon and Schuster.

Kenna, Margaret E. 1976. "Houses, Fields, and Graves: Property and Ritual Obligation on a Greek Island." *Ethnology* 15: 21–34.

———. 1991. "The Social Organization of Exile: The Everyday Life of Political Exiles in the Cyclades in the 1930s." *Journal of Modern Greek Studies* 9: 63–82.

Kertzer, David I. 1996. *Politics and Symbols: The Italian Communist Party and the Fall of Communism*. New Haven, CT: Yale University Press.

Kharalambous, Dimitris. 1989. *Pelatiakés skhésis ke laïkismós: I eksothesmikí sinénesi sto ellinikó politikó sístima*. Athens: Eksandas.

Kodrou, Eva. n.d. *Greekness in the Diaspora*. C-Level research paper, Department of Social Anthropology, Stockholm University, Sweden.

Koenig, Général Pierre. 1971. *Bir-Hakeim, 10 juin 1942*. Paris: Robert Laffont.

Koliopoulos, John S. 1987. *Brigands with a Cause: Brigandage and Irredentism in Modern Greece, 1821–1912*. Oxford: Clarendon Press.

Kondo, Dorinne K. 1990. *Crafting Selves: Power, Gender, and Discourses of Identity in a Japanese Workplace*. Chicago: University of Chicago Press.

Kordatos, Yanis K. 1924. *I kinonikí simasía tis ellinikís epanastáseos tou 1821*. Athens: I. Vassiliou.

Laffin, John. 1974. *The French Foreign Legion*. London: J. M. Dent.

Laiou-Thomadakis, Angeliki. 1977. *Peasant Society in the Late Byzantine Empire: A Social and Demographic Study*. Princeton: Princeton University Press.

———. 1992. *Gender, Society, and Economic Life in Byzantium*. Hampshire: Variorum.

Lambropoulos, Vassilis. 1988. *Literature as National Institution: Studies in the Politics of Modern Greek Criticism*. Princeton: Princeton University Press.

Lancaster, Roger N. 1988. *For God and the Revolution: Popular Religion and Class Consciousness in the New Nicaragua*. New York: Columbia University Press.

———. 1992. *Life Is Hard: Machismo, Danger, and the Intimacy of Power in Nicaragua*. Berkeley: University of California Press.

Leach, Edmund R. 1965. "The Nature of War." *Disarmament and Arms Control* 3: 165–83.

———. 1980. "On Reading *A Diary in the Strict Sense of the Term*: Or the Self-Mutilation of Professor Hsu." *RAIN* 36: 2–3.

Lefkowitz, Mary R. 1996. *Not Out of Africa: How Afrocentrism Became an Excuse to Teach Myth as History*. New York: Basic Books.

Leavitt, John. 1996. "Meaning and Feeling in the Anthropology of Emotions." *American Ethnologist* 23: 514–39.

Llewellyn Smith, Michael. 1965. *The Great Island: A Study of Crete*. London: Longmans.

Loizos, Peter. 1975. "Changes in Property Transfer among Greek Cypriot Villagers." *Man* (n.s.) 10: 503–23.

———. 1988. "Intercommunal Killing in Cyprus." *Man* (n.s.) 23: 639–53.

Machin, Barrie. 1983. "St. George and the Virgin: Cultural Codes, Religion and Attitudes to the Body in a Cretan Mountain Village." *Social Analysis* 14: 107–26.

Mackridge, Peter. 1985. *The Modern Greek Language: A Descriptive Analysis of Standard Modern Greek*. Oxford: Oxford University Press.

Macpherson, C. B. 1962. *The Political Theory of Possessive Individualism: Hobbes to Locke*. Oxford: Clarendon Press.

Maddox, Richard. 1993. *El Castillo: The Politics of Tradition in an Andalusian Town*. Urbana: University of Illinois Press.

Makriyannis, Ioannis. 1992. *Makriyanni apomnimonévmata*. Athens: Dorikos.

Maltezou, Chryssa. 1991. "The Historical and Social Context." In David Holton, ed., *Literature and Society in Renaissance Crete*, 17–47. Cambridge: Cambridge University Press.

Manganaro, Marc, ed. 1990. *Modernist Anthropology: From Field Work to Text*. Princeton: Princeton University Press.

Mazower, Mark. 1993. *Inside Hitler's Greece: The Experience of Occupation, 1941–44*. New Haven, CT: Yale University Press.

Mbembe, Achille. 1992. "Provisional Notes on the Postcolony." *Africa* 62: 3–37.

Meraklis, Mikhalis. 1984. *Ellinikí laoghrafía: kinonikí singrótisi.* Athens: Odysseas.

Mesevrinos. 1969. "Proleghómena." In Andreas Nenedakis, *O Kritikós Pólemos,* pp. 7–18. Lund: Tetradia tou Riga.

Meunier, Jacques. 1987. *Le monocle de Joseph Conrad: Ethnologie, exotisme et littérature.* Paris: La Découverte/*Le Monde.*

Mintz, Jerome R. 1982. *The Anarchists of Casas Viejas.* Chicago: University of Chicago Press.

Moore, Sally Falk. 1987. "Explaining the Present: Theoretical Dilemmas in Processual Ethnography." *American Ethnologist* 14: 727–36.

Mourellos, Ioannis D. 1931. *Kritiké vioghrafíe (Simvolí is tin istorían ton epanastáseon 1821–1866–1878–1896–1897.* Athens: Estia.

Needham, Rodney. 1972. *Belief, Language, and Experience.* Oxford: Blackwell.

Nenedakis, Andreas. 1955. "I teleftéa sinavlía." *Víma* [Rethemnos], 6 September.

————, ed. 1979. Marinos Tzane Bounialis. *O Kritikós Pólemos [The Cretan War].* Edited with an introduction by Andreas Nenedakis. Athens: n.p.

Nikolopoulous, Filippos. 1995. *Kinonioloyikí Proséngisi tou Loghotekhnikoú Erghou.* Athens: Enallaktikés Ekdhósis.

Obeyesekere, Gananath. 1992. *The Apotheosis of Captain Cook: European Mythmaking in the Pacific.* Princeton: Princeton University Press.

Okely, Judith. 1986. *Simone de Beauvoir.* London: Virago/New York: Pantheon.

————. 1992. "Anthropology and Autobiography: Participatory Experience and Embodied Knowledge." In Judith Okely and Helen Callaway, eds., *Anthropology and Autobiography,* pp. 1–28. *Association of Social Anthropologists' Monographs,* no. 29. London: Routledge.

Orso, Ethelyn G. 1979. *Modern Greek Humor: A Collection of Jokes and Ribald Tales.* Bloomington: Indiana University Press.

Orwell, George. 1970 [1968]. *The Collected Essays, Journalism and Letters of George Orwell: Volume 4: In Front of Your Nose,* edited by Sonia Orwell and Ian Angus. Harmondsworth: Penguin.

Panourgiá, E. Neni K. 1992. "O ratsistikós lóghos stin Elládha: i ithayenís stokhasmí." *O Polítis* 117 (January 1992): 38–43.

————. 1995. *Fragments of Death, Fables of Identity: An Athenian Anthropography.* Madison: University of Wisconsin Press.

Papadaki, Aspasia. 1995. *Thriskeftikés ke kosmikés teletés sti Venetokratoúmeni Kríti.* Rethimno: Nea Khristianiki Kriti.

Papagrigorakis, Idomenefs. 1964–65. *Ta Kritiká Rizítika Traghoúdia.* Khania.

Papakongos, Kostis. 1984 [1969]. *Ta kímata tis Ródhou.* Stockholm: Faros.

Papamanousakis, Stratis G. 1979. *I ksenokratía stin Kríti.* Athens: Kalvos.

Paparigopolous, Konstantinos. 1853. *Istoria tou ellinikou ethnous apo ton arkheotaton khronon mekhri tis simeron.* Athens: A. Koromilas.

Papataxiarchis, Evythmios. n.d. "The Dancing Efes: Notions of the Male Person in Aegean Greek Fiction." Manuscript. University of the Aegean, Mytilene, Greece.

Paraskhos, Kleon. 1954. Review of *Bir Hakeim. Kathimeriní,* 15 September.

Parmentier, Richard. 1996. "Haole-ing in the Wind: On the Rhetoric of Identity Anthropology." *Anthropological Quarterly* 69: 220–30.

Pesmazoglou, V. 1994. "Me kremmídhia, parakaló." *Víma,* 6 November 1994, p. B 6.

Petridis, Kostas. 1996. "Me aformí éna Vivlío." *Rethemniótika Néa,* 11 June, p. 2. [Unsigned.]

Petronikolos, Kosta Al. 1975. *I Eléftheri Poliorkiméni tou Dhionisíou Solomoú [The Free Besieged].* Athens: Sirios.

Politis, Alexis. 1983. *To Dhimotikó Traghoúdhi (Kléftika).* Athens: Ermis.

Porch, Douglas. 1991. *The French Foreign Legion: A Complete History of the Legendary Fighting Force.* New York: HarperCollins.

Porfiris, K. 1959. "*I áspri frákhtes* tou Andr. Nenedáki." *Avyí.*

Postel-Koster, Els. 1977. "The Indonesian Novel as a Source of Anthropological Data." In Ravindra K. Jain, ed., *Text and Context: The Social Anthropology of Tradition,* pp. 135–50. Philadelphia: Institute for the Study of Human Issues.

Poulianos, Aris. 1971. *I kataghoyí ton Kritón: Anthropoloyikí Erevna sto nisí tis Levendiás.* Athens: Vivliothiki Anthropoloyiks Eteras.

Poyatos, Fernando, ed., 1988. *Literary Anthropology: A New Interdisciplinary Approach to People, Signs, and Literature.* Amsterdam: J. Benjamins.

Prevelakis, Pandelis. 1961. *To khronikó mias politías [The Tale of a Town].* Athens: Galaxias.

Psikhoyos, Dimitris K. 1995. *Príkes, fóri, stafídha ke psomí.* 2d ed. Athens: National Center for Social Research (EKKE).

Psychoundakis, George. 1955. *The Cretan Runner: His Story of the German Occupation.* Translated by Patrick Leigh Fermor. London: John Murray.

Pushkin, Alexander Sergeevitch. 1983. *The Tales of Belkin.* London: Angel Books

Raftopoulos, Dimitris. 1959a. Review of Yannis M. Dalentzas, *To Khronikó tou Rethémnou* ([Athens]: Mavridis). *Epitheórisi Tékhnis* 57–58 (Sept.–Oct. 1959): 150.

———. 1959b. Review of Andreas Nenedakis, *White Fences. Epitheórisi Tékhnis* 57–58 (Sept.–Oct. 1959): 150–51.

———. 1963. "Traghoudhistís tis távlas, tou érota ke tis lefteriás." *Dhrómi tis Irínis* (May 1963): 46–47.

Rapport, Nigel. 1994. *The Prose and the Passion: Anthropology, Literature, and the Writing of E. M. Forster.* Manchester: University of Manchester Press.

Redfield, Robert. 1960. *The Little Community and Peasant Society and Culture.* Chicago: University of Chicago Press.

Ritsos, Yannis. 1961. *Epitafios.* Athens: Kedros.

———. 1974. *Romiosini.* Athens: Kedros.

Rorty, Amelie Oksenberg. 1995. "Understanding Others." In Lawrence Rosen, ed., *Other Intentions: Cultural Contexts and the Attribution of Inner States,* pp. 203–23. Santa Fe, NM: School of American Research.

Rosaldo, Renato. 1989. *Culture and Truth: The Remaking of Social Analysis.* Boston: Beacon.

Roseman, Sharon R. 1996. "How We Built the Road: The Politics of Memory in Rural Galicia." *American Ethnologist* 23: 836–60.

Rosen, Lawrence, ed. 1995. *Other Intentions: Cultural Contexts and the Attribution of Inner States.* Santa Fe, NM: School of American Research Press.

Sahlins, Marshall. 1985. *Islands of History.* Chicago: University of Chicago Press.

———. 1995. *How "Natives" Think: About Captain Cook, For Example.* Chicago: University of Chicago Press.

Sant Cassia, Paul, and Constantina Bada. 1992. *The Making of the Modern Greek Family: Marriage and Exchange in Nineteenth-Century Athens.* Cambridge: Cambridge University Press.

Sartre, Jean-Paul. 1949. *Literature and Existentialism.* Translated by Bernard Frechtman. Secaucus, NJ: Citadel Press.

Seferis, Yorgos. 1946. *Erotokritos.* [Athens]: Alpha.

Seferis, George, and Konstantinos Tsatsos. 1975. *Enas dhiáloghos ya tin píisi.* Athens: Ermis.

Seremetakis, C. Nadia. 1996. "In Search of the Barbarians: Borders in Pain." *American Anthropologist* 98: 489–91.

Skouteri-Didaskalou, Nora. 1991. *Anthropoloyiká ya to yinekío zítima.* 2d ed. Athens: O Politis.

Smith, Helena. 1996. "Island Paradise Where a Stolen Sheep Spells Death." *Observer* [London], 10 March 1996 ("The World").

Sontag, Susan. 1969. "A Letter from Sweden." *Ramparts* 23 (July 1969): 23–38.

Spiliadi, Veatriki. 1977. "Iroes antiroikís kathimerinótitas." *Kathimeriní,* 9 January, p. 4. [Review of *Manuscript.*]

St. Clair, William. 1972. *That Greece Might Still Be Free: The Philhellenes in the War of Independence.* London: Oxford University Press.

Stacy, R. H. 1977. *Defamiliarization in Language and Literature.* Syracuse, NY: Syracuse University Press.

Stamatiou, Kostas. 1985. "I zoí travá tin anifora." *Néa,* 2 February, p. 12.

Stephen, Lynn. 1995. "Women's Rights Are Human Rights: The Merging of Feminine and Feminist Interests among El Salvador's Mothers of the Disappeared." *American Ethnologist* 22: 807–27.

Stewart, Charles. 1991. *Demons and the Devil: Moral Imagination in Modern Greek Culture.* Princeton: Princeton University Press.

Stewart, Kathleen. 1996. *A Space on the Side of the Road: Cultural Poetics in an "Other" America.* Princeton: Princeton University Press.

Studies. 1987. *Studies in the History of the Greek Civil War, 1945–1949.* Copenhagen: Museum Tusculanum Press.

Sutton, David E. 1994. "'Tradition and Modernity': Kalymnian Constructions of Identity and Otherness." *Journal of Modern Greek Studies* 12: 239–60.

———. 1997. "Local Names, Foreign Claims: Family Inheritance and National Heritage on a Greek Island." *American Ethnologist* 24 (2): 415–37.

Svoronos, Nikos G. 1953. *Histoire de la Grèce moderne.* Paris: Presses Universitaires de France.

Syrimis, George. 1995. "Gender, Narrative Modes, and the Procreative Cycle: The Pregnant Word in Vizyenos." *Journal of Modern Greek Studies* 13: 326–49.

Taktsis, Costas. 1971. *The Third Wedding.* Translated by Leslie Finer. New York: Red Dust.

Tannen, Deborah. 1983. *Lilika Nakou.* Boston: Twayne.

Theodorakis, Mikis. 1987. *Ola ta traghoudhia.* Athens: Kaktos.

Tomadakis, Nikolaos V. 1979. Review of Nenedakis's edition of Marinos Tzane Bounialis, *The Cretan War. Athiná* 77: 397–405.

Trilling, Lionel. 1972. *Sincerity and Authenticity.* Cambridge, MA: Harvard University Press.

Troulis, Mikhalis. 1992. Review of Andreas Nenedakis, *Voukéfali. Kritoloyiká Grámmata* 5/6: 115–17.

Tsirkas, Stratis. 1976. *Khaméniániksi.* Athens: Kedros.

Tsoucalas, Constantine. *See* Tsoukalas, Konstandinos.

Tsouderos, Yannis E. 1995. *Afiéroma stin Istoría tis Krítis k' idhikótera tou Rethémnou, 1536 os 1924.* Rethemnos.

Tsoukalas, Konstandinos. 1996. *Taksídhi sto lógho ke tin istoría: Kímena 1969–1996.* 2 vols. Athens: Plethron.

Turner, V. W. 1974. *Dramas, Fields, and Metaphors: Symbolic Action in Human Society.* Ithaca, NY: Cornell University Press.

Tziovas, Dimitris. 1986. *The Nationism of the Demoticists and Its Impact on Their Literary Theory (1881–1930).* Amsterdam: Hakkert.

———. 1989. "Residual Orality and Belated Textuality in Greek Literature and Culture." *Journal of Modern Greek Studies* 7: 321–35.

Van Boeschoten, Riki. 1991. *From Armatolik to People's Rule*. Amsterdam: Adolf M. Hakkert.

Van Dyck, Karen. 1994. "Reading between Worlds: Contemporary Greek Women's Writing and Censorship." *Proceedings of the Modern Language Association* 109 (January 1994): 45–60.

———. 1997. *Kassandra and the Censors: Greek Poetry since 1967*. Ithaca, NY: Cornell University Press.

Vernier, Bernard. 1991. *La genèse sociale des sentiments: aînés et cadets dans l'île grecque de Karpathos*. Paris: Editions de l'École des Hautes Études en Sciences Sociales.

Verdier, Yvonne. 1995. *Coutume et destin: Thomas Hardy et autres essais*. Paris: Gallimard.

Vincent, Alfred. 1980. *Fortounatos Markou Andoniou Foskolou*. Iraklion: Eteria Kritikon Istorikon Meleton.

Vournas, Tassos. 1957. *Ghoudhi, to kínima tou 1909*. Athens: Ekdhosis Tekhni-Epistimi.

Wace, A. J. B., and M. S. Thompson. 1914. *Nomads of the Balkans: An Account of Life and Customs among the Vlachs of Northern Pindus*. London: Methuen.

Warren, Kay B. 1993. "Interpreting La Violencia in Guatemala: Shapes of Kaqchikel Silence and Resistance in the 1970s and 1980s." In Kay B. Warren, ed., *The Violence Within: Cultural and Political Opposition in Divided Nations*, pp. 25–56. Boulder, CO: Westview Press.

———. 1995. "Each Mind Is a World: Dilemmas of Feeling and Intention in a Kaqchikel Maya Community." In Lawrence Rosen, ed., *Other Intentions: Cultural Contexts and the Attribution of Inner States*, pp. 47–67. Santa Fe, NM: School of American Research Press.

———. 1997. "Narrating Cultural Resurgence: Genre and Self-Representation for Pan-Mayan Writers." In Deborah E. Reed-Danahay, ed., *Auto/Ethnography: Rewriting the Self and the Social*, pp. 21–45. Oxford: Berg.

Watson, Rubie S. 1994. "Memory, History, and Opposition under State Socialism: An Introduction." In Rubie S. Watson, ed., *Memory, History, and Opposition under State Socialism*, pp. 1–20. Santa Fe, NM: School of American Research Press.

Xenophon. 1972. *Xenophontis Expeditio Cyri*. [*Anabasis*.] Edited by J. Peters. Leipzig: Teubner.

Zambelios, Spiridon. 1852. *Asmata dhimotiká tis Elládhos, ekdhothénda meta melétis istorikís peri Meseonikoú Ellinismoú*. Athens: Ermis.

Zeï, Alki. 1987. *I aravoniastikiá tou Akhilléa*. Athens: Kedros. See also: 1991. *Achilles' Fiancée*. Translated by Gail Holst-Warhaft. Athens: Kedros.

INDEX

Venetians, Venice, 12, 13, 28, 29, 39n. 16, 52, 88, 211n, 232, 242, 251, 257, 260
Venizelos, Eleftherios, 33, 34, 44, 58, 59, 147, 198, 235
Venizelos, Sofoklis, 58
Verbalism, 54, 62, 179, 196, 198, 275, 279, 280
Verdier, Yvonne, 11n. 10
Vernier, Bernard, 148n. 4
Verse duels and couplets, 53, 54, 141, 142, 151, 167, 172, 174, 274, 277
Victimage: claims to political, 128, 129; sense of, 176
Víoma (pl. viómata), 265, 290
Vizyenos, George, 46n, 291
Vlastos, Pavlos, 53; archive of, 229
Voice: female, 46, 47, 144, 155, 157–58, 179–80, 182, 278, 291; female, as expressing masculinity, 276; narrator's, 133, 155, 179, 274, 277, 291; quality of, 17, 141–43, 167, 277; reproduction of speaking, 116, 141
Voukéfali (novel), 7, 30, 50, 227–31, 237–50, 253, 255, 256, 261, 262, 280, 281, 284, 285, 287
Voulgaris, Petros, 110

Wace, A. J. B., 256
Wages, 43
War, warfare, 80, 82, 87, 141; Civil, Greek, 20, 102, 106, 109, 111, 117, 118, 120, 122, 124, 136n. 10, 146, 193, 194, 213, 214, 216, 280, 288, 293; Cold, 135n; of Independence, Greek, 80n, 84, 85n, 87, 93–95, 98, 104, 106, 107, 180, 181, 195, 196, 199, 222, 229, 267, 277–78, 280; opposition to, 253. See also Asia Minor; World War II
War and Peace (novel by L. Tolstoy), 287
Warren, Kay B., 7n. 5, 8
Watson, Rubie S., 177, 296

Weber, Max, 113
White Fences (short stories), 89, 221, 242, 250
Widows, 134, 213
Women: agency of, denied, 278; as authors, 289–91; condition and roles of, 4, 16, 44, 45, 47, 48, 121, 134, 144–48, 150n, 152, 156–61, 172, 176, 180–82, 278, 279; as metaphor for male foes, 260; as painters, 147, 148, 179–80, 265; as prisoners, 106, 111
World War II, 20, 30, 31, 64, 89, 95, 117, 141; dilemmas of, as questioning state authority, 275–76. See also Allies; Bir Hakeim; Crete; Foreign Legion; Nazis; Resistance; Voice
Worth: of craft, 170; personal and social, 48, 81, 128, 156, 164, 172
Writing, 266–67; analogy of with artisanal craft, 268, 270; as basis of ambition, 197–98; as resistance to bureaucratic history, 284; as source of income, 197, 265, 286; as symbol of permanence and power, 291, 292; utilitarian view of, 268; by women, 289. See also Author; Novel

Xenophon, 79

Yalta, 96
Yaros. See Youra
Youra, 109, 111, 120, 122, 127, 130, 132–37, 185, 189, 197, 201, 209–10, 213–15, 219, 220, 222, 281, 289, 295–96
Youth, 41–42
Yugoslavs, 136, 253

Zambelios, Spiridon, 234, 254
Zeï, Alki, 216, 234
Zorba the Greek (novel by N. Kazantzakis and film by M. Cacoyannis), 293